PNG

The Definitive Guide

PNG
The Definitive Guide

Greg Roelofs

O'REILLY®

Beijing · Cambridge · Farnham · Köln · Paris · Sebastopol · Taipei · Tokyo

PNG: The Definitive Guide
by Greg Roelofs

Copyright © 1999 O'Reilly & Associates, Inc. All rights reserved.
Printed in the United States of America.

Published by O'Reilly & Associates, Inc., 101 Morris Street, Sebastopol, CA 95472.

Editor: Richard Koman

Production Editor: Nancy Wolfe Kotary

Printing History:

      June 1999:   First Edition.

This book is printed on acid-free paper with 85% recycled content, 15% post-consumer waste. O'Reilly & Associates is committed to using paper with the highest recycled content available consistent with high quality.

ISBN: 1-56592-542-4

To Dad, who missed so much. You've always been my role model.

Table of Contents

Preface

Once upon a time, the only images were those painted on the walls of caves. Then came papyrus, stucco walls (and a chapel ceiling), the printing press, photography, television, and computers. Whether it's progress or not is a question for philosophers, but there is no doubt that creating, copying, modifying, and transmitting images has never been easier or faster than it is today.

PNG, the Portable Network Graphics image format, is one little piece of the puzzle. In *PNG: The Definitive Guide*, I attempt to make PNG a little less puzzling by explaining the motivations behind PNG's creation, the ways in which it can be used, and the tools that can manipulate it. The intended audience is anyone who deals with PNG images, whether as an artist, a programmer, or a surfer on the World Wide Web.

About This Book

This book covers a lot of ground, as one would expect from anything with the word "Definitive" in its title. It is divided into three main parts. As much as possible, each part is written so that it can be read independently of the others. Even individual chapters are written this way, within reason; to avoid too much repetition, I'll periodically refer to other chapters.

Part I, Using PNG

Part I is intended for designers, web site owners, casual image creators, and web surfers—anyone who wants a quick start on using PNG images in a variety of applications. Such users may need only a brief overview of PNG features, but they want to know what applications support the format and to what extent, how to invoke PNG-specific features within the applications, and how to work around certain bugs or incompatibilities in the applications. Of course, a book like this cannot possibly stay current, particularly not when it comes to software, but every effort has been made to ensure that the information is accurate as of the day this is written (mid-April 1999).

Chapter 1, *An Introduction to PNG*, covers some basic concepts of computer images and file formats, explains how PNG fits in and where using it is most appropriate (and most inappropriate!), and ends with an in-depth look at an image-editing application with particularly good PNG support.

Chapter 2, *Applications: WWW Browsers and Servers*, looks at PNG support in web browsers and servers and shows how to use the HTML OBJECT tag and server-side content negotiation to serve PNG images to browsers capable of viewing them.

Chapter 3, *Applications: Image Viewers*, lists more than 75 applications capable of viewing PNG images, with support for a dozen operating systems. Viewers that are additionally capable of converting to or from other image formats are so noted.

Chapter 4, *Applications: Image Editors*, looks at PNG support in five of the most popular image editors, showing how to invoke such features as gamma correction and alpha transparency, and indicating some of the problems unwary users may encounter.

Chapter 5, *Applications: Image Converters*, covers five conversion applications in detail, including one specifically designed to optimize PNG images and another designed to test PNG images for conformance to the specification. In addition, the chapter lists another 16 dedicated image converters beyond those in Chapter 3.

Chapter 6, *Applications: VRML Browsers and Other 3D Apps*, looks at PNG as a required texture format of the VRML 97 specification and investigates the level of conformance of seven browsers. It also lists a dozen PNG-supporting applications designed for the editing or rendering of 3D scenes.

Part II, The Design of PNG

Part II looks at the PNG format from an historical and technical perspective, detailing its structure and the rationale behind its design. Part II is intended for more technical readers who want to understand PNG to its core.

Chapter 7, *History of the Portable Network Graphics Format*, looks at the events leading up to the creation of PNG, some of the design decisions that went into the format, how it has fared in the subsequent years, and what to expect for the future.

Chapter 8, *PNG Basics*, covers the basic "chunk" structure of PNG files and compares PNG's level of support for various fundamental image types against that of other image formats.

Chapter 9, *Compression and Filtering*, delves into the heart of PNG's compression engine, provides the results of some real-world compression tests, and offers a number of tips for improving compression to both users and programmers of the format.

Chapter 10, *Gamma Correction and Precision Color*, discusses one of the least understood but most important features of PNG, its support for platform-independent image display. That is, in order for an image to appear the same way on different computer systems or even different print media, it is necessary for both the user and the program to understand and support gamma and color correction.

Chapter 11, *PNG Options and Extensions*, details the optional features supported by PNG, including text annotations, timestamps, background colors, and other ancillary information.

Chapter 12, *Multiple-Image Network Graphics*, is a brief look at PNG's multi-image cousin, MNG, which supports animations, slide shows, and even highly efficient storage of some types of single images.

Part III, Programming with PNG

Part III covers three working, libpng-based demo programs in detail, and lists a number of other toolkits that offer PNG support for various programming languages and platforms. It is intended for programmers who wish to add PNG support to their applications.

Chapter 13, *Reading PNG Images*, is a detailed tutorial on how to write a basic PNG-reading display program in C using the official PNG reference library. The application is divided into a generic PNG backend and platform-specific frontends, of which two are provided (for 32-bit Windows and the X Window System).

Chapter 14, *Reading PNG Images Progressively*, inverts the logic of the previous chapter's demo program, simulating the design of a web browser's display-as-you-go PNG code. Progressive display of interlaced, transparent PNG images over a background image is supported.

Chapter 15, *Writing PNG Images*, shows how to create a basic PNG-writing program. The supplied code compiles into a simple command-line program under both Windows and Unix, and it includes support for interlacing, gamma correction, alpha transparency, and text annotations.

Chapter 16, *Other Libraries and Concluding Remarks*, lists a number of alternative libraries and toolkits, both free and commercial, including ones for C, C++, Java™,

Pascal, tcl/tk, Python, and Visual Basic. The chapter ends with a look back at what parts of the PNG design process worked and what didn't, and also a look forward at what lies ahead.

The *References* section lists technical references and resources for further information, both printed and electronic.

The *Glossary* defines a number of acronyms and technical terms used throughout the book.

Conventions Used in This Book

Italic is used for pathnames, filenames, program names, new terms where they are defined, newsgroup names, and Internet addresses, such as domain names, URLs, and email addresses.

`Constant width` is used to show code, commands, HTML tags, and computer-generated output.

`Constant width bold` is used in examples to show commands or other text that should be typed literally by the user.

`Constant width italic` is used in code fragments and examples to show variables for which a context-specific substitution should be made. The variable `email address`, for example, would be replaced by an actual email address.

 This type of boxed paragraph indicates a tip, suggestion, general note, or caution.

How to Contact Us

We have tested and verified all of the information in this book to the best of our ability, but you may find that features have changed (or even that we have made mistakes!). Please let us know about any errors you find, as well as your suggestions for future editions, by writing:

O'Reilly & Associates, Inc.
101 Morris Street
Sebastopol, CA 95472
800-998-9938 (in the U.S. or Canada)
707-829-0515 (international/local)
707-829-0104 (fax)

You can also send us messages electronically. To subscribe to the mailing list or request a catalog, send email to:

nuts@oreilly.com

To ask technical questions or comment on the book, send email to:

bookquestions@oreilly.com

In addition, the author has set up a web page to support users of the book at:

http://www.cdrom.com/pub/png/pngbook.html

This web page includes the complete source code for the demo programs described in Part III and may include additional fixes, improvements, new ports, and contributions. The page also includes an errata list. If the link ever breaks, check the following page for a pointer to the new location:

http://www.oreilly.com/catalog/pngdefg/

Acknowledgments

Though this book has only one author's name on the cover, it is the result of work by literally dozens of people. Glenn Randers-Pehrson's help was especially invaluable: he not only acted as a technical reviewer, but also contributed the interlace figure in Chapter 1 and the haiku in Chapter 7; he edited or co-edited not just one but all five of the PNG-related specifications available from the web site given in the previous section; and he authored virtually all of the MNG specification, wrote the incredibly useful pngcrush utility, and maintained libpng for the last year. On top of all that, his wife, Nancy, reviewed the book from a layperson's perspective; her insights were concise and invariably hit the mark. And Glenn's nephew, Michael, kindly contributed the haiku at the end of Chapter 16. Thanks to the whole family!

I'd also like to thank my two other reviewers and colleagues in the PNG Group, Adam Costello and Tom Lane. Adam's help was absolutely indispensable in explaining the subtle and sometimes complicated ramifications of gamma and color correction and of international text formats; he also supplied code for one class of background patterns in the progressive PNG viewer. Tom, leader of the Independent JPEG Group and a member of the TIFF advisory committee, supplied background, corrections, and additional information on two of the image formats most relevant to PNG users, and he provided the progressive JPEG images in the color insert.

Thanks to Pieter van der Meulen for providing the impressive icicles image and for generating the alpha channel for it on short notice. Pieter also supplied code for another class of background patterns in the progressive viewer and was an understanding colleague when book-related deadlines occasionally took precedence over work.

For the chapter on image editors, I enlisted the aid of several people to help test the level of PNG support in various products: Anthony Argyriou for Paint Shop Pro; Chris Herborth for Photoshop 4; and two fine Macromedia engineers, Steven Johnson and John Ahlquist, for Fireworks. Jim Bala and Richard Koman provided additional assistance with Photoshop.

Thanks also to Michael Stokes for information about the sRGB standard and ICC profiles; Chris Lilley for additional information on gamma and color correction (including an incredibly well-written tutorial distributed via the University of Manchester) and for the chromaticity diagram in Chapter 10; Jean-loup Gailly for an informal review of Chapter 9 and, together with Mark Adler, the zlib compression engine at the heart of PNG; and John Bowler for information about the private Windows clipboard for PNG and how to access it.

Jas Sandu, Jed Hartman, and François Vidal provided timely and detailed information about PNG support in 3D applications, and Mathew Ignash did so for Amiga applications and APIs. Thanks to Delle Maxwell for providing the images she used in part of a VRML course; they not only prompted me to do some serious and quantifiable comparisons of compression in PNG and related image formats but also helped nail down some of the myriad ways in which bad PNG encoders can write large PNG files.

Portions of Chapter 7 appeared in the April 1997 issue of *Linux Journal*; thanks to Marjorie L. Richardson and Specialized Systems Consultants for permission to reuse the historical material here.

On the O'Reilly side, many, many thanks to editor Richard Koman for his help and patience with a first-time author. He is also responsible for making sure that this book would be of interest to a wider audience than just programmers. Thanks also to Lenny Muellner for being so very responsive on all sorts of picky formatting questions, to Tara McGoldrick, to Rob Romano and Alicia Cech for issues relating to the figures, to Nancy Kotary for her incredible patience during production, and to Edie Freedman for doing her best to get me a "pnguin" for the cover.

A special thanks goes to Jennifer Niederst, who, while working on *Web Design in a Nutshell*, first suggested that I write this book. Many's the time over the past 10 months when I've debated whether it was a good suggestion or bad, but now that the book is done, I'm glad she did so.

Of course, without the patience of my sainted wife, Veronica, none of this could have happened. To little Lyra, I apologize for every time I uttered the phrase "Daddy is working"; you'll see a lot more of me now. And to little Delenn—well, you aren't here yet, but I know someday you'll be miffed if your sister is mentioned and you aren't. :-)

Finally, thanks to everyone in the PNG Development Group, the ISO/IEC standardization committee, and all of the countless contributors to the PNG home site, who provided (and continue to provide) information about new or updated PNG-supporting applications, broken links, and suggestions for improvement. And without the continued support of Walnut Creek CD-ROM, the site would not be nearly as accessible and complete as it is; a very special and ongoing thanks to Christopher Mann and David Greenman.

If there's anyone I've missed, please rest assured it was *not* intentional! The brain cell is going, as a certain compression colleague has been known to say.

PART I

Using PNG

1

An Introduction to PNG

PNG,* short for "Portable Network Graphics," is a computer file format for storing, transmitting, and displaying images. Similar to the GIF and TIFF image formats— in fact, designed to replace them in many applications—PNG supports lossless compression, transparency information, and a range of color depths. PNG also supports more advanced features such as gamma correction and a standard color space for precise reproduction of image colors on a wide range of systems and embedded textual information for storing such things as a title, the author's name, and explicit copyright.

In this chapter, we'll consider PNG from the perspective of a user who has some familiarity with the process of creating and using computer images, but insufficient knowledge of the technical differences between various formats to be certain when to use what. I won't dwell on features that are mostly of concern to developers; where I do bring up programming issues, it is principally to explain to the *user* why some software may not perform as well as expected. I'll concentrate on two areas to which PNG is particularly well suited: as an intermediate editing format for repeatedly saving and restoring images without loss, and as a final display format for the World Wide Web. And I'll finish up with an in-depth look at one application that has particularly good PNG support: Macromedia's Fireworks 1.0, an image-editing program specifically designed for creating web images.

---

* PNG is officially pronounced "ping" (at least in English) but never spelled that way. Yes, this was a major topic of discussion during its design, and it is explicitly noted in the specification. Believe it or not, in November 1998 the issue once again came under discussion, this time with greater emphasis on non-English pronunciation. Though the "three-letter" approach (i.e., *P–N–G* spoken as three separate letters) was not approved for inclusion in the spec, it may be considered an acceptable unofficial alternative.

Overview of Image Properties

Before we dive right into some of PNG's more interesting features, it might be helpful to introduce (or review) some essential image concepts and take a quick look at a few older image formats. Those who are already familiar with the most basic features of computer images can skip directly to the next section.

There are two main formats for computer images: raster, based on colored dots, which are almost always stored in a rectangular array and are usually packed so close together that individual dots are no longer distinguishable, and vector, based on lines, circles, and other "primitive" elements that typically cover a sizable area and are easily distinguishable from one another. Many images can be represented in either format; indeed, any vector-based image can be approximated by a raster image (lots of dots), and one could easily (though tediously) simulate a raster image in vector format by converting each dot to a tiny box.

The whole point of having two classes of image formats—and, indeed, of having numerous individual file formats—is implicit in the old saying, "Use the best tool for the job." Vector formats are appropriate for simple graphics and text, such as corporate logos, and their advantage is that they can be extremely compact and yet maintain perfect sharpness regardless of the size at which they are reproduced. But with the exception of pen-based plotters and some ancient vector-based displays, the end result is almost always a raster image.

For that reason, plus the fact that raster image formats are more common—and because PNG is one of them—we'll take a closer look at raster features. As I just noted, a raster image is composed of an array of dots, more commonly referred to as *pixels* (short for *picture elements*). One generally refers to a computer image's dimensions in terms of pixels; this is also often (though slightly imprecisely) known as its *resolution*. Some common image sizes are 640 × 480, 800 × 600, and 1024 × 768 pixels, which also happen to be common dimensions for computer displays.

In addition to horizontal and vertical dimensions, a raster image is characterized by depth. The deeper the image, the more colors (or shades of gray) it can have. Pixel depths are measured in *bits*, the tiniest units of computer storage; a 1-bit image can represent two colors (often, though not necessarily, black and white), a 2-bit image four colors, an 8-bit image 256 colors, and so on. To calculate the raw size of the image data before any compression takes place, one needs only to know that 8 bits make a byte. Thus a 320 × 240, 24-bit image has 76,800 pixels, each of which is 3 bytes deep, so its total uncompressed size is 230,400 bytes.

I'll return to the topic of compression in just a moment; first, let's take a closer look at the precise relationship between pixels and colors. Within the broad class of raster formats, there are three main image types: indexed-color, grayscale, and truecolor. The *indexed-color* method, also known as *pseudocolor, colormapped,* or *palette-based,* stores a copy of each color value needed for the image in a palette. The main image is then composed of index values referring to different entries in the palette. For example, imagine an image composed entirely of red, white, and blue pixels; the palette would have three entries corresponding to these colors, and each pixel would be represented by the value 0, 1, or 2. (The natural starting point for numbers on a computer is 0, not 1.) Since an image 2 bits deep can represent up to four colors, each pixel in this example would require only 2 bits, even though the precise shades of red, white, and blue might ordinarily require 24 bits each.

Grayscale and truecolor images are simpler in concept; the bytes used by each pixel correspond directly to shades of gray or to colors. In a *grayscale* image of a particular pixel depth, a 0 pixel usually (though not always) means black, while the maximum value at that depth corresponds to white. Intermediate pixel values are smoothly interpolated to shades of gray, though this is often not as straightforward as it might sound—*gamma correction,* a way of adjusting for differences in computer display systems, comes in here. I'll give a brief overview of gamma correction later in this chapter, and I'll discuss it at length in Chapter 10, *Gamma Correction and Precision Color*; for now, I'll merely note that it is a Good Thing, and image formats that provide support for it can be viewed on different platforms without appearing too light on one and too dark on another.

A *truecolor* image uses three separate values for each pixel, corresponding to shades of red, green, and blue. Such images are often also referred to as *RGB*. In Chapter 8, *PNG Basics*, I'll talk about human vision and the reasons why mixtures of just three colors can appear to reproduce all colors, or at least a sufficiently large percentage of them that one need not quibble over the difference. I'll also mention some common alternatives to the RGB *color space*. To be considered truly truecolor instead of merely "high color," an image must contain at least 8 bits for each of the three colors in each pixel; thus, at a minimum, a truecolor image has a depth of 24 bits.

Two other concepts—samples and channels—are handy when speaking of images, and RGB images are a good way to illustrate these concepts. A *sample* is one component of a single color value. For example, each pixel in a truecolor image consists of three samples: red, green, and blue. If the image is 24 bits deep, then each sample is 8 bits deep. A 256-shade grayscale image also has 8-bit samples, which means that one can speak of the "bits per sample" for either image type to indicate the level of precision of each shade or color. Note that I have been careful to distinguish between *sample depth* and *pixel depth*. The two terms are directly related in grayscale and truecolor images, but in indexed-color images they can be independent of each other. This is because the sample depth refers to the color values in the palette, while the pixel depth refers to the index values of each pixel (which reference the palette colors). To put it more concretely, the color values in the palette are usually 24-bit values (8 bits per sample), but the pixel indices are usually 8 bits or less. Our previous red, white, and blue example used only two bits per pixel.

A *channel*, on the other hand, refers to the collection of all samples of a given type in an image—for example, the green components of every RGB pixel. Thus a truecolor image has three channels, while a grayscale image has only one. (Ordinarily one does not speak of a palette-based image as having channels.) And when discussing transparency, yet another channel type is often used: the *alpha channel*. This is a special kind of channel in that it does not provide actual color information but rather a level of transparency for each pixel—or, more precisely, a level of *opacity*, since it is most common for the maximum sample value to indicate that the pixel is completely opaque and for zero to indicate complete transparency. A truecolor image with an alpha channel is often called an RGBA image; grayscale images with alpha channels are rarer and don't have a special abbreviation (although I may refer to them as "gray+alpha").

Palette-based images almost never have a full alpha channel, but another type of transparency is possible. Rather than associate alpha information with every pixel, one can instead associate it with specific palette entries. By far the most common approach is to specify that a single palette entry represents complete transparency. Then when the image is displayed against some sort of background, any pixel whose index refers to this particular palette entry will be replaced by the background at the pixel's location—or perhaps the pixel simply will not be drawn in the first place. But there is no conceptual requirement that only one palette entry can have transparency, nor that it must be fully transparent. As we'll see shortly, PNG effectively allows any number of palette entries to have any level of transparency.

While we're on the subject of colormapped images, two other concepts are worth mentioning: quantization and dithering. Suppose one has a 24-bit truecolor image, but it must be displayed on a 256-color, palette-based display. Since truecolor images typically use anywhere from 10,000 to 100,000 colors, the conversion to a colormapped image will involve substituting many of the color values with a much smaller range of colors. This process is known as *quantization*. Because the resulting images have such a limited palette of colors available to them, they often are unable to represent fine color gradients such as the different shades of blue seen in the sky or the range of facial tones in a softly lit portrait. One way around this is to *dither* the image, which is a means of mixing pixels of the available colors together to give the appearance of other colors (though generally at the cost of some sharpness). For example, a checkerboard pattern of alternating red and yellow pixels might appear orange. This effect is perhaps best illustrated with an example. Figure 1-1 shows a truecolor photograph (here rendered in grayscale) together with two 256-color versions of the same image—one simply quantized to 256 colors and the other both quantized and dithered. The insets give a magnified view of one region, showing the relative effects of the two procedures.

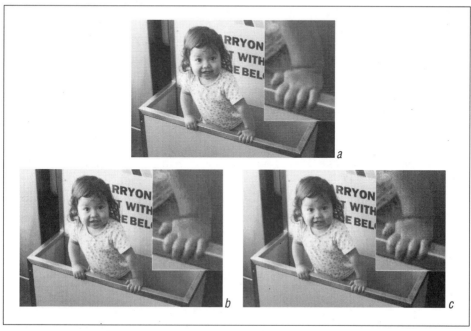

Figure 1-1: Original, 24-bit image (a); same image after quantization (b) and after quantization and dithering (c)

I'll round out our review of image properties and concepts with a quick look at compression. There are really only two flavors: lossless and lossy. *Lossless* compression preserves the exact image data down to the last bit, so that what you get out after uncompressing is exactly the same as what you started with. In contrast, *lossy* compression throws away some of the data in return for much better compression ratios. For photographic images, the best lossless methods may only manage a factor of two or three in compression, whereas lossy methods typically achieve anywhere from 8 to 25 times reduction with very little visible loss of quality. I'll discuss the details of compression, particularly the lossless variety, at greater length in Chapter 9, *Compression and Filtering*.

Finally, in describing the advantages of PNG, I will necessarily compare it with some older image formats. Although there are literally hundreds of different formats, we will be most concerned with just three: GIF, JPEG, and TIFF. GIF, short for the Graphics Interchange Format, and JPEG, short for the Joint Photographic

Experts Group (which defined the format), are both very common image types often seen on the Web. TIFF, on the other hand, short for Tagged Image File Format, is almost never used on the Web but is quite popular as an output format from scanners and as an intermediate "save format" while editing images. I'll touch on the properties of each of these formats as we go.

What Is PNG Good For?

For image editing, either professional or otherwise, PNG provides a useful format for storing the intermediate stages of an image. Since PNG's compression is fully lossless—and since it supports up to 48-bit truecolor or 16-bit grayscale—saving, restoring, and resaving an image will not degrade its quality, unlike standard JPEG (even at its highest quality settings). PNG also supports full transparency information, unlike JPEG (no transparency at all), GIF (no partial transparency), or even TIFF (full transparency is part of the specification but is not required for minimal conformance). And unlike TIFF, which is probably the most popular intermediate format today, the PNG specification leaves almost no room for implementors to pick and choose what features they'll support. What allowances are made, such as optional support for gamma correction, are tightly constrained. The result is that a PNG image saved in one application is readable and displayable in any other PNG-supporting program.

For the Web, as of early 1999, there are two image formats with ubiquitous support: JPEG and GIF. JPEG is very well suited to the task for which it was designed—namely, the storage, transmission, and display of photorealistic 8-bit grayscale and 24-bit truecolor images with good quality and excellent compression—and PNG was never intended to compete with JPEG on its own terms. But PNG, like GIF, is more appropriate than JPEG for images with few colors or with lots of sharp edges, such as cartoons or bitmapped text. PNG also provides direct support for gamma correction (loosely speaking, the cross-platform control of image "brightness") and transparency. I'll discuss these in more detail shortly.

GIF was the original cross-platform image format for the Web, and it is still a good choice in many respects. But PNG was specifically designed to replace GIF, and it has three main advantages over the older format: alpha channels (variable transparency), gamma correction, and two-dimensional interlacing (a method of displaying images at progressively higher levels of detail). PNG also compresses better than GIF in almost every case, but the difference is generally only around 5% to 25%, which is (usually) not a large enough factor to encourage one to switch on that basis alone. One GIF feature that PNG does *not* try to reproduce is multiple-image support, especially animations; PNG was and is intended to be a single-image format only. A very PNG-like extension format called MNG has been developed to address this limitation; it is discussed in Chapter 12, *Multiple-Image Network Graphics.*

Alpha Channels

Also known as a *mask channel,* an alpha channel is simply a way to associate variable levels of transparency (sometimes referred to as "translucency," though that may imply a diffuseness not present with alpha transparency) with an image. Whereas GIF supports simple binary transparency—any given pixel can be either fully transparent or fully opaque—PNG allows an additional 254 levels of partial transparency for "normal" images. It also supports a total of 65,536 transparency levels for the special "deeply insane" image types, but here we're concentrating on pixel depths that are useful on the Web.

All three of the basic PNG image types—RGB, grayscale, and palette-based—can have alpha information, but currently it's most often used with truecolor images. Instead of storing three bytes for every pixel, now four are required: red, green, blue, and alpha, or RGBA. The variable transparency allows one to create special effects that will look good on *any* background, whether light, dark, or patterned. For example, a photo-vignette effect can be created for a portrait by making a central oval region fully opaque (i.e., for the face and shoulders of the subject), the outer regions fully transparent, and a transition region that varies smoothly between the two extremes. When viewed with a web browser such as Acorn Browse or Arena, the portrait would fade smoothly to white when viewed against a white background or smoothly to black if against a black background. Both cases are shown in Figure 1-2.

This feature is especially important for the small web graphics that are typically used on web pages, such as colored (circular) bullets and fancy text. To avoid the jagged artifacts that really stand out on such images, most applications support *anti-aliasing,* a method for creating the illusion of smooth curves on a rectangular grid of pixels by smoothly varying the pixels' colors. The problem with anti-aliasing in the absence of variable transparency is that it must be done against a predetermined background color, typically either white or black. Reusing the same images on a different background usually results in an unpleasant "halo" effect, as shown in Figure 1-3. The standard approach is to create separate images for each background color used on a site, but this has negative implications both for the designer, who wastes time creating and maintaining multiple copies of each image, and for visitors to the site, who must download those copies.

Alpha blending, on the other hand, effectively uses transparency as a placeholder for the background color. Fully transparent regions will inherit the background color as is; fully opaque regions will show up as the foreground images. This is no different from the usual case, exemplified by transparent GIFs. But the anti-aliased

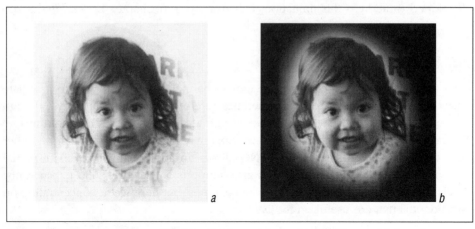

Figure 1-2: Portrait with an oval alpha mask against a white background (a) and against a black background (b)

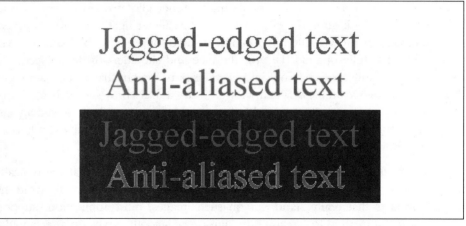

Figure 1-3: Gray text anti-aliased against a white background, displayed against both white and black backgrounds

regions in between the fully transparent and fully opaque areas are no longer premixed with an assumed background color; instead, they are partially transparent and can be mixed with whatever background on which the image happens to be placed.

Of course, effective replacements for GIF buttons and icons must not only be more useful but also of comparable or smaller size, and that mostly rules out true-color RGBA images. Fortunately, PNG supports alpha information with palette images as well; it's just harder to implement in a smart way. A PNG alpha-palette image is just that: an image whose palette also has alpha information associated with it, not a palette image with a full alpha mask. In other words, each pixel corresponds to an entry in the palette with red, green, blue, *and* alpha components. So if you want to have bright red pixels with four different levels of transparency, you must use four separate palette entries to accommodate them—all four entries will have identical RGB components, but the alpha values will differ. If you want all of your colors to have four levels of transparency, you've effectively reduced your total number of available colors from 256 to 64. In general, though, only some of the colors need more than one level of transparency, and recognizing which ones do is where things get tricky for the programmer.*

Gamma and Color Correction

Gamma correction basically refers to the ability to correct for differences in how computers (and especially computer monitors) interpret color values. Web authors in particular are probably aware that Macintosh-generated images tend to look too dark on PCs, and PC-generated images tend to look too light and washed out on Macs. An image that looks good on an SGI workstation won't look right on either a Macintosh or a PC, and even a PC-created image won't look right on all PCs.

Gamma information is a partial solution. It's a means of associating a single number with a computer display system, in an attempt to characterize the tricky physics lurking within a graphics card's digital-to-analog converter (RAMDAC) and within a monitor's high-voltage electron gun and display phosphors. Gamma is only a first approximation that accounts for overall "brightness," but it is generally sufficient for casual users. More demanding users will additionally want to adjust for differences in the individual red, green, and blue channels—the so-called *chromaticity* values, which are also supported by PNG. Even this is merely a second approximation, however.

The absolute best solution currently available is to use a complete *color management system*, which allows one to take into account things like the viewing environment (a "dim surround," for example) and its interaction with the human visual system. The International Color Consortium has defined a profile format that describes the relationship between an input color space (say, a digital camera or scanner) and the output color space that the user sees. This is the most general way to account for cross-platform differences (and, of course, PNG supports it via the iCCP chunk), but its flexibility comes at a cost: it tends to add at least 250 bytes and often 2,000 bytes or more to every image.

---

* As it happens, the same algorithm that allows one to quantize a 24-bit truecolor image down to an 8-bit palette image also allows one to reduce a 32-bit RGBA image to an 8-bit palette-alpha image. So it's not really that tricky for programmers; it's just not how they're used to thinking about such things.

Fortunately, a new proposal for operating systems and physical devices avoids the overhead of a complete ICC profile. Called *sRGB*, for Standard RGB color space, it defines just that: a standard, unified color space that devices can support, thereby allowing true color management with minimal file overhead and no need for the user to wade through a complicated end-to-end calibration procedure. As of January 1999, the sRGB proposal was in "Committee Draft for Voting," and it should be approved as an international standard* by mid-1999; conformant devices should start appearing shortly thereafter. PNG supports sRGB via a chunk called, logically enough, sRGB.

Gamma, chromaticity, and color management are described in more detail in Chapter 10; PNG's basic structure, including the means by which it can be officially or unofficially extended, is covered in Chapters 8 and 11.

Interlacing and Progressive Display

By now, just about everyone has seen interlaced GIFs in action; they first show up with a very stretched, blocky appearance and gradually get filled in until the full-resolution image is displayed. Their big advantage is that an overall impression of the image is visible after only one-eighth of the image data has been transferred; gross features such as embedded buttons or large text are often recognizable (and clickable) even at this stage.

But as useful as GIF's interlacing is, it has one big disadvantage: it is not symmetric. In other words, while GIF's first pass consists of one-eighth of the image data, that factor of eight comes entirely at the expense of vertical resolution. Horizontally, every line is at full resolution as soon as it is displayed, which means that each pixel in the first pass is stretched by a factor of eight. Needless to say, this does make text and other features much harder to recognize than they really need to be.

PNG's approach to interlacing is two-dimensional and involves no stretching at all on more than half of its passes. Even-numbered passes are stretched, but only by a factor of two—similar to the effect after GIF's third pass. Some applications display only the odd-numbered PNG passes, so their pixels always appear square. In addition, PNG's interlacing consists of seven passes, as opposed to GIF's four. This means that the user will see an overall impression of the image after only one-

---

* sRGB is Part 2 of IEC 61966 (*Colour Measurement and Management in Multimedia Systems and Equipment*), a proposed standard of Technical Committee 100 of the International Electrotechnical Commission. The IEC is a standards body similar to the International Organization for Standardization (ISO); in fact, international standards such as MPEG, VRML97, and the Latin-1 character set are all joint ISO/IEC standards, and PNG is on track to join them.

sixty-fourth of the data has arrived, eight times faster than GIF.* In the time it takes GIF to display its first pass, PNG displays four passes—and keep in mind that PNG's fourth pass is only one-quarter as stretched as GIF's first pass, with "pixels" that are basically 2 × 4 blocks instead of 1 × 8. As a general rule, text embedded in an interlaced PNG image becomes readable roughly twice as fast as in the identical interlaced GIF, as shown in Figure 1-4. The rows show the respective appearance after one-sixty-fourth, one-thirty-second, one-sixteenth, one-eighth, one-fourth, half, and all of the data has arrived. The first column shows GIF interlacing; the others show PNG interlacing, rendered in various styles: standard blocky rendering, interpolated rendering, and sparse rendering, respectively. Note that the word *Interlacing* has roughly the same readability in the fifth GIF row, the fourth blocky PNG row, and the third interpolated PNG row. In other words, the GIF text takes two to four times as long to become readable.

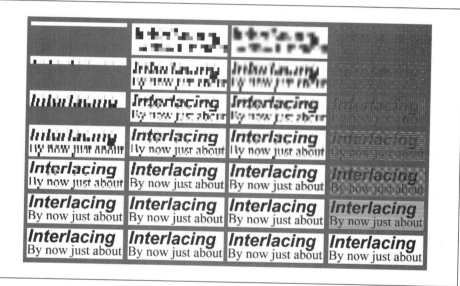

Figure 1-4: Comparison of GIF interlacing (far left), normal PNG interlacing (second from left), PNG with interpolation (second from right), and PNG with sparse display (far right)

JPEG doesn't support interlacing, per se, but it does support a method of progressive display that has been implemented in most browsers since late 1996. In fact, progressive JPEG is a two-dimensional scheme that is not only visually similar to

---

* I am implicitly assuming that one-sixty-fourth of the compressed data (the stuff that can be said to "arrive") corresponds to one-sixty-fourth of the *uncompressed* image data (what the user actually sees). This is not quite true for either PNG or GIF, though the difference is likely to be small in most cases—and other factors, such as network buffering, will tend to wash out any differences that do exist. See Chapter 9 for more details.

interlaced PNG but also somewhat superior. Loosely speaking, progressive JPEG uses the "average" color for any given block of pixels, whereas PNG uses the color of a single pixel in the corner of the block. Early JPEG passes also tend to be somewhat softer (smoother) than early PNG passes; some users find that effect more pleasing.

Finally, I should at least mention TIFF's potential for interlacing. Although no major browser supports TIFF as a native image format, it does offer a very general, random-access approach to image layout. Based either on groups of rows ("strips") or on rectangular blocks of pixels ("tiles"), a properly constructed TIFF could be used for some form of progressive display. But aside from complete lack of browser support (and very little interest from users), TIFF's compression works only within individual strips or tiles, not across them. So either the interlacing effect would be horrible or the compression would be (or quite possibly both), which is probably why no one seems to have tried it.

Compression

PNG's compression is among the best that can be had *without losing image data* and without paying patent or other licensing fees.* Patents are primarily of concern to application developers, not end users, but the decision to throw away some of the information in an image is very much an end-user concern. This information loss generally happens in two ways: in the use of a lesser pixel depth than is required to represent all of the colors in the image, and in the actual compression method (hence "lossy" compression).

PNG supports all three of the main image types discussed earlier: truecolor, grayscale, and palette-based. TIFF likewise supports all three; JPEG only the first two; and GIF only the third, although it can fake grayscale by using a gray palette. Both GIF and PNG palettes are limited to a maximum of 256 colors, which means that full-color images—which usually have tens of thousands or even hundreds of thousands of colors—cannot be stored as GIFs or palette-based PNGs without loss.† On the other hand, an image that does fit into a 256-color palette requires

---

* The "Burrows-Wheeler block transform coding" method used in the bzip2 utility is also unpatented and achieves somewhat better compression than PNG's low-level engine, but it wasn't publicly known at the time and is far, far slower for decoding. JPEG-LS, the new lossless JPEG standard, is fairly fast and performs somewhat better than PNG on natural images, but it does much worse on "artistic" ones. It's covered by patents held by Hewlett-Packard and Mitsubishi, but both companies are waiving license fees (i.e., allowing free use). And BitJazz has a new lossless technique called "condensation"; it appears to compress images 25% to 30% better than PNG, but it is patented and completely proprietary.

† Technically that's not *quite* true in the case of GIF; it supports the concept of multiple subimages, each of which may have its own palette and may be tiled side by side with other subimages to form a truecolor mosaic. This mode is not widely supported, however, particularly on 8-bit displays. Even where it is supported as intended by its proponents, it is an incredibly inefficient way to store and display truecolor image data.

only one byte per pixel, which leads to an immediate factor-of-three reduction in file size over a full RGB image before any "real" compression is done at all. This fact alone is an important issue for PNG images, since PNG allows an image to be stored either way.

It is worth mentioning that TIFF palettes support up to 65,536 colors, which is sufficient to handle many full-color images without loss. Any palette with more than 256 colors will require two bytes per pixel, eliminating much of the benefit of a palette-based image, but applications that support TIFF are usually more concerned with reading and writing speed than with file sizes.

So let's assume that the image type has been decided; that brings us to the compression method itself. Both GIF and PNG use completely lossless compression engines, and all but the most recently specified forms of TIFF do so as well. Standard JPEG compression is always lossy, however, even at the highest quality settings.* Because of this, JPEG images are usually three to ten times smaller than the corresponding PNG or TIFF images. This makes JPEG a very appealing choice for the Web, where small file sizes are important, but JPEG's compression method can introduce visible artifacts such as blockiness, color shifts, and "ringing" or "echos" near image features with sharp edges. The upshot is that JPEG is a poor choice for intermediate saves during editing, and for web use it is best suited to smoothly varying truecolor images, especially photographic ones, at relatively high quality settings. It is not well suited to simple computer graphics, cartoons, and many types of synthetic images. Figure C-3 in the color insert demonstrates this: notice the dirty (or "noisy") appearance of the blue-on-white text, the faint yellow spots above and below it, the darker blue spots in the upper half, and the hints of pink in the white-on-blue text.

Among the popular lossless image-compression engines, PNG's engine is demonstrably the most effective—even leaving aside the issue of prefiltering, which I'll discuss in the next section. TIFF's best classic compression method and GIF's (only) method are both based on an algorithm known as *LZW* (Lempel-Ziv-Welch), which is quite fast and was used in the Unix utility *compress* and in the early PC archiver ARC. PNG's method is called *deflate*, and it is used in the Unix utility *gzip* (which supplanted *compress* in the Unix world) and in PKZIP (which replaced ARC in the early 1990s as the preeminent PC archiver). Unlike LZW, deflate supports different levels of compression versus speed—a dial, if you will. At its lowest setting,† deflate is as fast as or faster than LZW and compresses

---

* There are two forms of truly lossless JPEG, which are discussed briefly in Chapter 8, but currently they are almost universally unsupported. There is also a relatively new TIFF variant that uses ordinary (lossy) JPEG compression, but it is likewise supported by very few applications.

† Actually I'm referring to deflate's second-lowest compression setting ("level 1"); the very lowest setting ("level 0") is uncompressed. Sadly, the dial only goes to 9, not 11.

roughly the same; at its highest setting, deflate is considerably slower but achieves noticeably better compression. (Decompression speed is essentially unaffected by the compression level, except insofar as a less compressed image may take more time to read from network or disk.) The deflate algorithm is described in more detail in Chapter 9.

Compression filters

Compression filters are a way of transforming the image data (without loss of information) so that it will compress better. Each row in the image can have one of five filter types associated with it; choosing which of the five to use for each row is almost more of a black art than a science. Nevertheless, at least one reasonably good algorithm is not only known but is also described in the PNG specification and is implemented in freely available software. Other algorithms are likely to perform even better, but so far this has not been an active area of research.

By way of example—admittedly an extreme case—a 512 × 32,768 image containing all 16,777,216 possible 24-bit colors compressed over 300 times better with filtering than without. The uncompressed image was 48 MB in size; the compressed but unfiltered version was around 36 MB; but the filtered version (using the "reasonably good algorithm" referred to earlier) was only 115,989 bytes (0.1 MB). And a version created by trying multiple filtering approaches was a mere 91,569 bytes, for a total compression ratio of 550:1 and an improvement over the unfiltered version of more than 400 times. Keep in mind that we're talking about *completely lossless compression* here. Yow.

Filtering is also described in more detail in Chapter 9.

Compression oopers

Despite PNG's potential for excellent compression, not all implementations take full advantage of the available power. Even those that do can be thwarted by unwise choices on the part of the user.

The most harmful mistake from the perspective of file size and apparent compression level is mixing up PNG image types. Specifically, forcing an application to save an 8-bit (or smaller) palette image as a 24-bit truecolor image is *not* going to result in a small file. This may be unavoidable if the original has been modified to include more than 256 colors (for example, if a continuous gradient background has been added or another image pasted in), but many images intended for the Web have 256 or fewer colors. These should almost always be saved as palette-based images.

Another simple mistake is creating interlaced images unnecessarily. Interlacing is a great benefit to users waiting for large images to download, but on small ones such as buttons and icons, it makes little difference. From a compression perspective, on the other hand, interlacing can have a significant impact, especially for small images. Compression works best where pixels are similar or identical, which is often the case in localized regions, but PNG's two-dimensional interlacing scheme mixes up pixels in an "unnatural" order that can destroy any compressor-friendly patterns.

Another "unnatural" image modification is standard JPEG compression. The echoes (or ringing) I mentioned earlier are almost never a good thing from PNG's point of view, regardless of their visual effect. For example, a blue image with white text could be saved natively as a two-color (1-bit) palette PNG. After JPEG compression, however, there will be a whole range of blues and whites in the image, and possibly even hints of some other colors. The image would then have to be saved as an 8-bit or even a 24-bit PNG, with obvious consequences for the file size. Bottom line: don't convert JPEGs to PNGs unless there is absolutely no alternative. Instead, start over with the original truecolor or grayscale image and convert *that* to PNG.

On the programmer's side, one common mistake is to include unused palette entries in a PNG image, which again inflates the file size. This error is most noticeable when converting tiny GIF images (bullets, buttons, and so on) to PNG format; these images are typically only 1,000 bytes or so in size, and storing 256 3-byte palette entries where only 50 are needed would result in over 600 bytes of wasted space. PNG's support for transparent palette images, which involves a secondary "palette" of transparency values that mirrors the main color palette, can also be misused in this way. Because all palette colors are assumed to be opaque unless explicitly given transparency, well-written programs will reorder the palette so that any transparent entries come first. That allows the remainder of the transparency chunk, containing only opaque entries, to be omitted.

Another common programmer mistake is to use only one type of compression filter, or to vary them incorrectly. As noted earlier, compression filters can make a dramatic difference in the compressibility of the image. However, this is not a feature that users need to know much about. For applications such as Adobe Photoshop that do allow users to play with filters, the best approach is to turn off filters for palette-based images and to use dynamic filters for all other types.

Finally, the low-level compression engine itself can be tweaked to compress either better or faster. Usually "best compression" is the preferred setting, but an implementor may choose to use an intermediate level of compression in order to boost the interactive performance for the user. In general, the difference in file size is negligible, but there are rare cases in which such a choice can make a big difference.

A more detailed list of compression tips for both users and programmers is presented in Chapter 9.

Summary of Usage

Table 1-1 summarizes the sorts of tasks for which PNG, JPEG, GIF, and TIFF tend to be best suited; question marks indicate debatable entries. (Keep in mind that there are always exceptions, though.)

Table 1-1: Comparison of Typical Usage for Four Image Formats

	PNG	GIF	JPEG	TIFF
Editing, palette image, fast saves	✓	✓		✓
Editing, truecolor image, fast saves	✓			✓
"Final" edit, best compression	✓			
Editing, maximal editor portability	?	?		?
Web, truecolor image, no transparency			✓	
Web, palette image, no transparency	✓	✓		
Web, image with "on/off" transparency	✓	✓		
Web, image with partial transparency	✓			
Web, cross-platform color consistency	✓			
Web, animation		✓		
Web, maximal browser portability	?	✓	✓	
Web, smallest possible images	✓		✓	

Several things are worth noting here. The first is that TIFF is not at all suited as a web format, simply because it is not supported by any major browser. (This will not be a big surprise to the web designers in the audience.) Even as an editing format, TIFF's main strength is its speed. With regard to portability between image-editing apps, the facts are a little murkier, however. GIF traditionally has been the best-supported format due to its simplicity, but a number of shareware and freeware applications have dropped support due to patent-licensing issues. TIFF has been widely supported, too, but it has also been widely cursed for its incompatibilities among apps. And PNG, of course, is still relatively new. By now it is supported by most of the main image editors, but some of its features (such as 48-bit truecolor) are often supported as read-only capabilities or ignored altogether.

The choice of a web format depends almost entirely on what features are required in the image. Transparency automatically rules out JPEG; partial transparency rules out GIF, as well. For animation, GIF is the only choice. For opaque, photographic images, JPEG is the only reasonable choice—its compression can't be beat. The truly critical issue, however, is portability across browsers. GIF and JPEG are relatively safe bets, but what about PNG? By late 1997, it was supported (at least minimally) in virtually all browsers; Microsoft's Internet Explorer 4.0 and Netscape's

Navigator 4.04 finally got native PNG support in October and November 1997, respectively.* But gamma correction was supported only by Internet Explorer, and PNG transparency was almost unusable. At the time of this writing, Navigator 5.0 is still unreleased, and IE 5.0 for Windows is unchanged from version 4.0. But there are strong indications that the Big Two will finally support both gamma and full alpha-channel transparency in their next major releases.

Of course, that begs the question of when it is safe to start using PNG on the Web. In theory, the extended OBJECT tag in HTML 4.0 provides the means to do so immediately. OBJECT is a "container" in HTML parlance, similar to FONT tags or BLOCKQUOTE; it affects the stuff inside it, between the <OBJECT> and </OBJECT> tags—including other (nested) OBJECTs. Unlike most container tags, however, OBJECTs refer to their own data (as part of the <OBJECT> tag itself), and this can include images. In fact, one can think of an OBJECT as an extremely enhanced IMG tag. Whereas IMG refers to a single datatype (just images) and can display a small amount of plain text if the image can't be rendered (via the ALT attribute), OBJECTs can refer to numerous datatypes (images, VRML, Shockwave, Java applets, and so on) and can display arbitrary HTML if their main datatype cannot be rendered (via the contents of the OBJECT container). Thus, browsers peel OBJECT blocks like onions, first trying to render the outermost layer and moving inward until they find something they can handle. As soon as they find something to render, the remainder of the block is discarded. (This is the sense in which the inner stuff is "affected": it may be completely ignored. Indeed, only one layer is *not* ignored . . . at least according to the HTML 4.0 specification.)

So the preferred approach for PNG images is simply to wrap an OBJECT tag around an old-style IMG tag, where the OBJECT refers to the PNG and the IMG refers to a JPEG or GIF version of the same image. I'll provide some concrete examples of this in Chapter 2, *Applications: WWW Browsers and Servers.* Newer browsers that support both PNG and OBJECT will render the PNG in the outer OBJECT, ignoring the IMG tag. Older browsers will either ignore OBJECT as an unknown tag or else parse it but recognize that they cannot render the PNG; either way, they will use the GIF or JPEG from the inner IMG tag, or the text in the ALT attribute if they do not support images.

At least, that's the theory. The main problem with this approach is that no version of Navigator or Internet Explorer up through the latest 4.x releases handles OBJECT tags correctly. Both browsers will attempt to find a plug-in to handle an OBJECT image; lacking that, they will either render the inner IMG or fail entirely. I'll look at this in more detail in Chapter 2.

---

* Most other web browsers have supported PNG natively since 1995 or 1996.

But plug-in oddities notwithstanding, the IMG-within-an-OBJECT approach works moderately well now and will only get better as browsers improve their conformance with WWW standards and as the need for external PNG plug-ins diminishes. Indeed, most of the images on the Portable Network Graphics home site are referenced in this manner. As for referring to PNG images directly in old-style IMG tags, which is more commonly thought of as "using PNG on the Web"—that depends on the images and on the target audience. For example, the Acorn home site already uses PNG images in places; their audience is largely Acorn users, and Acorn Browse has perhaps the best PNG support of any browser in the world. But sites targeted at the average user running Navigator or Internet Explorer must keep in mind that any given release of the Big Two browsers achieves widespread use only after a year or so, and even then, a large percentage of users continue to use older versions. From a PNG perspective, this means that late 1998 was about the earliest it would have been reasonable to begin using IMG-tag PNGs on general-purpose sites. Sites that would like to make use of PNG transparency or gamma support will have to wait until about a year after the 5.0 releases occur, which presumably means sometime in the year 2000. (PNG as the Image Format of the New Millennium* has a nice ring to it, though.)

Case Study of a PNG-Supporting Image Editor

Software development tends to be a dynamic and rapidly changing field, and even periodicals have trouble keeping up with what is current. To attempt to do so in a book—even one that uses the phrase "at the time of this writing" as often as I have here—borders on the ridiculous. Nevertheless, given PNG's unique feature set and its unfamiliarity to many of those who could make the best use of those features, I feel that it is worth the risk to explore in depth an application that appears to have, as of early 1999, the best PNG support of anything on the market: Macromedia's Fireworks 1.0, available for 32-bit Windows and Macintosh. (Version 2.0 was released while this book was in the final stages of production; information about it is noted wherever possible, but I did not have time to test it.)

Fireworks is an image editor with a feature set that rivals Adobe Photoshop in many ways, but with far more emphasis on web graphics and less on high-end printing support. In this, it is closer to Adobe ImageReady, a web-specific application intended to tune image colors and optimize file sizes. I'll come back to Photoshop and ImageReady in Chapter 4, *Applications: Image Editors*.

---

* That would be the millennium of four-digit years beginning with the numeral "2," which, of course, is what everyone will be celebrating on New Year's Eve, 1999. (The Third Millennium is the one that starts on January 1, 2001.)

PNG Feature Support in Fireworks

Fireworks 1.0 supports a good range of PNG features and image types, and it truly shines in its handling of transparency—indeed, its native internal format is 32-bit RGBA (truecolor with a full 8-bit alpha channel) for all images, and it can save this format, too. In addition, ordinary single-color (GIF-like) transparency is supported in both palette-based and RGB image types, and PNG's unique "RGBA palette" mode is also supported. Nor is this support limited to recognizing when an image contains 256 or fewer color-transparency combinations; with a suitable choice of export options, Fireworks can (within limits) quantize and optionally dither even a truecolor image with a nontrivial alpha channel to an 8-bit RGBA-palette image.

There are a couple of notable omissions from Fireworks's list of PNG features, however. The most painful is the lack of support for gamma and color correction; images created by the application will vary in appearance between different display systems just as much as any old-style GIF or JPEG image would, appearing too bright and washed out on Macintosh, SGI, and NeXT systems or too dark on just about everything else. Version 1.0 also cannot write interlaced PNGs, even though it provides a seemingly valid checkbox option for some PNG output types. Version 2.0 addresses this problem, but only in a very limited way: the original plans were to include a "hidden" preference that can be changed so that all exported PNG images are interlaced (instead of none of them).*

As one would expect of a graphics application targeted at the Web, Fireworks doesn't preserve 16-bit samples, although it will read 16-bit PNG images (for example, from a medical scan) and convert the samples to 8 bits. Slightly more surprising is its lack of support for true grayscale PNGs; Fireworks saves these as palette-based files, with a palette composed entirely of grayscale entries. This is a perfectly valid type of PNG file, but the required palette adds up to 780 bytes of unnecessary overhead, a distinct liability for icons and other tiny images. On the other hand, a palette-based grayscale image with transparency can include a colored palette entry to be used as the background color, something that PNG does not support for true grayscale files.

In addition to supporting PNG as an output format, Fireworks actually uses PNG as its native file format for day-to-day intermediate saves. This is possible thanks to PNG's extensible "chunk-based" design, which allows programs to incorporate application-specific data in a well-defined way. Macromedia has embraced this capability, defining at least four custom chunk types that hold various things pertinent to the editor. Unfortunately, one of them (pRVW) violates the PNG naming

---

* A tight release schedule was the main reason for the lack of a real fix in version 2.0; Macromedia engineers were fully aware of the deficiencies in the workaround and are expected to address them in the next release.

rules by claiming to be an officially registered, public chunk type, but this was an oversight and should be fixed in version 2.0.

Although it is entirely possible to use the intermediate Fireworks PNG files in other applications, including on the Web (in fact, one of the "frequently asked questions" on the Fireworks web site specifically mentions Netscape, Internet Explorer, and Photoshop), they are not really appropriate for such usage. One reason is that the native PNG format reflects Fireworks's internal storage format, which, as mentioned earlier, is 32-bit RGBA. Even if the image contains only two colors and no transparency, it is saved as a 32-bit PNG file. That certainly doesn't help the old compression ratio any, but the potential for expansion due to the image depth is often overshadowed by that due to the custom chunks, several of which are huge.* Thanks to these chunks (which are meaningless to any application but Fireworks), the intermediate PNG files can easily be larger than a completely uncompressed RGBA image would be.

Of course, Macromedia never intended for users to treat the native Fireworks PNG files as the final output format. The fully editable "fat" PNGs are produced by the Save menu option; to make final, highly compressed PNGs for web usage, use the Export option. While this might seem like an odd approach to someone unfamiliar with modern image editors, its only real difference from that of applications like Photoshop or Paint Shop Pro is the fact that the intermediate format is widely readable even by low-end apps and browsers (which is not the case for Photoshop's native *.psd* format or Paint Shop Pro's *.psp* format). For an in-house network with high-speed links—for example, in a design studio—this allows images to be easily browsable over the intranet, yet retain all of their object-level editing attributes.

Invoking PNG Features in Fireworks

Because Fireworks's internal format is 32-bit (i.e., truecolor plus a full alpha channel), working with transparency is as easy as opening an image and applying the Eraser tool to its background. For example, suppose you have a photograph of someone and want to focus on the face by making everything else transparent, leaving behind an oval (or at least roundish) portrait shot with a soft border. There are several ways to accomplish this, but the following prescription is one of the simplest:

---

* In a 590k tutorial image from Macromedia's web site, 230k is due to image data; 360k is due to custom chunks.

1. Open the original image (**File** → **Open**).

2. Pick the background image (**Modify** → **Background Image**).

3. Double-click on the **Lasso** tool (right side of tool palette, second from top).

4. In the **Tool Options** pop-up, pick **Feather** and a radius, perhaps 25.

5. Draw a loop around the face of the subject.

6. Invert the lasso selection so that the part *outside* the loop gets erased (**Select** → **Inverse**).

7. Erase everything outside the loop via **Edit** → **Clear** (or do so manually with the Eraser tool).

Note that the Lasso tool's feathering radius is subtly different from that available via the Select menu. The latter is a smoothing factor for the Lasso's *boundaries*; in this example, with an inverted selection so that the image's rectangular boundary is also lassoed, changing the value through the menu will round off the corners of the dashed Lasso boundary and may merge separated parts of it together. The feathering radius on the Tool Options pop-up affects only the width of the partially transparent region generated along the Lasso's boundary.

In any case, that's all there is to creating an image with transparency. The next step is to save it as a PNG file. As I just noted, the Save and Save As... menu items save the complete Fireworks "project," retaining information about the objects in the image and the steps used to create them, at a considerable cost in file size. It is generally worthwhile to save a copy that way in case further editing is needed later. But for publishing the image on the Web, it must be exported, and this is where it can be converted into a palette-based image with or without transparency—or left as a 32-bit RGBA image, but without all of the extra editing information included.

First let's consider the case of exporting the image as a full RGBA file. Here are the available options in the Export dialog box:

- **Format**: PNG
- **Bit Depth**: Millions +Alpha (32 bit)

Fireworks 1.0 provides no option to interlace the image, so the preceding steps represent the complete list of possibilities for this case. Things get more interesting when it comes to palette-based (or *indexed-color*) images. Then one has the option of choosing either single-color transparency or the nicer RGBA-palette transparency, in addition to a number of other palette-related options. Here are the options for the RGBA-palette case:

- **Format:** PNG
- **Bit Depth:** Indexed (8 bit) (this is the default)
- **Palette:** WebSnap Adaptive (default) or Adaptive
- **Dither:** Check on or off
- **Transparency:** Alpha Channel
- **Interlaced:** Checkbox may be checked but does nothing in version 1.0

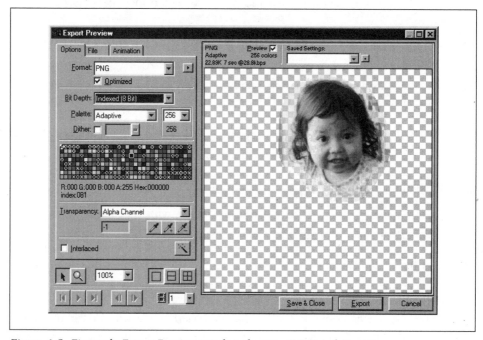

Figure 1-5: Fireworks Export Preview window showing RGBA-palette options

Note that the effects of the current options are reflected in the preview image to the right (as in Figure 1-5), which shows a limitation in Macromedia's original implementation of RGBA-palette mode. In particular, only four levels of alpha are used, two of which are either complete transparency or complete opacity (the other two represent one-third and two-thirds transparency), which results in very noticeable banding effects in Figure 1-6.

The four-level approach works quite well for anti-aliasing (that is, preventing "jaggies" on curved elements such as circles or text), which effectively involves a one-pixel-wide band of variable transparency lying between regions of complete transparency and complete opacity. But the previous example uses a 25-pixel-wide feathering radius, and the two partial-transparency bands both show up extremely well and have sharply defined edges even if dithering is turned on. Unfortunately, that rather defeats the purpose of alpha transparency in this case; the 32-bit

Figure 1-6: Example of Fireworks RGBA-palette image showing strong banding

version is the only alternative. Fortunately this was one of the areas that got fixed in version 2.0, and judging by one test image, the results are spectacular.

Very nearly the same procedure works if you want to save the image with single-color, GIF-like transparency; instead of picking Alpha Channel from the list of options in the Transparency pull-down box, this time pick **Index Color**. Doing so once will allocate a single palette entry, not used elsewhere in the image, to act as the fully transparent color. A strange feature of version 1.0 is that the Transparency pull-down will still indicate Alpha Channel the first time Index Color is chosen. Choosing it again will cause it to "stick," but at a cost: the entry chosen for transparency, which generally seems to be the last one (usually black), may now be used in the opaque parts of the image as well as the transparent regions. It is not clear whether this is a bug or an intentional feature of some sort, but it is fully reproducible. Figure 1-7 shows an example.

As with transparent GIFs, single-color PNG transparency requires that the image be displayed against a suitable background color—white, in our example—to look good. The opposite case, displaying against black, is shown in Figure 1-8.

Analysis of Fireworks PNG Support

I should note a few caveats about the implementation of indexed-color images and transparency in Fireworks 1.0. For example, the dither checkbox seems to have very little effect in any of the palette examples, and no effect at all on the alpha channel in RGBA images; in fact, the export "wizard" explicitly notes this and actually recommends against its use. And the palette-size pull-down seems to have been borrowed from the GIF user interface—it allows only power-of-two palette sizes (e.g., 64, 128, 256) even though PNG's palette chunk can have any

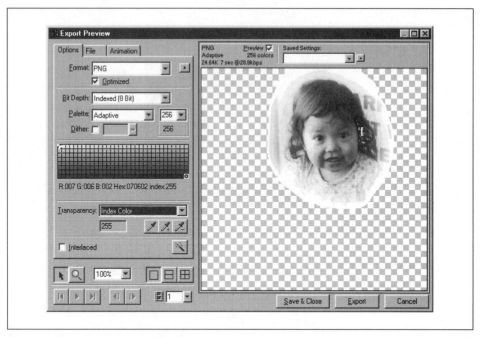

Figure 1-7: Fireworks Export Preview after choosing Index Color transparency twice, showing transparency (white artifacts) in opaque regions

Figure 1-8: Example of a Fireworks image with single-color transparency, displayed against the "wrong" background

number of entries from 1 to 256. The final jump is particularly abrupt; it may happen that 160 colors is the perfect trade-off between quality and image size, but such an image would have to be saved with either 128 or 256 colors.

With regard to transparency, the placement of transparent entries in the Export window's palette view is directly reflected in the PNG file's palette, whether Alpha Channel or Index Color is selected. This is regrettable, since the transparent colors are scattered all over the palette in the alpha case. The single-color case is even worse—the transparent color is the very last entry in the palette. As noted earlier, the preferred approach is to put all of the transparent entries at the beginning of the palette so that the redundant information about opaque colors can be eliminated from the transparency chunk. For a photographic image saved in palette format with single-color transparency, the cost is 127 or 255 bytes of wasted space.

PNG also supports a single-color (or single-shade) transparency mode that works with truecolor and grayscale images and avoids the need for a full alpha channel, but there is no way to invoke this feature in Fireworks. The lack of any grayscale support other than palette-based means that a gray image with an alpha channel must be saved either as RGBA, doubling its size, or as an indexed image with transparent palette entries, generally with some data loss. (The loss comes about because there are only 256 possible gray+alpha combinations in palette mode, whereas a full gray+alpha image supports up to 65,536 combinations.) There is also no support for a PNG background-color chunk.

Images that already have transparency are preserved quite well (recall that everything is stored internally as 32-bit RGBA), and Fireworks provides quite a number of options beyond what described earlier for adding or modifying transparency. One in particular that could be used for unsharp masking and other special effects is invoked via the **Xtras** menu. With the background image selected, choose **Other → Convert to Alpha**, which first converts the image to grayscale and then to an alpha mask. The lightest parts of the image become the most transparent, while the black parts remain opaque.

Fireworks's compression is reasonably good. Even though there are no user options to adjust the compression level, the default level is a good trade-off between speed and size. Truecolor images tend to be compressed within a few percent of the best possible size, while indexed-color images may see upward of 15% improvement when run through an optimization tool such as *pngcrush* (discussed in Chapter 5, *Applications: Image Converters*).

Fireworks also does a good job preserving PNG text annotations, albeit with a quirk: it removes all of the line breaks ("newlines"), for some reason. (Oddly enough, GIF and JPEG comments are not preserved.) The program adds its own Software text chunk; as one might expect, any incoming image that already includes such a chunk will find it replaced. This is a minor breach of PNG etiquette, but one that helps keep tiny image files from getting noticeably bigger because of text comments.

Fireworks 1.0 also adds a Creation Time text chunk to most images it exports. This is not really a problem, per se; what is unusual is that the chunk's contents are invariably "Thu, May 7, 1998"—a date that has nothing to do with any of the images or even with the release of Fireworks 1.0. See also Chapter 11 for a discussion of why "creation time" is a fuzzy concept. Version 2.0 was to have corrected this, replacing the Creation Time text chunk with PNG's officially defined timestamp chunk, tIME, but I did not have a chance to verify that. The tIME chunk indicates the time of last modification, which is a more precisely defined concept and one that is appropriate for an image editor.

As noted earlier, the ability to save interlaced PNG images will first be implemented as a global preference setting. As of January 1999, the plan was for this to require editing version 2.0's preferences file. Under Windows, this file is called *Fireworks Preferences.txt* and is in the Fireworks installation directory (*c:\Program Files\Macromedia\Fireworks*, by default); on the Macintosh, it is called *Fireworks Preferences* and is found in the *System Folder:Preferences* folder. Open the file in any text editor and find the line:

```
(ExportPngWithAdam7Interlacing) (false)
```

Change this to the following to make all exported images interlaced:

```
(ExportPngWithAdam7Interlacing) (true)
```

This change will only take effect after Fireworks 2.0 is restarted. Fortunately, later releases are expected to have a normal checkbox option.

Concluding Thoughts on Fireworks

Lest the preceding detailed list of caveats and oddities leave the reader with the impression that Fireworks's PNG support is not as good as I initially suggested, let me reiterate that it is, in fact, quite good overall. Version 2.0's improved support for RGBA-palette images puts Fireworks far ahead of any other image editor. The inability to set PNG interlacing is regrettable but is being addressed; lack of gamma support is the only truly unfortunate design choice, particularly for a product with both Windows and Macintosh versions. With luck, both gamma and color correction will become core features of the next major release.

2

Applications:
WWW Browsers
and Servers

Since the Web is where some of PNG's more uncommon features—alpha, gamma and color correction, two-dimensional interlacing—are most apparent and useful, it makes sense to begin our coverage of PNG-supporting applications with a look at web browsers and web servers.

WWW Browsers

Although there are dozens of web browsers available, most of which have supported PNG since 1995 or 1996, for the vast majority of users and webmasters there are only two that count: Netscape Navigator and Microsoft Internet Explorer. Collectively referred to as "the Big Two," these browsers' level of support for any given feature largely determines the viability of said feature. PNG support is a good example.

Netscape Navigator

Netscape's Navigator browser, which originally shipped standalone but more recently has been bundled as part of the Communicator suite, supplanted NCSA Mosaic late in 1994 as the standard browser by which all others were measured. Version 1.1N was released in the spring of 1995, at roughly the same time as the frozen PNG specification, but despite the hopes and efforts of the PNG developers, the first Navigator 2.0 betas shipped later that year with animated GIF support rather than PNG. Navigator 2.0 did offer the possibility of platform-specific, third-party PNG support via Netscape's new plug-in interface, but only for Windows and Macintosh. Alas, even that was fatally flawed from an image-support perspective: Navigator's native image-handling code (via the HTML IMG tag) had no provision for handing off unknown image types to plug-ins. That meant that even if PNG plug-ins were written for both supported platforms, and even if a majority of users downloaded and installed a plug-in, it would be useless for standard HTML—only pages using Netscape's proprietary EMBED tag would invoke the custom code. Moreover, Navigator 2.0 plug-ins were given no access to the existing page background, which meant that PNG transparency would be completely ignored.

The Navigator 3.0 betas in 1996 extended plug-in support to include Unix platforms as well, but they fixed none of the fundamental problems in the plug-in API.* The interface was considerably revamped in 1997 for the 4.0 betas, however, finally allowing transparency support via something called a *windowless plug-in*—though only for the Windows and Macintosh platforms. Support was also added for images referenced via the new HTML OBJECT tag. But the basic lack of a connection between plug-ins and the native IMG-tag code persisted, and this barrier extended to the new OBJECT-handling code as well—even a JPEG or GIF image in an OBJECT tag would fail unless an appropriate plug-in were found. Should the outer OBJECT happen to be a PNG, Navigator would fail to render even the inner GIF or JPEG in the absence of a PNG plug-in. Unlike IMG tags, Navigator required OBJECT tags to include the otherwise optional HEIGHT and WIDTH attributes to invoke a plug-in. In at least one version, the browser would ignore not only an undimensioned OBJECT but also all subsequent dimensioned ones.

But in November 1997, a year after the World Wide Web Consortium (W3C) officially recommended PNG for web use, Netscape released Navigator 4.04 with native PNG support—that is, it was at last capable of displaying PNG images referenced in HTML IMG tags without the need for a third-party plug-in. Unfortunately, versions 4.04 through 4.51 had no support for any type of transparency, nor did they support gamma correction, and their handling of OBJECT tags remained broken. At least a few of these releases, including 4.5, had a bug that effectively caused any PNG image served by Microsoft Internet Information Servers to be rendered as the dreaded broken-image icon. (I'll come back to this in the server section later in this chapter, but the bug is fixed in Navigator 4.51.) But the 4.x versions did support progressive display of interlaced PNGs, at least.

Concurrent with the later Communicator 4.0 releases, on March 31, 1998, Netscape released most of the source code to its development version of Communicator, nominally a pre-beta version "5.0." Developers around the world promptly dug into the code to fix their favorite bugs and add their pet features. One nice surprise was that the so-called Mozilla sources already contained a minimal level of

---

* Applications Programming Interface, the means by which one piece of code (in this case, the plug-in) talks to another (in this case, the browser). APIs are also how programs request services from the operating system or the graphical windowing system.

transparency support. There were two main problems with it, however: the transparency mask for all but the final pass of interlaced images was scaled incorrectly—a minor bug, hardly unexpected given the early stage of development—and the transparency was either fully off or fully on for any given pixel, regardless of whether multilevel transparency information (an alpha channel) was present. The latter problem proved to be more serious than it sounded. Because of the way Mozilla's layout engine worked, at any given moment the code had no idea what the background looked like; instead, it depended on the local windowing system to composite partly transparent foreground objects with the background image(s). In other words, adding full support for alpha transparency was not something that could be done just once in the image-handling code, but instead required modifying the "front end" code for each windowing system supported: at a minimum, Windows, Macintosh, and Unix's X Window System, plus any new ports that got added along the way.

Difficult as it may sound, fixing Mozilla's (and therefore Navigator's) support for PNG alpha channels is by no means an insurmountable challenge. But in one of life's little ironies, the person who initially volunteered to fix the code, and who thereafter nominally became responsible for it, also somehow agreed to write this book. Alas, when push came to shove, the book is what got the most attention. :-) But all is not lost; by the time this text reaches print, full alpha support should be well on its way into Mozilla and then into Navigator 5.0 as well.

Table 2-1 summarizes the status and level of PNG support in all of the major releases of Netscape's browser to date. The latest public releases, Navigator 4.08 and 4.51, are available for Windows 3.x, Windows 95/98/NT, Macintosh 68k and PowerPC, and more than a dozen flavors of Unix; the web page is at *http://home. netscape.com/browsers/*. Version 4.04 for OS/2 Warp is available only from IBM's site, *http://www.software.ibm.com/os/warp/netscape/*.

Table 2-1: PNG Support in Netscape Navigator and Mozilla

Version	PNG Support?	Level of Support
NN 1.x	No	N/A
NN 2.x	Plug-in (Win/Mac only)	EMBED tag only; no transparency
NN 3.x	Plug-in (all platforms)	EMBED tag only; no transparency
NN 4.0–4.03	Plug-in (all platforms)	EMBED or OBJECT; transparency possible on Windows and Macintosh
NN 4.04–4.51	Native (all platforms)	IMG; no transparency
Moz 4/98–4/99	Native (all platforms)	IMG; binary transparency
NN 5.0	Not yet released	To be determined (IMG with full alpha transparency?)

Table 2-2 summarizes the PNG support in a number of third-party plug-ins. Note that the Windows QuickTime 3.0 plug-in installs itself in every copy of Navigator and Internet Explorer on the machine, taking over the `image/png` media type in the process. This effectively breaks the browsers' built-in PNG support (if any) and may be true of other plug-ins as well. To remove the QuickTime plug-in from a particular instance of a browser, find its plug-ins directory—usually called *Plug-ins*—and delete or remove the file *npqtplugin.dll* (or move it elsewhere).

Table 2-2: PNG Support in Netscape Plug-ins

Name	Platform(s)	Plug-in API Level	Level of Support
PNG Live 1.0	Win 9x/NT, Mac PPC	2.0	No transparency, no gamma, no progressive display
PNG Live 2.0b5	Win 9x/NT	4.0	Full transparency if no background chunk, broken gamma, progressive display
QuickTime 3.0	Win 9x/NT, Mac 68k/PPC	2.0	No transparency, no progressive display
PNG Magick 0.8.5	Unix/X	3.0	No transparency, no progressive display, requires ImageMagick
G. Costa plug-in 0.9	OS/2	2.0	No transparency, progressive display

Netscape's online programming documentation for plug-ins may be found at *http://developer.netscape.com/docs/manuals/communicator/plugin/*. The PNG Live plug-in, versions 1.0 and 2.0b5, is available from *http://codelab.siegelgale.com/solutions/png_index.html* and *http://codelab.siegelgale.com/solutions/pnglive2.html*, respectively.* Apple's QuickTime is downloadable from *http://www.apple.com/quicktime/*. Rasca Gmelch's PNG Magick plug-in is available from *http://home.pages.de/~rasca/pngplugin/*, and the ImageMagick home page is at *http://www.wizards.dupont.com/cristy/ImageMagick.html*. And Giorgio Costa's OS/2 plug-in can be downloaded directly from *http://hobbes.nmsu.edu/pub/os2/apps/internet/www/browser/npgpng09.zip*.

Microsoft Internet Explorer

Microsoft's web browser lagged Netscape's in features and performance through its first two major releases, but with the release of Internet Explorer 3.0, general consensus was that it had largely caught up. IE 3.0 was the first Microsoft release

---

* The codelab site went offline in March 1999, and there has been no word from Siegel and Gale whether this is permanent.

to include support for Netscape-style plug-ins and, in that manner, became the first release to support PNG in any way—though only on the Windows platform. But with the release of the first IE 4.0 beta in the spring of 1997, followed by the official public release of version 4.0 in October 1997, Microsoft took the lead from Netscape, at least in terms of PNG support. IE 4.0 for Windows incorporated native PNG support, including progressive display, gamma correction, and some transparency. The latter was an odd sort of binary transparency, however, and apparently applied only to RGBA-palette images; images with a full alpha channel were rendered completely opaque, always against a light gray background. For palette images, IE's threshold for deciding which pixels were opaque and which were transparent was not set at 0.3%, as the PNG specification somewhat unfortunately recommends, nor at 50%, as one might intuitively expect, but instead at something like 99.7% opacity. That is, unless a given pixel were completely opaque, IE 4.0 would render it completely transparent. Needless to say, this resulted in some odd and unintended rendering effects that could have been mitigated by dithering the alpha channel down to a binary transparency mask.

Internet Explorer's handling of PNG images in HTML 4.0 OBJECT tags is decidedly buggy. Like Navigator, it will fail to render an OBJECT PNG with its native code, instead preferring to seek an ActiveX plug-in of some sort. But IE 4.0 does not necessarily limit itself to its own plug-ins; it has been observed to adopt Netscape plug-ins from elsewhere on the computer, and since it apparently doesn't support the Navigator 4.0 plug-in API, it fails on newer plug-ins such as PNG Live 2.0. Even worse, when two (or more) OBJECTs are nested, IE 4.0 will attempt to render *both* images.

It is also noteworthy that Internet Explorer 4.0 cannot be used to view standalone PNG images, even though it can do so if the images are embedded within a web page with IMG tags. Presumably this was simply an oversight, but it has ramifications for setting up the PNG media type within the Windows registry.

Internet Explorer 5.0 for 32-bit Windows was released in March 1999, and in most respects its PNG support was unchanged from version 4.0. The inability to view standalone PNGs was fixed (allowing IE 5.0 to be used as an ordinary image viewer), but in all other regards PNG support appears to have stagnated. OBJECT PNGs are still only displayed if the "Run ActiveX Controls and Plug-ins" setting is enabled (under **Tools** → **Internet Options** → **Security**), even though it ends up using the same internal PNG code as it does for IMG PNGs. Even worse, OBJECT PNGs are given a fat border, which results in the appearance of horizontal and vertical scrollbars around each one, and there is no transparency support at all for OBJECTs. As in IE 4.0, nested OBJECTs are all rendered, side by side. With ActiveX disabled, IE 5.0 does revert to whatever IMG tag is inside the OBJECTs, but not before it pops up one or two warning boxes every time it displays such a web page. Its transparency support is unchanged; only palette images are displayed with transparency, and the threshold for complete transparency is still set at 99.7% opacity.

Fortunately for Mac users, the development of Internet Explorer for Macintosh is handled by a separate group, and the yet-unreleased version 5.0 reportedly will have complete support for alpha transparency in PNG images. Of course, in the meantime, Mac fans are stuck with version 4.5, which has no PNG support at all.

Official releases of IE 5.0 exist for Windows 3.x, Windows 9x/NT, and two flavors of Unix (Solaris and HP-UX). PNG support in the Unix and 16-bit Windows versions is reported to be similar to that in the 32-bit Windows version.

Table 2-3 summarizes Internet Explorer's level of PNG support to date. The Internet Explorer home page is currently at *http://www.microsoft.com/windows/ie/*.

Table 2-3: PNG Support in Internet Explorer

Version	PNG support?	Level of Support
IE 1.x	No	N/A
IE 2.x	No	N/A
IE 3.x	Plug-in	EMBED tag only; no transparency
IE 4.0	Native (most platforms)	IMG; binary transparency (palette images only) with skewed threshold
IE 4.5	Plug-in (Macintosh only)	EMBED tag only; no transparency
IE 5.0	Native (most platforms)	IMG; binary transparency (palette images only) with skewed threshold
IE 5.0	Native (Macintosh—not yet released)	To be determined (IMG with full alpha transparency?)

Opera

Opera, the small-footprint, high-speed browser from Norway, is by some measures* the third most popular browser for the Windows 3.x and 95/98/NT platforms. Native ports to the Amiga, BeOS, Macintosh, OS/2, Psion, and Unix are also underway. Version 3.0 had no PNG support at all, while version 3.5 supported it only through old-style Netscape plug-ins (i.e., with no transparency support). Version 3.51, released in December 1998, includes native PNG support. Opera displays PNG images progressively and does gamma correction, but like Navigator, it does not invoke its internal image handlers for images in OBJECT tags. Transparency, unfortunately, is only partly supported. Truecolor and grayscale images with alpha channels are rendered completely opaque; most palette images are

---

* BrowserWatch statistics, anyway (*http://browserwatch.internet.com/stats/stats.html*).

rendered with binary transparency, although at least one palette-based example exists in which the image is rendered without any transparency.

Opera is available from the Opera Software home page, *http://www.operasoftware. com/*. News on the non-Windows ports can be found at *http://www.operasoftware. com/alt_os.html*.

Acorn Browse

At the other end of the popularity spectrum—at least to judge by overall statistics—lies a browser unique in its stellar support for PNG features: Acorn Browse. Available only for Acorn computers running RISC OS, Browse has always supported PNG and has offered full gamma and alpha-transparency support since version 1.25. Not only that, but (take a deep breath now) it actually supports full alpha transparency while doing replicating (blocky) progressive display of interlaced PNGs on top of arbitrary backgrounds. That's quite a mouthful, but in simple terms it means that the browser can display, in a very elegant manner, transparent, interlaced PNGs as they download. From a programmer's perspective it's even more impressive: consider that an opaque pixel from an early interlacing pass may get replicated and thereby hide background pixels that, due to transparency, should be visible when the image is completely displayed. So extra work is necessary to ensure that parts of the background covered up by early interlacing passes are still available for compositing during later passes. As of early 1999, there was no web browser in the world with better PNG support than Browse. Unfortunately, most development on Browse itself ended late in 1998, as a result of restructuring at Acorn; version 2.07 is the latest and possibly the final release, although the web page (*http://www.acorn.com/browser*) indicates that development "will continue . . . as a 'spare time' activity."

Arena

Arena was the World Wide Web Consortium's early test bed for HTML 3.0 and Cascading Style Sheets (CSS1). It also became one of the first browsers to support alpha transparency in PNG images (possibly the very first), although this feat was somewhat diminished by the fact that it didn't support background images at the time—except for its own "sandy" background. Nevertheless, it was a useful browser for testing PNG images under Unix.

Subsequent to the release of beta-3b in September 1996, Arena development was taken over by Yggdrasil Computing, which managed roughly 60 beta releases over the course of 16 months. The browser never achieved 1.0 status, however, and development essentially ended in March 1998 (though a final 0.3.62 release with minimal changes showed up in November 1998). Yggdrasil's Arena web page is at

http://www.yggdrasil.com/Products/Arena/, and old versions are still available from
the W3C's page at *http://www.w3.org/Arena/*.

Amaya

Amaya replaced Arena as the W3C's test-bed browser in 1996 and has always
included PNG support. Unlike Arena, it runs under not only various flavors of
Unix, but also Windows 95, 98, and NT. Although it supports transparency, its
implementation was still somewhat broken as of version 1.4; under Linux, it
appeared to support only binary transparency, and that only for palette-alpha
images (that is, images whose palette effectively consists of red, green, blue, and
alpha values). Amaya 1.4's support for gamma correction also appeared to be
incorrect but at least partially functional. On the positive side—and not surprisingly—it handled OBJECT image tags completely correctly, including those with
other OBJECTs nested inside. Amaya is freely available for download from
http://www.w3.org/Amaya/.

Other Browsers

PNG support in other browsers varies considerably by platform. On the Amiga, it
is ubiquitous, thanks to a technological marvel known as *datatypes* (a kind of
super-DLL that, among other things, provides generic image support); but under
operating systems like BeOS or Atari TOS, it is virtually nonexistent. The following
sections list many of the known PNG-supporting browsers, sorted by platform.

Amiga

Two datatypes provide PNG support for virtually every Amiga browser in existence: Cloanto's (*http://www.aminet.org/pub/aminet/util/dtype/PNG_dt.lha*) and
Andreas Kleinert's (*http://www.aminet.org/pub/aminet/util/dtype/akPNG-dt.lha*).
Cloanto made their first version of available within months of the PNG specification freeze, thereby making the Amiga the very first platform to support PNG in
web browsers. Andreas's datatype at one time was considered to have better overall PNG support, but the two datatypes appear to have comparable features as of
early 1999. Unfortunately, the datatype architecture itself currently precludes alpha
transparency and progressive display, but an operating system upgrade due in the
second quarter of 1999 is expected to add at least alpha support.

In the meantime, there are three Amiga browsers with native PNG support in addition to basic datatype support: AWeb (*http://www.xs4all.nl/˜yrozijn/aweb*),
iBrowse (*http://www.hisoft.co.uk/amiga/ibrowse*), and VoyagerNG (*http://www.
vapor.com/voyager*). The first two claim to support transparency, possibly including full alpha support. AWeb also does gamma correction, and all three display
PNGs progressively as they download.

Acorn

In addition to Browse, PNG is also supported on the Acorn platform by ANT Fresco (*http://www.ant.co.uk/prod/inetbroch/fresco2.html*), ArcWeb (*http://www. dsse.ecs.soton.ac.uk/~snb94r/arcweb*), and DoggySoft's Termite (*http://www.doggysoft.co.uk/trweb.html*) and Webite (*http://www.doggysoft.co.uk/prog4.html#web*) browsers, although the latter two do so via a third-party helper application called Progress from David McCormack (*http://www.atlantic.oaktree.co.uk/software/termite/progress.html*). Fresco is also notable as the browser chosen by Oracle for its network computer.

BeOS

As of this writing, the best bet for a PNG-capable web browser running under BeOS is a toss-up between the upcoming Opera port to BeOS, which will presumably include Opera Software's recently added PNG support, and the upcoming release of BeOS R4.1 and NetPositive 3.0 (*http://www.be.com/beware/Network/NetPositive.html*). The latter is Be's bundled web browser, which in its beta version already supports PNG—though not alpha transparency or gamma correction. BeOS R4.1 will ship with a PNG "Translator," which is the BeOS version of the Amiga datatype concept.

Macintosh

Surprisingly enough, given the Mac's popularity among graphic designers, there are only four PNG-supporting browsers for the platform, as of early 1999. That Netscape Navigator is one of them, and that Internet Explorer is also available (though without PNG support until version 5.0 is released) presumably has a great deal to do with this lack of other PNG support. Aside from Navigator, the only known PNG-supporting Macintosh browsers are iCab, Spyglass Mosaic, and versions 3.0A1 and later of NCSA MacMosaic, and development on both of the Mosaics ceased in 1996. iCab is a promising new browser for both Classic and Power Macintoshes; as of this writing, it is still in beta (Preview 1.3a) and has no gamma support or progressive display of interlacing, but it is reported to support alpha transparency. It is available from *http://www.icab.de/*.

There are also two or three plug-ins for Mac versions of Netscape prior to 4.04, depending on how one counts: the PNG Live 1.0 plug-in for PowerMacs, Sam Bushell's (beta) plug-in, and Apple's QuickTime 3.0 plug-in. Since Sam Bushell was also responsible for PNG support in QuickTime 3.0, it may be considered the successor to his own plug-in.

NeXTStep/OpenStep

Only one currently available browser for NeXTStep and OpenStep supports PNG natively: OmniWeb, versions 2.0 and later, available from *http://www.omnigroup. com/Software/OmniWeb/*. OmniWeb displays interlaced images progressively and does full gamma correction, but version 2.0 has no support for alpha transparency. (Version 3.0 is still in beta as of February 1999; its release notes do not mention PNG or alpha transparency.) Another NeXT browser, NetSurfer 1.1, once supported PNG, but it is no longer available.

OS/2

Until mid-1998, the options for native OS/2 PNG-supporting browsers were almost nonexistent: they included a widely distributed plug-in from Giorgio Costa and a beta plug-in from Panacea Software that was available for only two weeks. These could be used with IBM's OS/2 port of Netscape Navigator 2.02. (IBM's own Web-Explorer browser never supported PNG in any way.) But September 1998 saw the public release of IBM's Navigator 4.04 port (*http://www.software.ibm.com/os/warp/ netscape*), which includes native PNG support.

Client-Side Workarounds: The OBJECT Tag

Suppose that we would like to use PNGs wherever possible but still allow older browsers to see JPEGs or GIFs. Is there a way to do this? The answer is either "sort of" or "yes," depending on the approach one takes. In Chapter 1, *An Introduction to PNG*, I mentioned a client-side approach involving the HTML 4.0 OBJECT tag, but I also noted that neither of the Big Two yet handles such things correctly, and earlier in this chapter I enumerated some of the specific problems in the two browsers. The other approach is a server-side method involving content negotiation. We'll come back to that one later.

First, let us take a closer look at the client-side method. HTML 4.0's OBJECT tag was designed to be a generalized replacement for the HTML 3.2 IMG and APPLET tags and for Netscape's EMBED tag. Since OBJECT is a container, it can contain other elements inside it, including nested OBJECTs. The rules for rendering them are simple: start with the outermost OBJECT; if you can render that, do so, and ignore what's inside. Otherwise, continue peeling back the outer layers until you find something that *can* be rendered.

In the case of images, the following two elements are equivalent:

```
<IMG SRC="foo.png"
 ALT="[This text is visible if the image is not rendered.]">
```

```
<OBJECT TYPE="image/png" DATA="foo.png">
   [This text is visible if the image is not rendered.]
</OBJECT>
```

Because OBJECTs can be used for many things, the image/png MIME type in this example is strongly recommended so that the browser can unambiguously identify the data as an image (rather than, say, a Java applet) and, if it knows it has no support for the type, avoid contacting the server unnecessarily. For JPEGs or GIFs, the MIME type would be image/jpeg or image/gif, respectively. Both IMG and OBJECT tags may include optional HEIGHT and WIDTH attributes, but as we noted earlier, Netscape requires them in order to invoke an image-handling plug-in for an OBJECT tag.*

The trick that should allow both OBJECT-recognizing browsers and pre-OBJECT browsers to render something sensible is to wrap a GIF or JPEG version of an image, referenced via an old-style IMG tag, inside a new-style OBJECT tag that references a PNG version of the same image. In other words, one does something like the following:

```
<OBJECT WIDTH="160" HEIGHT="160" DATA="foo.png" TYPE="image/png">
   <IMG WIDTH="160" HEIGHT="160"  SRC="foo.jpg"
   ALT="[rare photo of the incredible foo]">
</OBJECT>
```

If we decide to accommodate only browsers that support either OBJECT or PNG (or both) but don't care about older browsers that support neither, we can get a little fancier with nested OBJECTs:

```
<OBJECT WIDTH="160" HEIGHT="160" DATA="foo.png" TYPE="image/png">
<OBJECT WIDTH="160" HEIGHT="160" DATA="foo.jpg" TYPE="image/jpeg">
   <IMG WIDTH="160" HEIGHT="160"  SRC="foo.png"
   ALT="[rare photo of the incredible foo]">
</OBJECT>
</OBJECT>
```

A browser that implements both PNG and HTML 4.0 will render the outer OBJECT PNG; one that implements HTML 4.0 but not PNG will render the inner OBJECT JPEG; and one that implements PNG but not HTML 4.0 will render the innermost IMG PNG. (And, of course, a browser with no image support will render the text in the IMG tag's ALT attribute.)

The reason these tricks don't work in practice is that some browsers—particularly Netscape Navigator and Microsoft Internet Explorer, but undoubtedly others as well—added incomplete or incorrect support for OBJECT before the HTML 4.0 specification was formally approved in December 1997. As I've already noted, no

---

* If Netscape ever modifies their plug-in code to work with IMG tags, presumably the HEIGHT and WIDTH attributes will be required there, as well. Fortunately, this is not a very onerous requirement for content producers.

released version of either of the Big Two browsers would invoke its native image-handling code when it encountered an OBJECT image, even as late as February 1999. Navigator always renders the inner IMG unless a plug-in is available; MSIE either pops up an error box claiming to need an ActiveX control or, in our tests, manages to crash while invoking a Netscape PNG plug-in installed elsewhere on the system. (I've also noted that Internet Explorer attempts to render all OBJECTs in a nested set, not just the outermost one.) Older versions of both browsers, and, likewise, all versions of Opera to date, behave as expected and simply ignore OBJECT images.

WWW Servers

On the server side of things, PNG support is much less of an issue. With one notable exception, server-side support involves, at most, adding a single line to a text configuration file and restarting the server to have it take effect. Smoothly upgrading web pages to use PNG images if possible—i.e., enabling content negotiation—requires additional effort, however.

"Standard" Servers

The first requirement for a web server to support PNG properly is to enable the correct MIME type, image/png. On most servers, including CERN/W3C (*http://www.w3.org/Daemon/Status.html*), NCSA (*http://boohoo.ncsa.uiuc.edu*), Apache (*http://www.apache.org*), Zeus (*http://www.zeus.co.uk/products*) and various flavors of Netscape servers (*http://home.netscape.com/servers*), this can be accomplished most easily by editing the *mime.types* file to include one of the following two lines:

```
image/png png
```

or:

```
type=image/png exts=png
```

The latter format is used by Netscape servers, but for any server, the correct format should be obvious from the other entries in the file (search for the image/gif or image/jpeg lines and use one of them as a template). Apache can also be configured via its *srm.conf* file (or, if AllowOverride FileInfo has been specified, in *.htaccess* files in individual directories) with the following line:

```
AddType image/png png
```

Note that the original PNG media type, image/x-png, has been obsolete since image/png was officially registered in October 1996. If the older type is present in either configuration file, change it to image/png or delete it altogether.

Once a change to the configuration files has been made, the server will need to be signaled to reread them. For some Unix servers, this can be done via the `kill -HUP` command, but restarting the server is a more portable method. Check the server's documentation for the recommended approach.

Internet Information Server

Microsoft's Internet Information Server (IIS) marches to its own drummer. Available as part of Windows NT Server (*http://www.microsoft.com/ntserver/web*), IIS uses the Windows registry in lieu of the traditional text-based configuration file for media (MIME) types. This part of the registry can be modified via Explorer to add the `image/png` type as follows; type the text printed in *italic*:

1. Open **Windows Explorer** (**Start** button → **Programs** → **Windows Explorer**).
2. Select **View** → **Options**.
3. Click on the **File Types** tab.
4. Click on the **New Type** . . . button.
5. Enter the following information:

   - **Description of type:** *Portable Network Graphics image*
   - **Associated extension:** *.png*
   - **Content Type (MIME):** *image/png*

6. Click on the **New** . . . button.
7. Enter the following information:

   - **Action:** Open.
   - **Application used to perform action:** *your full path to an image viewer.*
   - Uncheck **Confirm open after download** box.

8. Click on the **OK** button.
9. Click on the **Close** button.
10. Click on the **Close** button.

Since this setup takes place on the server itself, the application associated with the media type is not particularly important; it merely enables someone sitting at the server console to double-click on a PNG image to view it. The app can be any PNG-aware image viewer, including Netscape Navigator, but (as I noted before) not Microsoft's own Internet Explorer 4.0.

Setting up the media type is all that is required for basic, standards-compliant operation, but due to a bug that appears to exist in all PNG-supporting versions of Netscape's browser prior to 4.51 (and also due to particularly strict syntax checking on the part of Microsoft's server), IIS by default will refuse to serve PNG images to versions of Navigator up through 4.5. Instead, it returns an error ("HTTP/1.1 406 No acceptable objects were found," similar to the "404 Not found" error that is familiar to many web surfers), which Navigator renders as its broken-image icon. The cause is apparently a broken header that Netscape clients send as part of their HTTP content negotiation with the server:

```
Accept: image/gif, image/x-xbitmap, image/jpeg, image/pjpeg image/png
```

Note the missing comma after `image/pjpeg`. Because of this error, IIS does not recognize that `image/png` is an acceptable media type, and it therefore returns an error message instead of the image.

Reportedly, there is some form of workaround that involves tweaking the IIS-related parts of the Windows registry on the server, but as of early 1999, no one has yet come forth with the magic information. Semi-informed guesses include the possibilities of relaxing the strict HTTP syntax checking or of turning off content negotiation altogether, but it is not known whether either of these options actually exists in the server.*

Server-Side Workarounds: Content Negotiation

Serving PNG images with the correct MIME type is one thing, but there remains the issue of *when* to serve PNG images. As discussed earlier, the client-side method involving `OBJECT` tags really doesn't work very well. The only option that works is content negotiation, and, unfortunately, this only works for those who have control of the web server itself. Content negotiation is also dependent on the web server software being used. But it's conceptually a clean solution, and it has been proven in the field: the World Wide Web Consortium has successfully implemented it at *http://www.w3.org* since 1996. We'll take a look at how to enable and use content negotiation on the most popular web server in the world: Apache.†

Apache variants files

Apache actually supports two methods of content negotiation. The first involves "variants" files and is implemented in Apache's `mod_negotiation` module. To enable the module, the following line must be added to the *httpd.conf* configuration file:

```
AddHandler type-map var
```

---

* Another possibility (albeit a *truly* ugly and brutal one) is to forego the setup of the `image/png` media type that was described before—or, if the type already exists, eliminate it. Instead, register the .png file extension as belonging to another image type, such as `image/gif` or `image/jpeg`. But not only is this likely to break other browsers, it may not even fix the problem with Navigator; I mention it only as a last resort for desperate site administrators.

† The Zeus server is almost identical in configuration. See *http://www.zeus.co.uk/products/zeus1/docs/guide/features/content.html* for details.

The server must be restarted for this line to take effect. Then, for each image that is to be negotiated, create a `.var` file corresponding to the filename and refer to that in the HTML file. For example, to serve either *tux.gif* or *tux.png*, depending on each browser's capabilities, create a file called *tux.var* in the same directory and refer to it in the `IMG` tag in place of the actual image filename:

```
<IMG SRC="images/tux.var" ALT="[His Penguinness, Tux]">
```

The contents of *tux.var* should look something like this:

```
URI: tux.png
Content-Type: image/png;qs=0.7

URI: tux.gif
Content-Type: image/gif;qs=0.4
```

Each variant has a corresponding block of information, separated from that of the other variants by blank lines. The actual image filenames are given on the `URI` lines, and their corresponding MIME types are given on the subsequent `Content-Type` lines. In addition, a *quality of source* parameter `qs` is included for each image type. This is a number between 0.0 and 1.0 that indicates the relative preferences of the author for each image type. In this example, I've indicated that the PNG image (0.7) is preferred over the GIF (0.4). The default value of the `qs` parameter is 1.0.

A client browser requesting an image from the server also indicates its relative preferences, either explicitly or implicitly, via the HTTP Accept header. The web server then multiplies its quality parameter for each MIME type by the client's quality parameter* to get a composite value—this is the resolution phase of the negotiation. The highest composite value determines which image is sent.

In practice, things are a bit more complicated for the server, but this is usually hidden from the user. The problem arises when the client browser sends incomplete or even incorrect information. For example, some browsers send `Accept: image/*`, indicating that they can render any type of image. Others specify a list of image types but also include the catchall type `*/*`. And only rarely does a client include preference values for each type. As a result, the server must assume preference values for the client. By default, all types are given a value of 1.0, but Apache "fiddles" the values for wildcard types: `image/*` or `text/*` are assigned the value 0.02 instead, and `*/*` is assigned the value 0.01.

The variants file approach allows fine-grained control over every image in a web site, and has the distinct advantage that a site designer can use it at will, if the server administrator has enabled content negotiation. But maintaining parallel sets

---

* Multiplication is specified in the HTTP 1.1 spec; HTTP 1.0 said only to "combine" the values.

of images can be enough trouble all by itself; having to maintain a unique variants file for every image is enough to drive most site maintainers to distraction. Fortunately, Apache provides a partial alternative: *MultiViews*, a directory-wide (and potentially server-wide) method based on file extensions.

Apache MultiViews

Enabling MultiViews in Apache is accomplished by including it on an Options line in the *httpd.conf* configuration file:

```
Options +MultiViews
```

The option may appear inside a `<Directory>` container, in which case it applies only to the named directory tree rather than the entire server; inside a `<Virtual-Host>` container, in which case it applies only to a given virtual hostname; or, if `AllowOverride Options` has been specified, within *.htaccess* files in individual directories. As with variants, the server must be restarted before changes to the main configuration file are noticed.

Once MultiViews is enabled for a given directory—say, */www/htdocs/images*—a request for a file *foo* in that directory will either return *foo* if it exists or else negotiate between all *foo.** files.* So to serve either *tux.png* or *tux.gif*, for example, simply include both in the directory and refer to them as follows:

```
<IMG SRC="images/tux" ALT="[His Penguinness, Tux]">
```

Unfortunately, MultiViews has one great weakness: no version of Apache through 1.3.3 supports *multifile* quality-of-source settings. In particular, there is no way to add a line or two to one of the top-level configuration files to indicate that all PNGs on the site, or all in a particular directory tree, should have a source quality of, say, 0.7. Individual variants files are still allowed, and if found, their settings will override the Apache defaults. But the requirement to generate one variants file for every image is just as painful with MultiViews as with the standard variants file approach. The only alternative for now is to hack the source, which is precisely what was done at *http://www.w3.org*, the home of the W3C. The W3C programmers are working to get their patches cleaned up and incorporated into the stock Apache source tree, but there is no word on when that will occur, and in the meantime, the Apache developers "have no firm plans to add such functionality." As with many such things, multiple user requests for the feature would probably make a difference in the development plans.

---

* Version 1.3.4 was released a few weeks before this book's deadline; the "New Features in Apache 1.3" page (*http://www.apache.org/docs/new_features_1_3.html*) hinted at changes relevant to a global quality-of-source feature, but I did not have time to investigate fully. Specifically, the three server configuration files were merged (*srm.conf* and *access.conf* were absorbed into *httpd.conf*), and the `mod_negotiation` module was "completely overhauled." A comment in the `mod_negotiation` source code, however, indicates that the global setting still has not been implemented.

3

Applications:
Image Viewers

Unlike, say, image converters or editors, there is generally not a great deal to say about a PNG-supporting image viewer other than that it does, in fact, display PNG images. Gamma correction is the primary "special" feature one would like; color correction and the ability to view text annotations would be nice as well, but the reality is that most image viewers concentrate more on speed and breadth of support for different image formats and display depths than on features specific to any one format.

The list of viewers presented here is likewise long on breadth and short on specifics, simply because testing every viewer for every platform—or even a reasonable fraction of them—is impractical. Gamma and text support are noted wherever known, as is the ability to convert to or from other formats, but this is primarily a laundry list of viewers, sorted by platform. The current version of each, as of this writing, is listed wherever possible.

In addition to the viewing applications listed in the following discussion, two demo viewers are described in Chapter 13, *Reading PNG Images*, and Chapter 14, *Reading PNG Images Progressively.* They currently run under 32-bit Windows and Unix/X, and full source code is freely available. One other viewing application is also worth mentioning: Aladdin's Ghostscript, currently at version 5.50, which is (or has in the past been) available for every platform listed here. Ghostscript is a viewer for PostScript and Acrobat (PDF) files, but it can write PNG images and is therefore a special case.

Windows 95/98/NT

ACDSee32

Version 2.3, ACD Systems. Full gamma support; progressive display of interlaced images (sparse method); older versions ignored the background chunk and incorrectly displayed grayscale images with alpha channels. Not tested recently.

http://www.acdsystems.com/pages/acdsee32.htm

AI Picture Explorer

Version 1.2, Applied Insights. Conversion capabilities; can autogenerate web pages with thumbnail images.

http://users.aol.com/lgozum2/

AI Picture Utility

Version 2.5, Applied Insights. Conversion capabilities.

http://users.aol.com/aipict/aipict.html

Alter Image 32

Version 1.0a, Nun's Meadow Software. Conversion capabilities.

http://web2.airmail.net/nunnally/altimg.htm

CPIC

Version 1.80 ("build 273"), Photodex. Conversion capabilities; claims gamma support. CPIC is also sometimes known as CompuPic.

http://www.photodex.com/products/cpic/cpic_home.html

CryptaPix

Version 2.02, Briggs Softworks. Encryption capabilities. Versions prior to 2.0 were also available for Windows 3.x.

http://www.briggsoft.com/cpix.htm

DeBabelizer Pro

Version 4.5, Equilibrium. Conversion capabilities; claims gamma support.

http://www.equilibrium.com/ProductInfo/DBPro/ProNewFeatures.html

Drag And View

Version 4.0c, Canyon Software. Conversion capabilities.

http://www.canyonsw.com/dnv.htm

FmView

Version 2.0, WinCorner. Integrates into Windows File Manager and Explorer.

http://www.wincorner.com/home/fmview.html

GIF Construction Set

Version 1.0Q, Alchemy Mindworks.

http://www.mindworkshop.com/alchemy/gifcon.html

GrafCat

Alchemy Mindworks.

http://www.mindworkshop.com/alchemy/gctw.html

Graphic Viewer

Version 1.0, PrimaSoft PC.

http://www.primasoft.com/32org/32gview.htm

Graphic Workshop

Version 1.1Y, Alchemy Mindworks. Conversion capabilities; no gamma support in older versions. Not tested recently.

http://www.mindworkshop.com/alchemy/gww.html

HiJaak PRO

Version 4.5, IMSI. Conversion capabilities, but apparently not to PNG. HiJaak was originally developed by Inset, which was acquired by Quarterdeck, which finally sold the product to IMSI.

http://www.imsisoft.com/hijaak/hijaak.html

Imagenation

Version 5.0, Spicer Corporation. Conversion capabilities.

http://www.spicer.com/product/imagenation/imagenation_home.htm

ImgViewer/32

Version 2.31, Arcata Pet Software.* Conversion capabilities; claims gamma support. Related software includes WWPlus32 (multiformat wallpaper manager) and WWSaver32 (image-based screensaver).

http://www.arcatapet.com/imgv32.html

---

* Wacky fact: Arcata Pet Software's name comes from the associated pet store and supply shop.

IrfanView32

Version 2.90, Skiljan Irfan. Conversion capabilities.

http://stud1.tuwien.ac.at/~e9227474/

KeyView Pro

Version 6.0, Verity. Conversion and Netscape plug-in capabilities. FTP Software sold KeyView to Verity late in 1997.

http://www.keyview.com/

Makaha

Version 1.6, Brandyware Software. Conversion capabilities.

http://members.aol.com/brandyware/makaha.htm

Photonyx Viewer

Version 2.0, Chrome Imaging.

http://www.chrome-imaging.com/pview.html

PicaView32

Version 1.3, ACD Systems. Integrates into Windows Explorer menus.

http://www.acdsystems.com/pages/picaview32.htm

PicViewer

Version 1.81, Andrew Anoshkin.

http://www.strongsoftware.net/dronix/picview.html

PixelGraphicLibrary demo viewer

Version 1.0 beta 5, Peter Beyersdorf. Principally an imaging toolkit, but includes a demo viewer app.

http://www.beyersdorf.com/pgraphe.html

PixFolio

Version 2, ACK Software. Conversion capabilities.

http://www.frontpageaccess.com/acksoft/

PolyView

Version 3.10, Polybytes. Conversion capabilities.

http://www.polybytes.com/

QuickTime PictureViewer

Version 3.0, Apple Computer. Full gamma and color-correction support via ColorSync; claims full alpha support (but not clear in what form). Picture-Viewer completely supersedes the Tiny Viewer demo app that Sam Bushell included with his QuickTime 2.5 PNG-Importer. Note that any QuickTime-aware application (even Apple's SimpleText) can be used to view PNG images if QT3 is installed.

http://www.apple.com/quicktime/

Quick View Plus

Version 5.0, Jasc Software. This is software with *history*. Originally developed by Mastersoft as Viewer 95, both it and Mastersoft were acquired by Frame, which was almost immediately acquired by Adobe. The program and associated technologies were rereleased as Adobe File Utilities by Mastersoft in 1996, then sold to Inso in 1997. Inso gave the software its current name, but apparently sold or licensed the rights to the Windows version to Jasc in 1998. Inso still sells the Unix version and possibly the Windows version, but apparently only to government and "enterprise" customers.

http://www.jasc.com/qvp.html

Riptide Photo Studio

Version 1.0, Vorton Technologies. Conversion capabilities.

http://www.vorton.com/riptide.htm

Showcase

Version 1.2.00, CQuick Technologies.

http://www.cquick.com/Showcase/

ThumbsPlus

Version 3.30, Cerious Software. Conversion capabilities, but without the ability to write interlaced or transparent PNGs; possibly full gamma support; can autogenerate web pages with thumbnail images.

http://www.thumbsplus.com/

VidFun

Version 3.6, Lawrence Gozum. Conversion capabilities.

http://users.aol.com/lgozum/vidfun.htm

WebGraphics Optimizer

Version 4.0, Plenio Software Solutions. Conversion capabilities; Version 2.x had broken support for two-bit images, no gamma support, and no control over compression level or filtering (to the extent that it would happily write an output file larger than the input). Not tested recently.

http://www.webopt.com/

Windows 3.x

ACDSee16

Version 2.2, ACD Systems. (See also ACDSee32 earlier.)

> *http://www.acdsystems.com/pages/acdsee16.htm*

CPIC

Version 1.80 ("build 273"), Photodex. Conversion capabilities; claims gamma support. CPIC is also sometimes known as CompuPic.

> *http://www.photodex.com/products/cpic/cpic_home.html*

Drag And View

"Gold" version (possibly 1.3), Canyon Software. If the download filename, *dragvu13.zip*, can be trusted, and if the version numbering is the same as that for the 32-bit Windows version discussed earlier, then the 16-bit version may not include PNG support after all.

> *http://www.canyonsw.com/dnv.htm*

GIF Construction Set

Version 1.0Q, Alchemy Mindworks.

> *http://www.mindworkshop.com/alchemy/gifcon.html*

GrafCat

Alchemy Mindworks.

> *http://www.mindworkshop.com/alchemy/gctw.html*

Graphic Workshop

Version 1.1Y, Alchemy Mindworks. Conversion capabilities; no gamma support in older versions. Not tested recently.

> *http://www.mindworkshop.com/alchemy/gww.html*

GraphX Viewer

Version 1.51 only, Group 42. Conversion capabilities; full gamma support. Group 42 is the company for which Guy Schalnat worked while he wrote the first version of libpng. Unfortunately, there has been no further PNG-related work since he left.

Imagenation

Version 5.0, Spicer Corporation. Conversion capabilities.

> *http://www.spicer.com/product/imagenation/imagenation_home.htm*

KeyView Pro

Version 6.0, Verity. Conversion and Netscape plug-in capabilities. FTP Software sold KeyView to Verity late in 1997.

http://www.keyview.com/

PicaView16

Version 1.6, ACD Systems. Integrates into Windows File Manager.

http://www.acdsystems.com/pages/picaview16.htm

PixFolio

Version 2, ACK Software. Conversion capabilities.

http://www.frontpageaccess.com/acksoft/

QuickShow Lite

Alchemy Mindworks.

http://www.mindworkshop.com/alchemy/qshow.html

Quick View Plus

Version 5.0, Jasc Software. See its earlier listing in the 32-bit Windows section for a brief history.

http://www.jasc.com/qvp.html

ThumbsPlus

Version 3.30, Cerious Software. Conversion capabilities, but without the ability to write interlaced or transparent PNGs; possibly full gamma support; can autogenerate web pages with thumbnail images.

http://www.thumbsplus.com/

VidFun

Version 3.6, Lawrence Gozum. Conversion capabilities.

http://users.aol.com/lgozum/vidfun.htm

Viewer Pro!

Version 4.2, Brandyware Software. Conversion capabilities.

http://members.aol.com/brandyware/viewer.htm

VMS

The selection of PNG-supporting image viewers for VMS (or OpenVMS nowadays) is rather limited; indeed, I am aware of only two viewers, both ports of popular Unix/X viewers:

ImageMagick display
> Version 4.2.0, John Cristy. Conversion capabilities (mostly via accompanying *convert* utility); full gamma support; reported to include chromaticity support; partial MNG support. There is also a 32-bit Windows port, but it requires a third-party X server to run.
>
> > *http://www.wizards.dupont.com/cristy/ImageMagick.html*

XV Version 3.10a, John Bradley. Conversion capabilities, including interlacing support but without the ability to write transparent PNGs; full gamma support; preserves text information. XV is widely considered to be the preeminent image viewer for the X Window System. The only major drawback is that it was last released in December 1994, five days before the CompuServe/Unisys GIF announcement that began the PNG saga, and therefore does not include PNG support in the default distribution. Fortunately, it is available as C source code, and the home page includes not only the PNG patch but also several others, so it can be recompiled and tweaked at will. An upcoming patch will allow an image-background color to be set, similar to the `-bgcolor` option in the demo viewers in Chapters 13 and 14.

> *http://www.trilon.com/xv/*

Unix

Cameleo
> Version 3.0 beta, Caldera Graphics. Conversion capabilities; claims full 16-bit-per-sample support and strongly implies full gamma and color correction, including ICC profiles.
>
> > *http://www.caldera.fr/en/cameleo/*

Electric Eyes
> Red Hat Advanced Development Labs. Electric Eyes is a new, Linux/GNOME-based image viewer by The Rasterman (who's perhaps better known for his spectacularly fancy Enlightenment desktop). It is also one of the prototype

applications for *Imlib*, an X-based imaging toolkit described in Chapter 16, *Other Libraries and Concluding Remarks*.

> *http://www.labs.redhat.com/ee.shtml*

GRAV

Version 3.5, Michael Knigge. Broken support for 24-bit images. GRAV is a non-X-based image viewer for Linux, similar to Zgv, later in this list; it uses *svgalib* to display on a Linux console. It has not been updated since January 1996 and apparently is no longer under development.

> *http://metalab.unc.edu/pub/Linux/apps/graphics/viewers/svga/ grav-3.5.tar.gz*

Image Alchemy

Version 1.11, Handmade Software. Conversion capabilities (in fact, primarily a command-line conversion tool); claims full alpha support, gamma support, and support for ICC profiles via ColorSync. Note that only the versions for DOS and Macintosh and the commercial versions for Sun, SGI, and HP work-stations include viewing capability.

> *http://www.handmadesw.com/hsi/alchemy.html*

ImageMagick display

Version 4.2.0, John Cristy. Conversion capabilities (mostly via accompanying *convert* utility); full gamma support; partial MNG support. There is also a 32-bit Windows port, but it requires a third-party X server to run.

> *http://www.wizards.dupont.com/cristy/ImageMagick.html*

Photon Picture Viewer/pv

QNX Software Systems. No gamma support; QNX only. The Photon Picture Viewer is part of the Photon microGUI and can be downloaded as part of QNX's 1.44 MB "Internet Appliance" demo diskette.

> *http://www.qnx.com/products/photon/*

PingPong

Version 1.28, Willem van Schaik. Conversion capabilities (PNG to TIFF only, apparently, with preservation of alpha/transparency); NeXTStep and OpenStep only.

> *http://www.schaik.com/pingpong/*

Quick View Plus

Version 4.5, Inso. There is also a version 5.0 for Windows, sold by Jasc Software; see the listing in the 32-bit Windows section for at least part of the strange story.

http://www.inso.com/qvp/

ToyViewer

Version 3.02, Takeshi Ogihara. Conversion capabilities; transparency support; support for writing text comments; NeXTstep and OpenStep only. The latest NeXTStep version is 2.6a.

http://www.asahi-net.or.jp/~hq2t-oghr/next/toyv-eng.html

Viewpng

Version of May 9, 1997, Glenn Randers-Pehrson. Full alpha and gamma support; partial (out-of-date) MNG support; SGI Irix only. Viewpng requires the separate *pnggzip* utility (included) for its compression and decompression.

ftp://swrinde.nde.swri.edu/pub/mng/applications/sgi/

xli Version 1.16, Graeme Gill. Like XV, the next entry, xli (a modified version of xloadimage) has not been updated since 1994, before PNG was born. But it is available as C source code from *ftp.x.org* and elsewhere, and a PNG patch by Smarasderagd has been available for years, so compiling a PNG-capable version is straightforward.

http://web.access.net.au/argyll/xli.html
http://www.reptiles.org/~smar/xli-png.tar.gz

XV Version 3.10a, John Bradley. Conversion capabilities, including interlacing support but without the ability to write transparent PNGs; full gamma support; preserves text information. XV is widely considered to be *the* preeminent image viewer for the X Window System.[*] The only major drawback is that it was last released in December 1994, five days before the CompuServe/Unisys GIF announcement that began the PNG saga and therefore does not include PNG support in the default distribution. Fortunately, it is available as C source code, and the home page includes not only the PNG patch but also several others, so it can be recompiled and tweaked at will. An upcoming patch will allow an image-background color to be set, similar to the `-bgcolor` option in the demo viewers in Chapters 13 and 14.

http://www.trilon.com/xv/

---

[*] In fact, it is my preferred viewer.

Zgv

Version 3.0, Russell Marks. Zgv is a non-X-based image viewer for Linux, similar to GRAV, earlier in this list; it uses svgalib to display on a Linux console.

> *http://metalab.unc.edu/pub/Linux/apps/graphics/viewers/svga/*
> *zgv3.0-bin.tar.gz*

OS/2

Galleria

Version 2.31, Bitware Australia. Conversion capabilities in registered version.

> *http://ourworld.compuserve.com/homepages/bitware/*

PMJPEG

Version 1.9 only, PixVision Software. No alpha support; claims gamma support. Version 1.83 is the last version available as shareware from the web site; it is not clear whether version 1.9 was actually released or not.

> *http://www.pixvision.com/html/product_info_1.html*

PMView

Version 1.02, Peter Nielsen. Conversion capabilities; claims gamma support. Despite its seemingly interminable pre-1.0 beta period, PMView was probably the most popular image viewer for 32-bit OS/2.*

> *http://www.pmview.com/*

Macintosh

CPIC

Version 1.80 ("build 280"), Photodex. Conversion capabilities; claims gamma support. CPIC is also sometimes known as CompuPic.

> *http://www.photodex.com/products/cpic/cpic_home.html*

DeBabelizer

Version 3.0, Equilibrium. Conversion capabilities; claims gamma support.

> *http://www.equilibrium.com/ProductInfo/DB3/DB3NewFeatures.html*

GIFConverter

Version 2.4, Kevin Mitchell. Conversion capabilities; no transparency, gamma or text support.

> *http://www.kamit.com/gifconverter/*

---

* It was definitely my preferred OS/2 viewer.

GraphicConverter

Version 3.4.1, Lemke Software. Conversion capabilities; claims alpha and gamma support.

> *http://www.lemkesoft.de/us_gcabout.html*

Image32

Version 1.4.0, Mark Sproul.

> *http://msproul.rutgers.edu/macintosh/Image32Docs.html*

Image Alchemy

Version 1.11, Handmade Software. Conversion capabilities (in fact, primarily a conversion tool); claims full alpha support, gamma support and support for ICC profiles via ColorSync. Note that only the versions for DOS and Macintosh and the commercial versions for Sun, SGI, and HP workstations include viewing capability.

> *http://www.handmadesw.com/hsi/alchemy.html*

QuickTime PictureViewer

Version 3.0, Apple Computer. Full gamma and color-correction support via ColorSync; claims full alpha support (but not clear in what form). Picture-Viewer completely supersedes the Tiny Viewer demo app that Sam Bushell included with his QuickTime 2.5 PNG-Importer. Note that any QuickTime-aware application (even Apple's SimpleText) can be used to view PNG images if QT3 is installed.

> *http://www.apple.com/quicktime/*

ThumbsPlus

Beta 11/version 3.10, Cerious Software. Conversion capabilities, but without the ability to write interlaced or transparent PNGs; possibly full gamma support; can autogenerate web pages with thumbnail images.

> *http://www.thumbsplus.com/*
> *http://www.thumbsplus.com/macbeta.htm*

Java

As of January 1999 there were two Java viewers available, but with the recent addition of PNG support to the Java Advanced Imaging API, PNG-viewing capability can be expected soon in numerous Java applications and applets.

PNGImageViewer

    Neil Aggarwal. Requires Java (JDK) 1.1 or later.

        http://www.anet-dfw.com/~neil/PNGIVFrame.html

PngThing

    Sergey Kucherov. Requires Java (JDK) 1.1 or later.

        http://users.luckynet.co.il/~serge3/pngthing/PngThing.html

DOS

CompuShow

    Version 9.04, Bob Berry.* Conversion capabilities; gamma support; progressive display of interlaced images. Related software includes CompuShow 2000.

        ftp://ftp.simtel.net/pub/simtelnet/msdos/graphics/cshow904.zip
        ftp://ftp.simtel.net/pub/simtelnet/msdos/graphics/2show204.zip

Display

    Version 1.90t5 beta or 1.89, Jih-Shin Ho. Conversion capabilities; gamma support. Development apparently ended in June 1997.

        ftp://ftp.edu.tw/Graphics/Display/
        http://fn2.freenet.edmonton.ab.ca/~crnelson/display.html

Graphic Workshop

    Version 7.0f, Alchemy Mindworks. Conversion capabilities. Version 7.0f was the first and last DOS release to have PNG support. See also the 16-bit and 32-bit Windows versions earlier in this chapter.

        http://www.mindworkshop.com/alchemy/gws.html

Image Alchemy

    Version 1.11, Handmade Software. Conversion capabilities (in fact, primarily a command-line conversion tool); claims full alpha support, gamma support, and support for ICC profiles via ColorSync. Note that only the versions for DOS and Macintosh and the commercial versions for Sun, SGI, and HP workstations include viewing capability.

        http://www.handmadesw.com/hsi/alchemy.html

---

* Bob was also the inventor of the GIF image format, so one might consider him the grandfather of PNG. (Or not.)

NView

Version 1.5f, Jacques Nomssi Nzali. Development apparently ended in June 1996.

http://www.tu-chemnitz.de/~nomssi/nview.html

PictView

Version 1.80, Jan Patera. Conversion capabilities, but PNG support is read-only.

http://pascal.fjfi.cvut.cz/~patera/pictview/
http://www.geocities.com/SiliconValley/Pines/9994/

QPV/386

Version 1.7e, Oliver Fromme. QPV/386 is a multipurpose image viewer known for its speed; QPNG/386 is its free, PNG- and TGA-only sibling. Development on both apparently ended in November 1996.

http://www.tu-clausthal.de/~inof/q.html
ftp://ftp.cs.tu-berlin.de/pub/msdos/mirrors/stuba/pc/graph/qpng17e.zip

SEA

Version 1.34, Bart Wakkee, Ralph Gortzen, and Harold de Laat (distributed by Photodex). Conversion capabilities.

http://www.photodex.com/products/dos/dos_home.html#sea

BeOS

In addition to the following three viewers, Al Evans's BePNG and Jeremy Moskovich's BeShow were once available. But incompatibilities in the development versions of BeOS took their toll, and the two viewers were never updated to work with BeOS releases more recent than DR8 or DR9; they have since been moved to the "obsolete" area of Be's FTP site. BePNG was unique in having native support for PNG; all of the others use the *datatypes* facility developed by Jon Watte and later incorporated into the operating system as the BeOS translation kit. PNG support is provided via Simon Clarke's BPNGHandler:

http://www.be.com/beware/Datatypes/PNGHandler.html

It appeared in October 1998 that PNGHandler might have been renamed to PNG-Translator as of version 1.20 (see also the discussion in Chapter 16), but as of February 1999, the web page still referred to the original name.

DTPicView

Version 3.1.0, Edmund Vermeulen.

> *http://www.xs4all.nl/~edmundv/#DTPicView*
> *http://www.be.com/beware/Graphics/DTPicView.html*

LiView

Version 1.2 beta 5, Philippe Thomas.

> *http://aria.u-strasbg.fr/~thomasp/projets_be.html*

QuickPic

Version 0.90, Frank Fejes. Development apparently ended in February 1997; the app was never updated to work with BeOS versions more recent than DR8.

> *http://yoss.canweb.net/~frank/QuickPic/*

Atari

1stGuide

Version of June 10, 1997, Guido Vollbeding.

> *http://www.esc.de/homes/guivol/1stguide/*

GEM-View

Version 3.18, Dieter Fiebelkorn. GEM-View can view and save PNG images if Eric Prevoteau's PNG load/save modules have been installed.

> *http://www.castrop-rauxel.netsurf.de/homepages/dieter.fiebelkorn/*
> *GEMVIEW.HTML*
> *ftp://ftp.lip6.fr/pub/atari/Graphics/gvw_png.lzh*

Amiga

The Amiga includes a lovely facility known as *datatypes*, basically an extension of normal shared libraries (or DLLs) to provide generic data handling capabilities. With this facility, any datatypes-aware program—whether viewer, web browser, or image editor—can be extended after the fact, simply by adding the appropriate datatype for whatever new format comes along. In the case of PNG, two datatypes are available: Cloanto's and Andreas Kleinert's:

> *http://www.aminet.org/pub/aminet/util/dtype/PNG_dt.lha*
> *http://www.aminet.org/pub/aminet/util/dtype/akPNG-dt.lha*

Except where noted, all of the Amiga image viewers that follow require one of these datatypes for PNG support. (Indeed, there are probably many other datatypes-based viewers that are not listed here.)

Image Engineer

Version 3.41, Simon Edwards. Conversion capabilities. Image Engineer uses the SuperView Library (see Chapter 16) for its image support instead of datatypes.

http://amigaworld.com/support/imageengineer/

Multiview

Amiga. Multiview was apparently a standard, datatypes-aware viewer shipped as part of the Amiga operating system.

PPShow

Version 4.0, Nico François. Insofar as its last release was in February 1994—more than a year before the PNG specification was frozen—PPShow is a fine example of the power of Amiga datatypes.

http://www.aminet.org/pub/aminet/gfx/show/PPShow40.lha

SViewII

Version 8.10, Andreas Kleinert. Conversion capabilities. Formerly known as SuperView, SViewII includes the SuperView Library (discussed in Chapter 16) for all image I/O, instead of datatypes, despite the fact that Andreas wrote one of the available datatypes.

http://home.t-online.de/home/Andreas_Kleinert/sview.htm

ViewDT

Cloanto. ViewDT is a demo viewer included with Cloanto's PNG datatype; source code is included. Cloanto also once had a viewer called Personal View, but it no longer seems to exist.

http://www.aminet.org/pub/aminet/util/dtype/PNG_dt.lha

ViewTEK

Version 2.1, Thomas Krehbiel.

http://www.aminet.org/pub/aminet/gfx/show/ViewTEK21.lha

Visage

Version 39.21, Magnus Holmgren. Visage has had native PNG support since version 39.12.

http://www.algonet.se/~lear/visage.html

Acorn RISC OS

Although there are undoubtedly other image viewers available for the Archimedes, discovering them is tricky for those who are unacquainted with Acorn software sites. But at least one PNG-capable viewer exists:

Translator

Version 8.00, John Kortink. Conversion capabilities.

http://web.inter.nl.net/users/J.Kortink/indexsw.htm

4

Applications: Image Editors

To create a PNG image from scratch, one needs an image editor that understands PNGs. But there are many levels of understanding, and only a handful of editors exercise PNG's most interesting features. Here is a list of the support one would like to see in the ideal image editor:

- Basic image types: RGB, grayscale, and palette-based

- Images with fewer than 256 colors automatically saved as palette-based (or grayscale, if appropriate)

- Option to quantize and dither images with many colors down to 256 or fewer

- Simple transparency with any basic image type (i.e., single color marked as fully transparent)

- Full alpha transparency (also known as *alpha channel* or *alpha mask*)

- "Cheap" RGBA-palette transparency (i.e., where each palette entry has red, green, blue, and alpha components)

- Option to quantize and dither full RGBA images down to RGBA-palette images

- Option to enable interlacing

- Gamma correction, including calibration of display system

- Color correction: either chromaticity, sRGB, or full ICC profiles

- Ability to read, modify, and write 16-bit grayscale or 48-bit RGB images without conversion to lower bit depth

- Reasonable default compression settings: adaptive filtering turned on for all image types except palette-based; "medium" *zlib* compression level (say, between 3 and 7); unused palette entries omitted; if simple/cheap transparency, palette ordered so that opaque transparency entries can be omitted

- Options for both fast saves and best (slowest) compression

- Ability to preserve and store user-defined text information

Not every feature is vital, of course, and some users may want only a subset of these. But particularly when it comes to web design, one would like full support for gamma correction and for PNG's various transparency capabilities, preferably with an option for best (or at least good) compression. On the other hand, when it comes to compression, one does *not* want to be overwhelmed with the minutiae of PNG's many compression parameters, particularly when PNG-specific optimization products exist (one of which will be covered in Chapter 5, *Applications: Image Converters*).

In this chapter, I look at five of the most popular image-editing applications in detail, explaining how to invoke PNG-specific features and pointing out the limitations of each product. Because PNG's transparency options are among its most promising web-related capabilities, and because I wish to provide a concrete demonstration of the similarities and differences between the various editing programs, I will return to the sample editing task of Chapter 1, *An Introduction to PNG*—namely, the step-by-step procedure for creating a soft "portrait-style" transparency mask in an existing image. At the end of the chapter, I list a couple of dozen other editors with PNG support.

Photoshop 5

Photoshop 5.0.2, available for Macintosh and 32-bit Windows, is the latest version of Adobe's flagship image editor, as of this writing. It supports colormapped, grayscale, and RGB PNGs at sample depths of 8 bits, and images optionally can be saved as interlaced. Alpha transparency is supported in grayscale and truecolor images, but there appears to be no way to add any sort of transparency to a palette-based image. Gamma and color correction are also supported, with one caveat; I'll come back to that shortly.

Photoshop 5 is modal, which is to say that images of a given type (e.g., RGB) remain of that type until explicitly converted to something else—a process that must occur *before* one attempts to save the image. For example, to convert an RGB or grayscale image to palette-based, follow this prescription:

1. Choose **Image** → **Mode** → **Indexed Color**, which pops up a dialog box.

2. Choose an appropriate **Palette** type (typically **Adaptive**).

3. Set the number of colors, either via the **Color Depth** selector or by entering the number explicitly in the **Colors** entry field.

4. Select a dithering method: **None**, **Pattern**, or **Diffusion**.

5. Choose **Faster** or **Better** color matching, and optionally check the **Preserve Exact Colors** box (disabled if no dithering).

6. Click the **OK** button.

The Color Depth selector rather disingenuously indicates bits per pixel, but it is actually nothing more than a shortcut for specifying a power-of-two number of colors—that is, 3 bits/pixel is 8 colors, 4 bits/pixel is 16, and so on. All settings result in 8-bit-per-pixel PNG files.

Note also that the Pattern dither type is known as *ordered dithering* in other contexts, while the Diffusion choice corresponds to Floyd-Steinberg or something similar. The latter generally looks much better, since human eyeballs are very good at noticing the regular patterns of an ordered dither.

Photoshop 5 includes a wizard for creating transparent images, but we'll step through the procedure manually. The key is not to rely on background transparency but instead to add a new layer representing alpha transparency. More specifically, given an image with or without background transparency, do the following to add an alpha channel to it:

1. In the **Channels** palette, click on the arrow at the upper right and select **New Channel . . .** , which pops up a dialog box.

2. In the **Name:** entry field, give the new channel a name (for example, *Alpha*) and click the **OK** button; the other fields can be left with their default values.

3. In the **Channels** palette again, return to the original RGB or grayscale channel.

4. Click on the **Lasso** tool (left side of tool palette, second from top).

5. In the **Lasso Options** tab of the tool palette, set the **Feather** radius to some value, perhaps 13.

6. Draw a loop around the face of the subject.

7. Do *not* invert the Lasso selection; instead go back to the **Channels** palette and select the alpha channel (the lassoed loop will still be visible on the blank channel).

8. Erase everything outside the loop via **Edit → Clear**.

9. Once again, return to the original RGB or grayscale channel via the **Channels** palette, and optionally click on the visibility box of the alpha channel to show its effects overlaid on the main image.

The preceding Lasso-related operations differ from those in every other image editor that I investigated, including Adobe's own ImageReady 1.0. Specifically, the requirement *not* to invert the selection in order to erase the outer part of the alpha channel seemed counterintuitive.*

Having added an appropriate alpha channel to the image, it may now be saved as a 16-bit gray+alpha or 32-bit RGBA PNG:

1. Choose **File → Save a Copy . . .** , which pops up the usual file dialog box.

2. Pick an appropriate directory and filename for the image, choose PNG as the format, and make certain the Exclude Alpha Channels checkbox is *not* checked.

3. Click the **OK** button, which triggers yet another dialog box.

4. Optionally create an interlaced PNG by selecting **Adam7** as the interlacing type, and make sure the filter type is **Adaptive** for grayscale or truecolor images.

5. Click the **OK** button.

If transparency is only desired as an aid in creating the image, not as part of the actual file data, check the **Flatten Image** box in the Save dialog box.

Adobe made significant improvements to the overall handling of gamma and color correction in Photoshop 5, with explicit support for the new sRGB color space (see Chapter 10, *Gamma Correction and Precision Color*) and a number of other standard color spaces, as well. Photoshop 5 also includes an option to enable Monitor Compensation (which requires that the monitor be specified correctly first), and it always saves gamma and color-correction information with PNG images.

Unfortunately, the gamma information PS5 saves in PNG images is wrong; it is always too small by a factor of two, resulting in images that display much too darkly. This is a significant problem, because it appears *only* to affect PNG images. In other words, one cannot simply make the appropriate compensation in Photoshop's RGB setup panel and forget about it; either PNG images will be written incorrectly, or all other image types will be read and written incorrectly. The only workaround within Photoshop 5 is to misadjust the display gamma setting just before saving a PNG image and to reset it just after saving. For example, in a typical Windows PC (or other sRGB display system) with a gamma value of 2.2,

---

* It should be noted, however, that I am by no means an expert with any of the image editors described here! It is entirely possible that there are settings or alternative approaches that conform more closely to the "standard" Lasso procedure used in the other programs.

temporarily change the value to 1.1 in Photoshop's RGB Setup box (shown in Figure 4-1):

1. Choose **File** → **Color Settings** → **RGB Setup** . . .

2. Halve the **Gamma:** value (i.e., if it was 2.2, change it to 1.1).

3. Click the **OK** button.

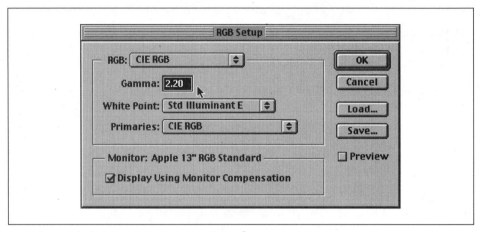

Figure 4-1: Photoshop 5 RGB Setup window

Then save the file in PNG format as before, but when finished, be sure to change the value back! Clearly, this is a crude and painful workaround.

An alternative, available at least to DOS, Windows, and Unix users, is to use a third-party utility to change the gamma values in all of the PNG files after they're saved. One such utility is *pngcrush*, which I'll discuss in some detail in Chapter 5, *Applications: Image Converters*. For a system with a gamma value of 2.2, which should correspond to a PNG file gamma of 0.454545 (or 1/2.2), the following command will replace the incorrect gamma information and write the fixed PNGs into a directory called *fixed/*:

```
pngcrush -d fixed -replace_gamma 0.454545 foo.png foo2.png ...
```

Newer versions of pngcrush support a simpler approach, tailor-made for Photoshop 5:

```
pngcrush -d fixed -double_gamma foo.png foo2.png ...
```

In addition to writing incorrect information in PNG files, Photoshop 5 appears to ignore any existing color space information when reading PNG files. Although one could, in principle, read the PNG gamma and chromaticity information and set up a custom RGB profile that matches it, this would have to be done manually and requires significant effort and knowledge on the part of the user. In other words, only the most dedicated experts are likely to be able to accomplish it, or even to bother with it in the first place.

Photoshop 5 has several other quirks, as well. As I mentioned earlier, palette-based images are always saved with 8-bit pixels and 256 palette entries, regardless of how few colors are actually used; for a bicolor image, this can result in a bloat factor of eight or more, compared to a properly optimized image. Adobe's rationale seems to be that this sort of optimization should be handled in a web-specific application like ImageReady. But leaving aside the fact that ImageReady 1.0 has similar problems, one would expect a high-end editing application like Photoshop (with its high-end price tag) to do much better.

Photoshop's PNG-related user options are overly technical and can also result in files that are larger than necessary. For example, for most users a simple Interlaced checkbox would suffice; there is no need to know that PNG's interlacing method is formally known as Adam7. Similarly, the ability to specify individual compression filters is nice from a theoretical standpoint, but 99% of users are not going to waste their time experimenting with the six choices Photoshop allows. Most will instead stick with the default value, which is often None (but sometimes Adaptive) and is rarely correct for the given image type. As a rule of thumb, palette-based images should always use None, and grayscale and truecolor images should always use Adaptive. There are very rare cases in which another choice will be better, but they are difficult to predict, and the difference in file size will usually be minimal anyway. In fact, Photoshop should probably offer only these two options in the first place. Oddly enough, Photoshop offers the user no control at all over the compression engine itself, even though this is much easier to understand conceptually and has a more predictable impact on the file size. Photoshop's hardwired compression setting seems to correspond to level 6 in most other implementations.

Photoshop 4 had little or no support for 16-bit-per-sample images; this, together with improved color management, was one of the major new features in version 5. Unfortunately, due to a programming oversight, 16-bit support was not extended to include PNG. On import, 16-bit PNG images are converted to 8-bit samples, and on export, PNG is not offered as an option for 16-bit images. Adobe has indicated that this will be addressed in the next major release.

Photoshop also lacks support for embedded PNG text annotations, despite allowing the user to enter an extensive set via the **File** → **File Info** . . . dialog box; these can only be saved to an external file. This is particularly surprising given the presence of checkboxes allowing one to Mark as Copyrighted (in the File Info dialog box, shown in Figure 4-2) and Exclude Non-Image Data (in the Save dialog box). The former option has to do with digital watermarking and the copyright symbol in Photoshop's titlebar. As to the latter option, text data is *always* excluded from the file.

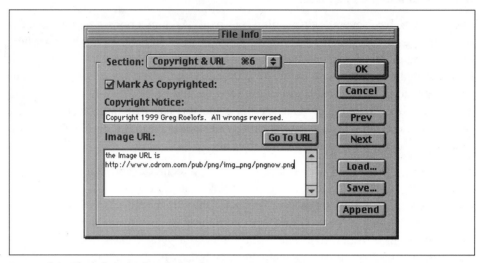

Figure 4-2: Photoshop 5 File Info window

Most critically, Photoshop has absolutely no support for transparency in color-mapped PNG images. When an RGBA or gray+alpha image has been converted to indexed mode, only the non-alpha data is affected; that is, Photoshop still indicates two channels, one for the indexed color data and one for the (unchanged) alpha channel. Attempting to save such an image is an exercise in frustration, however: in the Save As dialog, PNG is grayed out even though GIF is allowed (and indeed, a GIF saved in this way will have binary transparency corresponding approximately to the alpha channel). In the Save a Copy dialog, PNG is allowed, but the Exclude Alpha Channels box is both checked and grayed out.

Overall, it is evident that Adobe's attention was devoted more to enhancing generic editing features than to providing comprehensive support (or, in some cases, even basic support) for the three-year-old PNG format. In fact, PNG support seems almost to have been an afterthought, even in version 5.0. This may be reasonable from a business perspective, but it is nevertheless disappointing, given that PNG's capabilities map so closely into Photoshop's.

Further information about Photoshop is available from Adobe's web pages at *http://www.adobe.com/prodindex/photoshop/.*

Photoshop 4

Photoshop 4 is still in wide use and has a slightly different feature set from version 5, so we'll look at it in some detail, too. It supports the same basic PNG feature set the newer version does: colormapped, grayscale, RGB, and RGBA PNGs at sample depths of 8 bits or less, optionally interlaced, with no palette transparency or text support. Like PS5, it too has a gamma-related quirk, though not as severe. I'll discuss it in a moment.

Photoshop 4's support for PNG alpha channels is sufficiently well hidden that Jordan Mendelson set up a web page describing the step-by-step procedure for creating one, *http://jordy.wserv.com/experiments/png.html*. The approach is very similar to that in Photoshop 5, with the exception of the steps needed to actually modify the alpha channel for a portrait-style mask:

1. In the **Channels** palette, click on the arrow at the upper right and select **New Channel . . .**, which pops up a dialog box.

2. In the **Name:** entry field, give the new channel a name (for example, *Alpha*) and click the **OK** button; the other fields affect only how the alpha channel is displayed, not the actual image data, and can be left with their default values.

3. In the **Channels** palette again, leave the alpha channel as the selected one, but make the original RGB or grayscale channel visible by clicking on the small box to its left (an eyeball icon will appear in the box). The main image will now be visible under a 50% red "haze" that represents the alpha channel, assuming the default options in the previous step's dialog box were left unchanged.

4. Double-click on the **Lasso** tool (left side of tool palette, second from top).

5. In the **Lasso Options** tab of the tool palette, set the **Feather** radius to some value, perhaps 13.

6. Draw a loop around the face of the subject, but do *not* invert the selection.

7. Erase everything outside the loop via **Edit → Clear**; a soft-edged hole will appear in the red overlay, indicating that everything but the face of the subject is masked out.

Once the alpha channel is created, the whole image may be saved as a 16-bit gray+alpha or 32-bit RGBA PNG just as in Photoshop 5:

1. Choose **File → Save a Copy . . .**, which pops up the usual file dialog box.

2. Pick an appropriate directory and filename for the image, choose PNG as the format, and make certain the **Don't include alpha channels** checkbox is *not* checked.

3. Click the **OK** button, which triggers yet another dialog box.

4. Optionally create an interlaced PNG by selecting **Adam7** as the interlacing type, and make sure the filter type is **Adaptive** for grayscale or truecolor images.

5. Click the **OK** button.

If transparency is desired only as an aid in creating the image, not as part of the actual file data, go to the Layer menu and select **Flatten Image** before saving.

Gamma and color-correction information is always saved with PNG images, but in order for it to be meaningful (that is, not wrong), the monitor settings must be entered correctly in the Monitor Setup box, accessed via **File** → **Color Settings** → **Monitor Setup** (shown in Figure 4-3).

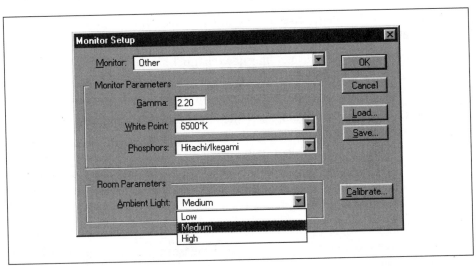

Figure 4-3: Photoshop 4 Monitor Setup window

The information can either be entered explicitly, by providing values for the display system's "gamma" value, white point, and phosphor types (see Chapter 10 for a more detailed explanation of these terms), or it can be done implicitly, by selecting a monitor type from a list of calibrated models. The implicit approach may not work exactly as intended, however; the default gamma value seems to be 1.8, whereas almost all PC display systems are closer to 2.2. Either way, there is one more setting, and this is where the caveat I mentioned earlier comes in. For the Ambient Light setting, only the Medium value will cause Photoshop to save correct gamma information in the PNG file. The High setting will result in a PNG gamma value that is too small by a factor of two,* while the Low setting results in a value that is 50% too large. Of course, this is still preferable to the case with Photoshop 5.0; at least Photoshop 4.0 has *one* setting that works correctly.

In other respects, Photoshop 4 is no different from version 5. It lacks support for text annotations, 16-bit samples, low-bit-depth samples and palette transparency, and its compression settings and interface are identical—that is, mediocre at best.

ImageReady

ImageReady is Adobe's Web-specific image editor for 32-bit Windows and the PowerPC-based Macintosh. It provides a number of ways to optimize the size and content of images and can be used either as a backend to Photoshop or as a standalone product. Its capabilities and structure are quite similar to those of Macromedia's Fireworks.

ImageReady 1.0 supports both 24-bit RGB PNGs and 8-bit palette-based PNGs, which it refers to as "PNG-24" and "PNG-8" files, respectively. There is no direct support for grayscale images, but it is possible to convert a color image to what is basically grayscale (**Image** → **Adjust** → **Desaturate**) and save it as an 8-bit color-mapped image with nothing but shades of near-gray in the palette. Interlacing, simple transparency, and full alpha transparency are supported, but the program appears not to allow single-color transparency in RGB images, and its implementation of PNG's RGBA-palette mode is almost useless. I'll take a closer look at that in just a moment.

The procedure for adding portrait-style transparency to an existing RGB image is similar to that for Fireworks and Photoshop. As before, open the file and use the Lasso tool to select the region of interest:

1. Choose **File** → **Open**.
2. Click on the **Lasso** tool (left side of tool palette, second from top).
3. Draw a loop around the face of the subject.
4. Invert the selection so that the part *outside* the loop gets erased (**Select** → **Inverse**).
5. **Select** → **Feather** . . . and set the **Feather Radius** to some value, perhaps 13.
6. Erase everything outside the loop via **Edit** → **Clear**.

Note that, unlike Fireworks's feather radius, ImageReady's extends to both sides of the lassoed path; that is, there will be partially transparent pixels both inside and

---

* Adobe's definition of "high" ambient light appears to involve something on the order of a spotlight shining in the user's face.

outside the selection. Thus, we drew our loop a bit bigger here and set the feather radius to roughly half of what it was in the Fireworks example.

Saving the newly cropped image as a 32-bit RGBA PNG is straightforward:

1. Open the **Optimize** palette (subwindow), shown in Figure 4-4, if it isn't already popped up (**Window → Show Optimize**).

2. Select **PNG-24** from the pull-down list at the upper left.

3. In the **Matte:** pull-down list, select **No Matte** (which will then display in the box as "None").

4. Check the **Transparency** checkbox.

5. Optionally check the **Interlaced** checkbox to make an interlaced PNG.

6. Choose **File → Save Optimized As** . . . and pick an appropriate directory and filename.

The PNG-24 Optimize palette is shown in Figure 4-4. The Transparency checkbox is rather misleading; leaving it unchecked indeed creates a completely opaque image, but ImageReady nevertheless writes a full 32-bit RGBA file! That is, the alpha channel is still there, but it is completely blank. One can only hope that this is an oversight and that it will be corrected in the next release; such files can hardly be considered "optimized."

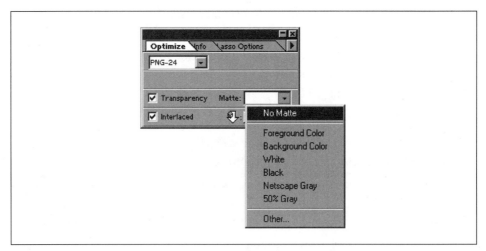

Figure 4-4: ImageReady Optimize palette for 24-bit PNG, with Matte pull-down menu

Things get more interesting in the palette-based case. As before, the action takes place in the Optimize palette, as shown in Figure 4-5:

1. Select **PNG-8** from the format pull-down list.

2. Select an appropriate palette type from the pull-down list on the second line (**Perceptual** is the default).

3. Select **No Matte** from the **Matte:** pull-down list.

4. Set **Colors:** to 256 or Auto.

5. Set **Levels:** to 1 (which will reduce the **Colors:** setting to 255).

6. Optionally check the **Interlaced** checkbox.

7. Choose **File** → **Save Optimized As** . . . and pick an appropriate directory and filename.

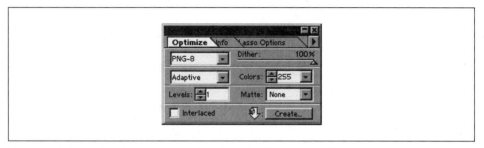

Figure 4-5: ImageReady Optimize palette for 8-bit (colormapped) PNG

Because the number of transparency levels was set to 1, this procedure will create an image with binary transparency; there will be a sharp cutoff at the lassoed boundary. (If the main image window is showing the Optimized tab instead of Original, the effects of the Optimize palette will be displayed in "real time," more or less.) How about a nice RGBA-palette image? One might imagine that between 4 and 16 transparency levels would suffice with dithering turned on, but the Levels spin button actually indicates the number of palette entries with transparency, not the number of transparency levels. Thus, even 160 "levels" is insufficient in our portrait example. This is largely due to ImageReady's strange optimization algorithm, which seems to prefer dark colors for transparency. Figure 4-6 shows the result; note the speckled appearance of the letters on the right side and the odd banding appearance (almost like an edge-detection algorithm) on the left.

For this image, a levels setting between 220 and 230 worked best, at least for transparency. The drawback is that this leaves only 26 to 36 colors for the opaque regions. For facial tones, that is simply not enough—one loses many of the saturated colors and most of the fine gradients and shading, leaving skin tones flat and grainy. And on top of that, the transparent regions show distinct banding, even with the large levels setting. See Figure 4-7 for an example with levels set at 224.

Figure 4-6: ImageReady optimized preview with 160 transparent entries, showing artifacts

Figure 4-7: ImageReady optimized preview with 224 transparent entries, showing degraded facial tones

Overall, ImageReady's PNG support is adequate, but it seems probable that GIF and JPEG were considerably higher priorities. The PNG-24 mode is excellent for images with full alpha channels, but the 33% size penalty incurred by opaque RGB images (thanks to the extraneous alpha channel) is unlikely to win friends in the web design crowd. PNG-8 is fine for opaque images with more than 16 colors, but low-color images are always saved at 8 bits per pixel, resulting in files that are too big by a factor of anywhere from two to eight. PNG-8 images with transparency, in addition to suffering the quantization problems noted previously, appear always to be saved with as many transparency entries as palette entries, resulting in up to 255 wasted bytes per image.

On the positive side, ImageReady supports interlacing with no trouble, and it preserves existing Copyright text chunks while allowing authors to change or add a new one. The procedure for adding one is simple:

1. Choose **File** → **Image Info** . . .
2. Fill in the **Copyright**: field appropriately (e.g., "Copyright 1999 O'Reilly and Associates. All rights reserved.").
3. Click the **OK** button.

The only other supported text keyword is Software, which ImageReady always writes automatically ("Adobe ImageReady"); it replaces any previous Software text chunk. All other text chunks are discarded, and there is no provision for authors to add others.

What about gamma and color correction? At first glance, ImageReady appears to support gamma, but this is mostly illusory. It does allow one to adjust the image appearance with a gamma slider (**Image** → **Adjust** → **Gamma** . . .), but doing so modifies the pixels directly, and information about the adjustment is not saved with the file. In other words, the same image will look different on different systems. Nor is the effect remembered, other than as part of ImageReady's Undo capability—changes to the gamma setting become permanent as soon as the OK button is clicked. PNG files that already have gamma chunks are treated the same as those without; the gamma information is discarded.

ImageReady's compression of PNG images is fair but by no means optimal. I already noted that colormapped images with just a few palette entries are saved at a higher bit depth than is necessary and that palette-based transparency information is stored inefficiently. On top of that, though, pngcrush (discussed in Chapter 5) was able to achieve compression improvements of between 6% and 45% on 22 variations of my test image, averaging around 12% overall. The reasons for this are not immediately obvious, however; ImageReady's compression settings seem reasonable, and it does use dynamic filtering on truecolor images.

The ImageReady home page is at *http://www.adobe.com/prodindex/imageready/*.

Paint Shop Pro

Jasc's Paint Shop Pro 5.0 is a capable and popular program for image editing; it is also quite affordable. Version 5.0 supports only 32-bit Windows, but version 3.12 is still available for Windows 3.x and NT 3.51 and also supports PNG. We'll only be looking at the newer release, however.

At the most basic level, PSP supports the three major PNG image types: color-mapped, grayscale, and RGB, both interlaced and noninterlaced. It provides options for converting between types, but it does not do so automatically; if a "16-million-color" image happens to use only 200 colors, it will still be saved as 24-bit RGB unless the user specifically asks for conversion to a palette image. Both GIF-style transparency (one completely transparent palette entry) and full 32-bit RGBA are supported, but RGBA-palette mode is not.

Paint Shop Pro's interface for adding an alpha mask to an image is quite elegant. First, open an ordinary RGB image, then pop up the **Add Mask From Image** dialog box, shown in Figure 4-8:

1. Choose **File** → **Open**.
2. Choose **Mask** → **New** → **From Image**.
3. Choose **Mask** → **Edit**.

The second step brings up the dialog box, shown in Figure 4-8. Setting the source to This Window guarantees that the size is correct, and basing it on the Source Opacity, where the original image had no transparency at all, will produce a blank slate on which gradients and other fills can be placed. Choosing the **Source luminance** button instead will generate transparency according to the light and dark areas in the image itself, and the areas that are considered transparent can be inverted by checking the **Invert mask data** checkbox at the bottom. Either way, the mask can be edited as an ordinary grayscale image after the third step.

Saving such an image is a two-step procedure. First, the alpha mask must be "glued" to the main image as its alpha channel, after which the standard save procedure applies:

1. Choose **Mask** → **Save To Alpha Channel**.
2. Choose **File** → **Save As** (or **Save Copy As**).

Converting an existing truecolor image to palette-based or creating a new palette-based image involves essentially the same procedure:

1. Choose **File** → **Open** or **New**.
2. Choose **Colors** → **Decrease Color Depth** → **256 Colors**.

Other depths are available, but most create the same size palette; indeed, the only other supported palette sizes in the output file are 2 and 16 colors. For an existing

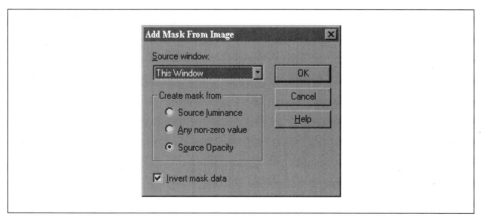

Figure 4-8: Paint Shop Pro alpha mask window

image, a dialog box will pop up offering different quantization methods (in the **Palette** section) and dithering methods (in the **Reduction method** section). Note that *Nearest color* means no dithering; *Error diffusion* is generally the nicest looking but slowest approach, sometimes known as Floyd-Steinberg or "FS" dithering in other programs. To add and view transparency, use the Colors menu again:

1. Choose **Colors** → **Set Palette Transparency**.
2. Choose **Set the transparency value to the current background color**.
3. Choose **Colors** → **View Palette Transparency**.

To set a color other than the background color as transparent, use the eyedropper tool to pick the color and find its index. Then, in place of the second step, select **Set the transparency value to palette entry** and enter the index value of the color.

Paint Shop Pro currently does not support gamma correction, even though it does provide a Monitor Gamma Adjustment window (via **File** → **Preferences** → **Monitor Gamma**) that could in theory be used to supply the appropriate information. PSP does add a modification-time chunk, but it is incorrectly written using the local time zone of the user rather than Universal Time as required by the PNG specification.

Text annotations, including those found in other file formats, are preserved and converted as needed. In addition, the user may add text chunks with the Title, Author, Copyright, and Description keywords via **View** → **Image Information** option. The program stores DOS-style line endings (both "carriage return" and "line feed" character codes) rather than following the PNG spec's recommendation to use Unix-style line endings (line-feed characters only).

With regard to file sizes, Paint Shop Pro always uses near-optimal compression and filtering settings on the image data. There is no option for faster compression, although PSP's own format is typically used for intermediate saves. The program's only major failing in this regard is that it always writes the maximum number of palette entries regardless of how many are used, and it doesn't reorder the palette so that the single transparent entry comes first, which would allow the remainder of the transparency chunk to be omitted. For a 50-color web icon with no transparency, this means the file will be 618 bytes larger than it should be, solely due to the overhead required to store a full 256 palette entries. With transparency, an average of 25 additional bytes would be wasted for this example, but the cost for true 256-color images may be as much as 255 bytes. As I've noted elsewhere, that can be a serious penalty for small images. In addition, PSP doesn't support writing three- or four-color images with 2 bits per pixel but instead will use 4 bits. Compression almost never makes up the difference; the output file will be roughly twice as large as it should be.

More information about Paint Shop Pro is available at Jasc's web site, *http://www. jasc.com/psp.html.*

The Gimp

The only offering in our roundup that is available for Linux, the GNU Image Manipulation Program, is also unique in that it may be obtained for free, with complete source code, if desired. Originally written for Unix and the X Window System, the Gimp (or GIMP) is also being ported to OS/2 and 32-bit Windows.* I tested version 1.0.2, the latest nondevelopment release as of this writing, under Linux 2.0. PNG support is handled via a plug-in with its own release schedule, though. A considerably improved version (1.1.7) was released in late February 1999, after my tests; I'll note its changes as we go.

Like Photoshop, the Gimp uses a modal approach to the basic image types, requiring an explicit conversion between RGB, grayscale, and indexed-color images. Both alpha channels and gamma correction are supported, albeit at a relatively basic level; I'll discuss the details shortly. Currently, the standard Gimp release does not support sample depths greater than 8 bits, but a separate development fork known as Gimp16 (or informally as "Hollywood") has extended the Gimp's core to operate on deep pixels and is expected to merge with the main development fork in the 2.0 time frame. There was no support for text annotations in the stock 1.0.2 release, but version 1.1.7 of the PNG plug-in appears to have added support for user-specified Title, Author, Description, Copyright, Creation Time, Disclaimer, Warning, Source, and Comment keywords; the Software keyword is

---

* Not only that, but the Windows port even runs under the Windows emulator WINE, making it one of the few large applications that can be run simultaneously as a native Linux application and as an emulated Windows program. Of course, that would be a fairly twisted thing to do.

added automatically. The newer plug-in release also supports timestamps via PNG's tIME chunk (described in Chapter 11, *PNG Options and Extensions*).

The Gimp employs Photoshop's layer-based editing model and in general will be familiar to anyone comfortable with Photoshop. The user interface does differ in one significant respect, however: instead of a large parent window with a main menu bar and various child windows inside, the Gimp uses separate, standalone windows for everything, and the functions corresponding to Photoshop's main menu are instead accessible via the righthand mouse button. At its most minimal, the Gimp consists only of the small tool-palette window, which contains a truncated File menu from which one can create a new image or open an existing file.

Conveniently enough, that leads us directly into our portrait example:

1. Choose **File** → **Open** and select an appropriate truecolor image.

2. Click the right mouse button over the image and select **Layers** → **Add Alpha Channel**, after which the titlebar will indicate **(RGB-alpha)** instead of just **(RGB)**.

3. Click on the **Lasso** tool (upper right corner of the tool palette).

4. Hold the right mouse button and choose **Dialogs** → **Tool Options** . . . .

5. Click on the **Feather** checkbox and set the **Feather Radius** slider to some value, perhaps 25.

6. Draw a loop around the face of the subject.

7. Invert the lasso selection: hold the right button and choose **Select** → **Invert**.

8. Erase everything outside the loop: hold the right button and choose **Edit** → **Clear**.

Aside from the use of the right mouse button instead of a menu bar, the procedure is almost identical to that in each of the other applications I've investigated. Note that the Gimp's feathering extends to both sides of the lassoed path, much as ImageReady's does. Unlike ImageReady, however (but similar to Fireworks), Gimp's "radius" appears to indicate the total width of the alpha band, not just half of it. The Lasso options box, the tool palette, and the main image window are shown overlapped in Figure 4-9. (Ordinarily, the first two float elsewhere on the desktop.)

To save the image as a 32-bit RGBA PNG, bring up the **Save as** dialog:

1. Hold the right mouse button and choose **File** → **Save as**.

2. Pick an appropriate directory and filename for the image, and either choose PNG explicitly from the drop-down file type list or do so implicitly by typing the *.png* filename extension.

3. Click the **OK** button, which brings up the **PNG Options** dialog box.

4. Set the **Compression level** slider to an appropriate value and optionally check the **Interlace** checkbox.

5. Click the **OK** button.

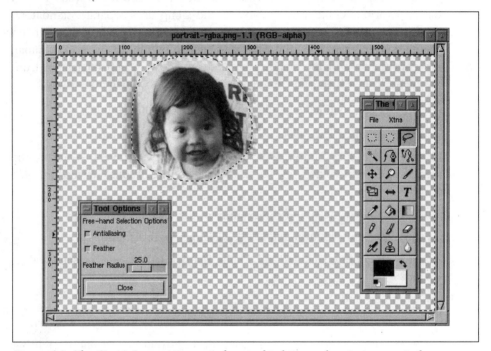

Figure 4-9: The Gimp's Lasso options window, tool palette, and main image window

The compression-level slider actually allows noninteger values, but it appears to truncate the fractional part. Thus, for maximum compression, the slider must be set at 9.0 exactly. For typical usage, 6.0 is fine, and for quick saves with decent compression, use 3.0.

Conversion of an RGB image (with or without an alpha channel) to grayscale or to indexed-color is accomplished via the right mouse button's **Image** submenu, either the **Grayscale** or **Indexed items**. Going from 32-bit RGBA to 16-bit gray+alpha is quite fast, and the Gimp saves the result properly as a gray+alpha PNG file. Similarly, converting plain RGB or grayscale to indexed-color mode works well and saves correctly. But conversion of RGBA or gray+alpha to Indexed is problematic with the stock 1.0.2 PNG plug-in. Gimp's internal palette model appears to be GIF-like in that there's no evidence that it supports partial transparency in indexed images; the main image display switches to a hard-edged mask with only fully transparent and fully opaque regions visible. More serious is the fact that even this much transparency results in a truncated file, a core dump (though not a termination of the other Gimp windows), and a pop-up error box indicating that the save failed. Perusal of the older PNG plug-in's source code strongly suggests that transparency support for indexed images was never implemented. Fortunately, Yamahata Kenichiro addressed this in version 1.1.7 of the plug-in, but I did not have a chance to investigate how it works.

Aside from that and a lack of support for text comments, the only other PNG-related problem seems to be in the gamma chunk. Version 1.0.2 of the Gimp has no support for monitor settings or calibration, and in the absence of those, it should assume a PC-like (or sRGB) environment on PCs and most workstations. That is, the gamma value it writes to file should be the inverse of 2.2. But the stock PNG plug-in actually writes 1.0, a value that causes images to appear extremely washed out when viewed with a gamma-aware application (unless the originating machine was a NeXT workstation). Fortunately, the developers addressed this problem within 24 hours of its having been reported, and version 1.1.7 of the PNG plug-in includes the fix (as will the next full release of the Gimp, presumably). Images saved under older versions can be corrected in a batch operation with a tool such as pngcrush. The following example performs a batch correction and puts all of the fixed images into a subdirectory called *fixed/*:

```
pngcrush -d fixed -replace_gamma 0.454545 foo.png foo2.png ...
```

The Gimp's compression of PNG files is excellent, with the program choosing the proper filtering strategies for both palette-based and continuous-tone images. pngcrush, covered in Chapter 5, was unable to eke out any improvement in file size beyond that due to eliminating the overhead of multiple image-data chunks, which amounts to a mere 12 bytes per 8,204-byte chunk, or less than 0.15% of the overall file size.

The main Gimp home page is at *http://www.gimp.org/*, with extensions available from the plug-in registry, *http://registry.gimp.org/* (including the PNG plug-in at *http://registry.gimp.org/detailview.phtml?plugin=PNG+for+GIMP+1.0/0.99.x*). The Gimp16 project has a separate home page at *http://film.gimp.org/*.

Other Image Editors

Many other editing applications also support PNG. All of the known ones are in the following list, with the version number of the latest release (as of early 1999) given wherever possible.

ArtEffect

Version 2.6, Haage & Partner Computer. Available for Amiga; read/write support for PNGs; full (32-bit) alpha support.

http://www.haage-partner.com/ae_e.htm

Becasso

Version 1.1, Sum Software. Available for BeOS PPC/x86; read/write support for PNGs; full (32-bit) alpha support; no gamma support.

http://www.sumware.demon.nl/products/becasso/

Canvas

Version 6.0, Deneba Software. Available for 32-bit Windows and Mac PPC; read/write support for PNGs. Emphasizes extensive support for transparency, alpha channels, and anti-aliasing, but the demo version does not allow images to be saved, so its level of PNG transparency support (if any) is not known.

http://www.deneba.com/dazroot/prodinfo/canvas6/info.html

ColorWorks:WEB

Version 4, SPG. Available for 32-bit Windows; read/write support for PNGs.

http://www.spg-net.com/product2.html

CorelDRAW

Version 8, Corel. Available for 32-bit Windows and Mac PPC; read/write support for PNGs.

http://www.corel.com/products/graphicsandpublishing/draw8/

CorelXARA

Version 1.5, Xara. Available for 16- and 32-bit Windows; read/write support for PNGs.

http://www.xara.com/noframes/corelxara/

Enhance

Version 4.0, MicroFrontier. Available for Mac 68k/PPC; read/write support for PNGs; no gamma support.

http://www.microfrontier.com/products/enhance40/

FreeHand Graphics Studio

Version 8.0.1, Macromedia. Available for 32-bit Windows and Mac PPC; read/write support for PNGs; full (32-bit) alpha support.

http://www.macromedia.com/software/freehand/

HoTMetaL PRO

Version 5.0, SoftQuad. Available for 32-bit Windows (version 3.0 was available for 16-bit Windows); read/write support for PNGs. This is actually an HTML editor, but versions 3.0 and later incorporate an image editor as well. In version 5.0, the bundled image application is Ulead's PhotoImpact 3.02 SE.

http://www.sq.com/products/hotmetal/

Illustrator

Version 8.0, Adobe. Available for 32-bit Windows and Mac PPC; read/write support for PNGs.

http://www.adobe.com/prodindex/illustrator/

Image Composer

Version 1.5, Microsoft. Available for 32-bit Windows; read/write support for PNGs; full (32-bit) alpha support. This was originally known as Altamira Composer and was bundled with FrontPage 98; it appears to have been superseded by PhotoDraw 2000.

http://www.microsoft.com/imagecomposer/

ImageFX

Version 3.2, Nova Design. Available for Amiga; read/write support for PNGs.

http://www.novadesign.com/fxinfo.htm

MediaStudio Pro

Version 5.2, Ulead Systems. Available for 32-bit Windows; read/write support for PNGs.

http://www.ulead.com/mspro5/

NetStudio

Version 1.0, NetStudio. Available for 32-bit Windows; read/write support for PNGs.

http://www.netstudio.com/product.html

Personal Paint

Version 7.1, Cloanto. Available for Amiga; read/write support for PNGs.

http://www.cloanto.com/amiga/programs_ppaint.html

PhotoDraw 2000

Microsoft. Available for 32-bit Windows; read/write support for PNGs.

http://www.microsoft.com/office/photodraw/

PhotoImpact

Version 4.2, Ulead Systems. Available for 32-bit Windows; read/write support for PNGs; no gamma support in version 3.0 (unknown in 4.0).

http://www.ulead.com/pi/

PhotoLine

Version 4.57, Computerinsel. Available for 32-bit Windows; read/write support for PNGs; version 2.x reportedly had problems saving alpha channels.

http://www.pl32.com/

Photonyx

Version 1.0, Chrome Imaging. Available for 32-bit Windows; read/write support for PNGs.

http://www.chrome-imaging.com/photonyx.html

Picnic

Version 0.4, Peder Blekken. Available for BeOS PPC; read/write support for PNGs (in fact, PNG is the only supported output format).

http://www.be.com/beware/Graphics/Picnic.html

Picture Publisher

Version 8, Micrografx. Available for 32-bit Windows; read/write support for PNGs.

http://www.micrografx.com/picturepublisher/

Satori

Version 2.5, Spaceward Graphics. Available for 32-bit Windows; read/write support for PNGs; full (32-bit) alpha support; may include support for images with 16-bit sample depth.

http://www.satoripaint.com/

Shake

Version 2.03, Nothing Real. Available for SGI Irix and 32-bit Windows; read/write support for PNGs; full support for images with 16-bit sample depth; full alpha support (32-bit and 64-bit); partial (write-only) gamma support.

http://www.nothingreal.com/Products/

VideoStudio

Version 3.0, Ulead Systems. Available for 32-bit Windows; read/write support for PNGs.

http://www.ulead.com/vs/

Visio

Version 5.0, Visio. Available for 32-bit Windows (version 4.1 is still available for Windows 3.x); read/write support for PNGs.

http://www.visio.com/products/

WebImage

Version 2.11, Group 42. Available for 32-bit Windows (version 1.72 is still available for Windows 3.x); read/write support for PNGs.

http://www.group42.com/webimage.htm

WebPainter

Version 3.0.5, Totally Hip Software. Available for Mac PPC and 32-bit Windows; read/write support for PNGs.

http://www.totallyhip.com/Link/ProductsWP3.html

WinImages

Version R5, Black Belt Systems. Available for 32-bit Windows; read/write support for PNGs.

http://www.blackbelt.com/wi_r5_dt.html

Xara Webster

Version 2.0, Xara. Available for 32-bit Windows; read/write support for PNGs.

http://www.xara.com/noframes/webster/

xart

Version of June 5, 1998, Rick Hohensee and others. Available for Unix/X; read/write support for PNGs; no alpha support. This is a "mutant spawn" of XPaint with emphasis on mouse-based freehand drawing.

http://cqi.com/~humbubba/quill/quill.html

XPaint

Version 2.5.6, David Koblas, Torsten Martinsen, and others. Available for Unix/X; read/write support for PNGs; no alpha support.

http://www.danbbs.dk/~torsten/xpaint/

xRes

Version 3.0, Macromedia. Available for 32-bit Windows and Mac 68k/PPC; read/write support for PNGs; full (32-bit) alpha support; no gamma support.

http://www.macromedia.com/software/xres/

New image editors with PNG support and updated information on the editors in the preceding list can be found at the *Image Editors with PNG Support* web page *http://www.cdrom.com/pub/png/pngaped.html*. This URL should remain valid for at least a few years, but there are never any guarantees on the World Wide Web. Should the link ever break, use a search engine to look for the page's title string or for one of the more oddly named utilities or companies listed.

5

Applications: Image Converters

Conversion to PNG from other image formats (or even from PNG) remains a popular approach for the simple reason that other formats have traditionally been better supported by applications. Even with good, current application support for PNG, users typically have large archives of older images, at least some of which may they desire to convert to PNG format.

Just as one would like to see certain basic PNG features supported in image editors (which may be thought of as a special case of conversion utilities, converting and optionally modifying a previously saved image file) one would like certain basic PNG features supported in converters. These include:

- Preservation of basic image types: RGB, grayscale, and palette-based

- Option to convert "truecolor" images with fewer than 256 colors to palette-based (or grayscale, if appropriate)

- Preservation of simple transparency in palette images (e.g., when converting from GIF), including the ability to reorder the palette so the transparent entry comes first, which avoids wasting space in PNG's transparency chunk

- Preservation of *unassociated* alpha transparency (e.g., when converting from TIFF)

- Preservation of gamma, chromaticity, sRGB, or full ICC profile information (see Chapter 10, *Gamma Correction and Precision Color*, for details)

- Option to preserve "deep" samples, such as from 12-bit JPEG or medical images or 16-bit-per-sample TIFF images

- Preservation of text information (e.g., from JPEG, GIF, and TIFF images)

- Preservation of interlacing or "progressiveness"

- Option to scan for unused palette entries and eliminate any from the palette

- Reasonable default compression settings: adaptive filtering turned on for all image types except palette-based; "medium" *zlib* compression level (say, between 3 and 7)

- Option for maximal (slowest) compression

Clearly, different users have different needs, but fundamental things that should be preserved when converting between image formats include the basic pixel information, transparency, and text. Items in the preceding list that involve optimization and compression of PNG images can be dealt with after the initial conversion is complete, but restoring text or transparency information that was lost in translation is tedious and to be avoided if at all possible.

In the next few sections, we will look at a number of conversion utilities in some detail. Most of these are command-line programs—not because we want the reader to suffer,* but because dedicated converters such as these typically do the best job and are often capable of batch (automated) conversions. I have also listed many image viewers with conversion capabilities in Chapter 3, *Applications: Image Viewers* and several image editors in Chapter 4, *Applications: Image Editors*; these are, by necessity, graphical and may be preferable for the casual user.

pngcrush

What may be the most useful conversion tool of all knows nothing of any image format other than PNG; it converts PNGs into other PNGs. pngcrush, by Glenn Randers-Pehrson, is a program for optimizing PNG images—specifically, for reducing their size as much as possible, although it can also perform simple housekeeping tasks such as removing or replacing specific chunks,† or adding gamma-correction information or simple transparency. It is an invaluable tool for use in conjunction with other converters and with commercial image editors, which may not always produce optimal PNG files.

pngcrush is currently available as a command-line, shareware program in DOS and Linux x86 flavors. The DOS version works under Windows 95/98/NT and can handle long filenames; it may also run in an OS/2 DOS box, but without long-file-name support. The current release, as of January 1999, is version 1.1.3 which has a home page at *http://www.netgsi.com/~glennrp/pngcrush/*.

---

* For *real* suffering, write a book.

† PNG's fundamental chunk structure is described in Chapter 8, *PNG Basics.*

The simplest pngcrush operation is a basic "crush" on a single file, specifying the output filename:

```
pngcrush foo.png foo-crushed.png
```

This results in output that looks something like the following:

```
pngcrush 1.1.3, Copyright (C) 1998, Glenn Randers-Pehrson.
 | This program was built with libpng version 1.0.3,
 |    Copyright (c) Guy Eric Schalnat, Group 42 Inc.,
 |    Copyright (c) 1996, 1997 Andreas Dilger,
 |    Copyright (c) 1998, 1999, Glenn Randers-Pehrson,
 | and zlib version 1.1.3, Copyright (c) 1998,
 |    Jean-loup Gailly and Mark Adler.

    foo.png IDAT length in input file =    148723
    IDAT length with method 1 (fm 0 zl 4 zs 0)=   147533
    IDAT length with method 2 (fm 1 zl 4 zs 0)=   124710
    IDAT length with method 3 (fm 5 zl 4 zs 1)=   110589
    IDAT length with method 9 (fm 5 zl 2 zs 2)=   880073
    IDAT length with method 10 (fm 5 zl 9 zs 1)=    85820
    best pngcrush method = 10 for foo-crushed.png (42.36% reduction)

    overall result: 42.36% reduction, 62903 bytes
```

pngcrush typically tries the five or six compression approaches that are, according to its heuristics, the most likely to compress the best. This involves varying the different filter and compression settings allowed by the PNG format (described in Chapter 9, *Compression and Filtering*). If pngcrush finds a method that produces a smaller file than the original, it saves the new file with that approach. (A 42% reduction as shown in the previous output is typical only of cases in which the original file was compressed particularly poorly.) Note that pngcrush operates completely losslessly with respect to the image data; the only loss of information it allows is the explicit removal or replacement of chunks at the user's direction. We'll come back to that shortly.

pngcrush also supports a truly brute-force approach that currently tests 102 different methods but may add more in the future. This rarely improves compression by more than a tenth of a percent over the default approach, but for busy sites looking to conserve bandwidth, saving even a dozen bytes may be well worth the cost of a very lengthy—but one-time—pngcrush session. The brute-force method is invoked with the –brute option, logically enough:

```
pngcrush -brute foo.png foo-crushed.png
```

In general, a site optimizing its content will want to crush all of its PNG images (by using batch-mode conversion), and pngcrush includes two options to support batch conversion. The first allows one to specify a new extension for converted images, which will be created in the same directory as the original:

```
pngcrush -e -crushed.png foo.png foo2.png foo3.png foo4.png
```

This example crushes four images, *foo.png* through *foo4.png*, giving them the extension *-crushed.png*; thus the output names are *foo-crushed.png*, *foo2-crushed. png*, and so on. Such an approach is handy for casual use, since an alphabetical directory listing will (usually) list the original and crushed versions in pairs, allowing quick, after-the-fact inspection of the changes in file sizes. But because it involves renaming files, this is probably not the preferred approach for a web site. The alternative is pngcrush's −d option, which allows one to specify an output directory in which to place the crushed images:

```
pngcrush -d crushed_images foo.png foo2.png foo3.png foo4.png
```

This example crushes the same four images, but leaves their filenames unchanged. The new versions will go in the *crushed_images* subdirectory, which will be created if it does not already exist.

The −**rem** option allows one to remove PNG chunks. This is quite handy, and is often a great way to trim a few dozen bytes from files (which can make a big difference in the case of small web graphics), but it does require knowledge of PNG's chunk names. The following example removes any timestamp chunks and both compressed and uncompressed text chunks from *foo.png* and places the result in the *crushed* subdirectory:

```
pngcrush -d crushed -rem tIME -rem zTXt -rem tEXt -rem iTXt foo.png
```

Note that this approach is somewhat akin to doing surgery with a hatchet: one has no control over specific instances of the listed chunks in the case of those (like zTXt, tEXt, and iTXt) that may appear more than once. In particular, the tEXt or iTXt chunk is where copyright info usually appears, and that is usually not something one wants to remove.*

One last option is worth a quick look. pngcrush's −g option allows one to set the gamma value of the image, which in turn provides for cross-platform consistency of the overall brightness of the image. Chapter 10 covers gamma and color correction in more detail, but the effect will be familiar to any site that uses both Macintoshes and PCs: images that look good on Macs tend to look too dark on PCs, and images that look good on PCs tend to look too bright and washed out on Macs.

---

* Of course, if a copyright is also embedded in the image data itself, the text version may be superfluous.

The solution is to include information about the system on which the image was created, and PNG's gAMA chunk is the simplest and most effective means of doing so. Unfortunately, not all image editors support gamma in PNG, and as you saw in the previous chapter, some of those that do support it store the wrong value. A site that has just received a batch of PNG images from its Mac-based design department might do something like the following:

```
pngcrush -d crushed -replace_gamma 0.65909 mac.png mac2.png mac3.png
```

For images from a PC-based design group, the corresponding command is:

```
pngcrush -d crushed -replace_gamma 0.45455 pc.png pc2.png pc3.png
```

In addition to optimizing the sizes of the images, these examples strip any existing gamma information out of the files, on the assumption that the values are known to be wrong and replace it with values that are appropriate for stock Macs (with a factory-default "system gamma" value of 1.8) or stock PCs. If it is known that the images that have gamma information are correct, use the -g option instead; it will add a gAMA chunk only to those images that do not already have one.

I should note that pngcrush is still a relatively new utility, and it does have a number of rough edges yet. For example, if an output file already exists, it will be overwritten without warning. There is also no recursion, no support for wildcards other than what the operating system provides (i.e., only under Unix), and no way to set a default extension or directory for crushed files (say, via an environment variable). The program's extended options also assume a fairly advanced knowledge of PNG files—for example, the official names of PNG chunks, in the case of the -rem option, or the numerical color types used internally by PNG, or the precise palette index of the color to be made transparent, in the case of the -trns option.* Nor is there yet support for counting colors in images and automatically converting from, say, RGB to palette format, although this is planned for a future version. But these are relatively minor user interface issues that will undoubtedly improve as the application matures. As regards its primary purpose of squeezing PNG images as tightly as possible, pngcrush is quite capable, and is likely to become an indispensable addition to the toolchest of any image-wrangler.

pnmtopng

Possibly the most complete conversion program in existence, at least with respect to support for PNG features, is *pnmtopng*. In conjunction with its inverse,

---

* Newer versions of pngcrush will print the palette, including indices, when given both the -n ("no crush") and -verbose options.

pngtopnm, and the rest of the NetPBM suite,* it is capable of handling basic conversions to and from virtually any image format. But pnmtopng really shines as a tool for adding and modifying PNG chunk information, including such things as text annotations, palette optimization, and support for adding or removing alpha (transparency) channels.

Currently, the latest version of pnmtopng is 2.37.2, released in March 1999; it can be found on the Source Code and Libraries web page of the PNG home site, *http://www.cdrom.com/pub/png/pngcode.html,* along with pointers to the libraries on which it depends.

Written and maintained by Alexander Lehmann and Willem van Schaik with contributions and fixes from others, pnmtopng is primarily a Unix-based tool, which unfortunately limits its usefulness to a minority of computer users. But other parts of the NetPBM suite have been ported to OS/2 and Windows, and it is likely that a future release of both pnmtopng and NetPBM will be more portable and may even include ready-to-go executables.

To begin explaining some of pnmtopng's features, it is first necessary to describe a little about the PBM format itself. If one wishes to be able to convert any of 100 possible image formats into any other, there are two options: write 10,000 individual converters to go directly from format A to format B for all possible pairs of A and B; or write only 200 converters, 100 to go from each of the image formats into some intermediate representation and another 100 to convert back from that intermediate format into the 100 target formats. Once the intermediate format exists, one need not stop at conversion programs; generic utilities to manipulate images suddenly become possible—for example, quantization, smoothing, cropping, contrast enhancement, and so on.

PBMplus/NetPBM is that intermediate format. It was originally designed by Jef Poskanzer and released as the PBMplus suite, with later "interim" packages released as NetPBM by Bill Davidsen. Since there has never been another PBMplus release, I will henceforth refer to the format as NetPBM, the name by which it is now most commonly known. The format is quite simple: three lines of text header—which may additionally include one or more comment lines—followed by the uncompressed image data. The image data may be stored as either text or binary values; the latter is more efficient and far more commonly used, but the existence of the text format means that one can actually create images or color palettes in an ordinary text editor. There are also three basic NetPBM image

---

* NetPBM originated as the PBMplus package, last released in December 1991. Subsequent third-party contributions from the Internet were gathered together and released as NetPBM in 1993 and early 1994, containing some 200 utilities for converting and manipulating images. The package has lain dormant since then, aside from the occasional appearance of utilities to support new image formats like PNG, but further news on this front is expected in 1999.

flavors: bilevel (or black and white), which is referred to as a *portable bitmap* or PBM file; grayscale, called a *portable graymap* or PGM; and truecolor (RGB), referred to as a *portable pixmap* or PPM file. Programs that can deal with more than one flavor usually have "PNM" in their names; this stands for *portable anymap*. There is currently no "real" PNM format; it is a virtual format and a convenient catchall name.

One notable feature missing from the NetPBM format is provision for alpha channels; this is a known limitation* with implications for converting between formats that support transparency, such as PNG, GIF, and TIFF. pnmtopng gets around this to some extent by the simple expedient of storing transparency information in a separate grayscale file. Before we get into that, let's look at some simpler cases.

pnmtopng is a command-line program, and, thanks to its Unix heritage, it is designed to operate as part of a multicommand pipeline. Unix pipes are a slick method of connecting the output of one program into the input of another; in principle there is no limit to how long such a chain can be, although in practice the amount of system resources that are available may constrain things. Here is a simple example that converts a GIF image into PNG:

```
giftopnm foo.gif | pnmtopng > foo.png
```

The file *foo.gif* is read by *giftopnm* (part of the NetPBM suite) and converted to NetPBM format, then piped into the input of pnmtopng, which converts the image to PNG format. Since there are no more programs to be run, pnmtopng's output is redirected into a file—in this case, *foo.png*.

Observant readers will recall that GIF images are always palette-based, yet I didn't say anything about palettes in describing the NetPBM format. In fact, NetPBM has no concept of palettes; giftopnm usually converts GIF images into PPM format (the RGB flavor). Fortunately, pnmtopng is smart enough to count the colors in an image and automatically write a palette-based PNG image if there are 256 or fewer colors. It will likewise detect if a color image is actually composed only of gray values; in that case, it will write either a grayscale PNG or a palette-based one, depending on which can be written with the fewest bits. This automatic checking comes at a cost, however: because it requires inspection of every pixel, it can be quite slow for large images. pnmtopng therefore includes a **-force** option to skip the checking. With this option, the previous example would result in a 24-bit truecolor PNG:

```
giftopnm foo.gif | pnmtopng -force > foo24.png
```

---

* Alpha support is a major reason behind the expected NetPBM revisions in 1999.

Here are examples for two other popular image formats, TIFF and JPEG:

```
tifftopnm foo.tiff | pnmtopng > foo-was-tiff.png
djpeg foo.jpg | pnmtopng > foo-was-jpeg.png
```

But these are all trivial conversions. Suppose I would like to convert an existing NetPBM image into an interlaced PNG, including gamma information, a timestamp, and some text—say, the author's name, the title of the image, its copyright, and perhaps the date on which the original photograph was taken. The first thing we need to do is create a small text file containing the text information. pnmtopng treats the first word on any line that does not begin with a blank (either a space or a tab character) as the keyword, with the actual text following. The text may stretch over several lines, and keywords with spaces in them must be quoted. Thus the following text file, containing four keywords and their corresponding values, would suffice:

```
Title           The Incredible and Rarely Seen Foo
Author          Greg Roelofs
Copyright       This image is hereby placed in the
                public domain by its author.
"Creation Time" 4 July 1976
     is the date on which this particular Foo was photographed.
```

Note that leading blanks (or "white space"), including any between the keywords and subsequent text, will not be included in the PNG text chunks. But any newlines (or "carriage returns," loosely speaking) will be included exactly as typed; thus, there will be one in the Copyright text chunk, right before the word "public," and another in the Creation Time text chunk, immediately after "1976." In addition, there is currently a bug in pnmtopng: when all of the text corresponding to a keyword appears on a line following the keyword—that is, the keyword is immediately followed by a carriage return—the program will sometimes crash. The problem will almost certainly be fixed by the time this book reaches print, but in the meantime, it can be avoided by adding a space after the keyword.

So assuming the text file were named *comments.txt* (and contains no keywords followed immediately by newlines), the following command would create the PNG image with the specified text and other information:

```
pnmtopng -interlace -gamma 0.65909 -text comments.txt \
   -time 1998-10-25 21:00:00 foo.ppm > foo.png
```

The first option is self-explanatory: the PNG image will be interlaced. For the -gamma option, we've used a value that corresponds to a typical Macintosh; we're imagining that the original image was scanned and tweaked on a Mac before being converted to PPM format (*foo.ppm*) on some other system. The -time option requires a little more explanation. First, note that it is distinct from the "Creation Time" text chunk we included; the -time option will write the special PNG tIME chunk, which represents the time the image was last modified. But the last modification time is clearly the time the image was converted into PNG format, so pnmtopng really should not require the user to specify the time information explicitly. This is particularly true, given that PNG's time chunk is supposed to be in Coordinated Universal Time, and most users are unlikely to know how to convert to that.* With luck, this oversight will also be corrected in the next release of the program.

Transparency is one of PNG's major strengths, so let's take a look at some of pnmtopng's options there. Suppose that we wish to vignette our treasured foo image—that is, we would like to apply an oval mask to it that gradually fades to complete transparency, in effect transforming our image from rectangular to rounded. This is easily accomplished by creating the oval mask as a grayscale (PGM) image, where white represents the regions that will be completely opaque (i.e., the main subject matter of the image) and black the outer, transparent regions. Then give the following command:

```
pnmtopng -alpha ovalmask.pgm foo.ppm > foo.png
```

This will ordinarily create a 32-bit RGBA image—in other words, truecolor with a full alpha channel. But if it happens that the combination of the original RGB image and the mask produces at most 256 RGBA combinations, pnmtopng is smart enough to detect that and write a palette-based image with transparency information instead. Moreover, it will automatically arrange the palette and transparency entries so that all of the completely opaque colors are at the end of the palette; the corresponding transparency entries may then be omitted, resulting in a smaller file.

In some cases, the transparency mask contains only fully opaque and fully transparent values, and it may happen (usually by design) that the parts of the underlying image that correspond to the transparent region are all one color, even though there may be thousands of colors in the opaque part. pnmtopng will again detect this, creating a palette-based image with just one transparency entry if possible; if there are too many colors, it will instead write a full grayscale or RGB image with a single color marked transparent. This results in a PNG file that's much more compact than one with a full alpha channel.

Transparent images intended for display only on web browsers will always have some sort of background specified as part of the web page, but for images that may be rendered by a standalone viewer, it is often desirable to include an explicit background color in the image. The **-background** option provides that capability; it accepts a color argument in almost any format allowed by MIT's X Window

---

* The example here corresponds to 1:00 p.m. in the US/Pacific time zone. But had the conversion taken place at 1:00 p.m. on the previous day, it would have been specified as 20:00:00 in Universal Time, thanks to the fact that daylight saving time had not yet ended.

System, including English text (assuming the X color database file can be found). Thus, the following three commands are equivalent (the `-alpha ovalmask.pgm` option has been omitted for brevity):

```
pnmtopng -background rgbi:1.0/0.855/0.726 foo.ppm > foo.png
pnmtopng -background "peach puff"         foo.ppm > foo.png
pnmtopng -background "#ffdab9"            foo.ppm > foo.png
```

For most users, the second form is probably the most easily understood but the least precise. Making it precise requires the finely honed ability to find the X color-database file, which can be difficult when it exists and impossible when it doesn't[*] (it is also explicitly platform-dependent; that is, the same color name is allowed to have different RGB values on different machines). Therefore, the first form is likely to be the most useful. It specifies the RGB values of the background color as decimal fractions between 0.0 and 1.0. The values are separated by forward slashes (/) and prefixed by `rgbi:`. The third form is the old-style hexadecimal format that is favored by programmers but almost no one else. (It also happens to be the format used in the demo programs I present in Chapters 13 and 14 on reading PNG images. Oh, the embarrassment.) The hex value need not be placed in quotation marks on a command line, but within a shell script it should be quoted, or the hash character (#) will be treated as the beginning of a comment.

pnmtopng also potentially supports the creation of 16-bit-per-sample images (that is, 16-bit grayscale, 32-bit gray+alpha, 48-bit RGB or 64-bit RGBA), but only with text (ASCII) NetPBM files, and only if the underlying NetPBM library supports 16-bit images, which is not the default behavior. The requirement to use ASCII format for the 16-bit NetPBM image files is a current limitation of the NetPBM suite. As with transparency and palettes, pnmtopng detects if 16-bit samples are really just scaled 8-bit samples; if so, it will automatically convert the image back to 8-bit samples unless the `-force` option is given. It can also be instructed to convert true 16-bit samples to 8-bit with the `-downsample` option.

Other supported features include chromaticity information, histograms, compressed text, explicit single-color transparency, physical pixel dimensions, and special compression options. Quantization of truecolor images to 256 or fewer colors is not supported by pnmtopng itself, but it is a straightforward part of the standard NetPBM package. For example, to quantize a 24-bit TIFF image to the 256 best colors, dither the result, and save it as a palette-based PNG, one can use:

```
tifftopnm foo.tiff | ppmquant -fs 256 | pnmtopng > foo.png
```

---

[*] For the record, it lives in */usr/openwin/lib/X11/rgb.txt* on Sun systems, */usr/X11R6/lib/X11/rgb.txt* on most Linux and FreeBSD systems, and */usr/lib/X11/rgb.txt* on "generic" Unix/X11 systems.

The `-fs` option to ppmquant instructs it to use Floyd-Steinberg dithering, which generally looks very nice but does require a fair amount of computation. The `256` parameter indicates the number of colors to be used in the final version; any value may be used (web-savvy designers might wish to use a smaller number of colors), but only values of 256 or less will result in a palette-based PNG image. What about images with an alpha channel? Unfortunately, those who wish to quantize 32-bit RGBA images down to a 256-entry "RGBA palette" are stuck for now. The ppmquant algorithm can easily be modified to support RGBA values in addition to ordinary RGB, but until NetPBM itself is updated, there is no way to pipe transparency information from one NetPBM utility into another.

For users of very large images, one other point is worth mentioning: pnmtopng currently reads the entire image into memory buffers before doing anything with it, which means that a 4000 × 4000 RGBA image would require 64 megabytes of real and/or virtual memory just for the uncompressed image itself. But all is not lost; in Chapter 15, *Writing PNG Images*, I present a very simple-minded NetPBM-to-PNG converter, and one of its design goals was the ability to convert images on the fly, requiring only a very small memory footprint. (Of course, this only works if the PNG image is not interlaced.) The demo program also has a `-time` option that automatically records the current time in the proper format, as well as one or two other potentially handy features.

gif2png

For simple batch conversion of GIF images into PNGs, pnmtopng is not only overkill but also somewhat tricky to automate. Such a task is more readily handled by *gif2png*, a special-purpose conversion program written by Alexander Lehmann. Besides the raw image pixels, there are three GIF features that translate directly into PNG features: transparency, text (comments), and interlacing. gif2png handles the first two automatically; only interlacing is not detected and automatically applied to the output image, although the program does include a `-i` option to force interlacing.

The simplest usage of gif2png is to give it the name of a GIF image:

```
gif2png foo.gif
```

The program will convert the image to a noninterlaced PNG, preserving any transparency, comments, and "graphic control" or "application extension" information. It will also add its own text chunk with the Software keyword, and it will automatically change the file extension from *.gif* to *.png*. There is one important caveat, however: the current version, gif2png 0.6, does not check for an existing file of the same name and will overwrite any such file without warning.

Because gif2png renames the files it converts without user input, it can be used to convert a whole directory of GIF files in a single command. Under Unix, where the shell expands wildcard filenames ("globbing"), this is as simple as:

```
gif2png *.gif
```

On other operating systems, the filenames must be specified explicitly:

```
gif2png a.gif b.gif c.gif d.gif e.gif foo.gif foo2.gif
```

To prevent gif2png from adding a Software text chunk to the output image(s), use the -s option:

```
gif2png -s foo.gif
```

To do the same conversion but to an interlaced PNG, include the -i option:

```
gif2png -s -i foo.gif
gif2png -si foo.gif
```

gif2png does have a few drawbacks, as might be expected given its pre-1.0 version number. In addition to the problem of overwriting existing files, gif2png's conversion of GIF transparency information is less than ideal; although it gets the job done, the program copies over the GIF palette without modification, which can result in useless transparency entries in the PNG file. For example, a 256-color GIF image whose last palette entry is the transparent one would result in a 256-entry transparency chunk in the PNG file, where one entry would suffice; in other words, it can waste up to 255 bytes in the output file. gif2png is also rather verbose and provides no option to keep it quiet; in fact, its progress meter (a simple percentage value, updated repeatedly) is supposed to be enabled only when the -p option is given, but it actually is on by default and can only be turned *off* with -p.

Despite all this, the program is quite stable and useful. It even converts GIF comments from IBM codepage 437 to PNG's Latin-1 format, and it will convert animated GIFs into multiple single-image PNGs. A planned option that would have automatically deleted the GIF input images after conversion was never implemented, nor was the capability of converting GIF Plain Text Extensions into PNG gIFt chunks. But these are minor issues; in fact, the gIFt chunk was officially declared Bad (that is, deprecated) in October 1998, so its lack of support in gif2png turned out to be prescient. Indeed, the only major problem with the program is the fact that it reads GIFs in the first place. It is therefore (according to Unisys) subject to the LZW patent and its associated licensing issues. Unisys initially claimed that freeware GIF programs would be granted a free LZW license, but that later changed, which was directly responsible for the cessation of further development on gif2png.

Pointers to the gif2png source code and to ready-to-go binaries for DOS, OS/2, Linux, Amiga, and Macintosh can be found on the Source Code and Libraries page of the PNG home site at *http://www.cdrom.com/pub/png/pngcode.html*. A graphical port written by Nigel Stewart for 32-bit Windows, called The Exorcist, supports drag and drop and is available from its own home page: *http://www.eisa.net. au/~nigels/Exorcist/Exorcist.html*. Version 1.1 is the latest release.

Tiff2png

The corresponding special-purpose conversion program for TIFF images was written by Willem van Schaik and is called, predictably, *Tiff2png*. By a strange coincidence, its latest version is also 0.6, but the program is perhaps slightly less robust than gif2png. This is primarily due to the fact that the TIFF format is hugely complex, supporting multiple forms of text annotations, both gamma and color correction, several flavors of transparency, many different sample depths, and numerous other options that might conceivably be carried over into a PNG image with a little effort (or, more likely, a lot of it).

Tiff2png's main features as a conversion program are its support for TIFF sample depths up to 16 bits and its support for transparency and alpha channels. Unlike gif2png, Tiff2png requires an explicit output filename and is therefore somewhat less convenient for batch conversions:

```
tiff2png foo.tiff foo.png
```

It is also completely quiet by default, although it supports a −v option to turn on its verbose mode:

```
tiff2png -v foo.tiff foo.png

Tiff2png: foo.tiff
TIFF Directory at offset 0x10008
  Image Width: 128 Image Length: 128
  Resolution: 72, 72 pixels/inch
  Bits/Sample: 8
  Compression Scheme: None
  Photometric Interpretation: RGB color
  Extra Samples: 1<assoc-alpha>
  Samples/Pixel: 4
  Rows/Strip: 16
  Planar Configuration: single image plane
Tiff2png: 128x128x32 image
Tiff2png: 8 bits/sample, 4 samples/pixel
Tiff2png: maxval=255
Tiff2png: color-type = truecolor + alpha
Tiff2png: bit-depth = 8
```

Unfortunately, Tiff2png does not distinguish between associated (premultiplied) alpha and unassociated alpha. The latter is the only form supported by PNG, but Tiff2png will happily store an associated alpha channel without conversion, as in the previous example.

The program also appears not to handle Intel-format ("little-endian": see the section entitled "Implementation" in Chapter 7) TIFF images with 16-bit samples correctly, instead storing the samples as is—which effectively means they are inverted, given that PNG samples must be stored in "big-endian" format. But lacking any such sample images, I was unable to verify this.

At any rate, Tiff2png is capable of converting at least some TIFF images with alpha transparency correctly, which gives it an advantage over the current NetPBM suite and pnmtopng. Although TIFF is subject to the same LZW licensing issues GIF is, it supports several other compression methods (including no compression) and is therefore less of a problem for program authors. In Tiff2png's case, all TIFF manipulations are handled via Sam Leffler's free **libtiff** library, which means Tiff2png itself can be updated at will without worrying about the sorts of legal issues that plagued gif2png. Source code for Tiff2png can be found on the *Source Code and Libraries* page of the PNG home site, *http://www.cdrom.com/pub/png/ pngcode.html*, but there are presently no prebuilt executables.

pngcheck

Finally, we should take a look at an extremely useful PNG utility that is not usually considered a conversion tool: *pngcheck*. pngcheck prints the chunks in a PNG file, along with their contents, in many cases; one can loosely think of it as a utility that "converts PNG images to text," although it does so in such a way that they could never be converted back to PNG format. (In particular, it provides no way to print the actual pixel data, although it can print just about everything else.)

Originally written by Alexander Lehmann as a simple tool to check PNG images for corruption, such as might occur if the file were transferred in text mode, pngcheck was subsequently extended by Andreas Dilger, Greg Roelofs, and others, evolving into a nearly complete PNG syntax checker and content dumper. The latest versions (1.99-grr1 is current as of this writing) even include partial support for MNG files, the multi-image PNG extension described in Chapter 12 (*Multiple-Image Network Graphics*). pngcheck is most often used to understand why a particular image is larger than expected—perhaps a 16-color image was saved in 24-bit RGB format instead of palette format, or a truecolor image was saved with minimal compression and no filtering. But it can also be used simply to test PNG files and print their dimensions, image types, and approximate compression ratios.*

The most basic use of pngcheck involves giving it one or more filenames and no options, like so:

```
pngcheck foo.png foo2.png foo3.png
```

This results in output similar to the following, except that here the lines have been wrapped to fit the page:

```
No errors detected in
    foo.png (578x802, 24-bit RGB, interlaced, 54.7%).
No errors detected in
    foo2.png (32x32, 4-bit colormap, interlaced, 36.1%).
No errors detected in
    foo3.png (32x32, 64-bit RGB+alpha, non-interlaced, 58.1%).
```

An image that has been corrupted in some way might cause an error message such as the following:

```
foo4.png:  File is CORRUPTED by text conversion.
foo4.png:  Chunk name 00 0d 49 48 doesn't conform to naming rules.
```

But pngcheck is most useful for seeing what's inside a PNG image. The −v option, for *verbose* mode, prints the name of each chunk within the file, along with some basic information wherever appropriate. Because it can be a tad lengthy, it is often a good idea to pipe the program's verbose output through a paging filter such as *more*. The following example works on both Unix-based systems and DOS, OS/2, and Windows command lines:

```
pngcheck -v imgcomp.png | more

File: imgcomp.png (34163 bytes)
   chunk IHDR at offset 0x0000c, length 13
     640 x 480 image, 32-bit RGB+alpha, non-interlaced
   chunk gAMA at offset 0x00025, length 4: 0.45455
   chunk IDAT at offset 0x00035, length 8192
     zlib:  deflated, 32K window, default compression
   chunk IDAT at offset 0x02041, length 8192
   chunk IDAT at offset 0x0404d, length 8192
   chunk IDAT at offset 0x06059, length 8192
   chunk IDAT at offset 0x08065, length 1274
   chunk IEND at offset 0x0856b, length 0
No errors detected in imgcomp.png (97.2% compression).
```

---

* The compression ratio is computed by dividing the total file size by the nominal size of the uncompressed IDAT data, which means the presence of ancillary information or even a required palette can produce negative compression ratios—i.e., "expansion"—in small images. In other words, don't take it too seriously.

In this example, we see a fairly basic PNG file, a truecolor image with an alpha channel, composed of only four chunk types: the required IHDR, IDAT, and IEND chunks (described in Chapter 8), plus the optional but highly recommended gamma-correction chunk, gAMA (Chapter 10). Because the image primarily consists of solid-colored regions and simple gradients, it compressed unusually well; this probably indicates that dynamic filtering was used, but there is no way to be certain, given the preceding information.

However, pngcheck can optionally use the zlib compression library in order to look *inside* the compressed image data. In this case, it supports a −vv option ("very verbose") that prints out all of the preceding information plus filtering information. The filter output can be extremely long; for just the first IDAT chunk in the preceding example, it looks like this:

```
chunk IDAT at offset 0x00035, length 8192
  zlib:  deflated, 32K window, default compression
  zlib line filters (0 none, 1 sub, 2 up, 3 avg, 4 paeth):
   0 0 0 0 0 0 0 0 0 0 0 0 0 0 0 0 0 0 0 0 0 0 0 0
   0 0 0 0 0 0 0 0 0 0 0 0 0 0 0 0 0 0 0 0 0 0 0 0
   0 0 0 0 0 0 0 0 0 0 0 0 0 0 0 0 0 0 0 0 0 0 0 0
   0 0 0 0 0 0 1 1 1 1 1 1 1 1 1 1 1 1 1 1 1 1 1 1
   1 1 1 1 1 1 1 1 1 1 1 1 1 1 1 1 1 1 1 1 1 1 1 1
   1 2 2 1 2 1 2 2 2 2 2 2 2 2 2 2 2 2 2 2 2 2 2 2
   2 2 2 2 2 4 4 4 4 4 4 4 4 4 4 4 4 1 4 1 4 1 4 2 4
   2 2 2 2 2 2 2 2 2 2 2 2 2 2 2 2 2 2 2 4 4 4 2
  (200 out of 480)
```

The details are too complex to cover right now, but filtering and compression are discussed in Chapter 9. All that matters here is that different filters have been used for different rows in the image, indicating that some sort of dynamic filtering was applied (which is generally good). Unfiltered images, on the other hand, will have all zeros for the filter numbers, and statically filtered images will use only a single filter type. In most cases, that means the image is not compressed as well as it could be. One major exception, however, is palette-based images; they rarely respond well to filtering, and most programs don't try.

pngcheck also supports more specific types of output. Its −p option, for example, is another rather verbose case; it prints the contents of the palette and optional transparency chunks for colormapped images.* This can be useful in conjunction with a program such as pngcrush, for example, when one wishes to specify a particular color as transparent, but more commonly it is used to check whether the transparency chunk is full of needless opaque values. Consider the following example:

---

* It will also print the contents of the optional histogram and suggested-palette chunks; see Chapter 11, *PNG Options and Extensions*, for details.

```
pngcheck -p foo5.png

File: foo5.png (146 bytes)
  PLTE chunk: 4 palette entries
    0:  (  0,255,  0) = (0x00,0xff,0x00)
    1:  (255,  0,  0) = (0xff,0x00,0x00)
    2:  (255,255,  0) = (0xff,0xff,0x00)
    3:  (  0,  0,255) = (0x00,0x00,0xff)
  tRNS chunk: 3 transparency entries
    0:  255 = 0xff
    1:  255 = 0xff
    2:    0 = 0x00
No errors detected in foo5.png (32x32, 2-bit colormap, non-interlaced,
43.0%).
```

Here we have a four-color image: bright green, red, yellow, and blue. The colors of the palette are listed as RGB triplets in both decimal and hexadecimal (base 16) for convenience. The palette itself is unremarkable; what is more interesting is the transparency chunk, tRNS. It includes three entries, but the first two have the value 255, which indicates that the corresponding palette entries should be treated as completely opaque. But all palette entries are considered opaque unless explicitly given a non-opaque transparency value—in other words, any transparency entries with the value 255 are redundant and represent wasted space. In this case, the only non-opaque entry corresponds to the third color, yellow; a smart PNG-writing program would have reordered the palette so that yellow was the first entry, thus shaving two bytes off the file. It is not uncommon to be able to save 100 or more bytes in this manner, which can represent 10% to 20% of the file size for small web graphics.* In rare cases, it may be worthwhile to waste a few transparency entries so that the most common pixels in the image are all at the beginning of the palette (i.e., so they all have index values near zero); with filtering enabled, the compression engine may be able to make up the difference and then some. But as of early 1999, filtering has yet to be demonstrated effective on essentially any kind of palette-based image, so the possibility of recovering wasted transparency entries with improved compression is a rather tenuous one.

The other type of verbose pngcheck output is more useful to ordinary users, not just content developers trying to optimize things. The −t option prints not only text chunks' keywords but also their contents:

```
pngcheck -t ct1n0g04.png

File: ct1n0g04.png (796 bytes)
Title:PngSuite
Author:Willem A.J. van Schaik
(gwillem@ntuvax.ntu.ac.sg)
```

---

* One of the images used on the VRML98 web site had 211 transparency entries, of which 210 were unnecessary.

```
Copyright:Copyright Willem van Schaik, Singapore 1995
Description:A compilation of a set of images created to test the
various color-types of the PNG format. Included are
black&white, color, paletted, with alpha channel, with
transparency formats. All bit-depths allowed according
to the spec are present.
Software:Created on a NeXTstation color using "pnmtopng".
Disclaimer:Freeware.
No errors detected in
    ct1n0g04.png (32x32, 4-bit grayscale, non-interlaced, -55.5%).
```

This example, using one of Willem van Schaik's test images from the PNG Suite, contains six text chunks with keywords Title, Author, Copyright, Description, Software, and Disclaimer. The content of each chunk immediately follows the keyword and colon; this is not the most readable approach, but the information is available and usually understandable with only a little squinting. One deficiency of the current version is that it does not display the contents of compressed text chunks (zTXt), even when using the zlib compression library. This is promised to be fixed in a future version, however.

The latest version of pngcheck can be found via the Source Code and Libraries web page of the PNG home site, *http://www.cdrom.com/pub/png/pngcode.html*.

Other Conversion Programs

The converters we've discussed so far barely scratch the surface of what is available. If one includes image editors and viewers that can convert images in addition to dedicated conversion tools, there are well over one hundred applications capable of converting to and from the PNG format. Many of these were listed in the previous two chapters and are well worth considering, particularly for users who may be uncomfortable dealing with command-line programs.

Here is a list of some of the other dedicated (or nearly dedicated) image converters that support PNG. The most recent version as of January 1999 is given wherever possible.

ColourEdit
> Version of April 3, 1997, Julian Highfield. Available as an OpenDoc part for Mac 68k/PPC (mostly tested with OpenDoc 1.1 and Mac OS System 7.1.2); read/write support for PNGs.
>
> *http://www.stile.lboro.ac.uk/~cojch/ColourEdit/*

Creator

Version 3.22, John Kortink. Available for Acorn RISC OS; read/write support for PNGs; no alpha or gamma support.

http://web.inter.nl.net/users/J.Kortink/indexsw.htm

dicom2

Version 1.8, Sébastien Barré. Available for Windows 9x/NT, Linux x86, SunOS/Solaris SPARC; write-only support for PNGs; supports conversion of 12-bit medical formats to 16-bit grayscale PNGs.

http://www.hds.utc.fr/~barre/medical/dicom2/

Ghostscript

Version 5.50, Aladdin Enterprises. Available for Unix, VMS, OS/2, Windows 9x/NT, and Mac 68k/PPC; older versions available for Windows 3.x, DOS, Amiga, Atari, and possibly Acorn RISC OS; write-only support for PNGs.

http://www.cs.wisc.edu/~ghost/

gj2png

Version of February 13, 1997, Neil Aggarwal. Available for any platform supporting Java 1.1 or later; write-only support for PNGs.

http://www.anet-dfw.com/~neil/gjFrame.html

Icons Control 95

Version 7.02, Chris Doan. Available for Windows 9x/NT; read-only support for PNGs (converts various image formats to Windows *.ico* format).

http://members.aol.com/doanc/icnctrl.html

Image Arithmetic

Version 2.2a, Richard van Paasen. Available for Windows 9x/NT; read/write support for PNGs.

http://huizen.dds.nl/~buddha/imgart.html

LatinByrd

Version III v6, Stefan Schneider Software. Available for NeXTStep/OpenStep on 68k/x86/HP-PA/SPARC; write-only support for PNGs; can quantize 32-bit RGBA TIFF images to 8-bit RGBA-palette PNGs.

http://members.ping.at/stefan/LatinByrdProductInfo.html

PicCon

Version 2.50, Morten Eriksen. Available for Amiga; read-only; requires a PNG datatype such as those from Cloanto or Andreas Kleinert.

http://www.aminet.org/pub/aminet/gfx/conv/PicCon250.lha
http://www.aminet.org/pub/aminet/util/dtype/PNG_dt.lha
http://www.aminet.org/pub/aminet/util/dtype/akPNG-dt.lha
http://home.t-online.de/home/Andreas_Kleinert/support.htm

PNG-Box

Version 3.25, Andreas Kleinert. Available for Amiga 68k/PPC; write-only support for PNGs; supports interlacing and single-color transparency. PNG-Box is a graphical "any to PNG" conversion utility that uses Andreas's own Super-View Library for its image support instead of datatypes.

http://www.amigaworld.com/support/png-box/
http://home.t-online.de/home/Andreas_Kleinert/support.htm
http://www.aminet.org/pub/aminet/gfx/conv/PNG-Box.lha

!Png2Spr

Version 1.14, Tom Tanner. Available for Acorn RISC OS; read-only support for PNGs (converts to Acorn sprite format).

http://www.argonet.co.uk/users/ttehtann/

ptot

Version of March 10, 1995, Lee Daniel Crocker. Available as portable source code (does *not* require libpng or zlib); read-only support for PNGs (converts to TIFF); full gamma support (writes TIFF TransferFunction tag); full alpha support for true alpha channels (no palette-alpha or "cheap transparency" support).

ftp://swrinde.nde.swri.edu/pub/png/applications/ptot.tar.gz

SmartSaver

Version 3.0, Ulead Systems. Available for 32-bit Windows; read/write support for PNGs; full alpha support, including at least single-color palette transparency (not clear whether full RGBA-palette translucency is supported); reportedly cannot write 1-bit (bilevel) images.

http://www.webutilities.com/ssaver/noslip.htm

Spr2Png

Version 0.04b, Darren Salt. Available for Acorn RISC OS; write-only support for PNGs; full alpha support via secondary sprite that is used as a transparency mask or alpha channel; supports interlacing and background color. An older version was reported to produce streaks in conversions of newer (post-RPC) sprites, but this appears to be fixed in the current release.

http://www.youmustbejoking.demon.co.uk/progs.html#spr2png

ThumbNailer

Version 5.2, Smaller Animals Software. Available for 32-bit Windows; read/write support for PNGs; supports transparency, background color, and text; claims full gamma support.

http://www.smalleranimals.com/thumb.htm

Ultraconv

Version 3.0p1, Felix Schwarz. Available for Amiga 68k/PPC; read/write support for PNGs (natively since version 1.6, or via a datatype for earlier versions); no alpha or gamma support.

http://home.pages.de/~uconv/

New conversion utilities and updated information on the ones listed here can be found at the *Image-Conversion Applications with PNG Support* web page at the PNG home site, *http://www.cdrom.com/pub/png/pngapcv.html.* This URL is expected to be stable for years, but of course there are no guarantees on the World Wide Web! Use a search engine to look for the title string or for one of the more oddly named utilities listed if the link should ever break.

6

Applications: VRML Browsers and Other 3D Apps

VRML, the Virtual Reality Modeling Language, is a file format and a language for defining three-dimensional virtual objects, their appearances and their behaviors. As of early 1999, it has seen two major versions, and the design of a third is currently underway. Version 1.0 included little more than static geometry and never saw wide use. Version 2.0, released in August 1996 and approved as an ISO/IEC international standard in December 1997, added animation, scripting, and a much more rigorous specification of all aspects of the format. It also mandated PNG as one of two image formats required for minimal conformance. (JPEG was the other.) No doubt due to PNG's rampant popularity,* VRML 2.0—or VRML97, as the ISO standard is known—achieved dramatically greater recognition and acceptance than VRML 1.0, with shipments of VRML97 browsers reaching levels of between 25 million and 75 million units by the autumn of 1998.

How is PNG actually used in a 3D, text-based file format? A complete answer would require considerable discussion of 3D rendering engines, CPU and memory performance, Moore's Law, and so forth. But in a nutshell, VRML is designed for interactive 3D—particularly Web-based, immersive, interactive 3D. A truly realistic animated object, such as the dinosaurs in the movie "Jurassic Park" or the flying cow in "Twister," would require far more computational power to render in "real time" at reasonable frame rates (say, more than 15 frames per second) than even today's fastest processors can manage. And that's just one object; imagine every rock, tree, bug, cloud, and blade of grass rendered at the same level of realism, responding to dynamic effects like wind, sunlight, and other moving objects.

---

* Well, in part, anyway . . .

Doing all of that is likely to remain out of reach of typical personal computers for a decade or more.

As a result, VRML is all about trickery, and one of the most efficient forms of 3D trickery is known as *texture-mapping*. Instead of creating a highly detailed 3D object out of many tiny polygons, it is often possible to create a very realistic approximation of it out of just a few polygons, with an appropriate image (or *texture*) drawn over them. Anyone who has studied a 3D game like Quake or Descent is probably familiar with the concept; the buildings and even the characters are actually quite crude, but with stone or metal textures and lighting effects applied, the world suddenly becomes a realistically gloomy dungeon or sewer system or a bright and shiny high-tech laboratory.*

PNG's role in this is as a format for the textures. VRML references PNG images in much the same way that HTML pages do, via a URL that points at the PNG file. A VRML viewer then fetches the PNG image, applies it to the polygons of the relevant object according to the rules in the VRML specification, and displays the result within the 3D scene.

Because both raw VRML objects and PNG textures support not only colors but also transparency and partial transparency (loosely, "translucency"), a number of interesting effects are possible. On the other hand, the potential number of interactions and combinations is immense, so the VRML97 spec defines some basic rules regarding VRML materials and how textures modify them:

- A one-component texture—i.e., grayscale—absorbs and modulates the underlying polygon's color and transparency. For example, an opaque yellow triangle with a gray, gradient texture applied to it will turn into an opaque triangle with a yellow gradient. The orientation of the gradient depends on how the author specified the coordinates of the texture.

- A two-component texture (grayscale plus an alpha channel) absorbs the underlying polygon's color, but any transparency in the base polygon is replaced by the transparency of the texture.

- A three-component texture (RGB color) replaces the underlying polygon's color but inherits its transparency (if any); a blue texture applied to a red polygon with 50% transparency turn its into a 50% transparent blue polygon.

- A four-component texture (RGB plus an alpha channel, or RGBA) completely overrides the color and transparency of the underlying polygon.

What about palette-based images? If every color in the palette is pure gray (that is, if the values for red, green, and blue are equal for each entry), then the image is

---

* In the case of characters, animation and sound effects also aid the illusion tremendously.

treated as grayscale. If even one palette entry is not gray, the image is treated as RGB color. And if the image includes a transparency chunk (more on that in Chapter 8, *PNG Basics*), it is treated as though it has a full alpha channel.*

These rules are worth keeping in mind because, alas, full support for PNG in VRML browsers is Not Quite There Yet. Just as there are two main web browsers, prior to August 1998 there were just three main VRML browsers: Cosmo Player, WorldView, and blaxxun CC3D.† Although PNG support in each of them was better than that in either of the Big Two web browsers, VRML applications are necessarily subject to quite a few more variables: different rendering engines, a myriad of third-party hardware and even more versions of device drivers, various browser performance options, and, of course, the list presented earlier of ways in which a PNG texture can interact with the objects to which it is applied. And texture support is just one small part of a VRML browser! In other words, because so many things *can* go wrong, quite a few things *do* go wrong... at least in some situations.

Despite that somewhat bleak disclaimer, PNG support in older VRML browsers has improved with each new release, and several new browsers are under development as this is being written. Most of the major ones are listed in the following sections, with known problems indicated. Unless otherwise noted, all are plug-ins to web browsers, which they typically use not only to enable the downloading of files over the Web but also to provide support for Java, and JavaScript (the standardized variant of which is known ECMAscript).

Cosmo Player

Cosmo Player, at least the completely rewritten 2.x version, was designed with conformance and rendering accuracy as the primary goals and performance second. Currently, the latest release is version 2.1, only available for Windows 9x/NT. (An early beta is available for the PowerMac, but it is reported to be somewhat unstable; a more mature beta is available for Irix 6.5.) With Nice Transparency turned off, Cosmo's PNG support is exemplary—aside from the fact that all partial

---

* The transparency chunk rule also applies to true RGB or grayscale PNGs, in which such a chunk indicates that a single color or shade of gray is to be considered fully transparent.

† Platinum Technology bought Intervista (maker of WorldView) in June 1998 and most of Cosmo Software (maker of Cosmo Player) in August. In September, they publicly announced their intention to merge the two browsers within a relatively short period, so for a brief period the VRML world appeared to be heading toward an even greater similarity to the world of HTML. Alas, the best-laid plans sometimes go awry; in February 1999, Platinum restructured and, among other things, shed its entire 3D team. As of mid-March, it appeared that Platinum was well on it way to releasing the source code to Cosmo Player under a completely open license (with somewhat more restrictive licenses for other 3D tools, such as WorldView for Developers and Cosmo Worlds). But in yet another unexpected twist, Computer Associates announced in late March that it was acquiring Platinum. As of early April 1999, no one yet knew the fate of any of the WorldView/Cosmo suite.

transparency is achieved by dithering fully transparent and fully opaque pixels, an approach known as *screendoor transparency* or *stippled alpha*, which is great for performance but cannot be considered true alpha support. With Nice Transparency turned on, and regardless of whether the rendering engine is OpenGL software, OpenGL hardware, or Direct3D hardware, Cosmo 2.x displays an odd "popping" behavior with respect to opaque textures on translucent materials. That is, from some viewing angles, the textures will be translucent, as they are supposed to be; but from other angles, they will be completely opaque. In addition, gray textures with transparency sometimes also inherit the underlying material's transparency.

On the SGI/Irix platform, Cosmo Player 1.0.3 is the latest official release as of March 1999.* Like the PC version, it has a Nice Transparency mode that incorrectly allows two-component textures (grayscale with transparency) to absorb material transparency. In addition, if two polygons with partly transparent textures intersect, it can render parts of the polygons that should be opaque as transparent instead. This latter problem can be avoided by designing the VRML world without intersecting polygons (which are often a performance problem anyway).

Further information about the Windows and Macintosh versions of Cosmo Player is available from *http://www.cosmosoftware.com/products/player/brief.html*. The web page for the Irix version is at *http://www.sgi.com/software/cosmo/player.html*.

WorldView/MSVRML

WorldView is available not only as an Internet Explorer and Navigator plug-in from Intervista, but also as a slightly modified Internet Explorer component from Microsoft. The latter is known as Microsoft's MSVRML browser, and up through the June 1998 end-user release of Windows 98, it corresponded to WorldView 2.0. Subsequent versions of Win98, at least on some new PCs, and Internet Explorer 5.0 included a VRML browser corresponding to WorldView 2.1, which was Intervista's final release.† (Intervista never released version 2.1 as a Navigator plug-in version, however, for either Windows or PowerMac.)

Unlike Cosmo Software's approach, Intervista's design philosophy for WorldView appears to have emphasized performance, particularly hardware-assisted performance. This is not necessarily a bad thing—with Direct3D acceleration under Windows 95, WorldView was usually faster than Cosmo Player in my tests, sometimes much faster—but it does mean that some design decisions adversely affect PNG

---

* SGI retained rights to the Irix version of Cosmo Player and was to release at least one more version, corresponding to Cosmo Player 2.1 for Windows, early in 1999. Indeed, the first 2.1 beta for Irix was released at the end of February.

† WorldView 2.1 was preinstalled on new machines that shipped with Intel's i740 3D accelerator.

rendering. For example, WorldView apparently does not support texture sizes greater than 256 × 256 pixels; instead, it automatically scales down large images. It also supports screendoor transparency rather than true alpha blending (similar to Cosmo Player's behavior with Nice Transparency disabled), and it defaults to a palette-like, limited-color rendering mode, although this can be overridden by choosing Full Color graphics mode from the Options pop-up.

Beyond the intentional limitations in PNG support, WorldView suffers from some transparency bugs similar to Cosmo's. For example, grayscale PNGs with transparency also inherit the underlying material's transparency, just as in Cosmo Player 1.x for Irix. Opaque textures, on the other hand, fail to absorb the underlying material transparency.

In addition, WorldView with hardware acceleration enabled is at the mercy of the user's graphics hardware, the quality of the video drivers supplied with the hardware, and Microsoft's DirectX (of which at least three major versions are available). Observed hardware-specific bugs include a lack of support for material transparency (3Dfx Voodoo Rush<enbased card) and a lack of support for material or texture transparency or for non-palette-based textures (ATI Rage Pro card). Many of these problems are likely to disappear as hardware manufacturers release more mature versions of their video drivers, but some of the limitations may simply be due to an overly aggressive use of DirectX in WorldView itself.

Note that the older WorldView 2.0 also had problems with so-called "RGBA-palette" PNGs, and with hardware acceleration enabled under Windows, it failed to display RGBA PNG textures at all (observed on a Rendition Vérité-based card).

WorldView is currently still available from *http://www.intervista.com/worldview/*, but as with *cosmosoftware.com*, the site may disappear when Computer Associates completes its acquisition of Platinum.

blaxxun Contact

blaxxun's Contact browser (the unified, version 4.0 name for the older CC3D and CCpro browsers) is available only for the Windows 9x/NT platform and is optimized primarily for performance, like WorldView. Unlike WorldView, however, CC3D also comes in an OpenGL version, and both that and the Direct3D version can support full alpha blending of PNG textures, at least in some modes. The Direct3D modes that support only screendoor transparency also support only 8-bit, palette-based rendering, however.

Because the selection of PC video cards with good, hardware-assisted OpenGL support was still fairly sparse in 1998, only the Direct3D version of Contact 4.002 was tested. It did not support transparency in RGBA-palette PNGs at all, regardless of the material transparency, and gray palette-based PNG textures with transparency failed to inherit the underlying material color. On the other hand, palette and grayscale textures with binary (or single-shade) transparency additionally inherited the underlying material transparency. Implementation problems were also probably to blame for the incorrect rendering of overlapping transparent textures.

Unlike older versions of the browser, which failed to render large textures at all, Contact 4.0 appeared to resample them to smaller sizes if the hardware had insufficient texture memory. In High Quality software-rendering mode, the newer release appeared not to have any size limitations—indeed, its rendering of large, opaque textures was distinctly better than that of Cosmo Player, which is otherwise considered to have a very high quality renderer. On the other hand, transparent textures reverted to stippled transparency in this mode. Contact 4.0 is available for download from *http://www.blaxxun.com/products/contact/*.

Viscape Universal

Superscape has been in the 3D business since before VRML existed, but the release of Viscape Universal 5.60 late in 1998 was its first nonbeta attempt at a VRML97 browser. As with Cosmo Player and CCpro, it supports both OpenGL and Direct3D rendering engines.

Version 5.60 comes reasonably close to achieving Superscape's claims of "full VRML97 compliance," at least with regard to textures. Alpha transparency is supported, but single-shade PNG transparency in grayscale or RGB textures is not, and palette-alpha PNGs are rendered mostly opaque. Material transparency has varying effects: with the OpenGL renderer, *all* textures are composed with the underlying transparency; with Direct3D, none of them are. Both behaviors are incorrect. Grayscale textures also fail to absorb the underlying material's color.

On a more amusing note, Viscape Universal has no support for GIF textures— which is allowed by the VRML specification—but it fails to render the underlying material correctly in the absence of the textures. The browser may be downloaded from *http://www.superscape.com/download/ViscapeUniversal/*.

LibVRML97/Lookat

LibVRML97 is Chris Morley's free VRML97 library, written in C++; Lookat is a simple browser based on the library. As of version 0.7.9, the library was known to compile under Linux, Solaris, and Windows 95; it should be portable to most platforms with a reasonably up-to-date C++ compiler. The Lookat sample browser (and its Motif- and GTK-based variants, xmLookat and gtkLookat) was originally specific to Unix and the X Window System, but a 32-bit Windows port was progressing quite rapidly as of January 1999.

Earlier versions had various minor texture problems, but version 0.7.9 earned a distinction shared by no other VRML browser: perfect texture-rendering compliance with the VRML97 specification for all combinations of texture types and material properties, as far as our tests can determine. The browser may have other limitations, but its PNG support is without parallel.*

LibVRML97 is freely available as C++ source code from *http://www.vermontel. net/~cmorley/vrml.html* under a BSD-like license. The Motif and GTK frontends are available under the GNU General Public License.

FreeWRL

Another Open Source VRML97 browser is Tuomas Lukka's FreeWRL, a Perl-based effort that uses OpenGL for 3D rendering and FreeType for font support. As such, it is one of the few VRML97 browsers that runs under Linux, but because of its dependence on a host of secondary Perl packages and external libraries,† it is not for the meek. Version 0.13 supported PNG, but just barely: only on primitive shapes (Box, Cylinder, and Sphere, not IndexedFaceSet, Extrusion, or Elevation-Grid nodes), and in a test world with both PNGs and JPEGs, the two JPEG textures appeared to be used on every textured surface, replacing all of the PNG textures. It also did not support material transparency, had problems with nonconvex, textured polygons, and, as a script-based browser, was rather slow.

Version 0.17 was Tuomas's final release (December 1998); as of January 1999, John Stewart was the maintainer, and the new web site was *http://debra.dgbt.crc. ca/~luigi/FreeWRL/*. Version 0.19 was the current release as of early April 1999.

VRMLView

VRMLView, from the Norwegian company Systems in Motion, is available for Windows 9x/NT, Irix, Linux/Intel, and BeOS, with an HP-UX port underway. As of early 1999, two betas of version 2.0 had been released: "2.0b1" in January 1998 and "2.0beta1" in August, available for Linux, Windows, and BeOS. The first had a fatal PNG bug, but support in the second was reasonably good and included full alpha blending.

Nevertheless, VRMLView 2.0beta1 had several problems with PNG textures, many similar to those seen in other browsers. Among them were the following:

---

* There was actually a tiny glitch: one pixel in the corner of one GIF texture was the wrong color. Oops.

† Perl 5.0; Perl modules libwww, libnet, MIME-Base64, MD5, HTML-Parser, and Data-Dumper; Mesa or a commercial OpenGL library; FreeType; libjpeg, libpng, and zlib; and optionally XSwallow, to enable its use in Netscape Navigator as an inline VRML plug-in.

- Gray palette-based textures do not inherit underlying material colors.
- Gray PNGs with transparency also inherit underlying material transparency.
- Gray non-palette-based PNG textures with transparency are rendered opaque.
- Opaque palette-based and RGB textures on partially transparent materials are rendered completely transparent.
- In some places, background polygons are rendered on top of foreground polygons.

The VRMLView 2.0 beta shipped with all texture support turned off, but textures could be enabled by selecting the Textures item in the View menu. Subsequently, textures were enabled from the outset. Also note that the Linux version required the 3.0 beta version of the Mesa OpenGL clone (subsequently released), which was not immediately obvious from the README file. Finally, keep in mind that the browser still lacked support for some basic VRML nodes, such as Background and Anchor. VRMLView's web page is at *http://www.sim.no/vrmlview.html*.

Other VRML Browsers

Other VRML97 browsers that included some level of PNG support were Dimension X's Liquid Reality, Netscape's Live3D, and Newfire's Torch. Dimension X was acquired by Microsoft in 1997, and its 3D technology was absorbed into the Liquid Motion animation tool. The Java-based Liquid Reality browser itself was discontinued, but since its PNG support was fairly buggy and usually crashed the browser (under both Solaris and Windows 95), it was never a truly usable PNG-supporting VRML browser.

Netscape's Live3D browser, based on a VRML 1.0 browser (WebFX) acquired from Paper Software, had good PNG support, aside from reversing all red and blue color values and supporting only screendoor transparency. The rights to version 2.0 were acquired by SGI early in 1997, and it was renamed and released as Cosmo Player 1.0 for the PC. With the Cosmo Player 2.0 rewrite, most traces of Live3D vanished, although it was still bundled with Netscape Communicator versions up through 4.04.

Newfire's Torch browser was a special-purpose, games-oriented VRML engine. It was designed purely for speed and interactive performance, but it nevertheless supported PNG, including a dithered form of screendoor transparency that looked better than the usual flavor. Aside from using an 8-bit color model regardless of display depth, its only known bug was a failure to compose grayscale textures with the underlying material color. Unfortunately, it disappeared when Newfire went bankrupt early in 1998.

In addition to the dead PNG-supporting browsers (let us hope there's no connection to PNG support there!), two other VRML97 browsers were still under active development in 1998: Sony's Community Place 2.0 (*http://www.community-place. com*) and VRwave 0.9 (*http://www.iicm.edu/vrwave*) from the Graz (Austria) University of Technology. Neither supported PNG as of early 1999, but PNG support was promised for both in upcoming releases.

Other 3D Applications

Quite a few other 3D applications support PNG, too. These range from VRML editors and high-end modeling programs to artificial terrain generators and font-extrusion utilities. In the next few pages, I list a number of these applications, together with the version number of the latest release and the current web site as of this writing.

3D Studio MAX

> Version R2.5, Kinetix/Autodesk. Available for 32-bit Windows; read/write support for PNGs. This is *the* reference software for high-end 3D modeling, much like Adobe Photoshop is the reference for high-end image editing; release 2.0 (and later) supports export of VRML 2.0.

> > *http://www.ktx.com/3dsmax/*
> > *http://www.ktx.com/3dsmaxr2/*

Cosmo Worlds

> Version 1.1 (Irix) and 2.0 (Win32), SGI Cosmo Software, Platinum Technology, Computer Associates, and/or Web3D Consortium. Available for SGI Irix and 32-bit Windows; read/write support for PNGs; full alpha support. This was Cosmo's flagship VRML 2.0 editing program. SGI retained the rights to the Irix version; as of early April 1999, the fate of the Windows version was up in the air. Platinum's plans to release it to the Web3D Consortium (as open source code, free for noncommercial use) may go forward, or it may remain proprietary software under Computer Associates' control.

> > *http://www.cosmosoftware.com/products/worlds/brief.html*
> > *http://www.sgi.com/software/cosmo/worlds.html*
> > *http://www.web3d.org*

Extreme3D

> Version 2.0, Macromedia. Available for 32-bit Windows and Mac PPC; read/write support for PNGs as textures and backgrounds; write-only support for PNGs as output format for rendered scenes, including interlacing and (32-bit) alpha support. This is a 3D modeling and animation tool.

> > *http://www.macromedia.com/software/extreme3d/*

Font F/X

Version 2.0, DCSi/Electric Rain. Available for 32-bit Windows; write-only support for PNGs. This is a 3D font-rendering program.

> *http://www.erain.com/*

gforge

Version 1.3a, John Beale. Available for Unix and DOS; write-only support for PNGs. This is a terrain generator that uses "random fractal forgery" to produce realistic mathematical representations of hills, mountains, and craters; its output must be fed into the POV-Ray ray tracer for rendering. The included Tcl/Tk interface is called Xforge.

> *http://www.best.com/~beale/gforge/*

LightWave 3D

Version 5.6, NewTek. Available for 32-bit Windows, Mac PPC, Irix, and Solaris. Read/write support for PNGs and full (32-bit) alpha support if James G. Jones's PNG loader/saver is installed as a plug-in. This is another 3D modeling and animation tool, with particular emphasis on film and video output.

> *http://www.newtek.com/products/lightwave/description.html*
> *http://datausa.com/pixelsys/plugins.htm*

Mathematica

Version 3.0.2, Wolfram Research. Available for 32-bit Windows, Mac 68k/PPC, and most flavors of Unix; version 2.2.3 is also available for 16-bit Windows, OS/2, and OpenVMS. Read/write support for PNGs, read-only support for 32-bit RGBA, and full 16-bit support if Jens-Peer Kuska's PNGBitmap package is installed. Mathematica is a graphical environment for interactive mathematics and technical computing; the add-on allows it to use PNGs for textures on surfaces and to save rendered output and other graphics elements in PNG format.

> *http://www.wri.com/mathematica/*
> *http://www.mpae.gwdg.de/~kuska/mcpng.html*

MathGL3d

Version 2.0, Jens-Peer Kuska. Available for 32-bit Windows, Linux, and Solaris; read/write support for PNGs. This is a standalone, interactive viewer for Mathematica 3D elements; it supports PNGs as textures on input and as an output format for rendered images. It can also produce POV-Ray or VRML 2.0 models with PNG textures.

> *http://www.mpae.gwdg.de/~kuska/mview3d.html*

Nendo

Nichimen Graphics. Available for 32-bit Windows and Solaris; read/write support for PNGs. This is a 3D modeling and 2D painting application with support for PNGs as textures and VRML 2.0 as both an input and output format. PNG images can be edited in the paint portion of the program.

> *http://www.nichimen.com/nendo/*

pf2wrl

Version 1.4, WareOnEarth. Available for SGI Irix; write-only support for PNGs. This is a simple (and free) command-line utility to convert IRIS Performer 3D files into VRML 2.0 format; it will optionally convert the SGI-specific texture formats into PNG and JPEG.

> *http://www.wareonearth.com/freesoft.html*

POV-Ray

Version 3.1a, Persistence of Vision Development Team. Available for 16- and 32-bit Windows, Unix, Mac 68k/PPC, DOS, and Amiga; read/write support for PNGs; full (32-bit) alpha support; full gamma support; full 16-bit-per-sample support. This is probably the most well known ray-tracing program; its file format has become an unofficial 3D standard.

> *http://www.povray.org/*

Rational Reducer

Version 2.2, Systems in Motion. Available for 32-bit Windows, Linux, and SGI Irix; read-only support for PNGs. This is a polygon-reduction tool for 3D models in VRML 1.0, VRML 2.0, AutoCAD (DXF), and 3D Studio MAX (3DS) formats. It supports PNGs for textures.

> *http://www.sim.no/reducer.html*

trueSpace

Version 4.1, Caligari. Available for 32-bit Windows; read/write support for PNGs. This is a 3D modeling and rendering program with support for radiosity, NURBS, and so on. It supports PNGs for textures and can write VRML 2.0 files.

> *http://www.caligari.com/products/*

Xara3D

Version 3.0, Xara. Available for 32-bit Windows; write support for PNGs (may also support reading PNGs as textures); full (32-bit) alpha support. This is a 3D font-rendering program.

http://www.xara.com/xara3d/

One other application is worth mentioning here. VermelGen, an all-Java VRML editor written by Justin Couch and Cameron Gillies, relies on Java's built-in image-handling support for textures. The most recent version of the app, beta 2, was released in mid-1997 when Java did not support PNG. But with native PNG support in the new Java Advanced Imaging API and in Justin's own Java Image Content Handlers (see Chapter 16 for both), it is possible that VermelGen will inherit PNG support as well. (Of course, it's also quite possible that some modifications would have to be made in order to work with the updated Java code.) VermelGen is available from *http://www.vlc.com.au/VermelGen*; it requires the JVerge VRML classes, available from *http://www.vlc.com.au/JVerge/*.

As with the other application categories, new VRML browsers and 3D applications with PNG support will be listed on the following two pages at the PNG home site:

http://www.cdrom.com/pub/png/pngvrml.html
http://www.cdrom.com/pub/png/pngap3d.html

PART II

The Design of PNG

7

History of the
Portable Network
Graphics Format

Internet GIF tax,
January '95.
PNG to the rescue!

—Glenn Randers-Pehrson[*]

The Portable Network Graphics image format, or PNG for short, is the first general-purpose image format to achieve wide, cross-platform acceptance[†] since JPEG/JFIF arrived in the early 1990s. Almost every major feature in PNG exists in other general-purpose formats—specifically, GIF, JPEG, and TIFF—yet in January 1995, a group of strangers felt compelled to band together and design another image format from scratch. To understand why, it is necessary to delve even further into history.

In 1977 and 1978, Israeli researchers Jacob Ziv and Abraham Lempel published a pair of papers on a new class of lossless data-compression algorithms in the journal *IEEE Transactions on Information Theory*. These algorithms, now collectively referred to as "LZ77" and "LZ78," formed the basis for an entire industry of software, hardware, and subsequent research papers. One of the follow-up papers was by Terry Welch and was published in the June 1984 issue of *IEEE Computer*. Entitled "A Technique for High-Performance Data Compression," it described his research at Sperry into a fast, efficient implementation of LZ78 called LZW.

---

[*] Alternatively, "Unisys bombshell, / Christmas 1994. / PNG to the rescue!"

[†] The choice of adjectives is intentional: there are other widely accepted formats, such as Windows BMPs, but they're not cross-platform, and there are cross-platform formats such as PostScript or the astronomical FITS format, but they're not general-purpose.

By 1987, when CompuServe's Bob Berry was busy designing the GIF image format, LZW was well established in the Unix world in the form of the *compress* command, and in the PC world in the form of SEA's ARC. As a fast algorithm with good compression and relatively low memory requirements, LZW was ideally suited to the PCs of the day, and it became Berry's choice for a GIF compression method, too. In turn, GIF became the image format of choice on the Internet, particularly on the worldwide discussion forum known as Usenet.

And so things remained largely unchanged until 1994. The introduction (from a practical standpoint) of JPEG around 1992 or 1993 may have slowed GIF's rising star slightly, but computational requirements and the limitations of then-current graphics cards limited JPEG's acceptance for several years. With the advent of graphical browsers for the World Wide Web in 1992 and 1993, GIF's popularity only increased: simple graphics with few colors were the norm, and those were ideally suited to GIF's palette-based format. With the release of Netscape Navigator 1.0 in 1994, progressive rendering of images as they downloaded suddenly became widespread, and GIF's interlacing scheme worked in its favor once more.*

Then, three days after Christmas 1994, CompuServe quietly dropped a small bombshell on an unsuspecting world: henceforth, all GIF-supporting software would require royalties. In fact, the announcement was apparently the culmination of more than a year of legal wrangling with Unisys, which had inherited the Welch LZW patent in the 1986 merger of Sperry and Burroughs, and which had by 1993 become considerably more aggressive about enforcing its patent in software-only applications.

In any case, shortly after the holidays ended, word of the announcement reached the Internet—specifically, the ever-volatile Usenet community. As one might expect, the results were spectacular: within days, a full-fledged conflagration of bluster, whining, flaming, vitriol, and general-purpose noise had engulfed several of the Usenet newsgroups, among them *comp.compression* and *comp.graphics*. But mixed in with the noise was the genesis of an informal Internet working group led by Thomas Boutell. Its purpose was to design not only a replacement for the GIF format, but also a successor to it: better, smaller, more extensible, and *free.*

---

* Progressive capability had for quite some time been part of the JPEG specification, too, but since the Independent JPEG Group's free library didn't support the progressive mode until August 1995, neither did any applications—including web browsers.

Anatomy of an Internet Working Group

What would become known as the "PNG Group" or "PNG Development Group" began as many such groups do—as a collection of participants in a Usenet newsgroup. When the discussion became both more detailed and considerably more verbose, it became a mailing list with an associated CompuServe forum. Tom Boutell posted the very first PNG draft—then known as "PBF," for Portable Bitmap Format*—to *comp.graphics, comp.compression,* and *comp.infosystems. www.providers* on Wednesday, 4 January 1995. It had a 3-byte signature, chunk numbers rather than chunk names, a maximum pixel depth of 8 bits, and no specified compression method, but even at that stage it had more in common with today's PNG than with any other existing format.

Within one week, most of the major features of PNG had been proposed, though by no means yet accepted: delta filtering for improved compression (Scott Elliott and Mark Adler), deflate compression (Tom Lane, the Info-ZIP Group and many others), 24-bit support (many folks), the PNG name itself (Oliver Fromme), internal CRCs (Greg Roelofs), gamma chunk (Paul Haeberli), and 48- and 64-bit support (Jonathan Shekter). That week also saw the first proto-PNG mailing list set up, Tom Boutell's release of the second draft of the specification, and Greg's posting of some test results that showed a 10% improvement in compression if GIF's LZW method were simply replaced with the deflate (LZ77) algorithm.

One of the real strengths of the PNG group was its ability to weigh the pros and cons of various issues in a (mostly) rational manner, reach some sort of consensus, and then move on to the next issue without prolonging discussion on "dead" topics indefinitely. In part this was probably due to the fact that the group was relatively small, yet possessed of a sufficiently broad range of graphics and compression expertise that no one felt unduly shut out when a decision went against him.† In part it was also due to a frequently updated "scorecard," which listed the accepted and rejected features and summarized any issues that were still undecided.

But the most important factor in the group's progress was the position of Benevolent Dictator, held by Tom Boutell. As with the very successful Linux development model, in which Linus Torvalds is trusted with the final say on anything having to do with the Linux kernel, so Tom, as the initiating force behind the PNG project, was granted this power. When consensus was impossible, Tom would make a

---

* Also known by some as the Peanut Butter Format, a.k.a. Chunky GIF.

† All of the PNG authors were male. Most of them still are. No doubt there's a dissertation in there somewhere.

decision, and that would settle the matter. On one or two rare occasions he might later have been persuaded to reverse the decision, but this generally happened only if new information came to light.

In any case, the development model worked: by the beginning of February 1995, seven drafts had been produced, and the PNG format was settling down. (The PNG name was adopted in Draft 5, after a great deal of fuss; GIF's indeterminate pronunciation* was the prime motivating factor, but the allure of an unofficial recursive acronym—PNG's Not GIF—was what decided the matter.) The next month was mainly spent working out the details: chunk-naming conventions, CRC size and placement, choice of filter types, palette ordering, specific flavors of transparency and alpha-channel support, interlace method, and so on. CompuServe was impressed enough by the design that on February 7, 1995, they announced support for PNG as the designated successor to GIF, supplanting what they had initially referred to as the GIF24 development project. By the beginning of March, PNG Draft 9 was released and the specification was officially frozen—just over two months from its inception. Although further drafts followed, they merely added clarifications, some recommended behaviors for encoders and decoders, and a tutorial or two. Indeed, Glenn Randers-Pehrson has kept some so-called "paleo PNGs" that were created at the time of Draft 9; they are still readable by any PNG decoder today.

Table 7-1 is a time line listing many of the major events in PNG's history.

Table 7-1: PNG Time Line

Date	Event
4 Jan 1995	PBF Draft 1 (Thomas Boutell)
4 Jan 1995	Delta filtering (Scott Elliott, Mark Adler)
4 Jan 1995	Deflate compression (Tom Lane and others)
4 Jan 1995	24-bit support (many)
5 Jan 1995	TeleGrafix LZHUF proposal
6 Jan 1995	PNG name (Oliver Fromme)
7 Jan 1995	PBF Draft 2 (Thomas Boutell)
7 Jan 1995	ZIF early results (Greg Roelofs)
7 Jan 1995	Internal CRC(s) (Greg Roelofs)
8 Jan 1995	Gamma chunk (Paul Haeberli)
8 Jan 1995	48-, 64-bit support (Jonathan Shekter)
9 Jan 1995	FGF proposal, implementation (Jeremy Wohl)
10 Jan 1995	First NGF/PBF/proto-PNG mailing list (Jeremy Wohl)
15 Jan 1995	PBF Draft 3 (Thomas Boutell)

---

* The author of the GIF specification pronounces it with a soft G, as "jif."

Table 7-1: PNG Time Line (continued)

Date	Event
16 Jan 1995	CompuServe announces GIF24 development (Tim Oren)
16 Jan 1995	Spec available on WWW (Thomas Boutell)
16 Jan 1995	PBF Draft 4 (Thomas Boutell)
23 Jan 1995	PNG Draft 5 (Thomas Boutell)
24 Jan 1995	PNG Draft 6 (Thomas Boutell)
26 Jan 1995	Final 8-byte signature (Tom Lane)
1 Feb 1995	PNG Draft 7 (Thomas Boutell)
2 Feb 1995	Adam7 interlacing scheme (Adam Costello)
7 Feb 1995	CompuServe drops GIF24 in favor of PNG (Tim Oren)
13 Feb 1995	PNG Draft 8 (Thomas Boutell)
7 Mar 1995	PNG Draft 9 (Thomas Boutell)
11 Mar 1995	First working PNG viewer (Oliver Fromme)
13 Mar 1995	First valid PNG images posted (Glenn Randers-Pehrson)
1 May 1995	pnglib 0.6 released (Guy Eric Schalnat)
1 May 1995	zlib 0.9 released (Jean-loup Gailly, Mark Adler)
5 May 1995	PNG Draft 10 (Thomas Boutell)
13 Jun 1995	PNG web site (Greg Roelofs)
27 Jul 1995	NCSA X Mosaic 2.7b1 with native PNG support (Dan Pape)
20 Sep 1995	Arena 0.98b with native PNG support (Dave Beckett)
8 Dec 1995	PNG spec 0.92 released as W3C Working Draft
23 Feb 1996	PNG spec 0.95 released as IETF Internet Draft
28 Mar 1996	Deflate and zlib approved as Informational RFCs (IESG)
22 May 1996	Deflate and zlib released as Informational RFCs (IETF)
17 Jun 1996	libpng 0.89c released (Andreas Dilger)
1 Jul 1996	PNG spec 1.0 released as W3C Proposed Recommendation
11 Jul 1996	PNG spec 1.0 approved as Informational RFC (IESG)
24 Jul 1996	zlib 1.0.4 released (Jean-loup Gailly, Mark Adler)
4 Aug 1996	VRML 2.0 spec released with PNG as requirement (VAG)
1 Oct 1996	PNG spec 1.0 approved as W3C Recommendation
14 Oct 1996	`image/png` approved (IANA)
6 Nov 1996	sRGB chunk registered (PNG Development Group)
9 Dec 1996	sPLT chunk registered (PNG Development Group)
15 Jan 1997	PNG spec 1.0 released as Informational RFC 2083 (IETF)
28 Jan 1997	pCAL chunk registered (PNG Development Group)
5 Apr 1997	libpng 0.95b released (Andreas Dilger)
1 Oct 1997	Internet Explorer 4.0 with native PNG support (Microsoft)
11 Nov 1997	Navigator 4.04 with native PNG support (Netscape)
28 Feb 1998	MHEG-5 UK profile for digital TV released (UK DTG)
9 Mar 1998	libpng 1.0 released (Glenn Randers-Pehrson)
9 Jul 1998	zlib 1.1.3 released (Jean-loup Gailly, Mark Adler)
17 Aug 1998	iCCP chunk registered (PNG Development Group)

Table 7-1: PNG Time Line (continued)

Date	Event
23 Oct 1998	PNG spec 1.1 approved (PNG Development Group)
21 Dec 1998	Opera 3.51 with native PNG support (Opera Software)
31 Dec 1998	PNG spec 1.1 released (PNG Development Group)
14 Jan 1999	libpng 1.0.3 released (Glenn Randers-Pehrson)
9 Feb 1999	iTXt chunk registered (PNG Development Group)
9 Jun 1999	*PNG: The Definitive Guide* published

Perhaps equally interesting are some of the proposed features and design suggestions that ultimately were not accepted: the Amiga IFF format; uncompressed bitmaps, either gzip'd or stored inside zipfiles; thumbnail images and/or generic multi-image support; "little-endian"* byte order; Unicode UTF-8 character set for text; YUV and other lossy (nonlossless) image-encoding schemes; vector graphics; and so forth. Many of these topics produced an amazing amount of discussion—in fact, the main proponent of the zipfile idea was still arguing about it more than two years later.

Implementation

A frozen spec opens the door to implementations, and many people set about writing PNG encoders and decoders as soon as Draft 9 appeared. The real glory, however, is reserved for the handful of people who took it upon themselves to write the free programming libraries supporting PNG: Jean-loup Gailly and Mark Adler, both of Info-ZIP and gzip fame, who rewrote the deflate compression engine in a form suitable for general-purpose use and released it as *zlib*; and Guy Eric Schalnat of Group 42, who almost single-handedly wrote the initial version of *libpng* (then known as *pnglib*). The first truly usable versions of the libraries were released two months after Draft 9, on May 1, 1995. Although both libraries were missing some features required for full implementation, they were sufficiently complete to be used in various freeware applications. Draft 10 of the specification was released at the same time, with clarifications and corrections resulting from these first implementations.

The pace of development slowed at that point, at least to outward appearances. Partly this was due to the fact that, after four straight months of intense

---

* The name stems from a reference in *Gulliver's Travels* to opposing factions of silly people, some of whom (Lilliputians) broke their eggs at the little end before eating them and some of whom (Blefuscudians) broke them at the big end. The argument over PNG's byte order was almost equally silly, but in the end (so to speak) big-endian was chosen for two reasons: it's easier for humans to read and debug in a "hex dump" (a textual rendering of a binary file), and it's the same as "network byte order," which is something of an Internet standard.

development and many megabytes of email, everyone was exhausted; partly it was due to the fact that Guy controlled the development of libpng, and he became busy with other things at work. Often overlooked is the fact that, while writing the spec was a very focused effort and writing the reference implementation was only slightly less so, once the library had been released in a usable form there were literally hundreds of potential applications pulling at developers' interests. And finally, there was the simple perception that PNG was basically done—a point that was emphasized by a CompuServe press release to that effect in June 1995.

Nevertheless, progress continued. June saw the genesis of the PNG web site, which has now grown to more than two dozen pages, and Kevin Mitchell officially registered the "PNGf" Macintosh file ID with Apple Computer. In August 1995, Alexander Lehmann and Willem van Schaik released a fine pair of additions to the NetPBM image-manipulation suite: pnmtopng and pngtopnm version 2.0. And in December, at the Fourth International World Wide Web Conference, the World Wide Web Consortium (W3C) released the PNG Specification version 0.92 as an official standards-track Working Draft.

February 1996 saw the release of version 0.95 as an Internet Draft by the Internet Engineering Task Force (IETF), followed in July by the Internet Engineering Steering Group's (IESG) approval of version 1.0 as an official Informational RFC. (It was finally released by the IETF as RFC 2083 in January 1997.) In early August, the Virtual Reality Modeling Language (VRML) Architecture Group adopted PNG as one of the two required image formats for minimal VRML 2.0 conformance. Meanwhile, the W3C promoted the spec to Proposed Recommendation status in July and then to full Recommendation status on the first of October. Finally, in mid-October 1996, the Internet Assigned Numbers Authority (IANA) formally approved "image/png" as an official Internet Media Type, joining image/gif and image/jpeg as non-experimental image formats for the Web. Much of this standardization would not have happened nearly as quickly without the tireless efforts of Tom Lane and Glenn Randers-Pehrson, who took over editing duties of the spec from Thomas Boutell.

MNG

Also in 1996 came the revival of efforts to produce a multiple-image variant of PNG suitable for slide shows, animations, and very efficient storage of certain simple kinds of images. Multi-image support had been left out of the PNG specification for several reasons: multi-image capability in GIF was supported by virtually no one; multi-image GIFs were indistinguishable from single-image GIFs (i.e., they had the same filename extension); including multi-image support in PNG would have delayed both its development and its acceptance in the marketplace, due to the burden of extra complexity, and creating a separate, PNG-based multi-image format not only would be a logical extension of PNG but also would be more appropriate to a group with backgrounds in animation and multimedia. As it happened, however, this latter group never materialized, and with the early-1996 release of Netscape Navigator 2.0 with support for GIF animations,* it became clear that the PNG Group needed to produce some sort of response.

Unfortunately there was a fairly fundamental disagreement within the group over whether the new format should be a very thin layer on top of PNG, capable of duplicating GIF animations but not much more, or whether it should be a full-fledged multimedia format capable of synchronizing images, sound, and possibly video. Although the former would have been trivial (and fast) to design and implement, proponents of the latter design held sway during the early discussions in the summer of 1996. In the end, however, something of a compromise was created— though possibly due more to attrition than consensus. Called Multiple-image Network Graphics, the MNG format design was largely shaped by Glenn Randers-Pehrson and included simple but general operations to manipulate sections of images, but no direct sound or video support. As of November 1998 the MNG specification was close to being frozen, but was also quite large and still awaiting implementation in the form of a reference library similar to libpng. Until such time as either a reference library or some other form of complete implementation exists, the MNG spec will not be approved as a standard, nor is it likely that more than a handful of third-party developers will offer support for it.

Mainstream Support and Present Status

If 1996 was the year of PNG's standardization, 1997 was the year of PNG applications. After having taken over libpng development from Guy Eric Schalnat in June 1996, Andreas Dilger shepherded it through versions 0.89 to 0.96, adding numerous features and finding and fixing bugs; application developers seemed not to mind the library's "beta" version number, and increasingly employed it in their mainstream apps. With native support in popular programs such as Adobe's Photoshop and Illustrator, Macromedia's Freehand, JASC's Paint Shop Pro, Ulead's PhotoImpact, and Microsoft's Office 97 suite, PNG's star was clearly rising. But perhaps the crowning moment came in the autumn, with fresh versions of the Big Two web browsers. Microsoft's Internet Explorer 4.0 in October and Netscape's Navigator 4.04 in November both included native, albeit somewhat limited, PNG support. At last, the widespread use of PNG on the Web came within the realm of possibility.

---

* Alas, Netscape's support of GIF animations probably did more to ensure the format's longevity than any other event in GIF's history.

The theme for 1998 seems to have been *maturity*. Having been handed the reins of principal libpng development at the beginning of the year, Glenn Randers-Pehrson fixed many bugs, finished the documentation and generally polished libpng into a stable release worthy of a "1.0" version number by early March—three years to the day, in fact, after the PNG specification was frozen. In February, the UK Digital Television Group released the MHEG-5 UK Profile for next-generation teletext on digital terrestrial television; the profile included PNG as one of its bitmap formats, and as a result, manufacturers such as Philips, Sony, Pace and Nokia were expected to be shipping digital televisions and set-top boxes with built-in PNG support by the time this book reaches print. At the very end of March 1998, Netscape released Mozilla, the pre-alpha source code to Communicator 5.0, which allowed interested third parties (like the PNG Group) to tinker with the popular browser and make it work as intended. In October, the PNG Group approved some important additions and clarifications to one of the more difficult technical aspects of the PNG spec, namely, gamma and color correction; these changes defined the PNG 1.1 specification—the first official revision in three and a half years. And at roughly the same time, a joint committee of the International Organization for Standardization (ISO) and the International Electrotechnical Commission (IEC) began the yearlong process to make Portable Network Graphics an official international standard (to be known as ISO/IEC 15948 upon approval).

But a history bereft of darker events is perhaps not so interesting... and, sadly enough, for a brief period in April 1998, it appeared that things might once again be percolating on the legal front. Specifically, there were rumors that Stac, Inc., believed the deflate compression engine in zlib (which is used by libpng) infringed on two of their patents. Careful reading of the patents in question, United States patents 4,701,745 and 5,016,009, suggests that although it is possible to write an infringing deflate engine, the one actually used in zlib does not do so.* Moreover, as this is written, a full year has passed with no public claims from Stac, no further private contacts, and no confirmation of the original rumors. However, until this is tested in court or Stac makes a public announcement clearing zlib of suspicion, at least a small cloud will remain over the Portable Network Graphics format as a whole. The irony should be evident to one and all.

---

* It should go without saying—but lawyers like it to be said anyway—that this is not official legal advice. Consult a patent attorney to be (more) certain. But note that deflate is also being standardized into open Internet protocols such as PPP.

8

PNG Basics

The fundamental building block of PNG images is the *chunk*. With the exception of the first 8 bytes in the file (and we'll come back to those shortly), a PNG image consists of nothing but chunks.

Chunks

Chunks were designed to be easily tested and manipulated by computer programs, easily detected by human eyes, and reasonably self-contained. Every chunk has the same structure: a 4-byte length (in "big-endian" format, as with all integer values in PNG streams), a 4-byte chunk type, between 0 and 2,147,483,647 bytes of chunk data, and a 4-byte *cyclic redundancy check* value (CRC). This is diagrammed in Figure 8-1.

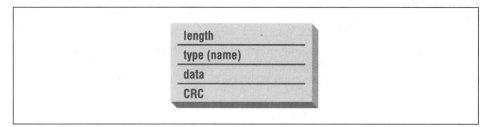

Figure 8-1: PNG chunk structure

The data field is straightforward; that's where the interesting bits (if any) go; specific content will be discussed later, as each chunk is described. The length field refers to the length of the data field alone, not the chunk type or CRC. The CRC, on the other hand, covers both the chunk-type field and the chunk data and is always present, even when there is no chunk data. Note that the combination of length fields and CRC values is already sufficient to check the basic integrity of a PNG file! The only missing information—not including the contents of the first 8 bytes in the file—is the exact algorithm (or "polynomial") used for the CRC. That turns out to be identical to the CRC used by gzip and many popular archiving programs; it is described in detail in Section 3.4 of the *PNG Specification, Version 1.1*, available from *http://www.cdrom.com/pub/png/pngdocs.html*.

The chunk type is possibly the most unusual feature. It is specified as a sequence of binary values, which just happen to correspond to the upper- and lowercase ASCII letters used on virtually every computer in the Western, non-mainframe world. Since it is far more convenient (and readable) to speak in terms of text characters than numerical sequences, the remainder of this book will adopt the convention of referring to chunks by their ASCII names. Programmers of EBCDIC-based computers should take note of this and remember to use only the numerical values corresponding to the ASCII characters.

Chunk types (or names) are usually mnemonic, as in the case of the IHDR or *image header* chunk. In addition, however, each character in the name encodes a single bit of information that shows up in the capitalization of the character.* Thus IHDR and iHDR are two completely different chunk types, and a decoder that encounters an unrecognized chunk can nevertheless infer useful things about it. From left to right, the four extra bits are interpreted as follows:

- The first character's case bit indicates whether the chunk is critical (uppercase) or ancillary; a decoder that doesn't recognize the chunk type can ignore it if it is ancillary, but it must warn the user that it cannot correctly display the image if it encounters an unknown critical chunk. The tEXt chunk, covered in Chapter 11, *PNG Options and Extensions*, is an example of an ancillary chunk.

- The second character indicates whether the chunk is public (uppercase) or private. Public chunks are those defined in the specification or registered as official, special-purpose types. But a company may wish to encode its own, application-specific information in a PNG file, and private chunks are one way to do that.

- The case bit of the third character is reserved for use by future versions of the PNG specification. It must be uppercase for PNG 1.0 and 1.1 files, but a decoder encountering an unknown chunk with a lowercase third character should deal with it as with any other unknown chunk.

---

* The ASCII character set was conveniently designed so that the case of a letter is always determined by bit 5. To put it another way, adding 32 to an uppercase character code gives you the code for its lowercase version.

- The last character's case bit is intended for image editors rather than simple
  viewers or other decoders. It indicates whether an editing program encountering an unknown *ancillary* chunk* can safely copy it into the new file (lowercase) or not (uppercase). If an unknown chunk is marked unsafe to copy,
  then it depends on the image data in some way. It must be omitted from the
  new image if any *critical* chunks have been modified in any way, including
  the addition of new ones or the reordering or deletion of existing ones. Note
  that if the program recognizes the chunk, it may choose to modify it appropriately and then copy it to the new file. Also note that unsafe-to-copy chunks
  may be copied to the new file if only ancillary chunks have been modified—
  again, including addition, deletion, and reordering—which implies that ancillary chunks cannot depend on other ancillary chunks.

PNG Signature

So chunk names encode additional information that is primarily useful if the chunk
is not recognized. The remainder of this book will be concerned with known
chunks, but before we turn to those, there is one more component of PNG files
that has to do with the unknown: the PNG file signature. As noted earlier, the first
8 bytes of the file are not, strictly speaking, a chunk.† They are a critical component of a PNG file, however, since they allow it to be identified as such regardless
of filename. But the PNG signature bytes are more than a simple identifier code:
they were cleverly designed to allow the most common types of file-transfer corruption to be detected. Web protocols these days typically ensure the correct transfer of binary files such as PNG images, but older transfer programs like the
venerable command-line FTP (File Transfer Protocol) often default to text-mode or
"ASCII" transfers. The unsuspecting user who transfers a PNG image or other
binary file as text is practically guaranteed of destroying it. The same is true of the
user who extracts a PNG file from a compressed archive in text mode or who
emails it without some form of "ASCII armor" (such as MIME Base64 encoding or
Unix uuencoding).

The 8-byte PNG file signature can detect this sort of problem because it simulates
a text file in some respects. The 8 bytes are given in Table 8-1.

---

* Since any decoder encountering an unknown critical chunk has no idea how the chunk modifies the
  image—only that it does so in a critical way—an editor cannot safely copy *or* omit the chunk in the
  new image.

† They can be thought of as such, however, since their length is known (8 bytes), their position and
  purpose are known (beginning of the file; signature), and their CRC is implied (the 8 bytes are constant, so effectively they amount to their own CRC).

Table 8-1: PNG Signature Bytes

Decimal Value	ASCII Interpretation
137	A byte with its most significant bit set ("8-bit character")
80	P
78	N
71	G
13	Carriage-return (CR) character, a.k.a. CTRL-M or ^M
10	Line-feed (LF) character, a.k.a. CTRL-J or ^J
26	CTRL-Z or ^Z
10	Line-feed (LF) character, a.k.a. CTRL-J or ^J

The first byte is used to detect transmission over a 7-bit channel—for example, email transfer programs often strip the 8th bit, thus changing the PNG signature. The 2nd, 3rd, and 4th bytes simply spell "PNG" (in ASCII, that is). Bytes 5 and 6 are end-of-line characters for Macintosh and Unix, respectively, and the combination of the two is the standard line ending for DOS, Windows, and OS/2. Byte 7 (CTRL-Z) is the end-of-file character for DOS text files, which allows one to TYPE the PNG file under DOS-like operating systems and see only the acronym "PNG" preceded by one strange character, rather than page after page of gobbledygook. Byte 8 is another Unix end-of-line character.

Text-mode transfer of a PNG file from a DOS-like system to Unix will strip off the carriage return (byte 5); the reverse transfer will replace byte 8 with a CR/LF pair. Transfer to or from a Macintosh will strip off the line feeds or replace the carriage return with a line feed, respectively. Either way, the signature is altered, and in all likelihood the remainder of the file is irreversibly damaged.

Note that the 9th, 10th, and 11th bytes are guaranteed to be 0 (that is, the ASCII NUL character) by the fact that the first chunk is required to be IHDR, whose first 4 bytes are its length—a value that is currently 13 and, according to the spec, will never change. (Instead, "new chunk types will be added to carry new information.") The fact that the 0 bytes in the length come first is another benefit of the big-endian integer format, which stores the high-order bytes first. Since NUL bytes are also often stripped out by text-mode transfer protocols, the detection of damaged PNG files is even more robust than the signature alone would suggest.

A Word on Color Representation

Before we start putting chunks together, however, a brief interlude on the representation and terminology of color is useful. Color fundamentally refers to a property of light—namely, its wavelength. Each color in the rainbow, from red to purple, is a relatively pure strain of wavelengths of light, and none of these colors can be generated by adding together any of the others.* Furthermore, despite what our eyeballs would have us think, the spectrum does not end at deep purple; beyond that are the ultraviolet, X-ray, and gamma-ray domains. Nor does it end at dull red—smoke on the water glows in the infrared, if only we could see it, and still further down the spectrum are radio waves.† Each of these wavelength regions, from radio on up to gamma, is a color.

So when someone refers to an RGB image—that is, containing only red, green, and blue values—as "truecolor," what twisted logic lies behind such a claim? The answer lies not in physics but in physiology. Human eyes contain only three classes of color sensors, which trigger color sensations in the brain in ways that are not yet fully understood. One might guess that these sensors (the *cones*) are tuned to red, green, and blue light, but that turns out not to be the case, at least not directly. Instead, signals from the three types of cones are added and sub-tracted in various ways, apparently in more than one stage. The details are not especially important; what matters is that the end result is a set of only three sig-nals going into the brain, corresponding to luminosity (or brightness), a red-versus-green intensity level, and a yellow-versus-blue level. In addition, the cones are not narrow-band sensors, but instead each responds to a broad range of wave-lengths. The upshot is that the human visual system is relatively poor at analyzing colors, so feeding it different combinations of red, green, and blue light suffices to fool it into thinking it is seeing an entire spectrum. Keep in mind, however, that while true yellow and a combination of red and green may look identical to us, to spectrometers (or nonhuman eyes) they are quite different.

In fact, even printers "see" color differently. Since they employ pigments, which absorb light rather than emit it, the RGB color space that works so well for com-puter monitors is inappropriate. Instead, use a "dual" color space based on cyan, magenta, and yellow, or CMYK for short.‡ And in video processing, television, and the JPEG image format, yet another set of color spaces is popular: YUV, YIQ, and YC_bC_r, all of which represent light as an intensity value (Y) and a pair of orthogo-nal color vectors (U and V, or I and Q, or C_b and C_r). All of these color spaces are beyond the scope of this book, but note that *every single one of them has its basis in human physiology.* Indeed, if YUV and its brethren sound quite a lot like the set of three signals going into the brain that I just discussed, rest assured that it's not

---

* Mathematically, this is known as *orthogonality* and is the basis for Fourier decomposition, among other things.

† It is probably not coincidence that the range of light visible to our water-filled orbs just happens to be the precise range of wavelengths that is *not* strongly absorbed by water.

‡ The *K* is for black. Since black is the preferred color for a huge class of printed material, including text, it is more efficient and considerably cheaper to use a single pigment for it than always to be mixing the other three. Some printing systems actually use five, six, or even seven distinct pigments.

coincidence. Not a single color space in common use today truly represents the full continuum of physical color.

Finally, note that image files may represent the appearance of a scene not only as a self-contained item, but also in reference to a background or to other images or text. In particular, transparency information is often desirable. The simplest approach to transparency in computer graphics is to mark a particular color as transparent, but more complex applications will generally require a completely separate channel of information. This is known as an *alpha channel* (or sometimes an alpha mask) and enables the use of partial transparency, such as is often used in television overlays. In the text that follows, I will refer to an RGB image with an alpha channel as an *RGBA* image. PNG adheres to the usual convention that alpha represents opacity; that is, an alpha value of 0 is fully transparent, and the maximum value for the pixel depth is completely opaque. PNG also uses only *unassociated* alpha, wherein the actual gray or color values are stored unchanged and are only affected by the alpha channel at display time. The alternative is *associated* or *premultiplied* alpha, in which the pixel values are effectively precomposited against a black background; although this allows slightly faster software compositing, it amounts to a lossy transformation of the image data and was therefore rejected in the design of PNG.

The Simplest PNG

We've looked at the fine details of a PNG file—the subatomic structure, if you will—so let us turn now to a few of the basic atoms (chunks) that will allow us to create a complete "molecule," or valid Portable Network Graphics file. The simplest possible PNG file, diagrammed in Figure 8-2, is composed of the PNG signature and only three chunk types: the image header chunk, IHDR; the image data chunk, IDAT; and the end-of-image chunk, IEND. IHDR must be the first chunk in a PNG image, and it includes all of the details about the type of the image: its height and width, pixel depth, compression and filtering methods, interlacing method, whether it has an alpha (transparency) channel, and whether it's a truecolor, grayscale, or colormapped (palette) image. Not all combinations of image types are valid, however, and much of the remainder of this chapter will be devoted to a discussion of what is allowed. IDAT contains all of the image's compressed pixel data. Although single IDATs are perfectly valid as long as they contain no more than 2 gigabytes of compressed data, in most images the compressed data is split into several IDAT chunks for greater robustness. Since the chunk's CRC is at the end, a streaming application that encounters a large IDAT can either force the user to wait until the complete chunk arrives before displaying anything, or it can begin displaying the image without knowing if it's valid. In the latter case, if the IDAT happens to be damaged, the user will see garbage on the display.

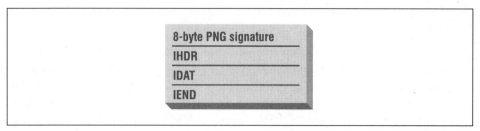

Figure 8-2: Layout of the simplest PNG

(Since the image dimensions were already read from a previously CRC-checked chunk, in theory the garbage will be restricted to the region belonging to the image.) Fortunately, small IDAT chunks are by far the most common, particularly in sizes of 8 or 32 kilobytes.

IEND is the simplest chunk of all; it contains no data, just indicates that there are no more chunks in the image. IEND is primarily useful when the PNG image is being transferred over the network as a stream, especially when it is part of a larger MNG stream (Chapter 12, *Multiple-Image Network Graphics*). And it serves as one more check that the PNG file is complete and internally self-consistent.

These three chunk types are sufficient to build truecolor and grayscale PNG files, with or without an alpha channel, but palette-based images require one more: PLTE, the palette chunk. PLTE simply contains a sequence of red, green, and blue values, where a value of 0 is black and 255 is full intensity; anywhere from 1 to 256 RGB triplets are allowed, depending on the pixel depth of the image. (That is, for a 4-bit image, no more than 16 palette entries are allowed.) The PLTE chunk must come before the first IDAT chunk; the structure of a colormapped PNG is shown in Figure 8-3.

PNG Image Types

I noted earlier that not all possible combinations of PNG image types and features are allowed by the specification. Let's take a closer look at the basic types and their features.

Palette-Based

Palette-based images, also known as colormapped or index-color images, use the PLTE chunk and are supported in four pixel depths: 1, 2, 4, and 8 bits, corresponding to a maximum of 2, 4, 16, or 256 palette entries. Unlike GIF images, however, fewer than the maximum number of entries may be present. On the other hand, GIF does support pixel depths of 3, 5, 6, and 7 bits; 6-bit (64-color) images, in particular, are common on the World Wide Web.

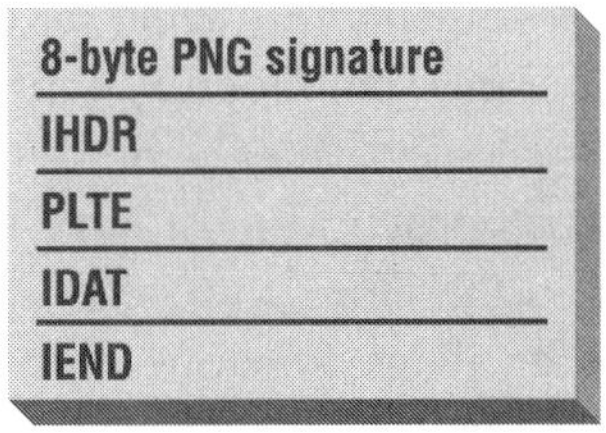

Figure 8-3: Layout of the second-simplest PNG

TIFF also supports palette images, but baseline TIFF allows only 4- and 8-bit pixel depths. Perhaps a more useful comparison is with the superset of baseline TIFF that is supported by Sam Leffler's free libtiff, which has become the software industry's unofficial standard for TIFF decoding. libtiff supports palette bit depths of 1, 2, 4, 8, and 16 bits. Unlike PNG and GIF, however, the TIFF palette always uses 16-bit integers for each red, green, and blue value, and as with GIF, all $2^{bit\ depth}$ entries must be present in the file. Nor is there any provision for compression of the palette data—so a 16-bit TIFF palette would require 384 KB all by itself.

Palette-Based with Transparency

The PNG spec forbids the use of a full alpha channel with palette-based images, but it does allow "cheap alpha" via the transparency chunk, tRNS. As its name implies—the first letter is lowercase—tRNS is an ancillary chunk, which means the image is still viewable even if the decoder somehow fails to recognize the chunk.[*] The structure of tRNS depends on the image type, but for palette-based images it is exactly analogous to the PLTE chunk. It may contain as many transparency entries as there are palette entries (more than that would not make any sense) or as few as one, and it must come after PLTE and before the first IDAT. In effect, it transforms the palette from an RGB lookup table to an RGBA table, which implies a potential factor-of-four savings in file size over a full 32-bit RGBA image. The icicle image used as a basis for Figure C-1 in the color insert is an RGBA-palette image; it is "only" 3.85 times smaller than the 32-bit original due to dithering (which hurts compression).

---

[*] Once again, the distinction between critical and ancillary chunks is largely irrelevant for chunks defined in the specification, since presumably they are known by all decoders. But even the names of standard chunks were chosen in accordance with the rules, as if they might be encountered by a particularly simple-minded PNG decoder. In fact, this was done in order to test the chunk-naming rules themselves: would a decoder that relied only on them behave sensibly? The answer was "yes."

By comparison, GIF supports only binary transparency, wherein a single palette color is marked as completely transparent, while all others are fully opaque. GIF has a tiny advantage in that the transparent entry can live anywhere in the palette, whereas a single PNG transparency entry should come first—all tRNS entries before the transparent one must exist and must have the value 255 (fully opaque), which would be redundant and therefore a waste of space. But the code necessary to rearrange the palette so that all non-opaque entries come before any opaque ones is simple to write, and the benefits of PNG's more flexible transparency scheme far outweigh this minor drawback.

The TIFF format supports at least three kinds of transparency information, two involving an interleaved alpha channel (*extra samples*) and the third involving a completely separate subimage (or *subfile*) that is used as a bilevel transparency mask. Baseline TIFF does not require support for any of them, but libtiff supports the two interleaved flavors directly, and could probably be manhandled into some level of support for the subfile approach, although the transparency mask is "typically at a higher resolution than the main image if the main image is grayscale or color," according to the TIFF 6.0 specification. On the other hand, with the possible exception of user-designed TIFF tags, there is no support at all for "cheap alpha," i.e., marking one or more palette entries as partially or completely transparent.

Grayscale

PNG grayscale images support the widest range of pixel depths of any image type. Depths of 1, 2, 4, 8, and 16 bits are supported, covering everything from simple black-and-white scans to full-depth medical and raw astronomical images.*

There is no direct comparison with GIF images, although it is certainly possible to store grayscale data in a palette image for both GIF and PNG. The only place a gray palette is commonly distinguished from a regular color one, however, is in VRML97 texture maps. Baseline TIFF images, on the other hand, support 1-bit "bilevel" and 4- and 8-bit grayscale depths. Nonbaseline TIFF allows arbitrary bit depths, but libtiff accepts only 1-, 2-, 4-, 8-, and 16-bit images. TIFF also supports an inverted grayscale, wherein 0 represents white and the maximum pixel value represents black.

The most common form of JPEG (the one that uses "lossy" compression, in which some information in the image is thrown away) likewise supports grayscale images

---

* Calibrated astronomical image data is usually stored as 32-bit or 64-bit floating-point values, and some raw data is represented as 32-bit integers. Neither format is directly supported by PNG, although one could, in principle, design an ancillary chunk to hold the proper conversion information. Conversion of data with more than 16 bits of dynamic range would be a lossy transformation, however—at least, barring the abuse of PNG's alpha channel or RGB capabilities.

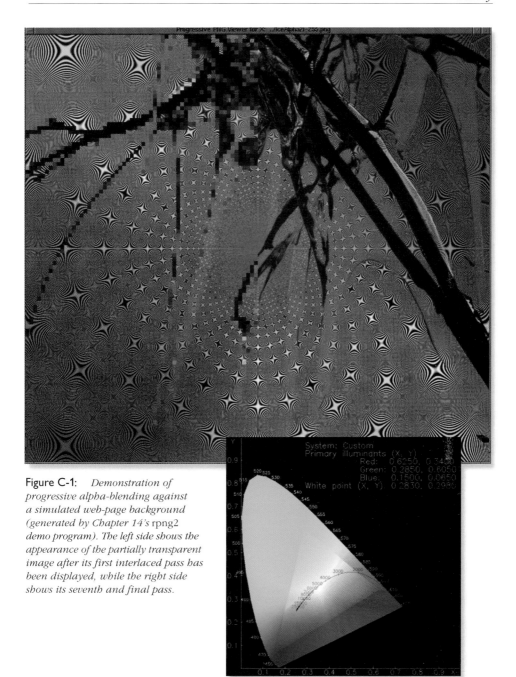

Figure C-1: *Demonstration of progressive alpha-blending against a simulated web-page background (generated by Chapter 14's* rpng2 *demo program). The left side shows the appearance of the partially transparent image after its first interlaced pass has been displayed, while the right side shows its seventh and final pass.*

Figure C-2: *Chromaticity diagram for a particular device (courtesy of Chris Lilley).*

Figure C-3: *Effects of JPEG compression on sharp-edged features. In the upper half, note the regions of darker blue, the lighter echos around the white text, and the faint pinkish areas (for example, in the curve of the "P"); the lower half has numerous dark echos around the text, bands of yellow above and below it, and very dark spots in some of the letters (particularly the "s"). Even at a very low quality setting (for emphasis), the JPEG is three times as big as the completely lossless PNG version.*

Figure C-4a: *Second pass (26%) of progressive JPEG, without smoothing by the decoder.*

Figure C-4b: *Second pass of progressive JPEG, with smoothing.*

Figure C-4c: *Fifth pass (40%) of progressive JPEG, with smoothing.*

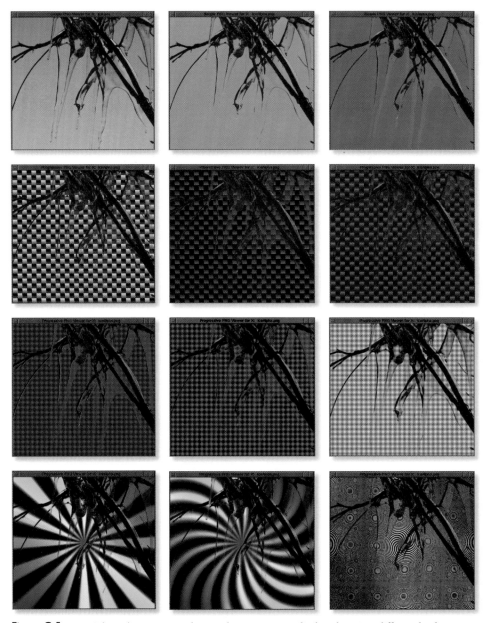

Figure C-5: *An 8-bit palette image with partial transparency, displayed against different backgrounds. The upper-left image is the original photograph (courtesy of Pieter van der Meulen), and to its right is the transparent version with its default background color; both are displayed by Chapter 13's simple* rpng *demo program. The upper-right image is the same thing with a different background color* (rpng-x -bgcolor #aa77ff IceAlpha.png). *The remaining three rows show some of the background patterns supported by Chapter 14's demo program,* rpng2. *(Subtlety was not one of our goals.)*

in depths of 8 and 12 bits. In addition, there are two variants that use truly lossless compression and support any depth from 2 to 16 bits: the traditional version, known simply as "lossless JPEG," and an upcoming second-generation flavor called "JPEG-LS."* But the first is extremely rare, and is supported by almost no one, despite having been standardized years ago, and the second is also currently unsupported (although that is to be expected for a new format). Lossy JPEG is very well supported, thanks largely to the Independent JPEG Group's free *libjpeg* (which, like libtiff, has become the de facto standard for JPEG encoding and decoding)—but, of course, it's lossy. Note that libjpeg can be compiled to support either 8-bit or 12-bit JPEG, but not both at the same time. Thus, from a practical standpoint, only 8-bit, lossy grayscale is supported.

Grayscale with Transparency

PNG supports two kinds of transparency with grayscale and RGB images. The first is a palette-style "cheap transparency," in which a single color or gray value is marked as being fully transparent. I noted earlier that the structure of tRNS depends on the image type; for grayscale images of any pixel depth, the chunk contains a 2-byte, unscaled gray value—that is, the maximum allowed value is still $2^{bit\ depth}-1$, even though it is stored as a 16-bit integer. This approach is very similar to GIF-style transparency in palette images and incurs only 14 bytes overhead in file size. There is no corresponding TIFF image type, and standard JPEG does not support any transparency.

Grayscale with Alpha Channel

The second kind of transparency supported by grayscale images is an alpha channel. This is a more expensive approach in terms of file size—for grayscale, it doubles the number of image bytes—but it allows the user much greater freedom in setting individual pixels to particular levels of partial transparency. Only 8-bit and 16-bit grayscale images may have an alpha channel, which must match the bit depth of the gray channel.

The full TIFF specification supports two kinds of interleaved "extra samples" for transparency: associated and unassociated alpha (though not at the same time). Unlike PNG, TIFF's alpha channel may be of a different bit depth from the main image data—in fact, every channel in a TIFF image may have an arbitrary depth. TIFF also offers the explicit possibility of treating a "subfile," or secondary image within the file, as a transparency mask, though such masks are only 1 bit deep, and therefore support only completely opaque or completely transparent pixels.

---

* Be aware that even at the highest quality settings, the common form of JPEG is never lossless, regardless of whether the setting claims 100% or something similar.

Baseline TIFF does not require support for any of this, however. Current versions of *libtiff* can read an interleaved alpha channel as generic "extra samples," but it is up to the application to interpret the samples correctly. The library does not support images with channels of different depths, and although it could be manipulated into reading a secondary grayscale subfile (which the application could interpret as a full alpha channel), that would be a user-defined extension—i.e., specific to the application and not supported by any other software.

As I just noted, standard JPEG (by which I mean the common JPEG File Interchange Format, or JFIF files) has no provision for transparency. The JPEG standard itself does allow extra channels, one of which could be treated as an alpha channel, but this would be fairly pointless. Not only would it require one to use a nonstandard, unsupported file format for storage, there would also tend to be visual artifacts, since lossy JPEG is not well suited to the types of alpha masks one typically finds (unless the mask's quality setting were boosted considerably, at a cost in file size). But see Chapter 12 for details on a MNG subformat called JNG that combines a lossy JPEG image in JFIF format with a PNG-style, lossless alpha channel.

RGB

RGB (truecolor) PNGs, like grayscale with alpha, are supported in only two depths: 8 and 16 bits per sample, corresponding to 24 and 48 bits per pixel. This is the image type most commonly used by image-editing applications like Adobe Photoshop. Note that pixels are stored in RGB order. (BGR is the other popular format, especially on Windows-based systems.)

Truecolor PNG images may also include a palette (PLTE) chunk, though the specialized suggested-palette (sPLT) chunk described in Chapter 11 is often more appropriate. But if present, the palette encodes a suggested set of colors to which the image may be quantized if the decoder cannot display in truecolor; the suggestion is presumed to be a *good* one, so decoders are encouraged to use it if they can. Of course, multi-image viewers such as web browsers often resort to a fixed palette for simplicity and rendering speed.

Baseline TIFF requires support only for 24-bit RGB, but libtiff supports 1, 2, 4, 8, and 16 bits per sample. Ordinary JPEG stores only 24-bit RGB,* though 36-bit RGB is possible with the seldom-supported 12-bit extension. The also seldom-supported lossless flavor of JPEG can, in theory, store any sample depth from 2 to 16 bits, thus 6 to 48 bits per RGB pixel.

---

* Technically, color JPEGs are almost always encoded internally in the YC_bC_r color space and converted to or from RGB by the decoder or encoder software.

RGB with Transparency

As mentioned previously, PNG supports cheap transparency in RGB images via the tRNS chunk. The format is similar to that for grayscale images, except now the chunk contains *three* unscaled, 16-bit values (red, green, and blue), and the corresponding RGB pixel is treated as fully transparent. This option adds only 18 bytes to the image, and there are no corresponding TIFF or JPEG image types.

RGB with Alpha Channel

Finally, we have truecolor images with an alpha channel, also known as the RGBA image type. As with RGB and gray+alpha, PNG supports 8 and 16 bits per sample for RGBA or 32 and 64 bits per pixel, respectively. Pixels are always stored in RGBA order, and the alpha channel is not premultiplied. ·

The use of PLTE for a suggested quantization palette is allowed here as well, but note that since the tRNS chunk is prohibited in RGBA images, the suggested palette can only encode a recommended quantization for the RGB data or for the RGBA data composited against the image's background color (see the discussion of bKGD in Chapter 11), not for the raw RGBA data. Disallowing tRNS is arguably an unnecessary restriction in the PNG specification; while a suggested RGBA palette would not necessarily be useful when compositing the image against a varied background (the different background pixel values would likely mix with the foreground pixels to form more than 256 colors), it would be helpful for cases where the background is a solid color. In fact, this restriction was recognized and addressed by an extension to the specification approved late in 1996: the suggested-palette chunk, sPLT, which is discussed in Chapter 11.

Although baseline TIFF does not require support for an alpha channel, libtiff supports RGBA images with 1, 2, 4, 8, or 16 bits per sample; both associated and unassociated alpha channels are supported. JPEG has no direct support for alpha transparency, but MNG offers a way around that (see Chapter 12).

Interlacing and Progressive Display

We'll wrap up our look at the basic elements of Portable Network Graphics images with a quick consideration of progressive rendering and interlacing. Most computer users these days are familiar with the World Wide Web and the method by which modern browsers present pages. As a rule, the textual part of a web page is displayed first, since it is transmitted as part of the page; then images are displayed, with each one rendered as it comes across the network. Ordinary images are simply painted from the top down, a few lines at a time; this is the most basic form of progressive display.

Some images, however, are in a format that allows them to be rendered as an overall, low-resolution image first, followed by one or more passes that refine it until the complete, full-resolution image is displayed. For GIF and PNG images this is known as *interlacing*. GIF's approach has four passes and is based on complete rows of the image, making it a one-dimensional method. First every eighth row is displayed; then every eighth row is displayed again, only this time offset by four rows from the initial pass. The third pass consists of every fourth row, and the final pass includes every other row (half of the image).

PNG's interlacing method, on the other hand, is a two-dimensional scheme with seven passes, known as the Adam7 method (after its inventor, Adam Costello). If one imagines the image being broken up into 8 × 8-pixel tiles, then the first pass consists of the upper left pixel in each tile—that is, every eighth pixel, both vertically and horizontally. The second pass also consists of every eighth pixel, but offset four pixels to the right.

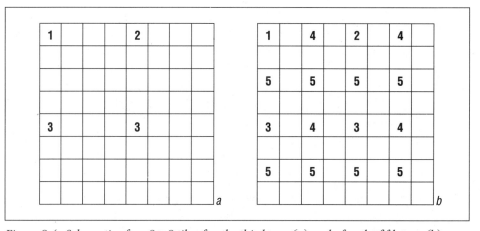

Figure 8-4: Schematic of an 8 × 8 tile after the third pass (a) and after the fifth pass (b)

The third pass consists of two pixels per tile, offset by four rows from the first two pixels (see Figure 8-4a). The fourth pass contains four pixels in each tile, offset two columns to the right of each of the first four pixels, and the fifth pass contains eight pixels, offset two rows downward (see Figure 8-4b). The sixth pass fills in the remaining pixels on the odd rows (if the image is numbered starting with row one), and the seventh pass contains all of the pixels for the even rows. Note that, although I've described the method in terms of 8 × 8 tiles, pixels for any given pass are stored as complete rows, not as tiled groups. For example, the fifth pass consists of every other pixel in the entire third row of the image, followed by every other pixel in the seventh row, and so on.

The primary benefit of PNG's two-dimensional interlacing over GIF's one-dimensional scheme is that one can view a crude approximation of the entire image roughly eight times as fast.* That is, PNG's first pass consists of one sixty-fourth of the image pixels, whereas GIF's first pass consists of one-eighth of the data. Suppose one were to save a palette image as both an interlaced GIF and an interlaced PNG. Assuming the compression ratio and download speeds were identical for the two files, the PNG image would have completed its fourth pass as the GIF image completed its first. But most browsers that support progressive display do so by replicating pixels to fill in the areas that haven't arrived yet. For the PNG image, that means each pixel at this stage represents a 2×4 block, whereas each GIF pixel represents a 1×8 strip. In other words, GIF pixels have an 8-to-1 aspect ratio, whereas PNG pixels are 2-to-1. At the end of the next pass for each format (GIF's second pass, PNG's fifth; one-quarter of the image in both cases), the PNG pixels are square 2×2 blocks, while the GIF pixels are still stretched, now as 1×4 strips. In practical terms, features in the PNG image—particularly embedded text—are much more recognizable than in the GIF image. In fact, readability testing suggests that text of any given size is legible roughly twice as fast with PNG's interlacing method.

JPEG also supports a form of progressive display, but it is not interlacing in the usual sense of reordering the pixels spatially. Rather, it involves reordering the frequency components that make up a JPEG image, first displaying the low-frequency ones and working up to the highest frequency band; this is known as *spectral selection*. In addition, progressive JPEG can transmit the most significant bits of each frequency component earlier than the less significant ones, a feature known as *successive approximation* that is very nearly the same as turning up the JPEG quality setting with each scan. The two approaches can be used separately, but in practice they are almost always used in combination. Because JPEG operates on 8×8 blocks of pixels, progressive JPEG bears a strong resemblance to interlaced PNG during the early stages of display, though it tends to have a softer, fuzzier look due to the initial lack of high-frequency components (which is often deliberately enhanced by smoothing in the decoder). This is visible in Figures C-4a and C-4b in the color insert, which represent the second pass of a progressive JPEG image (26% of the compressed data), both unsmoothed and smoothed. Note in particular the blockiness in the shadowed interior of the box and the "colored outside the lines" appearance around the child's arms and hands; the first effect is completely eliminated in the smoothed version, and the second is greatly reduced. JPEG's first pass is actually more accurate than PNG's, however, since the

---

* As I (foot)noted in Chapter 1, *An Introduction to PNG*, this implicitly assumes that one-eighth of the compressed data corresponds to one-eighth of the uncompressed (image) data, which is not quite accurate. The difference is likely to be small in most cases, however. I'll discuss this further in Chapter 9, *Compression and Filtering*.

low-frequency band for each 8 × 8 pixel block represents an average for all 64 pixels, whereas each 8 × 8 block in PNG's first pass is represented by a single pixel, usually in the upper left corner of the displayed block. By its fifth pass, which represents only 40% of the compressed data, the progressive JPEG version of this image (Figure C-4c) is noticeably sharper and more accurate than all but the final pass of the PNG version. Keep in mind also that, since the PNG is lossless and therefore 11 times as large as the JPEG, 40% of the compressed JPEG data is equivalent to only 3.5% of the PNG data, which corresponds to the beginning of PNG's third pass. This only emphasizes the point made previously: for non-transparent, photographic images on the Web, use JPEG.

Note that smoothing could be applied to the early passes of interlaced PNGs and GIFs, as well; tests suggest that this looks better for photographic images but maybe not as good for simple graphics. (On the other hand, recall that smoothing did seem to enhance the readability of early interlace passes in Figure 1-4.) As for representing blocks by the pixel in the upper left corner, it would be possible to replicate each pixel so that the original would lie roughly at the center of its clones, as long as some care were taken near the edges of the image. This would prevent the apparent shift in some features as later passes are displayed. But neither smoothing nor centered pixel replication is currently supported by the PNG reference library, *libpng*, as of version 1.0.3.

It is worth noting that TIFF can also support a kind of interlacing, although like everything about TIFF, it is much more arbitrary than either GIF's or PNG's method. Baseline TIFF includes the concept of *strips*, each of which may include one or more rows of image data though the number of rows per strip is constant. A list of offsets to each strip is embedded within the image, so in principle one could make each strip a row and do GIF-style line interlacing with any ordering one chose. But since TIFF's structure is fundamentally random access in nature, this approach would only work if one imposed certain restrictions on the locations of its internal directory, list of strip offsets, and actual strip data—that is, one would need to define a particular subformat of TIFF.

In addition, libtiff supports a TIFF extension called *tiles*, in which the image data is organized into rectangular regions instead of strips. Since the tile size can be arbitrary, one could define it to be 1 × 1 and then duplicate PNG's Adam7 interlacing scheme manually—or even extend it to 9, 11, or more passes. However, since every tile must have a corresponding offset in the TIFF image directory, doing something like this would at least double or triple the image size. Also, TIFF's compression methods apply only to individual strips or tiles, so there would be no real possibility of compression aside from reusing tiles in more than one location (that is, by having multiple tile offsets point at the same data). And, as with the strip approach, this would require restrictions on the internal layout of the file. Nevertheless, the capability does exist, at least theoretically.

9

Compression and Filtering

One of PNG's strengths, particularly in comparison to the GIF and TIFF image formats, is its compression. As I noted in Chapter 1, *An Introduction to PNG*, a primary motivation driving the design of the Portable Network Graphics format was to create a replacement for GIF that was not only free but also an improvement over it in essentially all respects. As a result, PNG compression is completely lossless—that is, the original image data can be reconstructed exactly, bit for bit—just as in GIF and most forms of TIFF.*

Filtering

We'll look at the compression engine itself shortly, but PNG's performance is not due solely to an improved compression algorithm. PNG also supports a precompression step called *filtering*. Filtering is a method of reversibly transforming the image data so that the main compression engine can operate more efficiently. As a simple example, consider a sequence of bytes increasing uniformly from 1 to 255. Since there is no repetition in the sequence, it compresses either very poorly or not at all. But a trivial modification of the sequence—namely, leaving the first byte alone but replacing each subsequent byte by the difference between it and its predecessor—transforms the sequence into an extremely compressible set of 255 identical bytes, each having the value 1.

As a real-life example of this (though still not particularly realistic), consider the image known as *16million.png*. This 24-bit, 512 × 32,768 RGB image contains one pixel of every possible color—more than 16 million of them altogether. As raw

---

* And as a corollary, PNG file sizes are usually considerably larger than ordinary JPEG, since the latter uses lossy compression—that is, it throws away some information. TIFF also supports JPEG compression as one of its many options, but the more common methods are lossless and based on either run-length encoding (RLE) or the same LZW algorithm used in GIF.

data, it therefore requires 48 MB to store. Simple PNG-style compression with no filtering brings it down to 36 MB, only a 25% reduction in size. But with filtering turned on, the same compression engine reduces it to 115,989 bytes, more than 300 times better than the nonfiltered case, for a total compression factor of 434!* *Zowie.*

Actual image data is rarely that perfect, but filtering does improve compression in grayscale and truecolor images, and it can help on some palette images as well. PNG supports five types of filters, and an encoder may choose to use a different filter for each row of pixels in the image. Table 9-1 lists the five filter types.

Table 9-1: PNG Filter Types

Name	Description
None	Each byte is unchanged.
Sub	Each byte is replaced with the difference between it and the "corresponding byte" to its left.
Up	Each byte is replaced with the difference between it and the byte above it (in the previous row, as it was before filtering).
Average	Each byte is replaced with the difference between it and the average of the corresponding bytes to its left and above it, truncating any fractional part.
Paeth	Each byte is replaced with the difference between it and the *Paeth predictor* of the corresponding bytes to its left, above it, and to its upper left.

The last method requires some explanation. Invented by Alan Paeth, the Paeth predictor is computed by first calculating a *base value*, equal to the sum of the corresponding bytes to the left and above, minus the byte to the upper left. (For example, the base value might equal 228 + 228 − 227 = 229.) Then the difference between the base value and each of the three corresponding bytes is calculated, and the byte that gave the smallest absolute difference—that is, the one that was closest to the base value—is used as the predictor and subtracted from the target byte to give the filtered value. In case of ties, the corresponding byte to the left has precedence as the predicted value, followed by the one directly above. Note that all calculations to produce the Paeth predictor are done using exact integer arithmetic. The final filter calculation, on the other hand, is done using base-256 modular arithmetic; this is true for all of the filter types.

Though the concept is simple, there are quite a few subtleties in the actual mechanics of filtering. Most important among these is that filtering always operates on bytes, not pixels. For images with pixels smaller than eight bits, this means that

---

* Actually, it gets even better. The dimensions of the image were chosen for convenient web-browser scrolling, but a 4096 × 4096 version created by Paul Schmidt is half the size—a mere 59,852 bytes (841 times compression). And just wait until we get to the chapter on MNG!

the filter algorithms actually operate on more than one pixel at a time; for example, in a 2-bit palette or grayscale image, there are four pixels per byte. This approach improves the efficiency of decoders by avoiding bit-level manipulations.

At the other end of the spectrum, large pixels (e.g., 24-bit RGB or 64-bit RGBA) are also operated on as bytes, but only *corresponding* bytes are compared. For any given byte, the corresponding byte to its left is the one offset by the number of bytes per pixel. This means that red bytes in a truecolor image are compared with red bytes, green with green, and blue with blue. If there's an alpha channel, the alpha bytes are always compared; if the sample depth is 16 bits, upper (most significant) bytes are compared with upper bytes in the same color channel, and lower bytes are compared with lower. In other words, similar values will always be compared and operated on, in hopes of improving compression efficiency. Consider an RGB image, for example; the red, green, and blue values of any given pixel may be quite different, but neighboring pairs of red, green, and blue will often be similar. Thus the transformed bytes will tend to be close to zero even if the original bytes weren't. This is the real point of filtering: most of the transformed bytes will cluster around zero, thus giving the compression engine a smaller, more predictable range of byte values to cope with.

What about edges? If the "corresponding byte" to the left or above doesn't exist, the algorithm does not wrap around and use bytes from the other side of the image; instead, it treats the missing byte as zero. The wraparound method was, in fact, considered, but aside from the fact that one cannot wrap the top edge of the image without completely breaking the ability to stream and progressively display a PNG image, the designers felt that only a few images would benefit (and minimally, at that), which did not justify the potential additional complexity.

Interlacing is also a bit of a wrench in the works. For the purposes of filtering, each interlace pass is treated as a separate image with its own width and height. For example, in a 256 × 256 interlaced image, the passes would be treated as seven smaller images with dimensions 32 × 32, 32 × 32, 64 × 32, 64 × 64, 128 × 64, 128 × 128, and 256 × 128, respectively.* This avoids the nasty problem of how to define corresponding bytes between rows of different widths.

So how does an encoder actually choose the proper filter for each row? Testing all possible combinations is clearly impossible: even a 20-row image would require testing over 95 trillion combinations, where "testing" would involve filtering and compressing the entire image. A simpler approach, though still computationally expensive, is to incrementally test-compress each row, save the smallest result, and

---

* Yes, that adds up to the right number of pixels. (Go ahead, add it up.) Note that things may not come out quite so cleanly in cases in which one or both image dimensions are not evenly divisible by eight; the width of each pass is rounded up, if necessary.

repeat for the next row. This amounts to filtering and compressing the entire image five times, which may be a reasonable trade-off for an image that will be transmitted and decoded many times.

But users often have barely enough patience to wait for a single round of compression, so the PNG development group has come up with a few rules of thumb (or heuristics) for choosing filters wisely. The first rule is that filters are rarely useful on palette images, so don't even bother with them. Note, however, that one has considerable freedom in choosing how to order entries in the palette itself, so it is possible that a particular method of ordering would actually result in image data that benefits significantly from filtering. No one has yet proven this, however, and the most likely approaches would involve doing statistics on every pair of pixels in the image. Such approaches would be quite expensive for larger images.

Filters are also rarely useful on low-bit-depth (grayscale) images, although there have been rare cases in which promoting such an image to 8 bits and then filtering has been effective. In general, however, filter type None is best.

For grayscale and truecolor images of 8 or more bits per sample, with or without alpha channels, dynamic filtering is almost always beneficial. The approach that has by now become standard is known as the *minimum sum of absolute differences* heuristic and was first proposed by Lee Daniel Crocker in February 1995. In this approach, the filtered bytes are treated as signed values—that is, any value over 127 is treated as negative; 128 becomes −128 and 255 becomes −1. The absolute value of each is then summed, and the filter type that produces the smallest sum is chosen. This approach effectively gives preference to sequences that are close to zero and therefore is biased against filter type None.

A related heuristic—still experimental at the time of this writing—is to use the *weighted* sum of absolute differences. The theory, to some extent based on empirical evidence, is that switching filters too often can have a deleterious effect on the main compression engine. A better approach might be to favor the most recently used filter even if its absolute sum of differences is slightly larger than that of other filters, in order to produce a more homogeneous data stream for the compressor—in effect, to allow short-term losses in return for long-term gains. The standard PNG library contains code to enable this heuristic, but a considerable amount of experimentation is yet to be done to determine the best combination of weighting factors, compression levels, and image types.

One can also imagine heuristics involving higher-order distance metrics (e.g., root-mean-square sums), sliding averages, and other statistical methods, but to date there has been little research in this area. Lossless compression is a necessity for many applications, but cutting-edge research in image compression tends to focus almost exclusively on lossy methods, since the payoff there is so much greater. Even within the lossless domain, preconditioning the data stream is likely to have less effect than changing the backend compression algorithm itself. So let's take a look at that next.

The Deflate Compression Algorithm

In some ways compression is responsible for the very existence of the Portable Network Graphics format (recall Chapter 1), and it is undoubtedly one of the most important components of PNG. The PNG specification defines a single compression method, the *deflate* algorithm, for all image types.

Part of the LZ77 class of compression algorithms, deflate was defined by PKWARE in 1991 as part of the 1.93a beta version of their PKZIP archiver. Independently implemented by Jean-loup Gailly and Mark Adler, first for Info-ZIP's Zip and UnZip utilities and shortly thereafter for the GNU *gzip* utility, the deflate algorithm is battle-tested and today is probably the most commonly used file-compression algorithm on the Internet. Although it is not the best-compressing algorithm known,* deflate has a very desirable mix of characteristics: high reliability, good compression, good encoding speed, excellent decoding speed, minimal overhead on incompressible data, and modest, well-defined memory footprints for both encoding and decoding.

As an LZ77-derived algorithm, deflate is fundamentally based on the concept of a *sliding window.* One begins with the premise that many types of interesting data, from binary computer instructions to source code to ordinary text to images, are repetitious to varying degrees. The basic idea of a sliding window is to imagine a window of some width immediately preceding the current position in the data stream (and therefore sliding along as the current position is updated), which one can use as a kind of dictionary to encode subsequent data. For example, if the text of this chapter is the data stream, then the current position at the very instant you read this is *here.* Preceding that point is a little more than 13,000 bytes of text, which includes, among other things, six copies of the fragment "or example" (whoa, there's another one!). Instead of encoding such strings as literal text, deflate replaces each with a pair of numbers indicating its length (in this case, 10 bytes) and the distance back to one of the previous instances (perhaps 950 bytes between the fifth and sixth). The greater the length of the string, the greater the savings in encoding it as a pointer into the window.

There are various ways to implement LZ77; the approach used by deflate is a "greedy" algorithm originally devised by James Storer and Thomas Szymanski—

---

* Arithmetic coding has been around for a long time and significantly outperforms deflate; the relatively recently published Burrows-Wheeler block transform coding (implemented in *bzip2,* for example) shows considerable promise as well; and the patented BitJazz condensation method is likewise quite impressive.

hence its name, LZSS. LZSS employs a look-ahead buffer and finds the longest match for the buffer within the sliding window. If the match exceeds a given threshold length, the string is encoded as a length/distance pair and the buffer is advanced a corresponding amount. If the longest match is *not* sufficiently long, the first character in the look-ahead buffer is output as a literal value, and the buffer is advanced by one. Either way, the algorithm continues by seeking the longest match for the new contents of the buffer.

The deflate algorithm is actually a bit more clever than the preceding description would suggest. Rather than simply storing the length/distance pairs and literal bytes as is, it further compresses the data by Huffman-encoding the LZ77 output. This approach is generically referred to as LZH; deflate's uniqueness lies in its method of combining literals and lengths into a single Huffman tree, its use of both fixed and dynamic Huffman codes, and its division of the output stream into blocks so that regions of incompressible data can be stored as is, rather than expanding significantly, as can happen with the LZW algorithm.

The PNG specification further dictates that the deflate data stream must conform to the zlib 1.0 format. In particular, the size of the sliding window must be a power of 2 between 256 bytes and 32 kilobytes, inclusive, and a small zlib header and trailer are required. The latter includes a 32-bit checksum on the *uncompressed* data; recall that the compressed stream is already covered by PNG's 32-bit CRC value in each IDAT chunk.

More detailed explanation of the deflate algorithm and the zlib data format is beyond the scope of this book, but the full zlib and deflate specifications are included in Appendixes D and E, respectively. In addition, a reference such as *The Data Compression Book*, by Mark Nelson and Jean-loup Gailly, is invaluable for understanding many compression algorithms, including LZ77 and LZSS.

Practically speaking, independent implementation of the deflate algorithm is both difficult and unnecessary. Almost every PNG implementation available today makes use of the freely available zlib compression library, and the examples in Part III, *Programming with PNG*, do so as well.* For now I merely note that zlib supports ten compression levels (including one with no compression at all), differing in the algorithms used to find matching strings and in the thresholds for terminating the search prematurely.

As an aside, note that the efficiency of the compression engine increases as more data is processed, with peak efficiency being reached when there is sufficient data to fill the sliding window. This occurs mainly because there are fewer strings

---

* Nevertheless, at least one alternative (in C++) is available as part of Colosseum Builders' Image Library, and it is also described in a book by John Miano, *The Programmer's Guide to Compressed Image Files.*

available in the "dictionary," but also, initially, because those strings that do exist are limited in length—obviously, they cannot be any longer than the amount of data in the window. Thus, for example, when 25% of the compressed data has been received, it may correspond to only 20% of the pixels. But because of data buffering in network protocols and applications, any large disparities due to the truly low-efficiency encoding at startup will tend to be washed out at the 512-byte level (or higher). That is, even though the first 50 bytes might represent only 1% compression, those bytes generally will not be available until after the 512th byte has been received, by which point the compression efficiency may have reached 10% or better. And since this is generally true of most compression algorithms, including those used by both GIF and PNG, it is reasonable to compare (as I did in Chapter 1) the appearance of the *uncompressed* pixels at an instant when equal amounts of *compressed* data have been received.

A Final Word on Patents

As mentioned at the end of Chapter 7, *History of the Portable Network Graphics Format*, Stac has reportedly claimed that the deflate algorithm is covered by two of their patents. In fact, there are a number of patents that *can* be infringed upon by a compliant deflate implementation, including one held by PKWARE itself that involves sorted hash tables. But the deflate specification includes a section on implementing the algorithm without infringing,* and, of course, zlib itself follows that prescription. While these things are never 100% certain unless and until they are tested in court, developers and users can be reasonably confident that the use of zlib and its implementation of the deflate algorithm is not subject to licensing fees.

Real-World Comparisons

The only convincing way to demonstrate the compression benefits of one image format over another is to do an actual comparison of the two on a set of real images. The problem is choosing the set of images—what works for one person may not work for another. What I've done here is to gather together results from a number of real-world tests performed over the past few years. Readers can expect to achieve similar results on similar sets of images, but keep in mind that one can always choose a *particular* set of images for which the results will be dramatically different. I'll explain that remark after we see a few cases.

---

* From Section 4 of the deflate specification, "Compression algorithm details": "...it is strongly recommended that the implementor of a compressor follow the general algorithm presented here,
  which is known not to be patented per se."

For starters, let's look at a small, very unscientifically chosen set of images: seven nonanimated GIF images that happened to be the only ones readily available on my machine one fine day in June 1998:

```
 38280 linux-penguins.gif
  1249 linux-tinypeng.gif
298529 linux_bigcrash.gif
 20224 linux_lgeorges.gif
  4584 linux_rasterman.gif
  1226 sun-tinylogo.gif
 27660 techweb-scsi-compare.gif
391752 TOTAL
```

The images ranged in size from just over a kilobyte to nearly 300 kilobytes (the exact byte sizes are given in the preceding list) and in dimension from 32 × 32 to 800 × 600. All but the first and last were interlaced. When converted to PNG with the gif2png utility (Chapter 5, *Applications: Image Converters*), preserving interlacing manually and introducing no new text annotations, things improved somewhat:

```
 35224 linux-penguins.png          -8.0%
   722 linux-tinypeng.png         -42.2%
283839 linux_bigcrash.png          -4.9%
 20476 linux_lgeorges.png          +1.2%
  4812 linux_rasterman.png         +5.0%
   566 sun-tinylogo.png           -53.8%
 20704 techweb-scsi-compare.png   -25.1%
366343 TOTAL                       -6.5%
```

Five of the images shrank when converted to PNG—three of them quite significantly—while two grew. Overall, the set achieved a 6.5% improvement in byte size. Since gif2png uses the standard settings of the libpng reference code,* its results may be considered typical of "good" PNG encoders. But the owner of a web site will often be willing to spend a little more time up front on compression in return for additional bandwidth savings in the long run. That's where pngcrush (also discussed in Chapter 5) comes in. Here are its results; the appended percentages are again relative to the original GIF file sizes:

```
 34546 linux-penguins.png          -9.8%
   710 linux-tinypeng.png         -43.2%
282948 linux_bigcrash.png          -5.2%
 19898 linux_lgeorges.png          -1.6%
  4731 linux_rasterman.png         +3.2%
   550 sun-tinylogo.png           -55.1%
 19155 techweb-scsi-compare.png   -30.7%
362538 TOTAL                       -7.5%
```

---

* libpng is discussed at length in Chapters 13, 14, and 15, which demonstrate how to use libpng to read and write PNG images.

So we see that the current state-of-the-art PNG encoder ekes out another percentage point in the total size, with all but one of the images now smaller than the original. That lone holdout is worth a closer look in this case. I already noted that *linux_rasterman.gif* was one of the interlaced images; suppose it had not been? The noninterlaced GIF version is 4,568 bytes, only 16 bytes smaller than the original. But the noninterlaced PNG version is either 4,067 bytes (gif2png) or 4,000 bytes (pngcrush)—a savings of 11.0% or 12.4% over the noninterlaced GIF. In other words, PNG's two-dimensional interlacing scheme can have a *significant negative impact on compression*, particularly for small images. This is an important point to consider when creating images: is interlacing really needed for a 152 × 96 image (as in this case) when the penalty is more than 18% of the file size?

This example may have been instructive, but seven images do not constitute a statistically valid sample.[*] So let's consider a few more data sets. One real-life example comes from the course entitled "Authoring Compelling and Efficient VRML 2.0 Worlds" at the VRML98 conference in Monterey, California. Though the content of the course was otherwise outstanding, one slide comparing image formats for 3D textures was rather alarming from a PNG perspective. It showed the following, together with the textures themselves (which are omitted here):

```
row 1:  ''linoleum1'' (128 × 128 grayscale)

    16008 linoleum1.png
    10956 linoleum1.jpg
     7055 linoleum1.gif

row 2:  ''doggie'' (128 × 256 color)

    89022 doggie.png
     9897 doggie.jpg
    24605 doggie.gif

row 3:  mixed

    26732 fog.png          (128 × 128 grayscale + alpha)
    15735 circlefade.png   (128 × 128 grayscale + alpha)
     4367 buttfly.gif      (128 × 128 color + transparency)
```

Even with no more details than are shown here, at least one problem is apparent: in row 2, the JPEG image is 24 bits deep, while the GIF is only 8 bits. Judging by the size of the corresponding PNG, one might assume (correctly) that the PNG is also 24 bits. So on the one hand, PNG is being compared with an image of the same depth that uses lossy compression, while on the other it is being compared with an image only one-third as deep, which also amounts to lossy compression. That hurts.

---

[*] That would be a small understatement.

As it turned out, there were other problems: the PNG images were created with an image editor not known for its compression capabilities, and some of the PNGs were interlaced even though their GIF counterparts were not. (And since this was a VRML course, I should note that no VRML browser in existence actually uses interlacing to render textures progressively, so there is generally no point in creating such images.) The upshot is that all of these factors—JPEG's lossy compression, mixing 24-bit and 8-bit images, mixing interlaced and noninterlaced images, and using a particularly poor encoder to compress the PNGs—worked against our favorite image format.

After evening the playing field by using the GIFs as the source images for the PNGs, turning off interlacing, and using a combination of conversion and encoding tools (including pngcrush), the results were considerably better for PNG, as shown in Table 9-2.

Table 9-2: PNG, GIF, and JPEG Comparison for VRML98 Course Images

Name	JPEG Size	GIF Size	Original PNG Size	Optimized PNG Size	PNG Change
linoleum1	10,956	7,055	16,008	**6,753**	−57.8%
doggie	9,897	24,605	89,022	**22,555**	−74.7%
fog	—	—	26,732	**16,221**	−39.3%
circlefade	—	—	15,735	**6,638**	−57.8%
buttfly	—	4,367	—	**3,965**	—

Here, I've marked the smallest version of each image in boldface type; the only one that isn't a PNG is the color JPEG, which is hardly surprising. What is interesting is that the grayscale JPEG (*linoleum1.jpg*) is larger than both the GIF and optimized PNG versions, despite the presumed benefits of lossy compression. There are at least three reasons for this. First, GIF and PNG both get an automatic factor-of-three savings from the fact that each pixel is only 1 byte deep instead of 3 bytes. Second, JPEG is at a relative disadvantage when dealing with grayscale images, because most of its compression benefits arise from how it treats the color components of an image. Third, this particular image is more artificial than natural, with quite a few relatively sharp features, which makes it particularly ill suited to JPEG-style compression.

But perhaps the most striking feature of Table 9-2 is just how poorly the original encoder did on its PNG images. Realizable savings of 40% to 75% are unusual, but thanks to poor encoding software, they are not as unusual as one might hope.

As another real example (but one that is perhaps more representative of what a typical web site might expect), the owner of *http://www.feynman.com* found that when he converted 54 nonanimated GIFs to PNGs, the collection grew in size from 270,431 bytes to 327,590 bytes. Insofar as all of the original images had depths of 8 bits or less—and even the worst PNG encoder will, on average, do as well or better than GIF on colormapped PNG images—the most likely explanation for the 21% increase in size is that the conversion utility produced 24-bit RGB PNGs. Indeed, the owner indicated that he had used ImageMagick's convert utility, older versions of which reportedly had the unfortunate habit of creating 24-bit PNGs unless explicitly given the `-depth 8` option. (This problem seems to have been fixed in more recent versions, however.) When the original GIFs were converted to PNG with gif2png instead, the total size dropped to 215,668 bytes, for a 20% overall savings over GIF. Individually, the GIFs were smaller in 15 of the 54 cases, but never by more than 340 bytes. Of the 39 images in which the PNG version was smaller, one-third of them differed by more than a kilobyte, and one was 14 KB smaller.

For the last GIF comparison, I downloaded the World Wide Web Consortium's icon collection, consisting of 448 noncorrupted GIF images. Of these, 43 had embedded text comments and 39 were interlaced. Most of the images were icon-sized (as would be expected), at 64 × 64 or smaller, but there were a handful of larger images, too. The total size of the files was 1,810,239 bytes. Conversion to PNG via *gif2png*, handling the interlaced and noninterlaced images separately in order to preserve their status, resulted in a total PNG size of 1,587,337 bytes, or a 12.3% reduction. Additional compression via pngcrush resulted in a total of 1,554,965 bytes, or a 14.1% reduction (relative to the GIF size). Out of the 448 images, PNG won the size comparison in 285 cases, lost in 161 cases, and tied in 2 cases. As in the previous test, however, the magnitude of the differences was the critical factor: GIF won by more than a kilobyte in only 1 case, while PNG won by that amount in 37 cases—4 of which were greater than 10 KB, 1 more than 64 KB. The average difference for the 285 cases in which PNG was smaller was 940 bytes; for the 161 GIF cases, it was a mere 78 bytes.

Finally, I've mentioned an upcoming JPEG standard for lossless compression a couple of times; it's worth a quick look, too. JPEG-LS, as the standard will be known,[*] is based on Hewlett-Packard's LOCO-I algorithm. As this is written, it is implemented in version 0.90 of HP's locoe encoder, available only in binary form for the HP-UX, Solaris, Irix, and 32-bit Windows platforms. (An independent implementation is available as C source code from the University of British Columbia.) In a comparison performed by Adam Costello, the HP encoder was tested against pnmtopng and pngcrush on the eight standard color images in the

---

[*] In December 1998 it became an ISO Draft International Standard, the final voting stage before becoming a full International Standard. It will officially be known as ISO/IEC 14495-1 upon approval. It has already been approved as International Telecommunication Union (ITU) Recommendation T.87.

Waterloo BragZone's ColorSet. pnmtopng is of interest only for speed reasons; even though it is moderately fast, locoe was considerably faster. I have omitted its size results from the comparison since, as expected, pngcrush outperformed it in all cases, though at a considerable cost in speed.

The results were fascinating. In the five test images categorized by the University of Waterloo as "natural," JPEG-LS beat PNG by between 5% and 11%—not a huge difference, but certainly significant. However, in the three images marked "artistic," PNG proved superior by wide margins, with one image more than three times smaller than the corresponding JPEG-LS version. These results are summarized in Table 9-3; once again, the byte size of the winning format for each image is highlighted in boldface type.

Table 9-3: PNG and JPEG-LS Comparison for Waterloo BragZone Color Images

Classification	Name	Total Pixels	JPEG-LS Size	PNG IDAT Size	Relative Difference
"natural"	lena	262,144	**445,799**	475,430	+6.6%
	monarch	393,216	**555,012**	615,260	+10.9%
	peppers	262,144	**385,047**	425,560	+10.5%
	sail	393,216	**767,374**	808,606	+5.4%
	tulips	393,216	**616,536**	680,881	+10.4%
"artistic"	clegg	716,320	653,299	**484,589**	−25.8%
	frymire	1,235,390	935,285	**251,865**	−73.1%
	serrano	499,426	293,532	**106,765**	−63.6%

Note that in the final column I used the JPEG-LS size as the reference, which effectively works against PNG—had I used PNG instead, the *frymire* image, for example, would show JPEG-LS as 271.3% larger, which looks much more impressive! Also note that I used the size of the PNG IDAT data for comparison rather than the actual PNG file size; this was done because locoe appears to encode raw JPEG data, with none of the overhead of standard JPEG file formats like JFIF and SPIFF.

In any case, the results are only slightly more statistically valid than the first comparison of GIF images was. Eight samples, even if they are a carefully chosen set of standard research images, cannot tell the full story. And results as intriguing as these certainly deserve more extensive testing, which will no doubt happen in due course.

Practical Compression Tips

I could hardly end this chapter without some practical pointers on optimizing PNG compression, both for users and for programmers. Herewith are some rough guidelines, arranged in descending order of effectiveness. Note that, as with any set of rules, there will always be exceptions.

Tips for Users

Following is a list of tips for users of PNG-supporting software:

Use the correct image format

If you have photographic images and their quality as JPEGs is acceptable, use JPEG! JPEG will almost always be smaller than PNG, especially for color images. Conversely, if you have images with just a few colors and/or sharp edges (such as text and simple graphics), JPEG is almost never the correct solution; use PNG or GIF instead. For binary transparency, also use PNG or GIF; for partial transparency or lossless RGB, use PNG or TIFF; for animations, use MNG or GIF.

Use the correct pixel depth

For example, don't convert a GIF (which, from a practical perspective, always has a depth of 8 bits or less) to a 24-bit PNG; that will automatically boost the file size by a factor of three. Similarly, if given the option, don't save a grayscale image as RGB; save it as grayscale or, at worst, as a palette-based PNG. Likewise, don't use a full alpha channel if single-color transparency (à la GIF) would suffice; it doubles the size of grayscale images and adds 33% to the size of RGB.

Corollary: Quantize and dither truecolor images to a palette if quality is acceptable

Likewise, quantize and dither RGBA or gray+alpha PNGs to a palette, if possible. This is something that only you, the user, can judge; no reasonable image application will ever quantize (which is a lossy transformation) unless instructed to do so by you. This is not an issue for GIF, which realistically supports *only* colormapped images (i.e., your choice of GIF as an output format amounts to an explicit instruction to quantize) nor is it an issue for JPEG, which supports only grayscale and truecolor. Only PNG supports colormapped, grayscale, and truecolor images, as well as alpha channels.

Use interlacing with care

Interlacing is a way to transmit the useful parts of an image more quickly, particularly on the Web, so that the end user can click on a hot-linked region before the image is fully downloaded, if she so chooses. But as I saw earlier, PNG's two-dimensional interlacing scheme can degrade compression by 15%

in some cases, especially for small images. Since small images are transmitted over the network fairly quickly anyway, they usually do not need to be interlaced.

Use the correct tools

In the first six chapters, I discussed a number of PNG-supporting applications and noted their limitations wherever possible; use that as a guide when choosing your tools, assuming you have a choice. Even if your program generally compresses PNG images well, consider using an optimizer such as pngcrush on everything when you're done;* definitely do so if your program is not known for its compression performance. For converting GIFs to PNGs, the dedicated gif2png is the most capable solution, even given its permanently beta version number; it preserves both transparency and embedded text comments.

Don't include unnecessary information

A lengthy copyright message or other text can add 100 bytes or more, which is a lot for icons and other small images.

Tips for Programmers

Following is a list of tips for programmers:

Use the correct pixel depth

Count colors! Or at least do so when the compression setting is "best" and you don't know that the image is grayscale—it doesn't take that long, and computers are good at that sort of thing. If there are 256 or fewer colors, write a colormapped image; doing so will translate to a factor-of-three savings in the PNG file size relative to an RGB image.

Use the correct pixel depth II

If the image is colormapped, don't assume that the pixels must be 8 bits deep. If there are only one or two colors, write a 1-bit image. If there are three or four colors, write a 2-bit image. If there are between 5 and 16 colors, write a 4-bit image. (These are the only useful cases for PNG.) The compression engine cannot compensate for bloated pixels! Choosing the correct depth for a palette-based image will reduce the file size by a factor of anywhere from two to eight relative to an 8-bit image.

Use grayscale if possible

If you know the image is gray, see if it can be written more compactly as a grayscale PNG than as a colormapped PNG—this is automatically true if there

---

* It is one of my favorite tools, in case that wasn't already apparent. As of April 1999, there are still a few optimization tricks it doesn't do, but its author is addressing those even as this is written.

are more than 16 shades of gray. Doing so will save up to 780 bytes by eliminating the palette. But don't assume that 16 or fewer shades automatically means the image can be written as 4-bit (or smaller) grayscale. Grayscale necessarily implies that the shades are evenly distributed from black to white. If, for example, the 16 shades are bunched up in one part of the gray spectrum, the image must be written as 8-bit grayscale or 4-bit palette-based. For larger images, the palette-based approach is almost certainly better; for small ones it depends, but the 8-bit grayscale case may end up being smaller. Try both, if possible; it's very fast for small images.

Set the compression and filtering options intelligently

For programs that use libpng (discussed at length in Part III), this is not a serious issue; it will automatically do the right thing if left to itself. But if you are writing custom PNG code, follow the guidelines in the PNG specification for matching filter strategies with image types. In particular, use filter type None for colormapped images and for grayscale images less than 8 bits deep. Use adaptive filtering (the "minimum sum of absolute differences" heuristic) for all other cases.

Truncate the palette

Unlike GIF, PNG's palette size is determined by the chunk size, so there is no need to include 256 entries if only 173 are used in the image. At 3 bytes per entry, wasted slots can make a big difference in icons and other small images.

Truncate the transparency chunk

It is extremely rare for every palette entry to be partially or fully transparent. If there are any opaque entries—in particular, if all but one are opaque—reorder the palette so that the opaque entries are at the end. The transparency entries corresponding to these opaque colors can then be omitted. The absolute worst possible approach is to put the single transparent entry at the *end* of the palette! Those 255 extra bytes are a lot for a file that would otherwise be 500 (or even 150) bytes long.

Do transparency intelligently

Understand how PNG's alpha channels and tRNS chunk work. If the alpha mask is binary (that is, either fully transparent or fully opaque), see if the transparent parts correspond to a single color or gray shade; if so, eliminate the alpha channel from the PNG file and use the tRNS chunk ("cheap transparency") instead. Alternatively, see if the total number of color+alpha combinations is 256 or fewer; if so, write a colormapped image with a tRNS chunk. If the user requests that an RGBA image be converted to indexed color, do so intelligently. The combination of PNG's PLTE and tRNS chunks amounts to a palette whose entries are RGBA values. The exact same algorithms that quantize and dither a 24-bit RGB image down to an 8-bit palette-based image can be used to quantize and dither a 32-bit RGBA or 16-bit grayscale+alpha image down to an 8-bit RGBA palette. In particular, you cannot treat color values and transparency values as if they are separate, unrelated entities; attempting to partition the palette into a "color part" and a "transparent part" makes no more sense than attempting to partition a standard RGB palette into red, green, and blue parts. If you do cheap transparency poorly, the user will be forced to use a full alpha channel, quadrupling her file size. For grayscale, an alpha channel "merely" doubles the size. Note that the icicle image in Figure C-1 in the color insert is actually colormapped. Aside from the garish background—which was actually generated by the viewing application—the full-resolution half looks pretty darned good, doesn't it?

Don't include unnecessary chunks in small images

Gamma information (or the sRGB chunk) is always good, but a full ICC profile may quadruple the size of a small image file. Consider not including a Software text chunk or tIME chunk, or do so only for images larger than, say, 100 × 100 pixels. Include dots-per-inch information (pHYs chunk) only if it is actually relevant to the image; but the user may be the only one who can make that call.

Offer the user reasonable options

Don't overwhelm him with unnecessary detail about filters or other technical jargon. For example, offer a simple checkbox to turn on interlacing. Offer a simple dial or even just two or three choices for compression level—*fastest*, *typical*, and *best*, perhaps. Even though it will make the file bigger, offer to include at least a few text annotations—Author, Title, Description, and/or Copyright, for example. On the other hand, offer to omit certain optional information, such as that described in the previous item.

Warn the user about data loss

If a region is completely transparent, don't zero out the underlying color pixels in order to improve compression unless you've notified the user in some way. Make sure she understands that quantization and dithering are lossy transformations, but don't make this an overly scary issue.

10

Gamma Correction and Precision Color

Anyone who has transferred images between a PC and a Macintosh—or even simply viewed on one platform an image created on another—has probably noticed one of the little gotchas of the computer world: images don't look the same on all systems. Images created on Macs tend to look too dark on PCs; images created on PCs tend to look too bright and washed out on Macs. A pure yellow on one machine may have an orange or greenish tint on another. Even on a single machine there are usually obvious changes in brightness and color as the monitor (CRT) warms up, not to mention when the user adjusts the screen controls. And in the absence of tedious calibration procedures and high-end color-conversion software, what comes out of the printer is, at best, only a vague approximation of what the screen shows.

PNG certainly doesn't solve all of these problems, but it does provide image authors with the means to minimize many of them, as long as the editing and viewing software is written properly. As recently proposed standards are approved and implemented in hardware, from graphics cards, to monitors, to printers and scanners, there is reason to expect that platform-independent color will become the norm, not the exception, in the new millennium.

Transfer Functions and Gamma

To understand the solutions, one must first become acquainted with the problems. I won't attempt to cover the subject in detail; an entire book could be written on it—and, indeed, Charles Poynton has done just that. But I will give a brief overview of the main issues and explain how some of the features of the Portable Network Graphics format fit into the picture. I may even mention some physics and an equation or three, but you shouldn't need a technical degree to be able to understand the basic ideas.

The ultimate goal of the entire process is for the light that leaves your monitor to produce the same *perception* as the light that originally entered the camera would have if it had entered your eyeballs instead. Alternatively, for images created with an image-editing application, the goal is for your display to produce the same perception (and basically the same light) as the artist's monitor produced while he was creating the image. Clearly this involves both the encoding process performed by the editor or conversion program that writes the image file, and the decoding process, perfromed by the viewer or browser that reads and displays the image, as well as aspects of human physiology and psychology. We'll refer to the combination of the encoding and decoding processes as the *end-to-end* process. PNG's role is to provide a way to store not only the image samples, that is, the color components of each pixel but also the information needed to relate those samples to the desired output of the display. A decoder that has both that information and knowledge of how the user's display system behaves can then deduce how the image samples must be transformed in order to produce the correct output.

Storing the image samples themselves is easy. The tricky part is figuring out the two additional pieces of critical information: when encoding, how the original light is related to the samples, and when decoding, how image samples are related to the display's actual output (i.e., the reproduced light). The fundamental problem is that working with and storing light is nearly impossible; instead, light is typically converted to electrical signals. Indeed, there are several more conversions along the way, each of which potentially modifies the data in some way.

As a concrete example, in an image captured via a video or electronic camera, light entering the camera is first converted to analog voltages, which are in turn converted to other voltages representing digital ones and zeros. These are stored in an image file as magnetic fields on a hard disk or as tiny pits on a CD-ROM. For display, the digital data in the file is optionally modified by the viewing application (this is where gamma correction and other tweaking is performed), then possibly converted again according to a lookup table (LUT), then generally converted by a graphics card ("frame buffer") back to an analog electrical signal.* This analog signal is then converted by the monitor's electronics into a directed beam of electrons that excites various phosphors at the front of the monitor and thereby is converted back into light. Clearly, there is a bit of complexity here (no pun intended).

But all is not lost! One can simplify this model in several ways. For example, conversions from analog to digital and from digital to analog are well behaved—they

---

* Early PC graphics cards (the "CGA" and "EGA" adapters, for example) communicated with the monitor digitally. Ironically, the burgeoning popularity of flat-panel displays and digital television is driving manufacturers back to using digital links between the frame buffer and display. As of early 1999, the standards and products were rare to nonexistent, but they're coming.

introduce minimal artifacts—so they can be ignored. Likewise, the detailed physics of the monitor's operation, from electrical signal to high-voltage electric fields to electrons to light, also can be ignored; instead, the monitor can be treated as a black box that converts an electrical signal to light in a well-defined way. But the greatest simplification is yet to come. Each of the conversions that remain, in the camera, lookup table, and monitor, is represented mathematically by something called a *transfer function*. A transfer function is nothing more than a way to describe the relationship between what comes out of the conversion and what went into it, and it can be a fairly complex little beastie. The amazing thing is that each of the preceding conversions can almost always be approximated rather well by a very simple transfer function:

```
output = input^exponent
```

where the output and input values are scaled to the range between 0 and 1. The two scaling factors may be different, even if "input" and "output" both refer to light; for example, monitors are physically incapable of reproducing the brightness of actual daylight. Even better, since the output of one conversion is the input to the next, these transfer functions combine in a truly simple fashion:

```
final output = ((input^exponent1)^exponent2)^exponent3
             = input^exponent1*exponent2*exponent3
```

This example happens to use three transfer functions, but the relation holds for any number of them. And the best part of all is that our ultimate goal, to have the final, reproduced output light be perceived the same as the original input light, is equivalent to the following trivial equation:

```
exponent1*exponent2*exponent3 = constant
```

Or in English: all of the exponents, when multiplied together, must equal a single, constant number. The value of the constant depends on the environments in which the image is captured and viewed, but for movies and slides projected in a dark room, it is usually around 1.5, and for video images shown in typical television or computer environments, it is usually about 1.14. Since the viewing application has the freedom to insert its own conversion with its own exponent, it could, in principle, ensure that the equation holds—if it knew what all the remaining exponents were. But in general, it lacks that knowledge. We'll come back to that in a moment.

In practice, images may be created with any number of tools: an electronic camera; the combination of a classic film-based camera, commercial developing process, and electronic scanner; an image-editing application; or even a completely artificial source such as a ray-tracing program, VRML browser, or fractal generator. To a viewing application, a file is a file; there is rarely any obvious clue as to the true origins of the image. In other words, the decoder can have no reasonable expectation of divining any of the transfer functions that came before the image data was saved to a file, even if it asks the user for help. The decoder's sole concern must therefore be the conversion of samples in the image file to the desired output on the display.

We'll come back and deal with encoders in a little while. For a decoder there are only two cases: either the file contains the additional information about how the samples are related to the desired output, or it doesn't. In the latter case, the decoder is no worse off than it would have been when dealing with a GIF or JPEG image; it can only make a guess about the proper conversion, which in most cases means it does nothing special.

But the case in which the file does contain conversion information is where things finally get interesting. Many types of conversion information are possible, but the simplest is a single number that is usually referred to as *gamma*. Gamma is a Greek letter (γ) that traditionally represents the exponent in the first equation I gave; the only problem is that, as we've seen, there are several exponents in the end-to-end process, and different people use the term "gamma" to mean different things. I will use "gamma" to refer to the exponent relating the image data and the desired display output. Not surprisingly, this is how PNG's gAMA chunk defines gamma, too.*

The gAMA Chunk

PNG's gAMA chunk basically says: if your overall display system's exponent (generally a combination of the system LUT exponent and the monitor or CRT exponent) is the same as the inverse of this gamma value, then the samples in the file are ready to go and need no further correction.† If not, the decoding correction can be computed from the product of the overall display-system exponent and the stored gamma value.

More precisely (and here we get into a bit of mathematics that will mainly be of interest to application developers), the stored gamma value represents the following relationship between the image samples and the desired output light intensity:

```
image_sample = light_outgamma
```

---

* Version 1.0 of the PNG specification discussed gamma in terms of the end-to-end transfer function from source to final display. This was deemed impractical and not necessarily indicative of real-world practice, so version 1.1 of the specification clarified all of the gamma-related discussion and reserved the actual term "gamma" solely for the usage described here.

† Practically speaking, values that are within about 5% of each other may be considered "the same."

or:

$$\texttt{image\_sample}^{1 / \texttt{gamma}} = \texttt{light\_out}$$

Once again, bear in mind that `light_out` and `image_sample` are scaled to the interval between 0 and 1; that is, if the sample depth is 8 bits, the file samples range between 0 and 255, so `image_sample` is obtained by dividing a given file sample by 255, in floating-point arithmetic.

The decoding pipeline is represented by this expression:

$$\texttt{image\_sample}^{\texttt{decoding\_exponent * LUT\_exponent * CRT\_exponent}} = \texttt{light\_out}$$

The `decoding_exponent` is simply the gamma correction that the application applies; the combination of the other two exponents is the "overall display system's exponent," to use the language with which we began this section. Notice that the preceding equation and the one before it are very similar—in fact, they imply the following relationship between the exponents:

```
(1 / gamma) = decoding_exponent * LUT_exponent * CRT_exponent
```

or, equivalently:

```
decoding_exponent = 1 / (gamma * LUT_exponent * CRT_exponent)
```

The gamma relationship given in English at the beginning of this section simply says that if the product on the right side of this equation equals one (which means `decoding_exponent` also equals one), then no further conversion is necessary—the image samples are ready to go as is. On the other hand, if the right-hand side of the equation differs from one, then that value is `decoding_exponent` and is what the decoder uses to correct the image samples before sending them to the display system:

$$\texttt{display\_input} = \texttt{image\_sample}^{\texttt{decoding\_exponent}}$$

Note that this procedure applies to each red, green, and blue value in a truecolor image or to each palette value in a colormapped PNG. But it does not apply to transparency values in an image with an alpha channel or a tRNS chunk; alpha samples are always assumed to be linear. Implementors should also be aware that there is no need to perform a computationally expensive exponentiation for every pixel in the image, or three times per pixel for an RGB image!. At most, there are only 65,536 possible sample values (for a 16-bit grayscale or 48-bit RGB image) and usually no more than 256, which means that gamma correction can be accomplished via a simple lookup table computed when the gAMA chunk is read.

That brings us to the gAMA chunk itself. Its contents are quite simple: a 4-byte, unsigned integer equal to gamma multiplied by 100,000 and rounded to the nearest integer. So if gamma is 1/2.2 (or 0.45454545 . . .), the value in the gAMA chunk is 45,455. There can be only one gAMA chunk, and it must appear before any IDATs and also before the PLTE chunk, if one is present.

As a practical matter, there is one more piece to the decoder half of the gamma puzzle. The issue of exponents for the lookup table and monitor on various systems is more complex than it should be, mainly because different systems use the term "gamma" in strange and sometimes sneaky ways. Table 10-1 summarizes the issue for some common platforms.

Table 10-1: Gamma Comparison Across Common Platforms

Platform	LUT_exponent	Default LUT_exponent	CRT_exponent	Default gAMA
PC	1.0	1.0	2.2	45,455
Macintosh	g/2.61	1.8/2.61	2.2	65,909
SGI	1/g	1/1.7	2.2	77,273
NeXT	1/g	1/2.2	2.2	100,000

The key thing to note, aside from the differences in default gAMA values across platforms, is that both Mac OS and SGI Irix allow the user to modify a "system gamma" setting that not only differs from the gamma definition we're using but also differs between platforms. These "gamma" values modify the lookup table, and SGI's is straightforward: *LUT_exponent* is simply the inverse of the SGI "gamma" value, which is denoted *g* in Table 10-1. (NeXT workstations use the same convention as SGI, but the only way to modify their setting is with third-party utilities.) The Macintosh, on the other hand, not only defines its "gamma" as directly proportional to *LUT_exponent* but also divides it by a constant factor (2.61). Thus, while the default Macintosh "gamma" of 1.8 appears close to SGI's default of 1.7, the actual lookup table exponents corresponding to these defaults are 1.8/2.61 and 1/1.7, respectively.

Encoding Gamma

That wraps up gamma correction on the decoding side of things, but what about encoders? After all, they must put the proper information into the PNG file in the first place, so that decoders can do their job correctly. The issue is more complex than for decoders, and not only because there are so many ways to generate an image. Consider the process of creating an image in an editor, which might seem the most straightforward case since it involves, in some sense, exactly the opposite procedure from that employed by the decoder. That is, the artist manipulates the image so that the displayed output has the desired appearance, then saves the result in a file with the proper gamma. Ordinarily, the editing application would simply write a gamma value that corresponds to the artist's display system. But if the image in question originated on another system, some editors will actually preserve its gamma setting by using a `decoding_exponent` for all manipulations on the artist's system—just as a normal viewer would. Thus the artist sees an image displayed in her own "gamma space," but the underlying image samples actually remain in the gamma space of the original system.

The case of an electronic camera that writes image files directly turns out to be the simplest possibility; as noted earlier, the camera has its own transfer function and exponent, and the camera's manufacturer should know precisely what that exponent is. When the camera saves an image, whether in PNG format or something else, the proper gamma value is simply the one that will make the end-to-end product of exponents equal to the correct constant—which, you'll recall, is around 1.14 in the case of images captured in a TV studio environment and intended for display on a computer system. But even under different lighting conditions, the camera knows what the conditions are and can correct for them accordingly, perhaps via preset gamma settings for half a dozen situations, for example: dimly lit, flash-illuminated, studio lighting, sunny day (high contrast), bright cloudy day (lower contrast), and so on.

For images captured with a traditional camera and scanned from a print, the issue is slightly fuzzier. If the scanner writes directly to an image file with no user control of brightness and contrast, the case is exactly analogous to that of the electronic camera: the scanner manufacturer knows what its transfer function is and can encode the proper gamma value in the file. But most scanners operate in conjunction with editing software that allows the user to tweak not only gamma-related settings but also color balance and saturation; this case is more like the first one considered (regardless of whether the user considers himself an "artist").

Ironically, images that are generated completely artificially are the most complicated case. Most calculations on artificial scenes, including those for VRML and ray-traced worlds, are done with "linear lighting" that would correspond to a gamma of 1.0. But in creating the scene, the artist usually makes adjustments based on how it displays on her system, and if she happens to use a viewer that performs no gamma correction, her feedback to the software that generates the images will be skewed—in effect, she will modify the colors, textures, lighting, and so forth, so that the gamma value corresponds to her display system. The solution, of course, is to use only software that supports gamma correction, both for generating the images and for viewing them.

Gamma Gotchas

Finally, as a prelude to the following sections, I'll note a few caveats. First, although I've referred to cathode-ray tube monitors (or CRTs) throughout the discussion so far, not all computers use them; in fact, notebook computers have long used liquid crystal displays, and LCDs are becoming increasingly popular on desktop systems as lightweight and space-saving alternatives to traditional monitors. Do the simple exponential (or power-law) transfer functions used earlier apply to LCDs as well? Yes, they do, but I need to qualify that answer. Raw LCDs are actually characterized by an S-shaped transfer function technically referred to as "sigmoid", for which the best exponential fit would have an exponent of 1.0. This is a lousy approximation, but fortunately, all real-world LCDs have corrective circuitry built in that makes them behave like monitors. So it is safe to use the same exponential transfer functions we discussed earlier. If the extra circuitry did *not* exist, the only reasonable-looking alternative would require support from both the encoding and decoding software. Specifically, an image editor running on an uncorrected LCD would need to include with the image a full International Color Consortium profile, which we'll discuss at the end of this chapter, and the decoder would in turn need to use it to correct the image on other display systems. Alternatively, the editor could precorrect the image samples to correspond to a normal CRT and include only gamma information, but this would be a lossy transformation of the image data.

A second caveat is that even when a monitor is the primary display device, other output devices such as grayscale or color printers are often used as well. Because of the vast differences in physics and technology between an image reproduced by emitting light directly from a monitor versus one reproduced as light reflected from printed paper, gamma correction is often of lesser relative importance than color correction. A full color management system may no longer be merely desirable but actually necessary. On the other hand, printers are sometimes calibrated to work properly with the local display, so an image that is gamma-corrected to look good on the monitor will also print properly.

A third caveat is that monitors are not perfectly described by exponential transfer functions, either. A better approximation is a combination of a linear function near zero and an exponential function elsewhere. But a simple exponential works well enough for most purposes.

The last thing to note is that even experts do not always agree, and the issue of what exponent to use to describe CRTs is one of those areas of disagreement. We've used 2.2 in the preceding discussion; that's the value used in the sRGB specification (more on that later) and the consensus of the color experts in the PNG Group. It is also the value used by manufacturers of professional, calibrated display equipment, such as Sony and Barco. On the other hand, Charles Poynton, one of the Web's leading color experts and the author of a number of technical papers and books, steadfastly maintains that 2.5 is more correct. At the time of this writing, things seem to be at an impasse, but there is hope for resolution as further test results become available in 1999.

In the meantime, Michael H. Brill has taken the initiative and written a poem that not only summarizes the gamma disagreement rather nicely but also does so with enviable wit and succinctness. It rhymes, too. The poem is entitled "Gamma and Its Bases" and may be found on Charles Poynton's web site: *http://home.inforamp. net/~poynton/notes/misc/Gamma_poem.html.*

Chromaticity

Adjusting the overall brightness of an image via gamma correction is a good first step, but it does not address the issue of color balance. Anyone who has visited a typical consumer electronics store has probably noticed that not every model on the wall of televisions displays the same way. Some may have a reddish tinge, some green; some usually display very bright, saturated colors, while others may opt for slightly paler but more realistic hues. Although one rarely sees a corresponding wall of computer monitors and LCDs all displaying the same image, there are similar differences between various manufacturers' models and even between monitors in the same production run.

The main contribution to such variations comes from the manufacturers' choices of light-emitting chemicals (phosphors) in monitors and of filters used in liquid crystal displays. In addition, some higher-end monitors (and all color TVs) allow one to adjust the color balance manually in one or more ways. The details are not particularly important; what matters is that there are differences—or to put it another way, the RGB color space is *device-dependent.* Understanding how one quantifies and corrects for these differences is most easily accomplished via a diagram.

Figure C-2 in the color insert, reproduced in grayscale as Figure 10-1, shows an interestingly shaped color blob with a numbered curve and a brighter triangle embedded in it and some numbers around its curved edge. The blob represents the complete range of hues and saturation levels that the human eye can discern; a true spectrum would wrap around the numbered edge* (albeit without the cyan region near the upper left). The middle is composed of smoothly interpolated mixtures, including "white." The numbers on the axes give the x and y values of each hue and are directly related to the International Commission on Illumination's (CIE, for Commission Internationale de l'Éclairage) XYZ color space, a standard

---

* The numbers give the wavelength (in nanometers) of the spectral colors along the edge. Visible light lies within the range 400 nm to 700 nm, roughly.

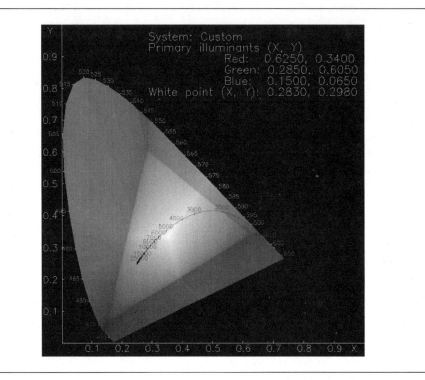

Figure 10-1: Grayscale version of typical chromaticity diagram.

and device-*independent* color space for well over half a century. We'll come back
to that shortly.

The brighter triangle in the middle represents the colors that can be displayed by a
particular monitor (not including any brightness information) and is known as the
color gamut of the display. The corners of the triangle give the maximum-intensity
red, green, and blue hues; these directly correspond to the physical characteristics
of the phosphors used in the display. LCDs, printers, color film, and even textile
dyes have similar gamuts, though not always triangular. Perhaps the most striking
feature is the fact that the monitor's gamut covers less than half of the complete
color range. In other words, there are many colors that the human eye can perceive but that cannot be correctly represented on a monitor. The fact that the chromaticity diagram can be displayed on a monitor at all means that the region
outside the triangle can be represented in *some* manner, just not the correct one.
This is the source of the cyan error noted previously.

Because the diagram has been projected down from a three-dimensional color
space (XYZ) to the two-dimensional *xy* plane, information about the *relative* intensities of red, green, and blue has been lost. That is, the *x,y* values for the red

phosphor indicate what color it emits at any given intensity level and similarly for the green and blue phosphors. But we still need to know the relative intensities of the three phosphors when they are all at full power. This is where the concept of "white" comes in. In fact, there are many candidates for "white," from the warm, yellowish whites produced by incandescent lightbulbs to the cool, bluish whites of electrical arcs and lightning.* The curved line in the middle represents all possible values of "white" for a given monitor, only one of which will be displayed as such. The associated numbers along the curve refer to the "blackbody temperature" or color temperature of any given white value; among other things, a star whose surface (photosphere) is at the given temperature will emit light of the given color most strongly.† Our Sun's surface temperature is around 6,000 degrees Kelvin, for example; not coincidentally, this is the color temperature most humans associate with "average" or "true" white.

How does all of this relate to color correction in PNG? If the encoding software knows the locations of the three corners of the triangle (the *primary chromaticities*) and of *white point*, it can save these values in PNG's chromaticity chunk, cHRM. When the image is decoded on another system with a different color range, the decoder can convert the *x,y* chromaticity values of both systems into XYZ space, calculate any necessary adjustments between the two, and use that calculation to convert the RGB values of the image into XYZ space and then into the RGB space of the display system.

The simple way to deal with such conversions is to feed the information to a *color management system* (CMS), assuming one is present. All of the tricky details of conversion between different color spaces and of mapping different monitor gamuts are handled by the CMS. Color management systems are not yet in wide use on typical users' platforms, however; a decoding application that wishes to maintain optimal color fidelity will need to handle the conversions on its own. The calculations to do so are not terribly difficult, but they do involve a number of matrix operations. These are detailed in Appendix B of the University of Manchester's excellent tutorial, *Colour in Computer Graphics*, and also in the "Color Tutorial" section of the *PNG Specification, Version 1.1*.

The structure of cHRM is shown in Table 10-2.

---

* It is slightly odd that humans perceive redder light as "warm" and bluer light as "cool" when, in fact, the opposite is true. Lightning is far hotter than the filament in an incandescent bulb.

† Keep in mind that we are still talking about *human perception*. A blackbody emits a true continuum of light; a monitor emits a more limited continuum composed of three broad, overlapping curves—corresponding to the red, green, and blue phosphors. Humans perceive the monitor's "white" output to be the same as that of a blackbody at a particular temperature, but a spectrometer would say otherwise.

Table 10-2: cHRM Chunk

Field	Length and valid range
White point x	4 bytes (0–2,147,483,647)
White point y	4 bytes (0–2,147,483,647)
Red x	4 bytes (0–2,147,483,647)
Red y	4 bytes (0–2,147,483,647)
Green x	4 bytes (0–2,147,483,647)
Green y	4 bytes (0–2,147,483,647)
Blue x	4 bytes (0–2,147,483,647)
Blue y	4 bytes (0–2,147,483,647)

Each of the eight values is an unsigned long integer, equal to the actual floating-point value multiplied by 100,000 and rounded to the nearest integer. Like the gAMA chunk, cHRM must precede all IDAT chunks and, if present, PLTE; only one cHRM chunk is allowed.

Color Management Systems and sRGB

The popularity of the RGB color space is at odds with its fundamentally device-dependent nature. In order to address this problem, a number of manufacturers of computer-related equipment and the International Color Consortium have cooperated to define a *standard* RGB space to which various devices such as monitors, printers, scanners, and electronic cameras can be calibrated. This specification, known as sRGB, is expected to be approved as an international standard by the International Electrotechnical Commission (IEC) by mid-1999; it will formally be known as IEC 61966-2-1.

sRGB allows one to create a PNG image on one system and print or display it on another with full color fidelity and without ever converting to XYZ or another device-independent color space. How well it works in practice remains to be seen, but a well-specified international standard—and manufacturers' evident interest in it—will go a long way toward ensuring that future devices are compatible at the RGB level.

In addition, an image that was created under sRGB can be flagged as such with very little overhead. Only one parameter, the rendering intent, is required; it is stored as a single byte in PNG's sRGB chunk. The rendering intent, also known as "artistic intent," indicates how the creator of the image wishes the colors to be mapped when the output device's color gamut (recall the discussion in the previous section) does not match that of the original device. For example, imagine that an artist creates an image on an sRGB-compliant monitor and graphics system, and when he's finished he sends it to an sRGB-compliant color printer. Because the light-emitting phosphors of the monitor and the light-reflecting inks of the printer and its paper will be able to represent somewhat different ranges of colors—ideally, mostly overlapping, but conceivably with only a little overlap—it is necessary for the artist to specify how he wishes the different color gamuts of the devices to be mapped to each other.

The simplest rendering intent (in concept) is known as *absolute colorimetric*. The word "colorimetric" means color-measuring, and this intent indicates that, for the region of overlap between source and destination gamuts, any given pixel will be measured to have identical colors on the two devices. When the output device is not capable of reproducing some of the colors of the input device (i.e., the gamut is more restricted in that region of color space), the colors are clipped to the nearest color that can be reproduced. The result is that dynamic range will be lost in some areas. For example, suppose that the image has a smoothly varying blue gradient and that the output device is restricted to only the darker blues. The output will show a smoothly varying gradient progressing from darkest blue to medium blue, but then it will saturate and render all of the remaining gradient as a constant, medium blue. Likewise, the intensity range may be clipped if the output device is incapable of rendering absolute black or the brightest shades of white. This rendering intent might be used in cases in which three or more profiles are involved—for example, when an image created on a computer display is intended for a particular typesetter but first needs to be proofed on a local printer.

A similar intent is *relative colorimetric*. As with the absolute flavor, RGB values correspond to precise CIE color measurements, but they are modified according to the intensity range and color cast (i.e., the white point) of the output medium. Referring to our artist again, his monitor may be capable of displaying true, 5,000K CIE white, but the paper in his printer generally will not uniformly reflect all of the wavelengths that hit it, regardless of the source.* To put it another way, the paper will have a different white point than the monitor. As a result, it may be desirable to sacrifice perfect color correspondence in favor of a similar dynamic range in intensities, by referencing the RGB values to whatever paper or other output medium is used. The output image may have an overall lighter or darker appearance or an overall color shift, but there will be no clipping of grayscale gradients, and the colors will *appear* to match—thanks to the human visual system's tendency to acclimate to an overall tint or, to put it another way, to the "prevailing white". The relative colorimetric intent is the ICC's default; it might be desirable for displaying and printing corporate logos.

---

* And if he's silk-screening white T-shirts, no amount of bleach will change that. There are some detergents that infuse clothing with small amounts of phosphorescent chemicals in order to make "whites whiter"; one's clothes are no longer strictly reflective, but actually glow slightly when exposed to blue or ultraviolet light. Such detergents are generally not part of an sRGB-compliant display system.

A still more approximate intent, but one that may capture more of the personality of the original image, is the *perceptual* rendering intent. The idea in this case is to map the full color ranges of source and destination devices as well as possible. This may involve either expansion, compression, or shifting of the color gamut. Even colors within the region where the gamuts overlap may be modified; in other words, absolute color fidelity is less important than preserving the dynamic range in both color and intensity of the image. This is often the most appropriate intent for rendering photographs.

Finally we have the *saturation-preserving* rendering intent, which is similar to perceptual rendering in that it doesn't necessarily enforce completely accurate color reproduction. But rather than favor overall gamut mapping like the perceptual intent does, this rendering intent specifies that the saturation of each color should remain constant. Saturation can be thought of as the amount of gray in a color of a given hue (say, greenish-aqua) and lightness. As the saturation approaches zero, the color approaches gray; maximum saturation gives the purest shade of the given hue. Since a cheap inkjet printer might have only two-thirds of the saturation range of an expensive dye-sublimation printer, colorimetric rendering might induce another kind of clipping in the inkjet's output. Saturation-preserving rendering would avoid that, but could possibly result in changes in hue and/or lightness. It might be the preferred intent for printing business charts and graphs.

PNG's sRGB chunk encodes the rendering intent with the same values specified by the International Color Consortium for ICC profiles: that is, byte value 0 for perceptual, 1 for relative colorimetric, 2 for saturation-preserving, and 3 for absolute colorimetric.

Because the sRGB color space encompasses gamma and chromaticity information, it is not strictly necessary for a PNG image to include gAMA and cHRM chunks in addition to the sRGB chunk. But since not all applications will know how to interpret sRGB, encoders should nevertheless include a gAMA chunk that corresponds to sRGB, and possibly a cHRM chunk as well. Decoders that know how to deal with cHRM are likely to know how to deal with sRGB, too, which is why cHRM may be omitted. The proper values for the two chunks are in Table 10-3.

An sRGB-aware decoder should ignore gAMA and cHRM whenever an sRGB chunk is present; the latter takes precedence. Less sophisticated applications can use gAMA and cHRM to render the image approximately as intended, even without knowledge of the sRGB color space. But note that there is no excuse for any application written after the PNG 1.1 specification not to recognize sRGB, at least; it is now part of the core spec, and new applications should know what gamma and chromaticity values correspond to it, regardless of whether the corresponding chunks—or even conflicting chunks—are actually present in the file. As with gAMA and cHRM, only one sRGB chunk is allowed, and it must appear before any PLTE and IDAT chunks.

Table 10-3: sRGB Gamma and Chromaticity Values

gAMA	Image gamma	45,455
cHRM	White point x	31,270
	White point y	32,900
	Red x	64,000
	Red y	33,000
	Green x	30,000
	Green y	60,000
	Blue x	15,000
	Blue y	6,000

ICC Profiles

For ultimate control over color fidelity and issues of device dependence, PNG supports the ability to embed a full International Color Consortium profile via the iCCP chunk. The ICC profile format, at version 3.4 as of this writing, is a relatively mature specification that is itself headed toward ISO standardization. The format is capable of describing not only computer monitors, but also printers, scanners, liquid crystal displays, film, transparencies, and so forth.

Though the profile format itself is understandably quite complex, given all of the devices and color-space conversions it must encompass, the format of PNG's iCCP chunk is independent of all that. Similar to the zTXt chunk (which will be described in Chapter 11, *PNG Options and Extensions*), iCCP contains only four elements, as shown in Table 10-4: a printable name terminated by a null byte; a byte indicating the compression method; and the compressed profile itself.

Table 10-4: iCCP Chunk

Field	Length and Valid Range
Profile name	1–79 bytes (Latin-1 text)
Null separator	1 byte (0)
Compression method	1 byte
Compressed ICC profile	n bytes

The profile name is for the convenience of the artist or user of the image; in practice, it will probably be similar to the profile description tag, which is embedded in the profile itself. The compression method byte currently must be zero, indicating a compressed stream in zlib format, using the deflate compression method. As with zTXt and the actual image data, a future major revision of the PNG spec may define other compression methods, in which case this byte will be allowed to take on other values.

Aside from uncompressing it, ordinary decoders will not be expected to know anything about the ICC profile other than the fact that they can be large (i.e., more than 64 KB); instead, they will simply hand it off to the local color management system for appropriate processing. Encoders should ensure two things: that the profile is a valid ICC profile and that it refers either to an RGB color space (for color images, including colormapped ones) or to a grayscale color space. CMYK color spaces, for example, are disallowed. Likewise, multiple copies of iCCP are disallowed; if the iCCP chunk is present, it must come before any PLTE or IDAT chunks.

By mid-1998, there were indications that something of a "TIFF effect" applied to the ICC profile format; that is, profiles from different vendors were not necessarily interoperable with each other or with different color management systems.* Presumably this will be worked out by the time the ICC specification becomes an official standard, but in the meantime, it is something of which PNG implementors should be aware.

---

* This is hardly surprising for a format that attempts to deal with such a thorny problem.

11

PNG Options and Extensions

In addition to the core chunk types described thus far, the Portable Network Graphics format supports a whole host of optional chunks for various purposes, from text annotations to conversion information. These are described in the following sections, very roughly in order of importance to the average user.

Background Color (bKGD)

Status: PNG Specification
Location: After PLTE, before first IDAT
Multiple: No

In some applications, notably web browsers, there is a natural background surrounding all images, against which images can be composited with transparency information. But standalone image viewers typically have no preferred background color or pattern and usually default to black, which may not be appropriate for some images. PNG therefore supports the concept of a preferred background color that can be used if nothing better is available.

The bKGD chunk is used for this purpose. Just as with the transparency chunk, tRNS (see Chapter 8, *PNG Basics*), the format of bKGD depends on the image type. For palette-based images it contains a single byte, whose value is the palette index of the color to be used for the background. For grayscale images, with or without alpha, the chunk contains a 2-byte, unscaled gray value, just as with tRNS—that is, the maximum allowed value is $2^{bit\ depth}-1$, even though it is stored as a 16-bit integer. And for truecolor images, the background chunk is exactly analogous to the grayscale version except that it contains three 16-bit, unscaled values representing the red, green, and blue components of the background color. There is no requirement in any of the three cases that the background color be present in the actual image data.

Note that colored backgrounds are not supported in grayscale images; while this is certainly a restriction, it appears not to be a particularly serious one, to judge by the lack of public comment to date. Note also that the background color should always be considered fully opaque, even if it happens to match a color marked by the tRNS chunk as partly or fully transparent.

Timestamp (tIME)

Status: PNG Specification
Location: Anywhere*
Multiple: No

The timestamp chunk provides a way for the author (or image-editing software) to record the time and date the image was last modified. The chunk contains 7 bytes of data, shown in Table 11-1.

Table 11-1: tIME Chunk

Field	Length and Valid Range
Year	2 bytes (0–65,535)
Month	1 byte (1–12)
Day	1 byte (1–31)
Hour	1 byte (0–23)
Minute	1 byte (0–59)
Second	1 byte (0–60)

As this book is being written before the Third Millennium begins, the first thing to notice is that PNG is not merely Y2K-compliant, but also Y2038, Y10K, and pretty much everything else on up through Y65K.† In addition, note that the seconds field is permitted to vary between 0 and 60; this allows for leap seconds, of which there have been roughly two dozen since 1972. (There has never been more than one leap second in any given minute, however.)

On a less technical level, why does tIME store the modification time rather than creation time? On the face of it, creation time would seem like a more useful piece of information, and indeed, it is explicitly supported in PNG via the text chunks described later. But whereas modification time is a well-defined quantity—even a computer program can determine whether the image data has been modified— creation time is ambiguous. If a scanned photograph of the Mona Lisa is converted

---

* Chunks with no explicit restrictions ("anywhere") are nonetheless implicitly constrained to come after the PNG signature and IHDR chunk, before the IEND chunk, and not to fall between multiple IDAT chunks.

† Presumably humanity will have come up with another image format or two by then.

to PNG format, is its creation time the time of image conversion, the time of the original scan, the time the photograph was taken, or even the time the painting was created? The case becomes even muddier if an artist creates a digital work partly based on the scanned image. So creation time is supported via one or more text chunks, which can also describe in precisely what sense the image was created.

Latin-1 Text Annotations (tEXt, zTXt)

Status: PNG Specification
Location: Anywhere
Multiple: Yes

That brings us to PNG's original text chunks, which are perhaps its most popular nonessential chunks. Regardless of how many words a picture is worth, it is often useful or necessary to add a few more in order to record pertinent information like title and author, store requisite legal notices such as a copyright or disclaimer, or merely to transfer text from one image to another.

PNG supports two types of Latin-1-based text chunks, uncompressed (tEXt) and compressed (zTXt). There is also a new Unicode-based chunk (iTXt) that we'll discuss next. For the first two, the format is basically the same: an uncompressed keyword or key phrase, a null (zero) byte, and the actual text. In zTXt the text is compressed; the first byte after the null indicates the compression method, for which only deflate is currently defined (method zero). The remainder is the compressed stream, which for method zero must be in zlib 1.x format, just as for image data. (The zlib 1.x format is described by revision 3.3 of the zlib specification, which is available from *http://www.cdrom.com/pub/infozip/zlib/zlib_docs.html.*)

Both keyword and raw text should be encoded with the Latin-1 (ISO/IEC 8859-1) character set; neither may contain null bytes. Since the keyword is intended to be recognizable by both humans and computer programs, additional restrictions are placed on it: it may not contain leading, trailing, or consecutive spaces, and it is restricted to characters in the range 32–126 and 161–255 (which, in particular, rules out both control characters and the nonbreaking space, decimal value 160). The only other restriction on the main text of the chunk is that newlines should be in Unix format, i.e., represented by a single line-feed character (decimal value 10).

I mentioned in Chapter 7, *History of the Portable Network Graphics Format*, that the Unicode UTF-8 character set was one of the items in the design of PNG that was voted down. In retrospect this was, perhaps, a lamentable decision; it was finally addressed early in 1999 with the iTXt chunk. But at the time, UTF-8 was very new and had not been extensively tested in the field. In particular, it had little or no operating-system support and no support in standard programming libraries, either for encoding and decoding or for the translation and display of UTF-8 characters in the native character set(s) of existing systems. Since PNG's design goals included both the use of well-tested technologies and the avoidance of undue burdens on developers of PNG applications, support for UTF-8 was dropped in favor of the more familiar Latin-1 character set.

The following list summarizes all of the keywords that are either included in the specification itself or officially registered as extensions to the spec:

Author

> The name of the author of the image. If the original image were a painting or other nonelectronic medium, both the original artist and the person who scanned the image might be listed.

Title

> A one-line title or caption. Longer captions should generally use the Description keyword, but see the end of this section for an unofficial alternative.

Description

> A longer description of or caption for the image, perhaps including details about the tools and settings used; the name, age, and/or location of the subject matter; or the mood the artist was trying to convey. See also the Software and Source keywords.

Creation Time

> The time the image was created, in whatever sense is most appropriate. The recommended format is that prescribed by Internet RFC 822 (Section 5), as amended by RFC 1123 (Section 5.2.14); specifically:

```
day month year hour:minute timezone
```

> where **day** is either one or two digits; **month** is a three-letter English abbreviation such as **Jun**; **year** is two or four digits (though the latter is strongly recommended); **hour** and **minute** are two digits each; and **timezone** is either a three-letter abbreviation (e.g., PST for Pacific Standard Time), or a one-letter U.S. military designation, or a four-digit number with a leading positive or negative sign indicating the hour:minute offset from Coordinated Universal Time (e.g., −0800 for Pacific Standard Time, which is eight hours and zero minutes earlier than UTC). In addition, the entire string may optionally be preceded by a **weekday** field, where **weekday** is a three-letter English abbreviation (e.g., **Fri**). A colon and two-digit **seconds** field may also be appended to the time (that is, **hour:minute:second**). Note that this is merely a recommendation; strings such as "circa 1492" are allowed, as is explanatory text following an RFC-style date string.

Copyright

The legal copyright notice for the image. For example, "Copyright 1999 by Greg Roelofs. This image may be freely used and distributed provided that it is not modified in any way and that this notice remains intact."

Disclaimer

A legal disclaimer notice for the image. This might include a company's standard boilerplate on all copyrighted works; in particular, it might be lengthy enough to store in a compressed (zTXt) chunk, while the copyright notice remains uncompressed.

Warning

A warning about the content or effects of the image. For example, certain types of popular material may not be suitable for minors, or a random-dot stereogram ("Magic Eye" 3D image) may induce headaches in some people.

Software

The name and possibly the version of the software used to create the image. This is most often generated automatically, but it need not be. More than one software application may be listed.

Source

Information about the device used to generate the image, such as a digital camera or a scanner.

Comment

A miscellaneous comment, often converted from a GIF comment (which lacks keywords).

In addition to these official keywords, one of the technical reviewers of this book and I have been known to make use of a few unofficial keywords. The Caption keyword is used to provide a brief description of an image that is more specifically tailored for use as a publishable caption than the generic Description keyword; it is also generally lengthier than is appropriate for the Title keyword. The E-mail keyword stores the email address of the author in standard Internet format (RFC 822, Section 6, as amended by RFC 1123, Sections 5.2.15 through 5.2.19); for example, *roelofs@pobox.com* . And the URL keyword is for a standard WWW Uniform Resource Locator (RFC 2068, Section 3.2); for example, *http://www.oreilly. com*. If the URL is reasonably self-explanatory, it is recommended that the chunk consist of the single URL and nothing else, but this is not a requirement. Multiple URLs should be separated by newline characters. Note that spaces and other white space (tabs, newlines, and so forth) are considered unsafe by the URL standard and therefore must be escaped within a conforming URL. For example, a space character must be encoded as %20. This allows easy parsing of optional explanatory text after a URL: the URL ends when the first white space (space, tab, or newline) is encountered.

International Text Annotations (iTXt)

Status: PNG Extensions*
Location: Anywhere
Multiple: Yes

I previously noted that, as of early 1999, PNG was in the midst of joint ISO/IEC standardization. One of the technical issues in the first Committee Draft vote was the lack of support for non-Western languages, specifically in the text chunks. In fact, the PNG Development Group had already discussed a more general text chunk in mid-1998, but its vote was deferred until there was external interest in it. The ISO comments from Japan and the United States clearly fell into the category of external interest, however, so the iTXt was voted on and approved as part of the PNG specification in early February 1999.

The layout of iTXt is a generalization of tEXt and zTXt, as shown in Table 11-2.

Table 11-2: iTXt Chunk

Field	Length and Valid Range
Keyword	1–79 bytes (Latin-1 text)
Null separator	1 byte (0)
Compression flag	1 byte (0, 1)
Compression method	1 byte (0)
Language tag	k bytes (ASCII text)
Null separator	1 byte (0)
Translated keyword	m bytes (Unicode UTF-8 text)
Null separator	1 byte (0)
Text	n bytes (Unicode UTF-8 text)

The first field is a keyword, with exactly the same restrictions and officially registered values (Author, Description, and so on) as the tEXt and zTXt chunks. Latin-1 (ISO/IEC 8859-1) was chosen so that existing PNG source code could be used without modification to parse and optionally recognize the keyword.

---

* As this book went to press, the iTXt chunk had just been approved for inclusion in the core PNG specification, but it was temporarily placed in the PNG extensions document pending completion and approval of extensive ISO-related changes to the core spec. (Note that these changes are almost entirely of an organizational or editorial nature; the technical content of the specification is expected to change only minimally from version 1.1.). Version 1.2 of the PNG specification is expected around mid-1999 or later. In the meantime, iTXt can be found in version 1.1.1 (and possibly later versions) of the extensions document, which is available electronically from *http://www.cdrom.com/pub/png/png-docs.html.*

The keyword is followed by a null separator byte and two compression-related bytes. The first indicates whether the main text is compressed (if its value is 1) or not (if it's 0). If the text is compressed, the next byte indicates its compression method, which currently must be zero for the zlib-encoded deflate algorithm. The two bytes could have been combined, but for historical reasons relating to the method byte in IHDR, the split approach was favored.

After the compression bytes is an optional *case-insensitive* field indicating the (human) language used in the remaining two text fields. This is necessary not only to render Unicode text properly but also to allow decoders to distinguish between multiple iTXt chunks, which may consist of the same text in different languages— but possibly identical keywords. Unlike both the keyword and the main text, the language tag is plain ASCII text (specifically, the "invariant" ASCII subset of ISO 646, which is itself a subset of both Latin-1 and Unicode UTF-8) conforming to Internet Standard RFC 1766. It consists of hyphen-separated "words" of between one and eight characters each, where the first word is either a two-letter ISO language code (ISO 639), the letter *i* for tags registered by the Internet Assigned Numbers Authority (IANA)* or the letter *x* for private tags. The second "word" is interpreted as an ISO 3166 country code if it is exactly two characters long or as an IANA-registered code if it is between three and eight characters. Subsequent "words" may be anything, as long as they conform to the general rules. Examples of language tags include cn (Chinese), en-US (American English), no-bok (Norwegian *bokmål* or "book language"), i-navajo (Navajo), and x-klingon (Klingon, from the fictional Star Trek universe).

A null separator byte terminates the language tag, which is followed by an optional translation of the keyword into the given language. The translated keyword is represented in the UTF-8 encoding of the Unicode character set, which is described in the International Standard ISO/IEC 10646-1, in Internet RFC 2279, and in the Unicode Consortium's reference, *The Unicode Standard*. Like the primary keyword, it should not contain any newline characters, and it is also followed by a null byte.

The remaining chunk data is the main UTF-8 text, either zlib-compressed or not, according to the compression flag. Since its length can be determined from the chunk length, it is not null-terminated. As with the other two text chunks, newlines should be represented by single line-feed characters (decimal 10), and all other control characters (1–9, 11–31, and 127–159) are discouraged. Note, however, that UTF-8 *encodings* may contain any of the bytes between 128 and 159; what is discouraged is the set of Unicode characters whose four-byte *integer values* are 128–159.

---

* As this is written, indications are that IANA will eventually be replaced by ICANN, the Internet Corporation for Assigned Names and Numbers. This transition may not occur until 2000, however.

That last point is confusing, so perhaps a quick primer on Unicode is in order. The Unicode *character set* is a mapping between graphic characters (or glyphs) and integers. The simplest representation is called UCS-4 and consists of 4-byte integers, potentially allowing more than two billion characters to be defined. On top of that are a number of possible transformations or *encodings* of the character set; UTF-8 is one of the more popular ones, encoding 4-byte UCS-4 characters into anywhere from 1 to 8 bytes. All Unicode characters below 128 are encoded as single bytes in UTF-8, and because Unicode characters 1–127 are identical to US-ASCII characters 1–127, the Unicode character set (and UTF-8 in particular) may be thought of as a very large superset of 7-bit ASCII.

Multibyte UTF-8 encodings, on the other hand, are composed entirely of byte values between 128 and 253—which means that bytes 1–9, 11–31, and 127 will never be found in valid UTF-8-encoded text except when representing the *characters* 1–9, 11–31, and 127. So about half of the control characters that are discouraged in iTXt can be detected simply by checking for those single bytes. The remaining half, characters 128–159, are all encoded with 2-byte sequences that happen to begin with byte value 194: 194 128 through 194 159. The fact that character 128 is discouraged in iTXt's UTF-8 text fields therefore means that the 2-byte encoding 194 128 is discouraged, but the 2-byte encoding 195 128 (À or "Latin capital letter A with grave accent") is completely acceptable.

Histogram (hIST)

Status: PNG Specification
Location: After PLTE, before first IDAT
Multiple: No

A histogram is nothing more than a frequency-of-occurrence table, and the PNG hIST chunk gives the approximate frequencies of occurrence for pixels of various colors. This information is typically used to decide which colors are the most important if the system is not capable of displaying all of them. Rather than force the decoder to count pixels every time the image is displayed, the histogram places the burden on the encoder, which performs the task only once.

PNG's hIST implementation is tied to the PLTE chunk; if there is no palette, hIST is not allowed. This and one or two other limitations were later recognized and addressed by the sPLT chunk, which we'll discuss next; it is generally favored over hIST, but the latter is smaller, and either may be used. The histogram must contain exactly as many entries as PLTE contains, and each entry is a 16-bit unsigned integer. Since such integers can only represent numbers in the range 0–65,535 and there may be millions of pixels of a given color, the histogram entries often must be scaled and are therefore inexact. The sole exception is the value zero; it is guaranteed to mean that there are *no* pixels of the corresponding color. A nonzero count that would otherwise be scaled and rounded to zero must instead be rounded up to one.

Truecolor images that include a PLTE chunk as a suggested quantization are a special case. The histogram counts are dependent on the algorithm used by the encoder for quantizing the pixels; if the decoder happens to use a different algorithm, its counts would be different, too. The upshot is that the histogram is particularly approximate in this case. Because truecolor images typically have far more colors than palette entries, the palette entries that do appear should always represent at least one pixel; thus there should be no zero counts in the histogram.

Suggested Palette (sPLT)

Status: PNG Specification
Location: Before first IDAT
Multiple: Yes

The suggested-palette chunk, sPLT, grew out of an acknowledgment of some limitations in PNG's PLTE, tRNS, and hIST chunks. I have already noted that PLTE is allowed only in palette, RGB, and RGBA images and that hIST is allowed only in images with PLTE; I also noted that tRNS is disallowed in images with alpha channels, which rules out the use of PLTE plus tRNS as a suggested gray/alpha or RGBA palette. sPLT eliminates these restrictions by merging all three of the older chunks into a general-purpose, suggested-RGBA-palette-plus-histogram chunk. In addition, sPLT may contain any number of entries (as long as it doesn't exceed the maximum chunk-size limit of two gigabytes); its entries may have either 8-bit or 16-bit sample depths; and multiple sPLT chunks encoding different suggested quantizations are allowed. A palette-based image may even have an sPLT chunk, perhaps representing a reduced palette for a particular web browser. The format of sPLT, given in Table 11-3, is straightforward.

Table 11-3: sPLT Chunk

Field	Length and Valid Range
Palette name	1–79 bytes (Latin-1 text)
Null separator	1 byte
Sample depth	1 byte (8 or 16)
Red value #1	1 byte (0–255) or 2 bytes (0–65,535)
Green value #1	1 byte (0–255) or 2 bytes (0–65,535)
Blue value #1	1 byte (0–255) or 2 bytes (0–65,535)
Alpha value #1	1 byte (0–255) or 2 bytes (0–65,535)
Relative frequency #1	2 bytes (0–65,535)
. . .	

The number of sPLT entries is implicitly given by the size of the chunk and the sample depth; in the more common case of 8-bit samples, it is obtained by dividing the chunk size, less the length of the palette name and the two subsequent bytes, by six. Entries are required to appear in decreasing order of frequency, but there is no requirement that all of them be different nor that all of them be used by the image. Furthermore, opaque images may include nonopaque sPLT entries, grayscale images may include colored entries, and the sample depth of sPLT is independent of that of the image.

Unlike the suggested practice for PLTE in RGBA images, the red, green, and blue values in sPLT are neither premultiplied by the alpha values nor precomposited against a background color. An encoder would still have to inspect every pixel if it wanted to compute an optimal palette for display of an RGBA image against a patterned background, but sPLT would enable a statistical approach based on the background image's own histogram in that case. And for solid backgrounds, sPLT provides the means to build an optimal palette regardless of the choice of background color.

As with the hIST chunk, frequency values are scaled to the range 0–65,535 and therefore are likely to be approximate. Inflating "important" colors based on the image's subject matter is allowed in sPLT, too. But whereas hIST requires a 0 frequency to correspond exactly to 0 pixels, sPLT allows the 0 value to represent infrequently used or unimportant colors. If all of the frequency values are 0, however, the histogram is undefined.

Note that multiple sPLT chunks are required to have different palette names.

Significant Bits (sBIT)

Status: PNG Specification
Location: Before PLTE and first IDAT
Multiple: No

The significant-bits chunk is used to indicate the nature of the source data in cases in which storing it in PNG form required a conversion. For example, gray pixels in medical images are often 12 bits deep, but PNG requires them to be scaled up to 16 bits for portability. Scaling the pixels does not alter the fact that they contain only 12 bits of real information, and the sBIT chunk stores this fact in a PNG file.

As with several other PNG chunks, the format of sBIT depends on the image type. Grayscale images are the simplest; sBIT then contains a single byte indicating the number of significant bits in the source data—in the preceding example, 12. For grayscale images with an alpha channel, sBIT contains 2 bytes, one for the gray channel and one for alpha; RGB images require 3 bytes, and RGBA images require 4. Palette-based images are treated like RGB except that the sBIT information refers to the palette entries, and the palette's effective sample depth is always 8, regardless of how many bits are used to index the palette. Note that the number of significant bits for any given channel must be greater than zero and less than or equal to the sample depth.

Ordinary PNG decoders need not worry about sBIT, but those that wish to recover the original image data can do so by right-shifting each image sample to leave only the number of bits indicated by sBIT. This implies that the scaling procedure used by the PNG encoder must not change the original bits; it can only append low-order bits to each sample.

Physical Pixel Dimensions (pHYs)

Status: PNG Specification
Location: Before first IDAT
Multiple: No

The pHYs chunk encodes the absolute or relative dimensions of pixels. For example, an image scanned at 600 dots per inch has pixels with known, absolute sizes—namely, one six-hundredth of an inch in both x and y directions. Alternatively, an image created on a 1280 × 1024 display will have nonsquare pixels, and the relative dimensions of each pixel, also referred to as the *aspect ratio*, may be stored so the image can be displayed as it was intended to be seen.

The layout of the chunk is shown in Table 11-4.

Table 11-4: pHYs Chunk

Field	Length and Valid Range
Pixels per unit, x axis	4 bytes (0–2,147,483,647)
Pixels per unit, y axis	4 bytes (0–2,147,483,647)
Unit specifier	1 byte (0, 1)

If the unit specifier byte is 1, the units are meters; if it is 0, the units are unspecified, and only the relative dimensions are known. Currently, no other values are valid. Note that the format of the chunk precludes pixel sizes greater than one meter, which should not be a significant hardship for most applications, but it allows pixels as small as 4.7 Ångstroms, which is roughly the size of a single atom.

For the previous scanning example, 600 dpi is equal to 23,622.05 pixels per meter, so both the x and y values would be 23,622, and the unit specifier would be 1. The second example is slightly trickier. First, it is necessary to know that practically all current computer displays have a physical aspect ratio of 4:3,* which means the viewable portion of the display (the glass) is three-quarters as high as it is wide. Thus, the horizontal pixels-per-unit in the case of a 1280 × 1024 display is proportional to (1280/4) or 320, while the vertical pixels-per-unit is proportional to (1024/3) or 341.333333. Because we don't have an absolute scale, we are free to multiply these values by a common factor; doing so will preserve some of the precision that would otherwise be lost due to truncation of the decimal part of the second value (the .3333 part). One choice would be a power of 10, such as 1,000; then the stored values would be 320,000 and 341,333, respectively. But in this case, we can do better: we know that the fractional part is simply one-third, so multiplying both values by 3 will preserve the aspect ratio exactly. Thus the chunk would contain the values (3 × 1280/4) or 960, (3 × 1024/3) or 1,024, and 0 for the unit specifier. Values of 15, 16, and 0 would work equally well.

A decoder that encounters a pHYs chunk with different values for the x and y axes has several options. The simplest and least correct approach is to ignore the chunk; most current viewers do this. A better approach is to interpolate the pixels in one of the dimensions; this gives the correct overall appearance but introduces noticeable artifacts—for the preceding example, it involves either duplicating every 15th column stretching the image horizontally, or deleting every 16th row shrinking the image vertically. The best approach is to resample the image, a procedure that amounts to converting the image to a continuous (or analog) representation and then overlaying the desired pixel grid on that. This is, by far, the most expensive approach in terms of CPU usage, but the results are excellent.

Physical Scale (sCAL)

Status: Officially registered (PNG Extensions)
Location: Before first IDAT
Multiple: No

PNG's sCAL chunk is similar to pHYs, except that instead of measuring the size of the image pixels relative to each other or to an original, physical image, sCAL measures their size relative to the actual subject matter of the image. For example, an astronomical image may span a certain number of radians in each direction, or an aerial photograph of Earth may cover a given number of kilometers.

Table 11-5 shows the format of sCAL; it is quite simple.

---

* This will change with the convergence of computers and high-definition TV. Displays for the latter have a 16:9 aspect ratio, which apparently is the geometric mean of standard television and computer displays (4:3) and of modern, panoramic films (typically 2.35:1, but it varies).

Table 11-5: sCAL Chunk

Field	Length and Valid Range
Unit specifier	1 byte (1, 2)
Units per pixel, x axis	m bytes (0–2,147,483,647)
Null separator	1 byte (0)
Units per pixel, y axis	n bytes (0–2,147,483,647)

Two units are defined: meters (unit specifier = 1) and radians (unit specifier = 2). The size of a pixel in the given units, both horizontally and vertically, is given by a pair of positive floating-point numbers encoded as ASCII strings and separated by a null byte. The most general form of a floating-point string includes an optional leading sign (+ or –), zero or more decimal digits (0–9, the "integer part"), an optional decimal point followed by zero or more decimal digits (the "fractional part"), and an optional e or E followed by an optional sign and one or more digits (the "exponent part"). Either the integer part or the fractional part must contain at least one digit, but everything else may be omitted. Thus, 1 and .1 are valid floating-point numbers, as is +123.4567e-089. Note that the exponent is interpreted as a power of 10 (10^{-89} in the third example) to be multiplied by the integer and fractional parts; this is the computer version of what is sometimes referred to as *scientific notation.*

Image Offset (oFFs)

Status: Officially registered (PNG Extensions)
Location: Before first IDAT
Multiple: No

For images that are available separately but envisioned as part of a greater whole, the image-offset chunk, oFFs, can be used to specify the absolute positioning of each. The most common example is positioning on a printed page, especially in conjunction with the pHYs chunk.

The layout of the chunk is given in Table 11-6.

Table 11-6: oFFs Chunk

Field	Length and Valid Range
Image position, x axis	4 bytes (−2,147,483,647–2,147,483,647)
Image position, y axis	4 bytes (−2,147,483,647–2,147,483,647)
Unit specifier	1 byte (0, 1)

Valid units are either pixels (unit specifier = 0) or microns* (unit specifier = 1). The image position is measured from the top and left edges of the page (whether real or virtual); an image that is intended to be partly cut off may have negative offsets.

Pixel Calibration (pCAL)

Status: Officially registered (PNG Extensions)
Location: After PLTE, before first IDAT
Multiple: No

The pCAL chunk is currently the only registered scientific-visualization extension to PNG, though it was moved into the regular PNG Extensions document as part of the general PNG spec revision process in October 1998. It is also the most mathematical of any approved chunk. Its purpose is to efficiently encode the relevant conversions between the integer samples in a PNG file and the physical quantity being represented by the image. Two conversions are represented: a linear conversion between the PNG samples and the original samples and a more general conversion from the original samples to the physical values they represent. The first mapping is often the identity mapping (i.e., the original samples are equal to the PNG samples), but it need not be.

The layout of the pCAL chunk is presented in Table 11-7.

Table 11-7: pCAL Chunk

Field	Length and Valid Range
Calibration name	1–79 bytes (Latin-1 text)
Null separator	1 byte
Original zero, X_0	4 bytes (signed integer)
Original maximum, X_{10}	4 bytes (signed integer)
Equation type	1 byte
Number of parameters, N	1 byte
Unit name	n bytes (Latin-1 text)
Null separator	1 byte
Parameter 0, P_0	p_0 bytes (ASCII floating-point text)
Null separator	1 byte
. . .	
Parameter L, P_L (Note: L = N−1)	p_L bytes (ASCII floating-point text)

---

* Microns are more properly known as micrometers (μm); there are one million of them in a meter, or 25,400 in an inch.

The unit name is a label, such as `kg/(m^3)` or `Mpc`, that applies to the physical quantity represented by the image samples. Dimensionless data may either include a descriptive string (e.g., "fractal iteration count") or leave the unit field a null string. There are no restrictions on the length of the unit name.

The X_0 and X_1 parameters encode the linear conversion. For an 8-bit sample depth, the PNG samples range from 0 to 255; more generally, they range from 0 to M, where $M = 2^{bit\ depth} - 1$. Most often, X_0 will equal 0 and X_1 will equal M, indicating that the PNG samples are the same as the original samples. But this need not be the case, and either of X_0 or X_1 may be positive or negative; the only restriction is that they may not be equal to each other. The conversion is done using integer arithmetic, according to the following equation:

```
original_sample = (PNG_sample * (X₁-X₀) + M/2) / M + X₀
```

The inverse mapping is:

```
PNG_sample = ((original_sample - X₀) * M + (X₁-X₀)/2) / (X₁-X₀)
```

Note that integer arithmetic here means that fractional values are rounded toward minus infinity, not toward zero; there's no difference for positive values, but for negative values, there is. Also keep in mind that the PNG samples are limited to the range [0,M] regardless of what the inverse mapping might give.

The more general conversion, between original samples and actual physical values, can be represented by one of four possible equation types: linear (type 0), exponential (type 1), exponential with arbitrary base (type 2), or hyperbolic sinusoidal (type 3). The number of parameters required by each is 2, 3, 3, and 4, respectively, and the parameters are stored in the same ASCII floating-point format as described for the sCAL chunk earlier. The equations use floating-point arithmetic, not integer, and are given by:

[0]   physical_value = $P_0 + P_1 *$ original_sample$/(X_1-X_0)$

[1]   physical_value = $P_0 + P_1 * e^{P_2\ *\ original\_sample/(X_1-X_0)}$

[2]   physical_value = $P_0 + P_1 * P_2^{\,original\_sample/(X_1-X_0)}$

[3]   physical_value = $P_0 + P_1 * \sinh(P_2*(original\_sample - P_3)/(X_1-X_0))$

Equation types 1 and 2 are equivalent in the sense that the same types of functions can be represented by either one; both are defined for convenience. For RGB or RGBA image types, the equations are applied to each of the color sample values independently, while for palette images, the equations are applied to the color sample values in the palette, not to the index values.

Equation type 3 may seem odd, but it allows floating-point data to be reduced to integer data in such a way that the resolution of the integer data is roughly proportional to the magnitude of the original floating-point data. That is, for 32-bit original data and 16-bit PNG samples, the resolution near zero is around 10^{-33}, and near $\pm 10^{31}$ it is around 10^{28}. To put it another way, the resolution everywhere is about 0.4% (or 1/256) of the magnitude.

Fractal Parameters (fRAc)

Status: Officially registered (PNG Extensions)
Location: Anywhere
Multiple: Yes

The fRAc chunk is unique in that it was officially registered as a PNG extension in 1995 but, as of early 1999, still had not actually been specified. Intended to store parameters pertaining to the generation of fractal images, the chunk is clearly useful only to a very specialized set of programs. As a result, its design was left in the hands of experts—specifically, the authors of Fractint, which is one of the most general fractal programs ever written and probably the most popular. But for technical reasons relating to Fractint's 16-bit origins, PNG support was not added as planned, so design of the fRAc chunk was deferred pending a rewrite of the program as a 32-bit application.

GIF Conversion Info (gIFg, gIFx)

Status: Officially registered (PNG Extensions)
Location: Anywhere
Multiple: Yes

Since PNG originated as an intended replacement for GIF, one requirement for the new format was to be able to store all possible GIF information in one form or another. Part of that requirement is addressed by chunks we've already described. Within GIF's Logical Screen Descriptor (the global header that immediately follows the GIF signature bytes), the Pixel Aspect Ratio, Color Resolution, and Background Color Index fields map to pHYs, sBIT, and bKGD, respectively. Note that Background Color Index only applies if there is a Global Color Table, however. Within the Image Descriptor, the Image Left Position and Image Top Position fields map to oFFs. And within the Graphic Control Extension, the Transparent Color Index maps to tRNS. This is summarized in Table 11-8.

Table 11-8: Correspondence Between GIF Fields and Standard PNG Chunks

GIF Block	GIF Variable Name	PNG Chunk
Logical Screen Descriptor	Pixel Aspect Ratio	pHYs
	Color Resolution	sBIT
	Background Color Index	bKGD
Image Descriptor	Image Left Position	oFFs
	Image Top Position	oFFs
Graphic Control Extension	Transparent Color Index	tRNS

The remainder of the requirement that PNG be able to store all GIF information is addressed by two of PNG's three GIF extension chunks. Both correspond directly to GIF89a extensions: the Graphic Control Extension (gIFg) and the Application Extension (gIFx). The third chunk, gIFt, turns out to be an unintended special case; it is discussed separately later.

GIF's Graphic Control Extension is most commonly used to indicate transparency, for which it corresponds most closely to PNG's tRNS chunk. But it is also used in multi-image GIFs to provide timing and compositing information. Although this is more properly the realm of MNG, PNG's multi-image cousin (which I'll discuss in Chapter 12, *Multiple-Image Network Graphics*, PNG also supports the conversion of a multi-image GIF into several single-image PNGs. The gIFg chunk is used to encode the nontransparency information in the GIF extension block so that loss-less conversion back to an animated GIF is possible.

The gIFg chunk, shown in Table 11-9, contains only three fields.

Table 11-9: gIFg Chunk

Field	Length and Valid Range
Disposal method	1 byte (0–3)
User input	1 byte (0, 1)
Delay time	2 bytes (0–65,535)

The interpretation and value of each field are identical to those in part 23 of the GIF89a Specification, with the exception that the 2-byte delay time is stored in big-endian order (most significant byte first) in gIFg, whereas GIF integers are stored in little-endian format. PNG decoders may treat the delay time (measured in hundredths of a second) as the maximum amount of time to display the image before going on to the next one, if any, but it is likely that most decoders will ignore the chunk entirely.

GIF's Application Extension is simply a way for an application to include its own information in the image; it corresponds exactly to a private chunk in a PNG image. The format is given in Table 11-10.

Table 11-10: gIFx Chunk

Field	Length and Valid Range
Application identifier	8 bytes (printable ASCII characters)
Authentication code	3 bytes
Application data	*n* bytes

The contents of gIFx are a direct transcription of the GIF data, with the sole exception that any GIF sub-blocks are deblocked into a flat stream.

GIF Plain Text (gIFt)

Status: Officially deprecated (PNG Extensions)
Location: Anywhere
Multiple: Yes

GIF's Plain Text Extension is a way to define an image composed entirely of text without actually storing the text as a bitmapped image. It defines a rectangular grid of character cells into which text characters of the specified foreground and background colors are placed, starting from the upper left and proceeding left to right and top to bottom; the decoder chooses the font that is the closest match to the specified size.

A casual reading of the GIF specification might suggest that the Plain Text Extension defines a method for cheaply overlaying fixed-width text on top of ordinary pixel data—and, indeed, that was probably the primary motivation behind the extension. But a more careful inspection reveals that the Plain Text Extension is treated as a separate subimage within the GIF stream, on equal terms with any block of bitmap data. It may, in fact, be the *only* graphic rendering block within the stream. And since PNG images are required to include bitmap data (i.e., IDAT chunks), allowing GIF Plain Text information to be included is perilously close to sanctioning multi-image PNGs. Largely because of this, the gIFt chunk was officially deprecated in October 1998. It is still allowed for backward compatibility (the horses have already left the barn, so to speak), but the current recommendation is that all decoders ignore the chunk and that encoders not write it in the first place. In fact, it is quite possible that no encoder or decoder ever did support gIFt; the Plain Text Extension was rarely used even in GIF's heyday, and even gif2png (see Chapter 5, *Applications: Image Converters*) never supported it.

In any case, the format of the gIFt chunk is as shown in Table 11-11.

Table 11-11: gIFt Chunk

Field	Length and Valid Range
Text grid left position, pixels	4 bytes (0–2,147,483,647)
Text grid top position, pixels	4 bytes (0–2,147,483,647)
Text grid width, pixels	4 bytes (0–2,147,483,647)
Text grid height, pixels	4 bytes (0–2,147,483,647)
Character cell width, pixels	1 byte (0–255)
Character cell height, pixels	1 byte (0–255)
Text foreground color	3 bytes (R, G, B samples, 0–255 each)
Text background color	3 bytes (R, G, B samples, 0–255 each)
Plain text data	n bytes

There are several differences from the GIF data structure. The actual text in the GIF block is divided into sub-blocks of between 1 and 255 bytes; the PNG plain text data is a single stream. In addition to the reversed order for integer values (big-endian in PNG), gIFt's width and height fields for the grid are 4 bytes each, twice as big as in GIF. The position fields are also twice as wide, which makes little sense from a preserve-the-GIF-data standpoint, but apparently was chosen for consistency with PNG's image-offset chunk. Both the Plain Text Extension and oFFs give positions relative to a logical page, not relative to the main image; thus, in the presence of oFFs data, the gIFt positions should be adjusted accordingly. Note that this may not be possible if the PNG image uses microns in the oFFs chunk and has no pHYs chunk—in that case, there is no conversion information between pixels (the only unit defined for gIFt) and microns.

Possibly the biggest difference, however, is that the Plain Text Extension is affected by the Graphic Control Extension, which means it implicitly includes transparency and timing effects. PNG's gIFt chunk does not include any transparency information, so effectively there is no way to float the gIFt text over the main image by giving it a transparent background color. This limitation appears to have been an oversight in the design of the PNG chunk and was another reason for its official deprecation. On the other hand, if the gIFt chunk appears before the first IDAT chunk, a hypothetical gIFt-aware PNG decoder might assume that the text amounts to a background image and render the pixel data on top of it, applying any transparency effects the main image possesses.

Other Chunks

Several other chunks were proposed but never approved as official extensions, mainly due to the perceived lack of need for them. The alignment chunk (aLIG, had it been approved) would have provided centering and baseline information about an image so that it could be aligned more cleanly with surrounding text; this would have been most useful for images with transparent edges. The fingerprint chunk (fING) would have provided a 16-byte MD5 fingerprint of the raw image data, a type of cryptographic signature that could be used to test whether two images were identical. Neither aLIG nor fING was ever put up for a vote, and both proposals have long since expired.

There were also three proposed scientific-visualization chunks, all of which were rejected in formal voting. The false-color chunk (fALS) would have provided false-color information for grayscale images, such as might be used to highlight a tumor in a medical scan or a shock front in a hydrodynamic simulation. The calibration chunks (xSCL and ySCL, but also known as xCAL and yCAL in later proposals) were similar to sCAL in providing information about the physical characteristics of an image subject but would have allowed offsets and different units along the two axes; they thus would have provided full calibration data, not just scaling information.

Note that any of these chunks may be resurrected in the future, as PNG becomes more widely used and as the needs of various PNG-using communities evolve.

12

Multiple-Image Network Graphics

The Multiple-image Network Graphics format, or MNG, is not merely a multi-image, animated extension to PNG; it can also be used to store certain types of single images more compactly than PNG, and in mid-1998 it was extended to include JPEG-compressed streams. Conceivably, it may one day incorporate audio or even video channels, too, although this is a more remote possibility. Yet despite all of this promise—or, rather, because of it—MNG was still a slowly evolving draft proposal nearly four years after it was first suggested.

As noted in Chapter 7, *History of the Portable Network Graphics Format*, MNG's early development was delayed due to weariness on the part of the PNG group and disagreement over whether it should be a heavyweight multimedia format or a very basic "glue" format. What it has evolved into, primarily due to the willingness of Glenn Randers-Pehrson to continue working on it, is a moderately complex format for composing images or parts of images, either spatially or temporally, or both. I will not attempt to describe it in full detail here—a complete description of MNG could fill a book all by itself and probably will, one of these days—but I will give a solid overview of its basic features and most useful applications. Further information on the format can be found at the MNG web site, *http://www.cdrom. com/pub/mng/*.

Common Applications of MNG

Perhaps the most basic, nontrivial MNG application is the slide show: a sequence of static images displayed in order, possibly looping indefinitely (e.g., for a kiosk). Because MNG incorporates not only the concepts of frames, clipping, and user input but also all of PNG's features, a MNG slide show could include scrolling, sideways transitions, fades, and palette animations—in other words, most of the standard effects of a dedicated presentation package and maybe a few nonstandard ones. Such an approach would not necessarily produce smaller presentations than the alternative methods (although the most popular alternatives tend to be rather large), and, as currently specified, it would be limited to a particular resolution defined by the component raster images. But MNG offers the *potential* of a more open, cross-platform approach to slide shows.

MNG also supports partial-frame updates, which not only could be used for further slide show transitions (for example, dropping bulleted items into place, one at a time) but also are able to support animated movies. Unlike animated GIFs, where moving a tiny, static bitmap (or "sprite") around a frame requires many copies of the sprite, MNG can simply indicate that a previously defined sprite should move somewhere else. It also supports nested loops, so a sprite could move in a zigzag path to the right, then up, then left, and finally back down to the starting position—all with no more than one copy of the background image (if any) and one copy of the moving bitmap. In this sense, MNG defines a true animation format, whereas GIF merely supports slightly fancy slide shows.

Images that change with time are likely to be some of the most common types of MNG streams, but MNG is useful in completely static contexts as well. For example, one could easily put together a MNG-based contact sheet of thumbnail images without actually merging the images into a single, composite bitmap. This would allow the same file to act both as an archive (or container) for the thumbnails, from which they could easily be extracted later without loss, and as a convenient display format.* If the number of thumbnails grew too large to fit on a single "page," MNG's slide show capabilities could be invoked to enable multipage display.

Other types of static MNGs might include algorithmic images or three-dimensional "voxel" (volume-pixel) data such as medical scans. Images that can be generated by simple algorithms are fairly rare if one ignores fractals. But *16million.png*, which I discussed in Chapter 9, *Compression and Filtering*, is such an image. Containing all 16.8 million colors possible in a 24-bit image, it consists of nothing but smooth gradients, both horizontally and vertically. While this allowed PNG's filtering and compression engine to squeeze a 48 MB image into just over 100 KB, as a MNG containing a pair of loops, move commands, and a few odds and ends it amounts to a mere 476 bytes. Of course, compression factors in excess of 100,000 times are highly atypical. But background gradient fills are not, and MNG effectively allows one to compress the foreground and background parts independently, in turn allowing the compression engine and the file format itself to work more efficiently.

---

* A file format encapsulating both data and a display method? Egad, it's object-oriented!

Ironically, one of the most popular nonanimated forms of MNG is likely to have no PNG image data inside at all. I've emphasized in earlier chapters that PNG's lossless compression method is not well suited to all tasks; in particular, for web-based display of continuous-tone images like photographs, a lossy format such as JPEG is much more appropriate, since the files can be so much smaller. For a multi-image format such as MNG, support for a lossy subformat—JPEG in particular—is a natural extension. Not only does it provide for the efficient storage of photographic backgrounds for composite frames (or even photographic sprites in the foreground), it also allows JPEG to be enhanced with PNG-like features such as gamma and color correction and (ta da!) transparency. Transparency has always been a problem for JPEG precisely because of its lossy approach to compression. What MNG provides is a means for a lossy JPEG image to inherit a loss less alpha channel. In other words, all of the size benefits of a JPEG image and all of the fine-tuned anti-aliasing and fade effects of a PNG alpha channel are now possible in one neat package.

MNG Structure

So that's some of what MNG can do; now let's take a closer look at what the format looks like and how it works. To begin with, MNG is chunk-based, just like PNG. It has an 8-byte signature similar to PNG's, but it differs in the first two bytes, as shown in Table 12-1.

Table 12-1: MNG Signature Bytes

Decimal Value	ASCII Interpretation
138	A byte with its most significant bit set ("8-bit character")
77	M
78	N
71	G
13	Carriage-return (CR) character, a.k.a. CTRL-M or ^M
10	Line-feed (LF) character, a.k.a. CTRL-J or ^J
26	CTRL-Z or ^Z
10	Line-feed (LF) character, a.k.a. CTRL-J or ^J

So while a PNG-supporting application could be trivially modified to identify and parse a MNG stream,* there is no danger that an older PNG application might mistake a MNG stream for a PNG image. Since the file extensions differ as well (*.mng* instead of *.png*), ordinary users are unlikely to confuse images with animations. The only cases in which they might do so are when an allowed component type

---

* Actually making sense of the MNG stream would require considerably more work, of course.

(e.g., a PNG or a JNG) is renamed with a *.mng* extension; such files are considered legal MNGs.

With the exception of such renamed image formats, all MNG streams begin with the MNG signature and MHDR chunk, and they all end with the MEND chunk. The latter, like PNG's IEND, is an empty chunk that simply indicates the end of the stream. MHDR, however, contains seven fields, all unsigned 32-bit integers: frame width, frame height, ticks per second, number of layers, number of frames, total play time, and the complexity (or simplicity) profile.

Frame width and height are just what they sound like: they give the overall size of the displayable region in pixels. A MNG stream that contains no visible images—say, a collection of palettes—should have its frame dimensions set to zero.

The ticks-per-second value is essentially a scale factor for time-related fields in other chunks, including the frame rate. In the absence of any other timing information, animations are recommended to be displayed at a rate of one frame per tick. For single-frame MNGs, the ticks-per-second value is recommended to be 0, providing decoders with an easy way to detect non-animations. Conversely, if the value is 0 for a multiframe MNG, decoders are required to display only the first frame unless the user specifically intervenes in some way.

"Number of layers" refers to the total number of displayable images in the MNG stream, including the background. This may be many more than the number of frames, since a single frame often consists of multiple images composited (or layered) on top of one another. Some of the layers may be empty if they lie completely outside the clipping boundaries. The layer count is purely advisory; if it is 0, the count is considered unspecified. At the other end of the spectrum, a value of $2^{31}-1$ (2,147,483,647) is considered infinite.

The frame-count and play-time values are also basically what they sound like: on an ideal computer (i.e., one with infinite processing speed), they respectively indicate the number of frames that correspond to distinct instants of time* and the overall duration of the complete animation. As with the layer count, these values are advisory; 0 and $2^{31}-1$ correspond to "unspecified" and "infinite," respectively.

Finally, MHDR's complexity profile provides some indication of the level of complexity in the stream, in order to allow simple decoders to give up immediately if the MNG file contains features they are unable to render. The profile field is also advisory; a value of zero is allowed and indicates that the complexity level is unspecified. But a nonzero value indicates that the encoder has provided

---

* MNG's concept of frames and subframes allows one to speak of two or more distinct frames with precisely zero delay between them, but these are considered just one frame for the purpose of counting the total number of frames in the stream.

information about the presence or absence of JPEG (JNG) chunks, transparency, or complex MNG features. The latter category includes most of the animation features mentioned earlier, including looping and object manipulation (i.e., sprites). All possible combinations of the three categories are encoded in the lower 4 bits of the field as odd values only—all even values other than zero are invalid, which means the lowest bit is always set if the profile contains any useful information. The remaining bits of the 2 lower bytes are reserved for public expansion, and all but the most significant bit of the 2 upper bytes are available for private or experimental use. The topmost bit must be zero.

Note that any unset (0) bit guarantees that the corresponding feature is not present or the MNG stream is invalid. A set bit, on the other hand, does not automatically guarantee that the feature *is* included, but encoders should be as accurate as possible to avoid causing simple decoders to reject MNGs unnecessarily.

The stuff that goes between the MHDR and MEND chunks can be divided into a few basic categories:

- Image-defining chunks
- Image-displaying chunks
- Control chunks
- Ancillary (optional) chunks

Note the distinction between *defining* an image and *displaying* it. This will make sense in the context of a composite frame made up of many subimages. Alternatively, consider a sprite-based animation composed of several sprite "poses" that should be read into memory (i.e., defined) as part of the animation's initialization procedure. The sprite frames may not actually be used until much later, perhaps only in response to user input.

Image-Defining Chunks

The most direct way to define an image in MNG is simply to incorporate one. There are two possibilities for this in the current draft specification: a PNG image without the PNG signature, or the corresponding PNG-like JPEG format, JNG (JPEG Network Graphics).* Just as with standalone PNGs, an embedded PNG must contain at least IHDR, IDAT, and IEND chunks. It may also include PLTE, tRNS, bKGD, gAMA, cHRM, sRGB, tEXt, iTXt, and any of the other PNG chunks we've described. The PLTE chunk is allowed to be empty in an embedded PNG, which indicates that the global MNG PLTE data is to be used instead.

---

* OK, that's a stretch, acronym-wise. But it's pronounceable, rhymes with PNG and MNG, and has a file extension, *.jng*, that differs by only one letter from *.jpg*, *.png*, and *.mng*.

An embedded JNG stream is exactly analogous to the PNG stream: it begins with a
JHDR chunk, includes one or more JDAT chunks containing the actual JPEG image
data, and ends with an IEND chunk. Standalone JNGs are also allowed; they must
include an 8-byte JNG signature before JHDR, with the format that's shown in
Table 12-2.

Table 12-2: JNG Signature Bytes

Decimal Value	ASCII Interpretation
139	A byte with its most significant bit set ("8-bit character")
74	J
78	N
71	G
13	Carriage-return (CR) character, a.k.a. CTRL-M or ^M
10	Line-feed (LF) character, a.k.a. CTRL-J or ^J
26	CTRL-Z or ^Z
10	Line-feed (LF) character, a.k.a. CTRL-J or ^J

JDATs simply contain JFIF-compatible JPEG data, which can be either baseline,
extended sequential, or progressive—i.e., the same format used in practically
every web site and commonly (but imprecisely) referred to as JPEG files. The
requirements on the allowed JPEG types eliminate the less-common arithmetic and
lossless JPEG variants, though the 12-bit grayscale and 36-bit color flavors are still
allowed.* To decode the JPEG image, simply concatenate all of the JDAT data
together and treat the whole as a normal JFIF-format file stream—typically, this
involves feeding the data to the Independent JPEG Group's free *libjpeg* library.

In order to accommodate an alpha channel, a JNG stream may also include one or
more grayscale IDAT chunks. The JHDR chunk defines whether the image has an
alpha channel or not, and if so, what its bit depth is. Unlike PNG, which restricts
alpha channels to either 8 bits or 16 bits, a JNG alpha channel may be any legal
PNG grayscale depth: 1, 2, 4, 8, or 16 bits. The IDATs composing the alpha channel may come before or after or be interleaved with the JDATs to allow progressive display of an alpha-JPEG image, but no other chunk types are allowed within
the block of IDATs and JDATs.

Although incorporating complete JNGs or PNGs is conceptually the simplest
approach to defining images in a MNG stream, it is generally not the most efficient
way. MNG provides two basic alternatives that can be much better in many cases;

---

* MNG optionally allows 12-bit-per-sample JPEG image data to follow the far more common 8-bit flavor, giving decoders the freedom to choose whichever is most appropriate. If both are included, it is
signalled in JHDR by a bit-depth value of 20 instead of 8 or 12, and the 8-bit and 12-bit JDATs are
separated by a special JSEP chunk. The 8-bit data must come first. Note that current versions of libjpeg can only be compiled to handle either 8-bit or 12-bit JPEG data, not both simultaneously.

the first of these is *delta images*.* A delta image is simply a difference image; combining it with its parent re-creates the original image, in much the same way that combining an "up"-filtered row of pixels with the previous row results in the original, unfiltered row. (Recall the discussion of compression filters in Chapter 9.) The difference of two arbitrary images is likely to be at least as large as either parent image, but certain types of images may respond quite well to differencing. For example, consider a pair of prototype images for a web page, both containing the same background graphics and much of the same text, but differing in small, scattered regions. Since 90% of the image area is identical, the difference of the two will be 90% zeros, and therefore will compress much better than either of the original images will.

Currently, MNG allows delta images to be encoded only in PNG format, and it delimits them with the DHDR and IEND chunks. In addition to the delta options for pixels given in DHDR—whether the delta applies to the main image pixels or to the alpha channel, and whether applying the delta involves pixel addition or merely replacement of an entire block—MNG defines several chunks for modifying the parent image at a higher level. Among these are the PROM chunk, for promoting the bit depth or color type of an image, including adding an alpha channel to it; the DROP and DBYK chunks, for dropping certain chunks, either by name alone or by both name and keyword; and the PPLT chunk, for modifying the parent's palette (either PLTE or tRNS, or both). The latter could be used to animate the palette of an image, for example; cycling the colors is a popular option in some fractal programs. PPLT could also be used to fade out an image by adding an opaque tRNS chunk and then progressively changing the values of all entries until the image is fully transparent.

The second and more powerful alternative to defining an image by including its complete pixel data is *object manipulation*. In this mode, MNG basically treats images as little pieces of paper that can be copied and pasted at will. For example, a polka-dot image could be created from a single bitmap of a circle with a transparent background, which could be copied and pasted multiple times to create the complete, composite image. Alternatively, tileable images of a few basic pipe fittings and elbow joints could be pasted together in various orientations to create an image of a maze. The three chunks used for creating or destroying images in the object sense are CLON ("clone"), PAST ("paste"), and DISC ("discard").

The CLON chunk is the only one necessary for the first example; it not only copies an image object in the abstract sense, but also gives it a position in the current frame—either as an absolute location or as an offset from the object that was copied. In order to change the orientation of objects, as in the maze example, the

---

* Named for the Greek letter *delta* (Δ or δ), which is often used in science and engineering to denote differences.

PAST chunk is required; as currently defined, it only supports 180° rotations and mirror operations around the x and y axes. (Ninety-degree rotations were ruled out since they are rarely supported in hardware, and abstract images are intended to map to hardware and platform-specific APIs as closely as possible.) PAST also includes options to tile an object, and not only to replace the underlying pixel data but also to composite either over or under it, assuming either the object or underlying image includes transparency information. Once component objects are no longer needed—for example, in the maze image when the maze is completely drawn—the decoder can be instructed to discard them via the DISC chunk.

Chunks for Image Display, Manipulation, and Control

MNG includes nine chunks for manipulating and displaying image objects and for providing a kind of programmability of the decoder's operations. The most complex of these is the framing chunk, FRAM. It is used not only to delimit the chunks that form a single frame, but also to provide rendering information (including frame boundaries, where clipping occurs) and timing and synchronization information for subsequent frames. Included in FRAM's timing and synchronization information is a flag that allows the user to advance frames, which would be necessary in a slide show or business presentation that accompanies a live speaker.

The CLIP chunk provides an alternate and more precise method for specifying clipping boundaries. It can affect single objects or groups of objects, not just complete frames, and it can be given both as absolute pixel coordinates and in terms of a relative offset from a previous CLIP chunk. Images that are affected by a CLIP chunk will not be visible outside the clipping boundary, which allows for windowing effects.

The LOOP and ENDL chunks are possibly the most powerful of all MNG chunks. They provide one of the most fundamental programming functions, the ability to repeat one or more image-affecting actions many times. I mentioned earlier that *16million.mng*, the MNG image with all possible 24-bit colors in it, makes use of a pair of loops; those loops are the principal reason the complete image can be stored in less than 500 bytes. Without the ability to repeat the same copy-and-paste commands by looping several thousand times, the MNG version would be at least three times the size of the original PNG (close to 1,000 times its actual size)—unless the PNG version were simply renamed with a *.mng* extension.

In addition to a simple iteration count, which can go as high as two billion, the LOOP chunk can provide either the decoder or the user discretionary control over terminating the loop early. It also allows for control via signals (not necessarily Unix-style signals) from an external program; for example, this capability might be invoked by a program that monitors an infrared port, thus enabling the user to control the MNG decoder via a standard television remote control.

Often used in conjunction with loops and clipping is the MOVE chunk, one of MNG's big advantages over animated GIFs. As one might expect, MOVE allows one or more already defined image objects to be moved, either to an absolute position or relative to the previous position of each object. Together with LOOP and ENDL, MOVE provides the basis for animating sprites. Thus, one might imagine a small Christmas MNG, where perhaps half a dozen poses of a single reindeer are cloned, positioned appropriately (with transparency for overlaps, of course!), and looped at slightly different rates in order to create the illusion of eight tiny reindeer galloping independently across the winter sky.*

Up until now, we've glossed over the issue of how or whether any given image is actually seen; the implication has been that any image that gets defined is visible, unless it lies outside the image frame or local clipping region. But an object-based format should have a way of effectively turning on and off objects, and that is precisely where the SHOW chunk comes in. It contains a list of images that are affected and a 1-byte flag indicating the "show mode." The show-mode flag has two purposes: it can direct the decoder to modify the potential visibility of each object, and it can direct the decoder to display each object that is potentially visible. Note that I say *potential* visibility; any object outside the clipping region or frame or completely covered by another object will clearly not be visible regardless of whether it is "on." Among the show modes SHOW supports is one that cycles through the images in the specified range, making one potentially visible and the rest not visible. This is the means by which a single sprite frame in a multipose animation—such as the reindeer example—is displayed and advanced.

In order to provide a suitably snowy background for our reindeer example, MNG provides the background chunk, BACK. As with PNG's bKGD chunk, BACK can specify a single color to be used as the background in the absence of any better candidates. But it also can point at an image object to be used as the background, either tiled or not. And either the background color or the background image (or both) may be flagged as mandatory, so that even if the decoder has its own default background, for example, in a web browser, it must use the contents of the BACK chunk. When both the background color and the background image are required, the image takes precedence; the color is used around the edges if the image is smaller than the frame and not tiled, or if it is tiled but clipped to a smaller region, and it is the "true" background with which the image is blended if it has transparency.

---

* Add a few more poses of a waving fat guy in a sleigh, and you'll swear you hear sleigh bells ringing and chestnuts roasting on an open fire.

Finally, MNG provides a pair of housekeeping chunks, SAVE and SEEK. Together, they implement a one-entry stack similar to PostScript's `gsave` and `grestore` commands; they can be used to store the state of the MNG stream at a single point. Typically, this point would represent the end of a prologue section containing such basic information as gamma and chromaticity, the default background, any non-changeable images (the poses of our reindeer, for example), and so forth. Once the SAVE chunk appears—and only one is allowed—the prologue information is effectively frozen. Some of its chunks, such as gAMA, may be overridden by later chunks, but they will be restored as soon as a SEEK chunk is encountered. Any images in the prologue are fixed for the duration of the MNG stream, although one can always make a clone of any such image and move that instead.

The SEEK chunk is allowed to appear multiple times, and it is where the real power lies. As soon as a decoder encounters SEEK, it is allowed to throw out everything that appeared after the SAVE chunk, flush memory buffers, and so forth. If a MNG were structured as a long-form story, for example, the SEEK chunks might be used to delimit chapters or scenes—any props used for only one scene could be thrown away, thus reducing the memory burden on the decoder.

That summarizes the essential structure and capabilities of MNG. I've skipped over a few chunks, mostly ancillary ones, but the basic ideas have been covered. So let us now take a look at a few examples.

The Simplest MNG

Arguably the absolute simplest MNG is just the simplest PNG (recall Chapter 8, *PNG Basics*), renamed with a *.mng* extension. Another truly simple one would be the empty MNG, composed only of MHDR, FRAM, and MEND chunks, which could be used as a spacer on web pages—it would generate a transparent frame with the dimensions specified in MHDR. But if we consider only nontrivial MNGs, the most basic one probably looks like Figure 12-1.

This is a very basic, two-image slide show, consisting of a pair of grayscale or truecolor PNG images (note the absence of PLTE chunks, so they cannot be colormapped images) and nothing else. In fact, the MNG stream is a little too basic; it contains no color space information, so the images will not display the same way on different platforms. It includes no explicit timing information, so the decoder will display the images at a rate of one frame per tick. At the minimum value of MHDR's ticks-per-second field, that translates to a duration of just one second for the first image and one or more seconds for the second image (in practice, probably indefinitely). There is no way to use this abbreviated method to define a duration longer than one second. To avoid those problems, sRGB and FRAM chunks could be added after MHDR; the latter would specify an interframe delay—say, five seconds' worth. Thus the simplest reasonable MNG looks like Figure 12-2. Of

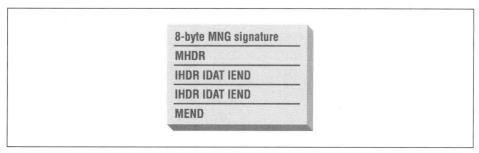

Figure 12-1: Layout of the simplest MNG

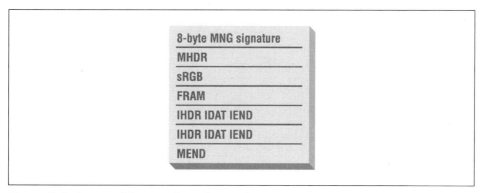

Figure 12-2: Layout of the second simplest MNG

course, sRGB should only be used if the images are actually in the standard RGB color space (see Chapter 10, *Gamma Correction and Precision Color*); if not, explicit gamma and chromaticity chunks can be used. Note that sRGB is only 13 bytes long, so its overhead is negligible.

An Animated MNG

As a more complex example, let us take a closer look at how we might create the animated reindeer example I described earlier. I will assume that a single cycle of a reindeer's gallop can be represented by six poses (sprite frames), and I'll further assume that all but the first pose can be efficiently coded as delta-PNGs. The complete MNG of a single reindeer galloping across the screen might be structured as shown in Figure 12-3. As always, we begin with MHDR, which defines the overall size of the image area. I've also included a gamma chunk so that the (nighttime) animation won't look too dark or too bright on other computer systems. The animation timing is set by the FRAM chunk, and then we begin loading sprite data for the six poses. The DEFI chunk ("define image") is one I haven't discussed so far; it is included here to set the potential visibility of the first pose explicitly—in this case, we want the first pose to be visible. After the IHDR, PLTE, IDAT, and IEND

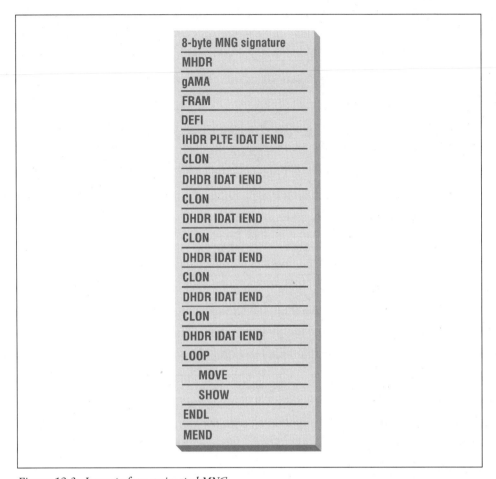

Figure 12-3: Layout of an animated MNG

chunks defining the first pose is a clone chunk, indicating that the second object
(the second pose in the six-pose sequence) is to be created by copying the first
object. The CLON chunk also indicates that the second object is *not* potentially visible yet. It is followed by the delta-PNG chunks that define the second image; we
can imagine either that the IDAT represents a complete replacement for the pixels
in the first image, with the delta part referring to the inheritance of the first image's
palette chunk, or perhaps the second image is truly a pixel-level delta from the
first image. Either way, the third through sixth images are defined similarly.

The heart of the animation is the loop at the end. In this case, I've included a
MOVE chunk, which moves the animation objects to the left by a few pixels every
iteration, and a SHOW chunk to advance the poses in sequence. If there are 600
iterations in the loop, the animation will progress through 100 six-pose cycles.

The complete eight-reindeer version would be very similar, but instead of defining full clones of the sprite frames, each remaining reindeer would be represented by partial clones of the six original poses. In effect, a partial clone is an empty object: it has its own object ID, visibility, and location, but it points at another object for its image data—in this case, at one of the six existing poses. So the seven remaining reindeer would be represented by 42 CLON chunks, of which seven would have the potential-visibility flag turned on. The loop would now include a total of eight SHOW chunks, each advancing one of the reindeer sprite's poses; a single MOVE chunk would still suffice to move all eight forward. Of course, this is still not quite the original design; this version has all eight reindeer galloping synchronously. To have them gallop at different rates would require separate FRAM chunks for each one.*

An Algorithmic MNG

Another good delta-PNG example, but one that creates only a single image algorithmically, is *16million.mng*, which I mentioned once or twice already. Figure 12-4 shows its complete contents. The initial FRAM chunk defines the structure of the stream as a composite frame, and it is followed by a DEFI chunk that indicates the image is potentially visible. The IHDR...IEND sequence defines the first row of the image (512 pixels wide), with red changing every pixel and blue incrementing by one at the halfway point. Then the outer loop begins—we'll return to that in a moment—followed immediately by the inner loop of 255 iterations. The inner loop simply increments the green value of every pixel in the row and moves the modified line down one. The DHDR, IDAT, and IEND chunks represent this green increment; the delta pixels are simply a sequence of 512 "0 1 0" triples. As one might guess, they compress extremely well; the 1,536 data bytes are packed into a total of 20 zlib-compressed bytes, including six zlib header and trailer bytes.

The outer loop has the task of resetting the green values to 0 again (easily accomplished by incrementing them by one more, so they roll over from 255 to 0) and of incrementing the blue values by two—recall that the first block of rows had blue = 0 on the left side and blue = 1 on the right. Thus the delta-PNG data at the bottom of the outer loop consists of 512 "0 1 2" triples, which compress to 23 bytes. Because the blue increments by two, this loop only needs to interate 128 times. It actually produces one extra row at the very end, but because this appears outside the frame boundary (as defined by the MHDR chunk), it is not visible.

---

* Note that Rudolph could be encoded as a set of six tiny delta-PNGs relative to the six original poses. Of course, to get that realistic Rudolph glow would require a semitransparent reddish region around his olfactory appendage, which necessarily involves either an alpha channel or a full tRNS chunk. But now we're talking True Art, and no sacrifice is too great.

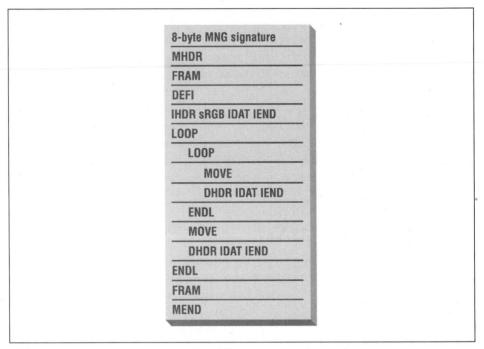

Figure 12-4: Layout of an algorithmic MNG

A JPEG Image with Transparency

Finally, let's look at an example of a JPEG image with an interleaved alpha channel. The particular example shown in Figure 12-5 is still wrapped inside a MNG stream, but it could as easily exist standalone if the MHDR and MEND chunks were removed and the signature changed to the JNG signature.

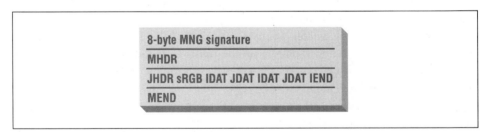

Figure 12-5: Layout of an alpha-JNG MNG

The JHDR chunk introduces the embedded JNG, defines its dimensions, and declares it to have an alpha channel. It is followed by an sRGB PNG chunk that indicates the image is in the International Color Consortium's standard RGB color space; decoders without access to a color management system should instead use the predetermined gamma and chromaticity values that approximate the sRGB color space (see Table 10-3).

The color-space chunk is followed by the IDAT chunks that define the image's alpha channel and the JDAT chunks that define its main (foreground) image. We've included a two-way interleave here in order to allow some possibility of progressive display, but in general one would want to interleave the IDATs and JDATs after perhaps every 16 or 32 rows—16 is a special number for JPEG decoders, and 16 or 32 rows is usually a reasonable amount to display at a time unless the image is quite skinny. On the other hand, keep in mind that each interleave (interleaf?) adds an extra 24 bytes of IDAT/JDAT wrapper code; this overhead should be balanced against the desired smoothness of the progressive output.

Note that we've included an IDAT first. This may be a good idea since the decoder often will be able to start displaying the image before all of the JDAT arrives, and we've assumed that the alpha channel is simple enough that the PNG data compressed extremely well (i.e., the IDAT is smaller than the JDAT of the same region). If the reverse is true, the JDAT should come first so that the image can be displayed as each line of alpha channel arrives and is decoded.

Also note that, although I've referred to "progressive" display here, I am not necessarily referring either to progressive JPEG or to interlaced PNG. In fact, MNG prohibits interlaced PNG alpha channels in JNG streams, and progressive JPEG may not mix well even with noninterlaced alpha channels, depending on how the application is written. The reason is that the final value of any given pixel will not be known until the JPEG is almost completely transmitted, and "approximate rendering" of partially transparent pixels (that is, rendering before the final values are known) requires that the unmodified background image remain available until the end, so that the approximated pixels can be recomputed during the final pass. Of course, a sophisticated decoder could display such an image progressively anyway, but it would incur a substantially greater memory and computational overhead than would be necessary when displaying a nonprogressive JPEG interleaved with an alpha channel. Instead, most decoders are likely to wait for sections of the image (e.g., the first 32 rows) to be competely transmitted before displaying anything. If progressive JPEG data *is* interleaved with the alpha channel, then such decoders will end up waiting for practically the entire image to be transmitted before even starting to render, which defeats the purpose of both interleaved JNG and progressive JPEG.

MNG Applications

As of April 1999, there were a total of six applications available that supported MNG in some form or another, with at least one or two more under development. The six available applications are listed; four of them were new in 1998.

viewpng

> The original MNG application, viewpng was Glenn Randers-Pehrson's test bed for PNG- and MNG-related features and modifications. It has not been actively developed since May 1997, and runs only under Irix on Silicon Graphics (SGI) workstations.
>
> *ftp://swrinde.nde.swri.edu/pub/mng/applications/sgi/*

ImageMagick

> This is a viewing and conversion toolkit for the X Window System; it runs under both Unix and VMS and has supported a minimal subset of MNG (MHDR, concatenated PNG images, MEND) since November 1997. In particular, it is capable of converting GIF animations to MNG and then back to GIF.
>
> *http://www.wizards.dupont.com/cristy/ImageMagick.html*

MNGeye

> Probably the most complete MNG decoder yet written, MNGeye was written by Gerard Juyn starting in May 1998 and runs under 32-bit Windows. Its author has indicated a willingness to base a MNG reference library on the code in MNGeye.
>
> *http://www.3-t.com/3-T/products/mngi/Homepage.html*

pngcheck

> A simple command-line program that can be compiled for almost any operating system, pngcheck simply prints the PNG chunk information in human-readable form and checks that it conforms to the specification. Partial MNG support was added by Greg Roelofs beginning in June 1998. Currently, the program does minimal checking of MNG streams, but it is still useful for listing MNG chunks and interpreting their contents.
>
> *http://www.cdrom.com/pub/png/pngcode.html#testers*

Paint Shop Pro

> PSP 5.0 uses MNG as the native format in its Animation Shop component, but it is not clear whether any MNG support is actually visible to the user. Paint Shop Pro runs under both 16-bit and 32-bit Windows.

> *http://www.jasc.com/psp.html*

XVidCap

> This is a free X-based video-capture application for Unix; it captures a rectangular area of the screen at intervals and saves the images in various formats. Originally XVidCap supported the writing of individual PNG images, but as of its 1.0 release, it also supports writing MNG streams.

> *http://home.pages.de/~rasca/xvidcap/*

While support for MNG is undeniably still quite sparse, it is nevertheless encouraging that a handful of applications already provide support for what has been, in effect, a moving target. Once MNG settles down (plans were to freeze the spec by May 1999) and is approved as a specification, and once some form of free MNG programming library is available to ease the burden on application developers, broader support can be expected.

New programs will be listed on the MNG applications page, *http://www.cdrom. com/pub/mng/mngapps.html.*

The Future?

MNG's development has not been the same success story that PNG's was, primarily due to a lesser interest in and need for a new animation format. Especially with the advent of the World Wide Web, people from many different walks of life have direct experience with ordinary images, and, in particular, they are increasingly aware of various limitations in formats such as GIF and JPEG. All of this worked (and continues to work) in PNG's favor. But when it comes to multi-image formats and animation, not only do these same people have much less experience, what need they do have for animation is largely met by the animated GIF format that Netscape made so popular. Animated GIFs may not be the answer to all of the world's web problems, but they're good enough 99% of the time. All of this, of course, works against MNG.

In addition, MNG is decidedly complex; objects may be modified by other objects, loops may be nested arbitrarily deeply, and so on. While it is debatable whether MNG is *too* complex—certainly there are some who feel it is—even its principal author freely admits that fully implementing the current draft specification is a considerable amount of work.

On the positive side, animated GIFs often can be rewritten as MNG animations in a tiny fraction of the file size, and there are no patent-fee barriers to implementing MNG in applications. Moreover, the Multiple-image Network Graphics format *is* making progress, both as a mature specification and as a supported format in real applications, and versions released since March 1999 now include implementor-friendly subsets known as MNG-LC and MNG-VLC (for Low Complexity and Very Low Complexity, respectively). Its future looks good.

PART III

Programming with PNG

13

Reading PNG Images

As with almost any kind of programming project, there are numerous alternatives one can take when writing a PNG-supporting program. Complete or partial code for reading and/or writing PNGs is available for the C, C++, Java, Pascal, tcl/tk, Python, and Visual Basic languages, at a minimum; some of it is in the form of commercial libraries, some as free source code, and some as a combination of both. Many of these in alternatives are listed in Chapter 16, *Other Libraries and Concluding Remarks*. One can even read and write PNG images directly, in effect implementing one's own PNG library, but this is a rather large undertaking and is generally not recommended except under special circumstances.

The granddaddy of all PNG libraries is *libpng*, the free reference library available as Standard (ANSI) C source code and used by many, if not most, PNG-supporting applications. It uses the similarly free zlib library (portable C source code) for compression and decompression, and in these next few chapters I'll provide detailed demonstrations of how to write programs with both.

A libpng-Based, PNG-Reading Demo Program

In order to provide a concrete demonstration of how to use libpng to read PNG images, I have written a complete (albeit basic) PNG viewer in Standard C. It consists of two main source files: a platform-independent one that includes all of the PNG- and libpng-specific code (*readpng.c*), and a platform-dependent file that contains all of the user interface and display code. The idea is that the PNG code (the "backend") is generic enough that it can be dropped into almost any image-reading C program, whether a viewer, editor, converter, or something else; it is the part that is of primary interest to us. The platform-dependent code ("frontend") is functional—yes, it really works!—but it is not complete or robust enough to be considered a final product.

The backend code was written for libpng version 1.0.3, but it should work with any 1.x release of the library. Later releases of libpng may add new interfaces, but the functions used here are expected to remain available more or less indefinitely, for backward compatibility. As for the frontend code, two versions are currently available: one for the X Window System (*rpng-x.c*; mainly for Unix systems, but also potentially VMS and OS/2), and one for Windows 95/98 and NT (*rpng-win.c*). I will avoid getting into the details of these as much as possible, but where it is unavoidable, I will either use excerpts that are common to both or else point out the differences between the two versions. Complete source listings for both flavors can be found at *http://www.cdrom.com/pub/png/pngbook.html*.

The basic PNG reader has the following features: it is file-based, it reads and displays a single image and then quits, and it is concerned only with reading and decoding that image—it has nothing better to do and can afford to wait on file input/output (I/O) and other potentially slow but non-CPU-intensive tasks. In other words, its characteristics are typical of standalone image viewers, converters, and many image editors, but not of web browsers. Browsers usually read from a network, which is often extremely slow compared to disk access (for example, due to limited modem bandwidth or just congested Internet sites), and they are usually busy formatting text and decoding several images at the same time—they *do* have something better to do than to wait for the rest of the file to show up. I'll address these issues in Chapter 14, *Reading PNG Images Progressively*, with the second demo program.

Preliminaries

Before we get into the heart of our basic demo program, I'll touch on a couple of mundane but nevertheless important details. The first is the libpng header file, *png.h*, which defines all of the libpng datatypes, declares all of the public function prototypes, and includes some useful macros. It must be included in any module that makes libpng function calls; in our case, we've segregated all of those in *readpng.c*, so that's the only place we need to include *png.h*:

```
#include "png.h"
```

Because *png.h* includes *zlib.h*, we need not include it explicitly, and most programs need not even worry about it, since there is rarely a need for the user's program to call zlib routines directly. But in our case we do want to make sure *zlib.h* is included somewhere. The reason for this is the second mundane detail: programs tend to be updated over time, and this often involves plugging in a newer version of a support library like libpng or zlib. When following up on a bug report, particularly with regard to software for which the source code is available (like the demo programs in this book), it is generally useful to know as much as possible about the version that exhibits the bug. In the presence of shared (dynamically linked) libraries, that's even more important. So as part of our demo program's usage screen—the poor man's version of an "about box"—we call a very small routine in *readpng.c* that indicates not only the versions of libpng and zlib with which it was compiled, but also the versions it is currently using:

```
void readpng_version_info()
{
    fprintf(stderr, "   Compiled with libpng %s; using libpng %s.\n",
      PNG_LIBPNG_VER_STRING, png_libpng_ver);
    fprintf(stderr, "   Compiled with zlib %s; using zlib %s.\n",
      ZLIB_VERSION, zlib_version);
}
```

The uppercase values here are macros defined in the *png.h* and *zlib.h* header files; they indicate the compile-time versions. The lowercase variables are globals exported by the two libraries, so they give the versions actually in use at the time the program is run. Ideally, each pair of version numbers will match, but it is not unusual for the user, and sometimes even the programmer, to be caught by an unsuspected mismatch.

readpng_init()

The "real" code in the basic PNG reader begins when the image file is opened (in *binary* mode!) and its stream pointer passed to our libpng-initialization routine, `readpng_init()`. `readpng_init()` also takes two pointers to long integers representing the height and width of the image:

```
int readpng_init(FILE *infile, long *pWidth, long *pHeight)
```

We can get away with using `longs` instead of `unsigned longs` because the PNG specification requires that image dimensions not exceed $2^{31} - 1$.* `readpng_init()` returns a status value; zero will be used to indicate success, and various nonzero values will indicate different errors.

The first thing we do in `readpng_init()` is read the first 8 bytes of the file and make sure they match the PNG signature bytes; if they don't, there is no need to waste time setting up libpng, allocating memory and so forth. Ordinarily one would read a block of 512 bytes or more, but libpng does its own buffered reads

---

* Of course, an image with dimensions that big is likely to exhaust the real and virtual memory on most systems, but we won't worry about that here.

and requires that no more than 8 bytes have been read before handing off control. So 8 bytes it is:

```
uch sig[8];

fread(sig, 1, 8, infile);
if (!png_check_sig(sig, 8))
    return 1;   /* bad signature */
```

There are two things to note here. The first is the use of the **uch** typedef, which stands for **unsigned char**; we use it for brevity and will likewise employ **ush** and **ulg** for **unsigned short** and **unsigned long**, respectively.* The second is that **png_check_sig()** and its slightly more general sibling **png_sig_cmp()** are unique among libpng routines in that they require no reference to any structures, nor any knowledge of the state of the PNG stream.

Assuming the file checked out with a proper PNG signature, the next thing to do is set up the PNG structs that will hold all of the basic information associated with the PNG image. The use of two or three structs instead of one is historical baggage; a future, incompatible version of the library is likely to hide one or both from the user and perhaps instead employ an image ID tag to keep track of multiple images. But for now two are necessary:

```
png_ptr = png_create_read_struct(PNG_LIBPNG_VER_STRING, NULL, NULL,
  NULL);
if (!png_ptr)
    return 4;   /* out of memory */

info_ptr = png_create_info_struct(png_ptr);
if (!info_ptr) {
    png_destroy_read_struct(&png_ptr, NULL, NULL);
    return 4;   /* out of memory */
}
```

The struct at which **png_ptr** points is used internally by libpng to keep track of the current state of the PNG image at any given moment; **info_ptr** is used to indicate what its state will be after all of the user-requested transformations are performed. One can also allocate a second information struct, usually referenced via an **end_ptr** variable; this can be used to hold all of the PNG chunk information that comes after the image data, in case it is important to keep pre- and post-IDAT information separate (as in an image editor, which should preserve as much of the existing PNG structure as possible). For this application, we don't care

---

* Other typedefs, such as **uchar** and **u_char**, are more common and recognizable, but these are sometimes also defined by system header files. Unlike macros, there is no way to test for the existence of a C typedef, and a repeated or conflicting typedef definition is treated as an error by most compilers.

where the chunk information comes from, so we will forego the `end_ptr` information struct and direct everything to `info_ptr`.

One or both of `png_ptr` and `info_ptr` are used in all remaining libpng calls, so we have simply declared them global in this case:

```
static png_structp png_ptr;
static png_infop info_ptr;
```

Global variables don't work in reentrant programs, where the same routines may get called in parallel to handle different images, but this demo program is explicitly designed to handle only one image at a time.

The pointers are now set up and pointing at allocated structs of the proper sizes— or else we've returned to the main program with an error. The next step is to set up a small amount of generic error-handling code. Instead of depending on error codes returned from each of its component functions, libpng employs a more efficient but rather uglier approach involving the `setjmp()` and `longjmp()` functions. Defined in the standard C header file *setjmp.h* (which is automatically included in *pngconf.h*, itself included in *png.h*), these routines effectively amount to a giant `goto` statement that can cross function boundaries. This avoids a lot of conditional testing (if `(error) return error;`), but it can make the program flow harder to understand in the case of errors. Nevertheless, that's what libpng uses by default, so that's what we use here:

```
if (setjmp(png_ptr->jmpbuf)) {
    png_destroy_read_struct(&png_ptr, &info_ptr, NULL);
    return 2;
}
```

The way to read this code fragment is as follows: the first time through, the `setjmp()` call saves the state of the program (registers, stack, and so on) in `png_ptr->jmpbuf` and returns successfully—that is, with a return value of zero—thus avoiding the contents of the if-block. But if an error later occurs and libpng invokes `longjmp()` on the same copy of `png_ptr->jmpbuf`, control suddenly returns to the if-block as if `setjmp()` had just returned, but this time with a nonzero return value. The if-test then evaluates to TRUE, so the PNG structs are destroyed and we return to the main program.

But wait! Didn't I just finish lecturing about the evils of direct access to structure members? Yet here I am, referring to the `jmpbuf` member of the main PNG struct. The reason is that there is simply no other way to get a pointer to the `longjmp` buffer in any release of libpng through version 1.0.3. And, sadly, there may not be any clean and backward-compatible way to work around this limitation in future releases, either. The unfortunate fact is that the ANSI committee responsible for defining the C language and standard C library managed to standardize `jmp_buf` in such a way that one cannot reliably pass pointers to it, nor can one be certain

---

The Dark Side

Let's take a brief break in order to make a couple of points about programming practices, mostly bad ones. The first is that old versions of libpng (pre-1.0) required one to allocate memory for the two structs manually, via `malloc()` or a similar function. This is strongly discouraged now. The reason is that libpng continues to evolve, and in an environment with shared or dynamically linked libraries (DLLs), a program that was compiled with an older version of libpng may suddenly find itself using a new version with larger or smaller structs. The `png_create_XXXX_struct()` functions allow the version of the library that is actually being used to allocate the proper structs for itself, avoiding many problems down the road.

Similarly, old versions of libpng encouraged or even required the user to access members of the structs directly—for example, the image height might be available as `info_ptr->height` or `png_ptr->height` or even (as in this case) both! This was bad, not only because similar struct members sometimes had different values that could change at different times, but also because any program that is compiled to use such an approach effectively assumes that the same struct member is always at the same offset from the beginning of the struct. This is not a serious problem if the libpng routines are statically linked, although there is some danger that things will break if the program is later recompiled with a newer version of libpng. But even if libpng itself never changes the definition of the struct's contents, a user who compiles a new DLL version with slightly different compilation parameters—for example, with structure-packing turned on—may have suddenly shifted things around so they appear at new offsets. libpng can also be compiled with certain features disabled, which in turn eliminates the corresponding structure members from the definition of the structs and therefore alters the offsets of any later structure members. And I already mentioned that libpng is evolving: new things get added to the structs periodically, and perhaps an existing structure member is found to have been defined with an incorrect size, which is then corrected. The upshot is that direct access to struct members is very, very bad. Don't do it. Don't let your friends do it. We certainly won't be doing it here.

---

that its size is constant even on a single system. In particular, if a certain macro is defined when libpng is compiled but not for a libpng-using application, then `jmp_buf` may have different sizes when the application calls `setjmp()` and when libpng calls `longjmp()`. The resulting inconsistency is more likely than not to cause the application to crash.

The solution, which is already possible with current libpng releases and will probably be required as of some future version, is to install a custom error handler.

This is simply a user function that libpng calls instead of its own longjmp()-based error handler whenever an error is encountered; like longjmp(), it is not expected to return. But there is no problem at all if the custom error handler itself calls longjmp(): since this happens within the application's own code space, its concept of jmp_buf is completely consistent with that of the code that calls setjmp() elsewhere in the application. Indeed, there is no longer any need to use the jmpbuf element of the main libpng struct with this approach—the application can maintain its own jmp_buf. I will demonstrate this safer approach in Chapter 14.

Note the use of png_destroy_read_struct() to let libpng free any memory associated with the PNG structs. We used it earlier, too, for cases in which creating the info struct failed; then we passed png_ptr and two NULLs. Here we pass png_ptr, info_ptr and one NULL. Had we allocated the second info struct (end_ptr), the third argument would point at it, or, more precisely, at its pointer, so that end_ptr itself could be set to NULL after the struct is freed.

Having gotten all of the petty housekeeping details out of the way, we next set up libpng so it can read the PNG file, and then we begin doing so:

```
png_init_io(png_ptr, infile);
png_set_sig_bytes(png_ptr, 8);
png_read_info(png_ptr, info_ptr);
```

The png_init_io() function takes our file stream pointer (infile) and stores it in the png_ptr struct for later use. png_set_sig_bytes() lets libpng know that we already checked the 8 signature bytes, so it should not expect to find them at the current file pointer location.

png_read_info() is the first libpng call we've seen that does any real work. It reads and processes not only the PNG file's IHDR chunk but also any other chunks up to the first IDAT (i.e., everything before the image data). For colormapped images this includes the PLTE chunk and possibly tRNS and bKGD chunks. It typically also includes a gAMA chunk; perhaps cHRM, sRGB, or iCCP; and often tIME and some tEXt chunks. All this information is stored in the information struct and some in the PNG struct, too, but for now, all we care about is the contents of IHDR—specifically, the image width and height:

```
png_get_IHDR(png_ptr, info_ptr, &width, &height, &bit_depth,
   &color_type, NULL, NULL, NULL);
*pWidth = width;
*pHeight = height;

return 0;
```

Once again, since this is a single-image program, I've been lazy and used global variables not only for the image dimensions but also for the image's bit depth (bits per sample—R, G, B, A, or gray—or per palette index, *not* per pixel) and color type. The image dimensions are also passed back to the main program via the last two arguments of `readpng_init()`. The other two variables will be used later. If we were interested in whether the image is interlaced or what compression and filtering methods it uses, we would use actual values instead of NULLs for the last three arguments to `png_get_IHDR()`. Note that the PNG 1.0 and 1.1 specifications define only a single allowed value (0) for either the compression type or the filtering method. In this context, compression type 0 is the deflate method with a maximum window size of 32 KB, and filtering method 0 is PNG's per-row adaptive method with five possible filter types. See Chapter 9, *Compression and Filtering*, for details.

That wraps up our `readpng_init()` function. Back in the main program, various things relating to the windowing system are initialized, but before the display window itself is created, we potentially make one more `readpng` call to see if the image includes its own background color. In fact, this function could have been incorporated into `readpng_init()`, particularly if all program parameters used by the backend `readpng` functions and the frontend display routines were passed via an application-specific struct, but we didn't happen to set things up that way. Also, note that this second `readpng` call is unnecessary if the user has already specified a particular background color to be used. In this program, a simple command-line argument is used, but a more sophisticated application might employ a graphical color wheel, RGB sliders, or some other color-choosing representation.

readpng_get_bgcolor()

In any case, assuming the user did not specify a background color, we call `readpng_get_bgcolor()` to check the PNG file for one. It takes as arguments pointers to three unsigned character values:

```
int readpng_get_bgcolor(uch *red, uch *green, uch *blue)
```

As before, we start with a `setjmp()` block to handle libpng errors, then check whether the PNG file had a bKGD chunk:

```
if (!png_get_valid(png_ptr, info_ptr, PNG_INFO_bKGD))
    return 1;
```

Assuming the `png_get_valid()` call returned a nonzero value, we next have libpng give us a pointer to a small struct containing the bKGD color information:

```
png_color_16p pBackground;

png_get_bKGD(png_ptr, info_ptr, &pBackground);
```

(pBackground was defined at the top of the function.) `pBackground` now points at a `png_color_16` struct, which is defined as follows:

```
typedef struct png_color_16_struct
{
    png_byte index;
    png_uint_16 red;
    png_uint_16 green;
    png_uint_16 blue;
    png_uint_16 gray;
} png_color_16;
```

As suggested by the struct members' names, not all of them are valid with all PNG image types. The first member, `index`, is only valid with palette-based images, for example, and `gray` is only valid with grayscale images. But it is one of libpng's handy little features (presently undocumented) that the `red`, `green`, and `blue` struct members are always valid, and those happen to be precisely the values we want.

The other thing to note, however, is that the elements we need are defined as `png_uint_16`, i.e., as 16-bit (or larger) unsigned integers. That suggests that the color values we get back may depend on the bit depth of the image, which is indeed the case. In fact, this is true regardless of whether the calling program requested libpng to convert 16-bit values or 1-, 2-, and 4-bit values to 8-bit; this is another currently undocumented tidbit. We'll be feeding all of these little gotchas back to the libpng maintainer, however, so one can assume that the documentation will be slightly more complete by the time this book is published.

Since we'll be dealing only with 8-bit samples in this program, and, in particular, since the arguments to `readpng_get_bgcolor()` are pointers to unsigned (8-bit) characters, we need to shift the high-order bits down in the case of 16-bit data or expand them in the case of low-bit-depth values (only possible with grayscale images). And either way, we need to pass the values back to the main program. Thus:

```
        if (bit_depth == 16) {
            *red   = pBackground->red   >> 8;
            *green = pBackground->green >> 8;
            *blue  = pBackground->blue  >> 8;
        } else if (color_type == PNG_COLOR_TYPE_GRAY && bit_depth < 8) {
            if (bit_depth == 1)
                *red = *green = *blue = pBackground->gray? 255 : 0;
            else if (bit_depth == 2)    /* i.e., max value is 3 */
                *red = *green = *blue = (255/3) * pBackground->gray;
            else /* bit_depth == 4 */   /* i.e., max value is 15 */
                *red = *green = *blue = (255/15) * pBackground->gray;
        } else {
            *red   = pBackground->red;
            *green = pBackground->green;
```

```
        *blue  = pBackground->blue;
    }

    return 0;
```

With that, the main program now has enough information to create an image window of the proper size and fill it with the background color, which it does. The top row of Figure C-5 in the color insert shows the two cases: the middle image is displayed with the background color specified in the PNG file itself, while the image on the right is shown with a user-specified background color.

The main program next calls the heart of the `readpng` code: `readpng_get_image()`, which sets the desired libpng transformations, allocates a PNG image buffer, decodes the image, and returns a pointer to the raw data. Before we look at that in detail, we should first discuss some of the design decisions that led to it.

Design Decisions

We decided at the outset that we didn't want to deal with a lot of PNG bit depths; we have plenty of that in the frontend code (at least for the X version ... sigh). Being fond of alpha transparency and the nice effects it can produce, we did want to retain full transparency information, however. In both cases, we were willing to sacrifice a minimal memory footprint in favor of simplicity and, to some extent, speed. Thus, we chose to expand or reduce all PNG image types to 24-bit RGB, optionally with a full 8-bit alpha channel. In other words, the output would always be either three channels (RGB) or four channels (RGBA).

Handling *all* alpha blending on our own, in the frontend, is not strictly necessary. In the case of a flat background color, which is all I've discussed so far, libpng can be instructed to blend the background color (either from the PNG file or as supplied by the user) with the foreground pixels, thereby eliminating the alpha channel; the relevant function is `png_set_background()`. The result would have been a single output format to deal with: three-channel, 24-bit RGB. But we had in mind from the outset the possibility of loading or generating a complete background image, not just a background color, and libpng currently has no provision for blending two images.

Gamma and Color Correction

Since this routine is also where any gamma and color correction (recall Chapter 10, *Gamma Correction and Precision Color*) would take place, we should step back a moment and look at how the main program deals with that. First I have a confession: I did not attempt any color correction. (Truly, I am scum.) But this does not excuse you, the reader, from supporting it, at least in higher-end applications! The X Window System's base library, Xlib, has included the X Color Management System since X11R5; it is accessed via the Xcms functions, an extensive API supporting everything from color-space conversion to gamut compression. Apple supports the ColorSync system on the Macintosh and will be releasing a version for Windows. And Microsoft, if not already supporting the sRGB color space natively in recent releases of Windows, certainly can be assumed to do so in coming releases; they and Hewlett-Packard collaborated on the original sRGB proposal.

But where color correction can be a little tricky, gamma correction is quite straightforward. All one needs is the "gamma" value (exponent) of the user's display system and that of the PNG file itself. If the PNG file does not include a gAMA or sRGB chunk, there is little to be done except perhaps ask the user for a best-guess value; a PNG decoder is likely to do more harm than good if it attempts to guess on its own. We will simply forego any attempt at gamma correction, in that case. But on the assumption that most PNG files will be well behaved and include gamma information, we included the following code at the beginning of the main program:

```
    double LUT_exponent;
    double CRT_exponent = 2.2;
    double default_display_exponent;

#if defined(NeXT)
    LUT_exponent = 1.0 / 2.2;
    /*
    if (some_next_function_that_returns_gamma(&next_gamma))
        LUT_exponent = 1.0 / next_gamma;
     */
#elif defined(sgi)
    LUT_exponent = 1.0 / 1.7;
    /* there doesn't seem to be any documented function to
     * get the "gamma" value, so we do it the hard way */
    infile = fopen("/etc/config/system.glGammaVal", "r");
    if (infile) {
        double sgi_gamma;

        fgets(fooline, 80, infile);
        fclose(infile);
        sgi_gamma = atof(fooline);
        if (sgi_gamma > 0.0)
            LUT_exponent = 1.0 / sgi_gamma;
    }
#elif defined(Macintosh)
    LUT_exponent = 1.8 / 2.61;
    /*
    if (some_mac_function_that_returns_gamma(&mac_gamma))
        LUT_exponent = mac_gamma / 2.61;
     */
```

```
#else
    LUT_exponent = 1.0;     /* assume no LUT:  most PCs */
#endif

    default_display_exponent = LUT_exponent * CRT_exponent;
```

The goal here is to make a reasonably well informed guess as to the overall display system's exponent ("gamma"), which, as you'll recall from Chapter 10, is the product of the lookup table's exponent and that of the monitor. Essentially all monitors have an exponent of 2.2, so I've assumed that throughout. And almost all PCs and many workstations forego the lookup table (LUT), effectively giving them a LUT exponent of 1.0; the result is that their overall display-system exponent is 2.2. This is reflected by the last line in the ifdef block.

A few well-known systems have LUT exponents quite different from 1.0. The most extreme of these is the NeXT cube (and subsequent noncubic models), which has a lookup table with a 1/2.2 exponent, resulting in an overall exponent of 1.0 (i.e., it has a "linear transfer function"). Although some third-party utilities can modify the lookup table (with a "gamma" value whose inverse is the LUT exponent, as on SGI systems), there appears to be no system facility to do so and no portable method of determining what value a third-party panel might have loaded. So we assume 1.0 in all cases when the NeXT-specific macro **NeXT** is defined.

Silicon Graphics workstations and Macintoshes also have nonidentity lookup tables, but in both cases the LUT exponent can be varied by system utilities. Unfortunately, in both cases the value is varied via a parameter called "gamma" that matches neither the LUT exponent nor the other system's usage. On SGI machines, the "gamma" value is the inverse of the LUT exponent (as on the NeXT) and can be obtained either via a command (**gamma**) or from a system configuration file (*/etc/config/system.glGammaVal*); there is no documented method to retrieve the value directly via a system function call. Here we have used the file-based method. If we read it successfully, the overall system exponent is calculated accordingly; if not, we assume the default value used on factory-shipped SGI systems: "gamma" of 1.7, which implies a display-system exponent of 2.2/1.7, or 1.3. Note, however, that what is being determined is the exponent of the console attached to the system running the program, not necessarily that of the actual display. That is, X programs can display on remote systems, and the exponent of the remote display system might be anything. One could attempt to determine whether the display is local by checking the **DISPLAY** environment variable, but to do so correctly could involve several system calls (**uname()**, **gethostbyname()**, etc.) and is beyond the scope of this demo program. A user-level workaround is to set the **SCREEN_GAMMA** variable appropriately; I'll describe that in just a moment.

The Macintosh "gamma" value is proportional to the LUT exponent, but it is multiplied by an additional constant factor of 2.61. The default gamma is 1.8, leading to an overall exponent of (1.8/2.61) × 2.2, or 1.5. Since neither of the two frontends (X or Windows) is designed to work on a Mac, the code inside the Macintosh if-def (and the `Macintosh` macro itself) is intended for illustration only, not as a serious example of ready-to-compile code. Indeed, a standard component of Mac OS 8.5 is Apple's ColorSync color management system (also available as an add-on for earlier systems), which is the recommended way to handle both gamma and color correction on Macs.

It is entirely possible that the user has calibrated the display system more precisely than is reflected in the preceding code, or perhaps has a system unlike any of the ones we have described. The main program also gives the user the option of specifying the display system's exponent directly, either with an environment variable (`SCREEN_GAMMA` is suggested by the libpng documentation) or by direct input. For the latter, we have once again resorted to the simple expedient of a command-line option, but a more elegant program might pop up a dialog box of some sort, or even provide a calibration screen. In any case, our main program first checks for the environment variable:

```
if ((p = getenv("SCREEN_GAMMA")) != NULL)
    display_exponent = atof(p);
else
    display_exponent = default_display_exponent;
```

If the variable is found, it is used; otherwise, the previously calculated default exponent is used. Then the program processes the command-line options and, if the `-gamma` option is found, its argument replaces all previously obtained values.

That turned out to be a moderately lengthy explanation of the demo program's approach to gamma correction (or, more specifically, to finding the correct value for the display system's exponent), mostly because of all the different ways the value can be found: system-specific educated guesses at the time of compilation, system-specific files or API calls at runtime, an environment variable, or direct user input. The actual code is only about 20 lines long.

readpng_get_image()

Once the display-system exponent is found, it is passed to the `readpng` code as the first argument to `readpng_get_image()`:

```
uch *readpng_get_image(double display_exponent, int *pChannels,
                       ulg *pRowbytes)
```

As with the previous two `readpng` routines, `readpng_get_image()` first installs the libpng error-handler code (`setjmp()`). It then sets up all of the

transformations that correspond to the design decisions described earlier, starting
with these three:

```
if (color_type == PNG_COLOR_TYPE_PALETTE)
    png_set_expand(png_ptr);
if (color_type == PNG_COLOR_TYPE_GRAY && bit_depth < 8)
    png_set_expand(png_ptr);
if (png_get_valid(png_ptr, info_ptr, PNG_INFO_tRNS))
    png_set_expand(png_ptr);
```

The astute reader will have noticed something odd in the first block: the same
function, **png_set_expand()**, is called several times, in different contexts but
with identical arguments. Indeed, this is perhaps the single most confusing issue in
all versions of libpng up through 1.0.3. In the first case, **png_set_expand()** is
used to set a flag that will force palette images to be expanded to 24-bit RGB. In
the second case, it indicates that low-bit-depth grayscale images are to be
expanded to 8 bits. And in the third case, the function is used to expand any tRNS
chunk data into a full alpha channel. Note that the third case can apply to either of
the first two, as well. That is, either a palette image or a grayscale image may have
a transparency chunk; in each case, **png_set_expand()** would be called twice
in succession, for different purposes (though with the same effect—the function
merely sets a flag, independent of context). A less confusing approach would be
to create separate functions for each purpose:

```
/* These functions are FICTITIOUS!  They DO NOT EXIST in any
 * version of libpng to date (through 1.0.3). */

if (color_type == PNG_COLOR_TYPE_PALETTE)
    png_set_palette_to_rgb(png_ptr);
if (color_type == PNG_COLOR_TYPE_GRAY && bit_depth < 8)
    png_set_gray_1_2_4_to_8(png_ptr);
if (png_get_valid(png_ptr, info_ptr, PNG_INFO_tRNS))
    png_set_tRNS_to_alpha(png_ptr);
```

With luck, these functions will be accepted for libpng version 1.0.4 (and later).

Getting back to the real code, the next pair of transformations involves calls to two
new functions, one to reduce images with 16-bit samples (e.g., 48-bit RGB) to 8
bits per sample and one to expand grayscale images to RGB. Fortunately these are
appropriately named:

```
if (bit_depth == 16)
    png_set_strip_16(png_ptr);
if (color_type == PNG_COLOR_TYPE_GRAY ||
    color_type == PNG_COLOR_TYPE_GRAY_ALPHA)
    png_set_gray_to_rgb(png_ptr);
```

The final transformation sets up the gamma-correction code, but only if the file
contains gamma information itself:

```
double  gamma;

if (png_get_gAMA(png_ptr, info_ptr, &gamma))
    png_set_gamma(png_ptr, display_exponent, gamma);
```

Once again, the declaration of **gamma** is included here for context; it actually occurs at the beginning of the function. The conditional approach toward gamma correction is on the assumption that guessing incorrectly is more harmful than doing no correction at all; alternatively, the user could be queried for a best-guess value. This approach was chosen because a simple viewer such as we describe here is probably more likely to be used for images created on the local system than for images coming from other systems, for which a web browser might be the usual viewer. An alternate approach, espoused by drafts of the sRGB specification, is to assume that all unlabeled images exist in the sRGB space, which effectively gives them gamma values of 0.45455. On a PC-like system with no lookup table, the two approaches amount to the same thing: multiply the image's gamma of 0.45455 by the display-system exponent of 2.2, and you get an overall exponent of 1.0—i.e., no correction is necessary. But on a Macintosh, SGI, or NeXT system, the sRGB recommendation would result in additional processing that would tend to darken images. This would effectively favor images created on PCs over (unlabeled) images created on the local system. The upshot is that one is making assumptions either way; which approach is more acceptable is likely to be a matter of personal taste. Note that the PNG 1.1 Specification recommends that the viewer "choose a likely default gamma value, but allow the user to select a new one if the result proves too dark or too light."

In any case, once we've registered all of our desired transformations, we request that libpng update the information struct appropriately via the **png_read_update_info**() function. Then we get the values for the number of channels and the size of each row in the image, allocate memory for the main image buffer, and set up an array of pointers:

```
png_uint_32  i, rowbytes;
png_bytep  row_pointers[height];

png_read_update_info(png_ptr, info_ptr);

*pRowbytes = rowbytes = png_get_rowbytes(png_ptr, info_ptr);
*pChannels = (int)png_get_channels(png_ptr, info_ptr);

if ((image_data = (uch *)malloc(rowbytes*height)) == NULL) {
    png_destroy_read_struct(&png_ptr, &info_ptr, NULL);
    return NULL;
}

for (i = 0;  i < height;  ++i)
    row_pointers[i] = image_data + i*rowbytes;
```

The only slightly strange feature here is the **row_pointers[]** array, which is something libpng needs for its processing. In this program, where we have allocated one big block for the image, the array is somewhat unnecessary; libpng could just take a pointer to **image_data** and calculate the row offsets itself. But the row-pointers approach offers the programmer the freedom to do things like setting up the image for line doubling (by incrementing each row pointer by **2*rowbytes**) or even eliminating the **image_data** array entirely in favor of per-row progressive processing on a single row buffer. Of course, it is also quite a convenient way to deal with reading and displaying the image.

In fact, that was the last of the preprocessing to be done. The next step is to go ahead and read the entire image into the array we just allocated:

```
png_read_image(png_ptr, row_pointers);
```

The **readpng** routine can return at this point, but we added one final libpng call for completeness. **png_read_end()** checks the remainder of the image for correctness and optionally reads the contents of any chunks appearing after the IDATs (typically tEXt or tIME) into the indicated information struct. If one has no need for the post-IDAT chunk data, as in our case, the second argument can be NULL:

```
png_read_end(png_ptr, NULL);

return image_data;
```

readpng_cleanup()

With that, **readpng_get_image()** returns control to our main program, which closes the input file and promptly calls another **readpng** routine to clean up all allocated memory (except for the image data itself, of course):

```
void readpng_cleanup(int free_image_data)
{
    if (free_image_data && image_data) {
        free(image_data);
        image_data = NULL;
    }

    if (png_ptr && info_ptr) {
        png_destroy_read_struct(&png_ptr, &info_ptr, NULL);
        png_ptr = NULL;
        info_ptr = NULL;
    }
}
```

That is, the main program calls **readpng_cleanup()** with a zero (FALSE) argument here so that **image_data** is not freed. If it had waited to clean up until after the user requested the program to end, it would have passed a nonzero (TRUE) argument instead. Setting `png_ptr` and `info_ptr` to NULL is unnecessary here, since `png_destroy_read_struct()` does that for us; but we do it anyway, since it's a habit that tends to save on debugging time in the long run.

Compositing and Displaying the Image

What one does at this point is, of course, entirely application-specific. Our main program calls a display routine that simply puts the pixels on the screen, first compositing against the desired background color if the final image has four channels (i.e., if it includes an alpha channel). Then it waits for the user to quit the program, at which point it destroys the window, frees any allocated memory, and exits.

The compositing step is perhaps interesting; it employs a macro copied from the *png.h* header file, albeit renamed to avoid problems, should *png.h* ever be included in the main program file, and using equivalent typedefs:

```
#define alpha_composite(composite, fg, alpha, bg) {              \
    ush temp = ((ush)(fg)*(ush)(alpha) +                         \
                (ush)(bg)*(ush)(255 - (ush)(alpha)) + (ush)128); \
    (composite) = (uch)((temp + (temp >> 8)) >> 8);              \
}
```

The unique thing about this macro is that it does *exact* alpha blending on 8-bit samples (for example, the red components of a foreground pixel and a background pixel) without performing any division. This macro and its 16-bit-per-sample sibling have been tested on a number of PC and workstation architectures and found to be anywhere from 2 to 13 times faster than the standard approach, which divides by 255 or 65,535, depending on sample size. Of course, hardware-assisted alpha compositing will always be faster than doing it in software; many 3D accelerator cards provide this function, and often they can be used even in 2D applications. Approximate methods (which divide by 256 of 65,536 by bit-shifting) are another fast alternative when absolute accuracy is not important.

Getting the Source Code

All of the source files for the *rpng* demo program (*rpng-x.c, rpng-win.c, readpng. c, readpng.h*, and makefiles) are available both in print and electronically, under a BSD-like Open Source license. The files will be available for download from the following URL for the foreseeable future:

> *http://www.cdrom.com/pub/png/pngbook.html*

Bug fixes, new features and ports, and other contributions may be integrated into the code, time permitting.

Alternative Approaches

It should go without saying that the program presented here is among the simplest of many possibilities. It would also have been possible to write it monolithically, either as a single `readpng` function or even as inlined code within `main()`, which is precisely how the sample code in the libpng documentation reads. Libpng allows user-defined I/O routines (in place of standard file I/O), custom memory allocators, and alternate error handlers to be installed, although there is currently no provision for an error-handling function that returns control to the libpng routine that called it.

There are also other options for the platform-dependent frontends, of course; reading an image from a file is often undesirable. One method in particular is worth mentioning, since it does not appear to be documented anywhere else at the time of this writing. On the 32-bit Windows platform, a "private" clipboard may be used to transfer PNG images between applications. The data format is simply the normal PNG stream, beginning with the signature bytes and ending with the IEND chunk. An application like *rpng-win* would register the private clipboard and then read PNG data from it in the usual way. The following code fragment outlines the essential steps:

```
UINT clipbd_format = RegisterClipboardFormat("PNG");

if (clipbd_format == 0) {
    /* call failed:  use GetLastError() for extended info */
} else if (OpenClipboard(NULL)) {
    HANDLE handle = GetClipboardData(clipbd_format);

    if (handle == NULL) {
        /* call failed:  use GetLastError() for info */
    } else {
        int data_length = GlobalSize(handle);   /* upper bound */

        if (data_length == 0) {
            /* call failed:  use GetLastError() for info */
        } else {
            BYTE *data_ptr = GlobalLock(handle);

            if (data_ptr == NULL) {
                /* call failed:  use GetLastError() for info */
            } else {

                /*================================================*/
                /* copy PNG data immediately, but don't flag an   */
                /* error if there are some extra bytes after IEND */
                /*================================================*/

                if (GlobalUnlock(handle) == 0) {
                    /* call failed:  use GetLastError() for info */
```

```
                        }
                    }
                }
            }
            if (CloseClipboard()) {
                /* call failed:  use GetLastError() for info */
            }
        } else {
            /* another window has the clipboard open */
            /* (can use GetOpenClipboardWindow() to get handle to it) */
        }
```

That one can do something like this in principle isn't new or unusual; what is new is that the "PNG" clipboard has already been implemented in some Microsoft apps, including Office 2000. All any other application needs in order to interoperate via this clipboard is its name and data format, which I've just described. Thanks to John Bowler for providing this information to the PNG Development Group.

In the next chapter, I'll look at a more radical alternative to the basic PNG decoder: a version that feeds libpng data at its own pace, rather than letting libpng read (and possibly wait for) as much data as it wants. Progressive viewers are at the heart of most online browsers, so we'll look at how to write one for PNG images.

14

Reading PNG Images Progressively

As I noted in Chapter 13, *Reading PNG Images*, the basic style of PNG viewer that reads each image from a file in a single gulp is appropriate to some applications, but not all. In particular, web browsers and the like tend to read images from a network, and they often download more than one image at the same time. It is usually desirable for them to display whatever is available at regular intervals so the user can get some idea of the contents of the page as quickly as possible. The alternative—waiting the minute or more that some web pages take to download—went out of style almost as soon as Netscape Navigator became available late in 1994.

This style of display is known as *progressive*, and as one might imagine, it places strong constraints on the structure of the program. In fact, in many ways a progressive reader is completely inverted from the basic design showed in the last chapter: instead of giving the image library control for the duration of the decoding process, in a progressive reader, the main program retains control, effectively throttling the library by restricting the amount of encoded image data it makes available per call. This will become much clearer with a concrete example, so let us jump right in.

Preliminaries

As in the first demo program, I have divided this program into a PNG-specific file (*readpng2.c* this time) and a platform-dependent file whose filename, logically enough, depends on the platform. I refer to these two parts as the "backend" and "frontend," respectively; I'll once again concentrate on the libpng-specific backend. This time through, I'll skim over many of the most basic libpng concepts, however. Indeed, most of the individual blocks of PNG code are virtually identical to their counterparts in the basic reader. What has changed is their overall order in the grand scheme of things.

I'll first note some of the things that haven't changed. As before, our overall design choices include a desire to deal only with 24-bit RGB or 32-bit RGBA data; I will instruct libpng to transform the PNG image data exactly as before. I will also make a game attempt at doing proper gamma correction; the main program not only calculates reasonable defaults based on the platform but also gives the user a chance to specify things precisely. The code for this is unchanged and will not be presented again. Likewise, I will continue to use the abbreviated typedefs uch, ush, and ulg in place of the more unwieldy unsigned char, unsigned short, and unsigned long, respectively.

Within the PNG-specific module, I will once again begin with the inclusion of the libpng header file, *png.h*, which in turn includes the *zlib.h* header file. (The latest releases at the time of this writing are libpng 1.0.3 and zlib 1.1.3, which are the versions used by the demo programs.) The four-line readpng2_version_info() routine is no different from that in the first demo program.

Because this style of PNG reader is intended for the kind of application that decodes multiple images simultaneously (read: browsers), one difference from the first program is the lack of global or static variables in the PNG code. Instead, all image-specific variables are embedded in a structure, which could be allocated repeatedly for as many images as desired. Although some globals are still used in the frontend code, they are all either truly global (that is, they could be used in a multi-image program without problems), or else they could be moved into the per-image struct, too.

readpng2_init()

The serious PNG code once again begins with the main program opening the PNG file, and I emphasize that it is opened in *binary* mode—hence the "b" flag in the second argument to fopen() ("rb"). A real browser would open an HTTP connection to a remote server and request the image instead of opening it as a local file. Rather than immediately jumping into our PNG initialization routine, readpng2_init(), as was the case in the first demo, this version first reads a block of data from the file and checks the first eight bytes for the PNG signature:

```
    if (!(infile = fopen(filename, "rb")))
        /* report an error and exit */
    } else {
        incount = fread(inbuf, 1, INBUFSIZE, infile);
        if (incount < 8 || !readpng2_check_sig(inbuf, 8)) {
            /* report an error and exit */
        } else {
```

```
            rc = readpng2_init(&rpng2_info);

            [etc.]
        }
    }
```

The `readpng2_check_sig()` function is nothing more than a wrapper to call
`png_check_sig()`. It would also have been possible to call the libpng routine
directly; libpng is unique in that it does not require any special setup or datatypes,
and it returns an integer value, which is the default for C functions. But that would
violate our separation of libpng and non-libpng code, if only in a tiny way, and it
would prevent the compiler from checking the argument and return types against
a prototype, in case the libpng function should ever change.

Sharp-eyed readers will have noticed that I call `readpng2_init()` with a different argument than last time:

```
    int readpng2_init(mainprog_info *mainprog_ptr)
```

The difference from the first version is that the function now has only one argument, a pointer to an object type called **mainprog_info**. This is just the per-
image struct mentioned earlier. It is defined as follows:

```
    typedef struct _mainprog_info {
        double display_exponent;
        ulg width;
        ulg height;
        void *png_ptr;
        void *info_ptr;
        void (*mainprog_init)(void);
        void (*mainprog_display_row)(ulg row_num);
        void (*mainprog_finish_display)(void);
        uch *image_data;
        uch **row_pointers;
        jmp_buf jmpbuf;
        int passes;
        int rowbytes;
        int channels;
        int need_bgcolor;
        int done;
        uch bg_red;
        uch bg_green;
        uch bg_blue;
    } mainprog_info;
```

I'll explain each member as we need it, but it is clear that many of the variables
that were formerly global or passed as arguments to functions now reside in this
struct. Note that similar variable types have been grouped, with the smallest ones
at the end, so that the larger types will be aligned on even memory boundaries by
default, minimizing the amount of padding the compiler has to add to the
structure.

`readpng2_init()` begins by calling libpng to allocate the two PNG structs:

```
png_structp  png_ptr;
png_infop  info_ptr;

png_ptr = png_create_read_struct(PNG_LIBPNG_VER_STRING,
    mainprog_ptr, readpng2_error_handler, NULL);
if (!png_ptr)
    return 4;   /* out of memory */

info_ptr = png_create_info_struct(png_ptr);
if (!info_ptr) {
    png_destroy_read_struct(&png_ptr, NULL, NULL);
    return 4;   /* out of memory */
}
```

I have used a pair of local variables here, **png_ptr** and **info_ptr**, for convenience. The **mainprog_info** struct also includes these variables, but because it's used in the main program, which has no knowledge of libpng datatypes, the struct versions of the two variables are simply declared as pointers to void. To use them directly in **readpng2_init()**, we would need to typecast them repeatedly, which is annoying and makes the program harder to read and somewhat slower. So I spent a few bytes on the temporary (local) variables to make life easier.

The next step is to set up one of those **setjmp()** calls. This differs from the previous version only in that now we're using our own struct's **jmpbuf** member instead of the one in the main PNG struct:

```
if (setjmp(mainprog_ptr->jmpbuf)) {
    png_destroy_read_struct(&png_ptr, &info_ptr, NULL);
    return 2;
}
```

The second big difference from the basic PNG reader is what comes next:

```
png_set_progressive_read_fn(png_ptr, mainprog_ptr,
    readpng2_info_callback, readpng2_row_callback,
    readpng2_end_callback);
```

Here we get a glimpse of the inversion of the program logic. The original approach was to call libpng and wait for it to return the requested image data, whether header information or actual pixels. That doesn't really work in a progressive program—if you give the library a hunk of data and wait for it to return, you may end up with nothing if the hunk was too small, or you may get the entire image back. More commonly, it is impossible to return a completely sensible result, due to the way compression works. The end of a buffer of compressed data may correspond to the first two bits of the red sample of a single pixel, for example, or it may cut off a piece of a compressed token that is therefore meaningless. Either way, what we really want is a way for the decoding library to provide us with data in a more controlled manner. Callbacks are the answer.

readpng2_error_handler()

In addition to the new local variables, I replaced two of the NULL arguments to `png_create_read_struct()` with meaningful pointers. This allows us to set up our own error handler and thereby avoid the ugly problem discussed in the previous chapter, where the size of the `setjmp()` buffer (`jmp_buf`) could differ between the application and the PNG library. All we've really done is duplicate libpng's error-handling code in the demo program: our `mainprog_info` struct now includes a `jmp_buf` to replace the one in the main PNG struct, and we've created a `readpng2_error_handler()` function that is almost identical to libpng's default error handler. Because the `jmp_buf` problem doesn't affect libpng's warning handler, we left that alone; thus the fourth argument to `png_create_read_struct()` is still NULL.

Our version of libpng's error handler looks like this:

```
static void readpng2_error_handler(png_structp png_ptr,
                                   png_const_charp msg)
{
    mainprog_info  *mainprog_ptr;

    fprintf(stderr, "readpng2 libpng error: %s\n", msg);
    fflush(stderr);

    mainprog_ptr = png_get_error_ptr(png_ptr);
    if (mainprog_ptr == NULL) {
        fprintf(stderr,
          "readpng2 severe error:  jmpbuf not recoverable;
        terminating.\n");
        fflush(stderr);
        exit(99);
    }

    longjmp(mainprog_ptr->jmpbuf, 1);
}
```

The main difference is that, unlike libpng, we have to retrieve the pointer to our error struct (which happens to be the same as our main struct) as an additional step. And since we know *something* went wrong (or we wouldn't be executing this code), it is particularly important to make sure the pointer is valid—or at least not NULL. If it is NULL, we're in big trouble: we have no way to retrieve our `jmp_buf` and therefore no way to return to the main application code and exit somewhat cleanly. In that case, we simply print an error message and give up. Otherwise, we retrieve `mainprog_ptr->jmpbuf` and `longjmp()` back to the most recently invoked `setjmp()`, just as libpng would do.

A callback is just what it sounds like: if our main routine calls the library with a chunk of data, the library will call us back when a certain amount has been processed—say, one row of image pixels. The function it calls (back in the main program, presumably) can then handle the decoded data, return, possibly get called again, and so forth. Eventually the library will exhaust the data it was given and return to the original routine. That routine can then read some more data from the network and pass it back to libpng, go and decode part of another image, respond to user input, or do anything else that needs doing.

The progressive handler in libpng is set up to work with three callback functions: one to be called when all of the header information has been read (i.e., everything prior to the first IDAT), one for when each row of the image is decoded (which includes "short" rows if the image is interlaced), and one for when the complete PNG stream has been read. These are the last three arguments to `png_set_pro-gressive_read_fn()`, and our versions are called `readpng2_info_call-back()`, `readpng2_row_callback()`, and `readpng2_end_callback()`, respectively. They are all required to have the same two arguments: `png_ptr` and `info_ptr`, the pointers to the two standard PNG structs. But in order for the application to associate image-specific data with each callback, libpng makes available a user-specified pointer, embedded somewhere within the PNG structs; it can be retrieved via a libpng function. In our case, we provide a pointer to the `main-prog_info` struct for the image. This is the second argument to `png_set_pro-gressive_read_fn()`. (The first argument is just the `png_ptr` itself.)

As it turns out, the call to `png_set_progressive_read_fn()` is essentially the whole point of our readpng2 initialization routine. The only remaining detail is to save the two temporary pointers into the `mainprog_info` struct before returning to the main program:

```
mainprog_ptr->png_ptr = png_ptr;
mainprog_ptr->info_ptr = info_ptr;

return 0;
```

These pointers will be used in the readpng2 decoding routine that calls libpng, which in turn sends the pointers back to the callback functions.

readpng2_decode_data()

Back in the main program, after dealing with various windowing-system chores, the code sets a few variables in the `mainprog_info` struct. The following excerpt is from the X version of the code, but the Windows code is the same, aside from prefixing function names with **rpng2_win_** instead of **rpng2_x_**:

```
if (user_did_not_specify_a_background_color_or_pattern)
    rpng2_info.need_bgcolor = TRUE;

rpng2_info.mainprog_init = rpng2_x_init;
rpng2_info.mainprog_display_row = rpng2_x_display_row;
rpng2_info.mainprog_finish_display = rpng2_x_finish_display;
```

Unlike the basic viewer, where the main program called a special function to check for and retrieve the image's background color, the progressive viewer simply sets the **need_bgcolor** flag in the struct. It also sets three function pointers corresponding to the three readpng2 callbacks. The reason for this apparent duplication will become clear when we look at the callbacks in detail.

Having prepared everything for decoding, the main program begins the data loop that is at its core, reading file data into a buffer and passing it to the PNG-decoding function:

```
for (;;) {
    if (readpng2_decode_data(&rpng2_info, inbuf, incount))
        ++error;
    if (error || feof(infile) || rpng2_info.done)
        break;
    if (timing)
        sleep(1);
    incount = fread(inbuf, 1, INBUFSIZE, infile);
}
```

Note the call to **readpng2_decode_data()** at the beginning of the loop, before **fread()**; it handles the initial chunk of data we read prior to calling **readpng2_init()**.

The only remarkable feature of the loop itself is the conditional call to the **sleep()** function. Because this is a demo program, and because it is intended to be a rough simulation of how a web browser functions, I chose to give the user the option of simulating how an image download over a fast modem would appear. The **sleep()** function is an extremely crude method of doing this—it has only one-second precision, which is too coarse to allow for a smooth simulation— but it is relatively portable and ubiquitous. Less portable but more precise alternatives include **usleep()** and various Windows API calls. But since no sane programmer would intentionally add a delay like this to the inner loop of a program except for demonstration purposes, I judged that **sleep()** was good enough for this. The combination of a one-second sleep interval and the default buffer size of 4096 bytes results in an apparent download speed that is 10% to 20% faster than a 33.6K modem can manage. In fact, it's close to the average connection speed of a 56K modem over typical phone lines.

As to `readpng2_decode_data()` itself, it is little more than a wrapper function for the libpng routine `png_process_data()`. Its arguments include a pointer to our `mainprog_info` struct, a pointer to the input buffer, and the number of bytes of input data; the only things it does besides calling libpng are copy the struct pointers and set up the usual error-handling code:

```
int readpng2_decode_data(mainprog_info *mainprog_ptr, uch *rawbuf,
                         ulg length)
{
    png_structp png_ptr = (png_structp)mainprog_ptr->png_ptr;
    png_infop info_ptr = (png_infop)mainprog_ptr->info_ptr;

    if (setjmp(mainprog_ptr->jmpbuf)) {
        png_destroy_read_struct(&png_ptr, &info_ptr, NULL);
        mainprog_ptr->png_ptr = NULL;
        mainprog_ptr->info_ptr = NULL;
        return 2;
    }

    png_process_data(png_ptr, info_ptr, rawbuf, length);

    return 0;
}
```

The struct pointers are copied merely because the alternative is to typedef them; the latter may be more efficient (though not necessarily, due to the extra level of indirection inherent in the `->` operator), but it is also uglier and makes the code somewhat less readable.*

readpng2_info_callback()

`png_process_data()` is, in some sense, the last real libpng function that the main program calls—yet so far we haven't set any transformations and have virtually no information about the PNG image except that its signature is correct. The solution to these little mysteries lies within the first of the callback routines, `readpng2_info_callback()`. In most respects, it functions as the second half of our libpng initialization routine: it gets the PNG image's header information, including the image dimensions and perhaps the background color; it sets all of the transformations, including gamma correction; and it calls a routine in the main program to initialize the viewing window. In short, it does everything except handle actual pixels.

One important thing it does *not* do, however, is set up the usual error-handling code via the `setjmp()` function. The reason for this is simple: libpng requires

---

* Clarity and expediency, that's what I like. Well, I like efficiency, too, but not at the cost of clarity when writing a book on programming PNG.

that control never return to it when an error occurs; ordinarily, it longjumps to a user routine, which then returns an error value to the main program. But in this case it is libpng itself that calls `readpng2_info_callback()`, so a longjump back to here would make no sense—the only things we could do would be to return to libpng or call `exit()` without cleaning up, which is a rather brutal method of handling an error. (Well, actually we could do our own longjump back to the main program, but that's effectively what we are already doing. And in the last chapter I noted my dislike of big `goto` statements.) By not calling `setjmp()` within the callback, any errors will return to the location of the previous `setjmp()` call, which was in `readpng2_decode_data()`. It can then return a proper error value to the main program.

There is a feature in the callback routine that has no analogue in the basic PNG reader, however:

```
mainprog_info  *mainprog_ptr;

mainprog_ptr = (mainprog_info *)png_get_progressive_ptr(png_ptr);

if (mainprog_ptr == NULL) {
    fprintf(stderr, "readpng2 error:  "
      "main struct not recoverable in info_callback.\n");
    fflush(stderr);
    return;
}
```

This is the way we retrieve our image-specific pointer from the bowels of the PNG structs. (If it's invalid, we're in big trouble already, but there's no need to compound the problem by dereferencing a NULL pointer and crashing immediately.) Having done so, we can now stuff the image dimensions into it, where they'll be used by the main program very shortly:

```
int  color_type, bit_depth;

png_get_IHDR(png_ptr, info_ptr, &mainprog_ptr->width,
    &mainprog_ptr->height, &bit_depth, &color_type, NULL, NULL, NULL);
```

As before, we called a libpng utility routine to retrieve information about the image. There are also so-called easy access functions to retrieve each item separately; the choice of one function call or several is purely a matter of taste.

 This is an appropriate point at which to comment once again on the evils of accessing PNG structures directly, so let us all repeat our favorite mantra: Friends don't let friends access elements of PNG structs directly. Bad, bad, bad!

See Chapter 13 for the detailed explanation, but trust me: it's not good karma.

As soon as we know the bit depth and color type of the image (via the `png_get_IHDR()` call we just made), we can check for a PNG bKGD chunk and, if it's found, adjust its values in exactly the same way as before:

```
if (mainprog_ptr->need_bgcolor &&
    png_get_valid(png_ptr, info_ptr, PNG_INFO_bKGD))
{
    /* do the same png_get_bKGD() call and scale the RGB values as
     * required; put results in mainprog_ptr->bg_red, bg_green,
     * and bg_blue */
}
```

This time, instead of passing the red, green, and blue values back through the arguments to a readpng2 function, we place them into the `bg_red`, `bg_green`, and `bg_blue` elements of our `mainprog_info` struct.

The next step is to set up the desired libpng transformations; this is completely identical to the code in the first demo program. It is followed by the gamma-correction setup, but here we depart slightly from the previous example:

```
if (png_get_gAMA(png_ptr, info_ptr, &gamma))
    png_set_gamma(png_ptr, mainprog_ptr->display_exponent,
        gamma);
else
    png_set_gamma(png_ptr, mainprog_ptr->display_exponent,
        0.45455);
```

Because this program is intended to provide an example of how to write a PNG reader for a web browser, we imagine that the files it will be viewing are coming from the Internet—even though the frontends we provide only read from local files, just as in the basic version. Because images from the Internet are more likely to have been either created on PC-like systems or intended for display on PC-like systems, we follow the recommendation of the sRGB proposal (see Chapter 10, *Gamma Correction and Precision Color*) and assume that all unlabeled images live in the sRGB color space—which, among other things, means they have a gamma of 1/2.2 or 0.45455, the same as most PCs and workstations. This does mean that unlabeled images created on a Macintosh, SGI, or NeXT workstation and intended for display on one of these systems will appear too dark. But that, of course, is why including a gamma value in the image file is so vitally important.

There is one last "transformation" to register after the gamma handling is out of the way; we want libpng to expand interlaced passes for us. This is signaled by calling `png_set_interlace_handling()`. It returns the number of passes in the image, which we save in case the main program wants to report to the user whether the image is interlaced (seven passes) or not (one pass):

```
mainprog_ptr->passes = png_set_interlace_handling(png_ptr);
```

Then we have libpng update the PNG struct information and return to us the final number of channels in the image and the size of each row:

```
png_read_update_info(png_ptr, info_ptr);

mainprog_ptr->rowbytes = png_get_rowbytes(png_ptr, info_ptr);
mainprog_ptr->channels = png_get_channels(png_ptr, info_ptr);
```

The very last thing `readpng2_info_callback()` does is call its corresponding function in the main program, which allocates the image memory, initializes the windowing system, and creates the display window with the proper dimensions:

```
(*mainprog_ptr->mainprog_init)();

return;
```

Recall that we saved pointers to three functions in the `mainprog_info` struct; this calls the first of the three. If we didn't care about separating PNG code from the main program routines, we could use just one routine per callback. But this way is a bit cleaner, and the performance hit is minimal.

readpng2_row_callback()

The heart of the progressive reader is the row-callback function. As with the other two callbacks, it is called by `png_process_data()` after some amount of image data is read; unlike them, it gets called multiple times, at least once for every row in the image.* `readpng2_row_callback()` has four arguments: the main PNG struct pointer, a pointer to the row of image data, the row number, and the pass number. Its structure is actually quite simple; most of the action occurs within libpng or back in the main program:

```
static void readpng2_row_callback(png_structp png_ptr,
                                  png_bytep new_row,
                                  png_uint_32 row_num,
                                  int pass)
{
    mainprog_info  *mainprog_ptr;
```

---

* For interlaced images, it gets called (with real data) an average of 1.875 times per row and at most 4 times per row (for a one-row image that is more than four pixels wide). Once per row is still a possibility, however, if the image has only one column.

```
        if (!new_row)
           return;

        mainprog_ptr = (mainprog_info *)png_get_progressive_ptr(png_ptr);

        png_progressive_combine_row(png_ptr,
          mainprog_ptr->row_pointers[row_num], new_row);

        (*mainprog_ptr->mainprog_display_row)(row_num);

        return;
    }
```

The first thing the routine does is check whether libpng provided any row data; if not, it returns immediately. Otherwise the function needs access to our **main-prog_info** struct, so it retrieves the pointer to that. Recall that the definition of this struct included two members that should look familiar: **image_data** and **row_pointers**. The first is the pointer to our image buffer; the second is an array of pointers giving the locations of every row within the buffer. Both were allocated and initialized when **readpng2_info_callback()** called its corresponding function in the main program. libpng does not require a row-pointers array in a progressive reader, but it happens to be a convenient and reasonably efficient way to access the image buffer.

In any case, the row-callback function calls **png_progressive_combine_row()** to combine the new image data with the existing pixels or, in the case of a noninterlaced image, to copy the row of data into the image buffer. Then it transfers control to its counterpart in the main program in order to composite the new pixels with the background, convert the row to a platform-dependent format, and optionally display it.

Compositing and Displaying the Image

The main-program code to do all of this is almost identical to that in the first demo program, but this time around we've added a small twist: the code now supports not only a user-defined background color but also a background image of sorts. Specifically, the user has the option of choosing one of a set of predefined background patterns that simulate a tiled background image. The patterns currently include gradient-filled checkerboards (three of which are shown in the second row of Figure C-5 in the color insert), smoothly interpolated diamonds (third row of Figure C-5), and radial waves (Figure C-1 and fourth row of Figure C-5); eventually, other patterns may be defined. This approach is simple enough that it could be generated on the fly, as the image is displayed, but in the interests of speed and simplicity, I chose to define a second complete image buffer in the **main-prog_init()** function. The background buffer is filled as follows for the diamond pattern (contributed by Adam M. Costello):

```
hmax = (bgscale-1)/2;   /* half the max weight of a color */
max = 2*hmax;           /* the max weight of a color */

for (row = 0;  row < rpng2_info.height;  ++row) {
    yidx = row % bgscale;
    if (yidx > hmax)
        yidx = bgscale-1 - yidx;
    dest = bg_data + row*bg_rowbytes;
    for (i = 0;  i < rpng2_info.width;  ++i) {
        xidx = i % bgscale;
        if (xidx > hmax)
            xidx = bgscale-1 - xidx;
        k = xidx + yidx;
        *dest++ = (k*r1 + (max-k)*r2) / max;
        *dest++ = (k*g1 + (max-k)*g2) / max;
        *dest++ = (k*b1 + (max-k)*b2) / max;
    }
}
```

With this approach, the inner display loop requires only a tiny change to support the background image instead of just a background color:

```
r = *src++;
g = *src++;
b = *src++;
a = *src++;
if (bg_image) {                       /* NEW */
    bg_red   = *src2++;               /* NEW */
    bg_green = *src2++;               /* NEW */
    bg_blue  = *src2++;               /* NEW */
}                                     /* NEW */
if (a == 255) {
    red   = r;
    green = g;
    blue  = b;
} else if (a == 0) {
    red   = bg_red;
    green = bg_green;
    blue  = bg_blue;
} else {
    /* this macro (copied from png.h) composites
     * the foreground and background values and
     * puts the result into the first argument */
    alpha_composite(red,   r, a, bg_red);
    alpha_composite(green, g, a, bg_green);
    alpha_composite(blue,  b, a, bg_blue);
}
```

In other words, the background color used for compositing is now changed once per pixel. (Note that the `src2` pointer is initialized just once per call. That's the only other change to the display routine to support the background image.) The cases in which the alpha component is either 255 or 0 are handled separately for performance reasons only; using the `alpha_composite()` macro would produce identical results. But because the macro employs multiplication, addition, and bit-shifting for every pixel (in fact, three times per pixel) and because fully opaque and fully transparent pixels are generally by far the most numerous, the difference in speed would probably be noticeable. It therefore makes sense to handle the two special cases separately. Whether full opacity or full transparency is handled first is less obvious; I guessed that opaque pixels are likely to be more common in images with transparency, so the 255 case is checked first.

The results, using one of the more exotic radial-wave patterns as the background, are shown in Figure C-1 in the color insert. The base image consists of partially transparent icicles hanging from opaque tree branches, seen against a completely transparent sky. The figure is a composite of the appearance after the first PNG pass (left half) and the final pass (right half).

readpng2_end_callback()

Once the last row-callback has been made, the program is basically done. Because of the way the main program's row-display code was written to deal with interlaced images, when the last row of pixels is sent, it is guaranteed to be flushed to the display immediately. Thus, when libpng calls our final callback routine, `readpng2_end_callback()`, it does nothing more than retrieve the pointer to our `mainprog_info` struct and call the corresponding `mainprog_finish_display()` function, which in turn merely sets a "done" flag and lets the user know that the image is complete:

```
static void rpng2_x_finish_display()
{
    rpng2_info.done = TRUE;
    printf("Done.  Press Q, Esc or mouse button 1 to quit.\n");
}
```

It would also have been reasonable to free both the `image_data` and `bg_data` buffers at this point, and a memory-constrained application certainly would do so—or, more likely, it would never have allocated full buffers in the first place, instead handling everything on a per-row basis and calculating the background pattern on the fly. Regardless, I chose to free *all* frontend buffers in the frontend cleanup routine, which is the last function called before the program exits.

readpng2_cleanup()

Before that happens, though, the `mainprog_finish_display()` routine returns control through `readpng2_end_callback()` to libpng and eventually back to the main program loop, which is now finished. The main program then closes the PNG file and calls `readpng2_cleanup()` to deallocate the PNG structs:

```
void readpng2_cleanup(mainprog_info *mainprog_ptr)
{
    png_structp png_ptr = (png_structp)mainprog_ptr->png_ptr;
    png_infop info_ptr = (png_infop)mainprog_ptr->info_ptr;

    if (png_ptr && info_ptr)
        png_destroy_read_struct(&png_ptr, &info_ptr, NULL);

    mainprog_ptr->png_ptr = NULL;
    mainprog_ptr->info_ptr = NULL;
}
```

Once that is done, the program waits for user input to terminate, then it exits.

Getting the Source Code

All of the source files for the *rpng2* demo program (*rpng2-x.c*, *rpng2-win.c*, *readpng2.c*, *readpng2.h*, and makefiles) are available via the web, under a BSD-like Open Source license. The files will be available for download from the following URL for the foreseeable future:

> *http://www.cdrom.com/pub/png/pngbook.html*

Bug fixes, new features and ports, and other contributions may be integrated into the code, time permitting.

15

Writing PNG Images

Writing PNG images is both simpler and more complex than reading them. Weighing in on the side of simplicity is the fact that there is no need for a lot of platform-specific code, particularly platform-specific graphical code—unless, of course, the application already is graphical. In general, there is also no need for a special progressive mode; writing a PNG file, or almost any image format, for that matter, is more or less progressive by nature, although some complexity creeps in when the image is interlaced.

Writing PNGs is more explicitly complex when it comes to dealing with ancillary information like text annotations, timestamps, and so forth. A simple PNG viewer can ignore all of that; its only concern is with displaying the pixels correctly and in a timely manner. But a PNG-writing application should be prepared to preserve any existing textual information and to give the user the option of adding new information—for example, a title, the author's name, and copyright information. One wants to avoid adding too much baggage to the image, but the user should also be given the option of adding a timestamp (e.g., the tIME chunk for time of last modification, or perhaps a tEXt chunk indicating the creation time).

When it comes to the actual image data, at a minimum, the application should be able to detect when there are no more than 256 colors or color-transparency pairs, including a possible background color, and write a palette-based image if that is the case. Ideally, it should also be able to write a grayscale image as grayscale instead of RGB, but unless there is already information available that indicates the pixels are gray, or the user indicates that the image is to be converted to grayscale, detecting such images can be both CPU- and memory-intensive.

It should go without saying that any such application should include gamma-correction information with the image whenever possible, and that it should be correct information; this may entail providing the user with a calibration screen. And image converters must be much more careful, since most images lacking explicit gamma information also lack any information from which one can infer the gamma value unambiguously; guessing incorrectly is worse than omitting the gamma info in the first place.

High-end, professional applications should also provide chromaticity information, if it is known, and mark any images created in the standard RGB color space with an appropriate sRGB chunk. They may also want to include a complete International Color Consortium embedded profile (iCCP chunk), but given the size of such profiles, this should always be an option given to the user, and generally it should not be the default option. See Chapter 10, *Gamma Correction and Precision Color*, for a more detailed discussion of gamma correction and color spaces.

Applications such as image editors, which usually include the generation of web-friendly graphics as one of their features, should also provide the user with the option of converting truecolor images into colormapped ones. This is known as quantization, and it should include images with an alpha channel. As I described in Chapter 8, *PNG Basics*, PNG's tRNS chunk effectively transforms a palette from RGB samples into RGBA; thus, any program that can quantize a 24-bit RGB image down to a 256-color palette-based image should also be capable of quantizing a 32-bit RGBA or 16-bit gray/alpha image down to a 256-entry PLTE/tRNS-based image. But because quantization is a lossy procedure, it should never be the default—unless, of course, the entire purpose of the application is the lossy conversion of truecolor images into colormapped ones.

Special-purpose applications that deal with sampled data from scientific or medical apparatus will often encounter odd bit depths or oddly calibrated data, at least compared with standard computer images. For example, medical tomographic (CT) images are usually stored as 16-bit integer samples, but the implied upper bound of 65,535 is misleading. Such images rarely use more than 10 to 12 bits of each sample, their maximum intensity value is typically less than 4,096 and sometimes less than 1,024, though rarely less than 256. When stored as PNG images, their samples should be scaled up so that the maximum value is near 65,535. For example, an image whose raw data has a maximum value of 1,891 is using only 11 bits of each sample—i.e., the next power of two is 2,048, or 2^{11}. It should be scaled up either by a factor of 32 (2^5), which corresponds simply to shifting the bits five to the left, or more properly by a factor of 65,535/2,047, which happens to be very closely approximated by what the PNG spec calls "left bit replication." These two approaches are more easily understood as C code:

```
    /* how to scale 11-bit data up to 16 bits */
#ifdef LEFT_BIT_REPLICATION
    new_sample = (old_sample << 5) | (old_sample >> 3);
```

```
#else
    new_sample = (old_sample << 5);     /* simple shift method */
#endif
```

Either way, the application should write an sBIT chunk into the file to indicate the number of significant bits in the original data; in this case, the sBIT value would be 11. It might also want to write a pCAL chunk indicating the calibration of the sample values relative to the physical quantity being measured. It is not intuitively obvious how one would allow the user to provide information for the pCAL chunk interactively, however; more likely, a programmer would hardcode things like the pCAL equation type directly into the application, given advance knowledge of the type of data being collected or manipulated.

A libpng-Based, PNG-Writing Demo Program

The demo program I present here is intentionally more limited than it should be if it were a "real" program, in order that the basic concepts of writing PNG images with libpng not be lost in the details. For simplicity's sake, I chose to write a basic command-line image-conversion program in ANSI C, with the PNG-specific "back-end" code in one file (*writepng.c*) and the single, cross-platform "frontend" in another file (*wpng.c*). As with the PNG-reading demo programs, this uses libpng, which is very complete, well-tested, and by far the most commonly used PNG library. This program also keeps all image-related variables in a single struct; as with the one described in Chapter 14, *Reading PNG Images Progressively*, this approach would enable a multithreaded program to handle several images at the same time. Finally, *wpng* uses NetPBM (or PBMplus) binary files for input, since there are few image formats that are simpler to read (or write, for that matter).

But recall from Chapter 5, *Applications: Image Converters*, that there is already an extremely capable NetPBM conversion program called *pnmtopng*, by Alexander Lehmann and Willem van Schaik. It supports practically all PNG chunks and all possible variants of image data, and its source code is freely available and reusable, subject to minimal restrictions. Rather than duplicate many of its functions, we chose to stick to a minimal subset and instead concentrate on a few features not currently supported* by the larger program: incremental (or progressive) conversion, automatic timestamping, interactive input of text fields, and support for a very unofficial NetPBM extension format: type P8 files, containing 32-bit RGBA data. Supported PNG output types include basic 8-bit-per-sample grayscale, RGB and RGBA images, either interlaced or not. The program will write a gamma chunk if the user supplies an explicit value, but not otherwise; it cannot know a

---

* The most recent release as of this writing is version 2.37.2.

priori in what color space the original NetPBM image was created. The background chunk is also supported if the user supplies a background color, but it is ignored if the input image has no alpha channel.

Readers with more advanced needs should study pnmtopng, which can be found on the PNG Source Code and Libraries page of the PNG home site: *http://www. cdrom.com/pub/png/pngcode.html*. It includes such features as rescaling low-bit-depth samples, reordering the palette so that opaque entries of the tRNS chunk may be omitted, and support for explicitly specifying a separate PGM file as the alpha channel. libpng and zlib can both be found in the same location.

Gamma Correction

Before diving into the PNG-specific code, there are a couple of items in the main program (frontend) that are worth a quick look. The first has to do with our old friend, gamma correction (see Chapter 10). As I noted earlier, in general there is no way to know what the gamma value of the input file is, so the output PNG file's gamma cannot be set automatically. But we do know that if the input file looks OK when displayed on the user's display system—which is presumed to be the one in use when the conversion program is run—then the file gamma is roughly equal to the inverse of the display system's exponent. So *wpng* calculates a default value for the display-system exponent just as our two PNG-reading demo programs did; the difference is that its calculated value is purely advisory. Here is the code to calculate the default gamma value:

```
        double default_gamma = 0.0;

    #if defined(NeXT)
        default_exponent = 1.0;   /* 2.2/next_gamma for 3rd-party utils */
    #elif defined(sgi)
        default_exponent = 1.3;   /* default == 2.2 / 1.7 */
        /* there doesn't seem to be any documented function to get the
         * "gamma" value, so we do it the hard way */
        if (tmpfile = fopen("/etc/config/system.glGammaVal", "r")) {
            double sgi_gamma;

            fgets(fooline, 80, tmpfile);
            fclose(tmpfile);
            sgi_gamma = atof(fooline);
            if (sgi_gamma > 0.0)
                default_exponent = 2.2 / sgi_gamma;
        }
    #elif defined(Macintosh)
        default_exponent = 1.5;   /* default == (1.8/2.61) * 2.2 */
        /*
        if (mac_gamma = some_mac_function_that_returns_gamma())
            default_exponent = (mac_gamma/2.61) * 2.2;
         */
```

```
#else
    default_exponent = 2.2;    /* assume std. CRT, no LUT:  most PCs */
#endif

    default_gamma = 1.0 / default_exponent;

    if ((p = getenv("SCREEN_GAMMA")) != NULL) {
        double exponent = atof(p);

        if (exponent > 0.0)
            default_gamma = 1.0 / atof(p);
    }
```

The first section calculates a platform-dependent exponent for the display system, which is then inverted to give a default file-gamma value. But it is possible that the user has calibrated the display system more precisely and has defined the **SCREEN_GAMMA** environment variable as suggested by the libpng documentation. If so, this value is used instead.

Note that the Macintosh code is incomplete. The `Macintosh` macro, presumed to be defined already, most likely would need to be set on the basis of compiler-specific macros. For example, the following preprocessor code would work for Metrowerks CodeWarrior and the Macintosh Programmer's Workbench, although **MPW** is not terribly specific and might be defined on non-Macintosh systems, too:

```
#if !defined(Macintosh)
#   if defined(__MWERKS__) && defined(macintosh)
#     define Macintosh
#   elif defined(MPW)   /* && defined(MCH_MACINTOSH) */
#     define Macintosh
#   endif
#endif
```

In any case, the calculated file gamma is presented as part of *wpng*'s usage screen but thereafter ignored.

Text Chunks

The other item worth looking at is the interactive text-entry code. Most windowing systems will have more elegant ways to read in text than I use here, but even they should ensure that the entered text conforms to the recommended format for PNG text chunks. PNG text is required to use the Latin-1 character set; strictly speaking, that does not restrict the use of control characters (character code 127 and any code below 32 decimal), but in practice only line feeds (code 10) are necessary. The use of carriage-return characters (code 13) is explicitly discouraged by the spec in favor of single line feeds; this has implications for DOS, OS/2, Windows, and Macintosh systems. Horizontal tabs (code 9) are discouraged as well since they don't display the same way on all systems, but there are legitimate uses for tabs in text. The section of the spec dealing with security considerations implicitly recommends against the use of the escape character (code 27), which is commonly used to introduce ANSI escape sequences. Since these can include potentially malicious macros, encoders should restrict the use of the escape character for the sake of overly simple-minded decoders. That leaves codes 9, 10, 32–126, and 160–255 as valid from a practical standpoint, with use of the first (tab) discouraged. Note that codes 128–159 are *not* valid Latin-1 characters, at least not in the printable sense. They are reserved for specialized control characters.

The specification also recommends that lines in each text block be no more than 79 characters long; I've chosen to restrict mine to 72 characters each, plus provide for one or two newline characters and a trailing NULL. The spec does not specifically address the issue of the final newline, but does require omitting the trailing NULL; logically, one might extend that to include trailing newlines, so I have.

Finally, I have arbitrarily allowed only six predetermined keywords: `Title`, `Author`, `Description`, `Copyright` (all officially registered), and `E-mail` and `URL` (unregistered). `Description` is limited to nine lines, mainly so that the little line-counter prompts for each line are single digits and therefore line up nicely; the others are limited to one line each. Thus the code for reading the `Title` keyword, once the text buffer (`textbuf`) has been allocated, looks like this:

```
    do {
        valid = TRUE;
        p = textbuf + TEXT_TITLE_OFFSET;
        fprintf(stderr, "  Title: ");
        fflush(stderr);
        if (FGETS(p, 74, keybd) && (len = strlen(p)) > 1) {
            if (p[len-1] == '\n')
                p[--len] = '\0';     /* remove trailing newline */
            wpng_info.title = p;
            wpng_info.have_text |= TEXT_TITLE;

            if ((result = wpng_isvalid_latin1((uch *)p, len)) >= 0) {
                fprintf(stderr, "  " PROGNAME " warning:  character"
                  " code %u is %sdiscouraged by the PNG\n"
                  "    specification [first occurrence was at"
                  " character position #%d]\n", (unsigned)p[result],
                  (p[result] == 27)? "strongly " : "", result+1);
                fflush(stderr);
#ifdef FORBID_LATIN1_CTRL
                wpng_info.have_text &= ~TEXT_TITLE;
                valid = FALSE;
#else
                if (p[result] == 27) {        /* escape character */
                    wpng_info.have_text &= ~TEXT_TITLE;
                    valid = FALSE;
                }
#endif
```

```
        }
      }
   } while (!valid);
```

Aside from some subtlety with the **keybd** stream that I won't cover here (it has to do with reading from the keyboard even if standard input is redirected), the only part of real interest is the test for nonrecommended Latin-1 characters, which is accomplished in the **wpng_isvalid_latin1()** function:

```
static int wpng_isvalid_latin1(uch *p, int len)
{
    int i, result = -1;

    for (i = 0;  i < len;  ++i) {
        if (p[i] == 10 || (p[i] > 31 && p[i] < 127) || p[i] > 160)
            continue;
        if (result < 0 || (p[result] != 27 && p[i] == 27))
            result = i;
    }

    return result;
}
```

If the function finds a control character that is discouraged by the PNG specification, it returns the offset of the first one found. The only exception is if an escape character (code 27) is found later in the string; in that case, its offset is what gets returned. The main code then tests for a non-negative value and prints a warning message. What happens next depends on how the program has been compiled. By default, the presence of an escape character forces the user to re-enter the text, but all of the other discouraged characters are allowed. If the FOR-BID_LATIN1_CTRL macro is defined, however, the user must re-enter the text whenever any of the "bad" control characters is found. The default behavior results in output similar to the following:

```
Enter text info (no more than 72 characters per line);
to skip a field, hit the <Enter> key.
  Title: L'Arc de Triomphe
  Author: Greg Roelofs
  Description (up to 9 lines):
    [1] This line contains only normal characters.
    [2] This line contains a tab character here: ^I
    [3]
  wpng warning:  character code 9 is discouraged by the PNG
  specification [first occurrence was at character position #85]
  Copyright: We attempt an escape character here: ^[
  wpng warning:  character code 27 is strongly discouraged by the PNG
  specification [first occurrence was at character position #38]
  Copyright: Copyright 1981, 1999 Greg Roelofs
  E-mail: roelofs@pobox.com
  URL: http://www.cdrom.com/pub/png/pngbook.html
```

Note that the `Copyright` keyword had to be entered twice since the first attempt included an escape character. The `Description` keyword also would have had to be reentered if the program had been compiled with `FORBID_LATIN1_CTRL` defined.

Returning to more mundane issues, `wpng_info` is the struct by which the frontend communicates with the PNG-writing backend. It is of type `mainprog_info`, and it is defined as follows:

```
typedef struct _mainprog_info {
    double gamma;
    long width;
    long height;
    time_t modtime;
    FILE *infile;
    FILE *outfile;
    void *png_ptr;
    void *info_ptr;
    uch *image_data;
    uch **row_pointers;
    char *title;
    char *author;
    char *desc;
    char *copyright;
    char *email;
    char *url;
    int filter;
    int pnmtype;
    int sample_depth;
    int interlaced;
    int have_bg;
    int have_time;
    int have_text;
    jmp_buf jmpbuf;
    uch bg_red;
    uch bg_green;
    uch bg_blue;
} mainprog_info;
```

As in the previous programs, we use the abbreviated typedefs uch, ush, and ulg in place of the more unwieldy **unsigned char**, **unsigned short**, and **unsigned long**, respectively. The `title` element is simply a pointer into the text buffer, and the struct contains similar pointers for the other five keywords. `have_text` is more than a simple Boolean (TRUE/FALSE) value, however. Because the user may not want all six text chunks, the program must keep track of which ones were provided with valid data. Thus, `have_text` is a bit flag, and `TEXT_TITLE` sets the bit corresponding to the `Title` keyword—but only if the length of the entered string is greater than one.

The user indicates that a field should be skipped by hitting the Enter key, and the fgets() function includes the newline character in the string it returns; thus a string of length one contains nothing but the newline.

writepng_version_info()

We'll turn now to the PNG-specific backend code in *writepng.c*. As with any module that calls libpng functions, it begins by including the *png.h* header file, which in turn includes *zlib.h*. This particular program also includes *writepng.h*, which defines our mainprog_info struct, various text-related macros, and prototypes for the externally visible functions that we'll be discussing in detail. Indeed, the first of these functions is almost trivial:

```
#include "png.h"       /* libpng header; includes zlib.h */
#include "writepng.h"  /* typedefs, common macros, public prototypes */

void writepng_version_info()
{
    fprintf(stderr, "   Compiled with libpng %s; using libpng %s.\n",
        PNG_LIBPNG_VER_STRING, png_libpng_ver);
    fprintf(stderr, "   Compiled with zlib %s; using zlib %s.\n",
        ZLIB_VERSION, zlib_version);
}
```

writepng_version_info() simply indicates the versions of libpng and zlib with which the application was compiled, as well as the versions it happens to be using at runtime. Ideally the two pairs of version numbers will match—in the case of a statically linked executable, they always will—but if the program was dynamically linked, it is possible that the program loader has found either an older or a newer version of one or both libraries, in which case strange problems may arise later. Making this information easily available to the user, whether in a simple text-mode usage screen as I do here or via a windowed "about box" or even a fancy, automated, troubleshooting function, can be helpful in dealing with the bug reports that inevitably show up sooner or later.

writepng_init()

Back in the main program we conditionally fill in various elements of our main-prog_info struct based on the user's command-line options: interlaced, modtime, have_time, gamma, bg_red, bg_green, bg_blue, and have_bg. Note that have_bg is set only if the user provides a background color *and* the PNM image type is the experimental "type 8" binary RGBA file. Also, whereas pnmtopng currently requires the user to provide a text version of the current time

for use in the tIME chunk, *wpng* automatically determines the current time if the
-time option is given:

```
if (user_specified_time_option) {
    wpng_info.modtime = time(NULL);
    wpng_info.have_time = TRUE;
}
```

After finishing the command-line options, we next open the input file (in *binary*
mode!), verify that it's in the proper format, and read its basic parameters: image
height, width, and depth. We also generate an output filename based on the input
name and verify both that the output file does not already exist and that it can be
opened and written to (also in binary mode!). That provides enough information
to fill in most of the rest of **mainprog_info**: **infile**, **pnmtype**, **have_bg**,
width, **height**, **sample_depth**, and **outfile**.

If any errors have occurred by this point, *wpng* prints the usage screen—including
the libraries' version information—and exits. Otherwise it optionally prompts the
user for PNG text information and then, finally, calls our PNG initialization routine,
writepng_init(). It is declared as follows:

```
int writepng_init(mainprog_info *mainprog_ptr)
```

where **mainprog_ptr** just points at the **mainprog_info** struct we filled in in
the main program. **writepng_init()** begins with some fairly standard libpng
boilerplate:

```
png_structp  png_ptr;
png_infop  info_ptr;

png_ptr = png_create_write_struct(PNG_LIBPNG_VER_STRING,
  mainprog_ptr, writepng_error_handler, NULL);
if (!png_ptr)
    return 4;   /* out of memory */

info_ptr = png_create_info_struct(png_ptr);
if (!info_ptr) {
    png_destroy_write_struct(&png_ptr, NULL);
    return 4;
}
```

This fragment allocates memory for the two internal structures that libpng currently requires and sets up a custom error handler. Note that while the structs have
the same names and types as those used in our PNG-reading demo programs,
libpng provides separate functions to create and destroy them. The first function,
png_create_write_struct(), also checks that the compile-time and runtime
versions of libpng are reasonably compatible. Of course, any change to the library
may create unforeseen incompatibilities, so passing this test does not absolutely

guarantee that everything will work. Failing it, on the other hand, is a pretty good indication that things will break.

The second and third arguments to `png_create_write_struct()` are the keys to installing a custom error handler. The second argument is a pointer to application data (`mainprog_ptr`, in this case) that will be supplied to the error handler; the third argument is the custom error-handling routine itself. I will explain why it is important to use a custom routine as soon as we take a look at the next section of code.

Once the structs have been allocated, it is necessary to set up the "receiving end" of the error-handling code for this particular function. Essentially every user function that calls a libpng routine will need code like this; it amounts to more standard boilerplate, and in general, the only difference between applications will be where the `jmpbuf` member is stored. In this program, as with the one in the previous chapter, we store `jmpbuf` in our own struct instead of relying on the one in the main PNG struct:

```
if (setjmp(mainprog_ptr->jmpbuf)) {
    png_destroy_write_struct(&png_ptr, &info_ptr);
    return 2;
}
```

I discussed the semantics of `setjmp()` and `longjmp()` in Chapter 13, *Reading PNG Images;* effectively they amount to a really big `goto` statement. The problem is not so much with the precise storage location of `jmpbuf`, but rather that its type, `jmp_buf`, can be different sizes depending on whether certain sytem macros have been defined. When one uses the default libpng error handler, `setjmp()` is called from the application, but `longjmp()` is called from within libpng. Since it is not uncommon for the library to be compiled separately from the application—indeed, it may not even have been compiled on the same system—there is no guarantee that the `jmp_buf` sizes in libpng and the application will be consistent. If they are not, mayhem ensues. See the sidebar for a solution.

As long as we're on the subject of alternatives, libpng also supports user-defined input/output functions. But its default is to read from or write to PNG files, and since that is precisely what we want to do here, I chose to stick with the standard I/O-initialization call and pass the output file's pointer to libpng:

```
png_init_io(png_ptr, mainprog_ptr->outfile);
```

Next we deal with compression. libpng has pretty good defaults, and many programs (possibly most) will not need to do anything here. But in our case we're converting from an uncompressed image format to PNG; for any given image, we're unlikely to do so more than once, and even if we convert many images, *wpng* is a command-line program and can easily be incorporated into a script for

---

writepng_error_handler()

The solution is a "custom" error handler, though that's a slight misnomer in our case. Completely custom error handlers can certainly be installed, but libpng currently assumes that its error-handling routine will never return. This rather drastically limits the options for alternatives—basically, one can use `longjmp()` or `exit()`, which amounts to an even larger `goto` statement.* Here, as in Chapter 14, *Reading PNG Images Progressively,* I have merely taken libpng's default error handler and modified it slightly to use `mainprog_ptr` instead of `png_ptr`:

```
static void writepng_error_handler(png_structp png_ptr,
png_const_charp msg)
{
    mainprog_info  *mainprog_ptr;

    fprintf(stderr, "writepng libpng error: %s\n", msg);
    fflush(stderr);

    mainprog_ptr = png_get_error_ptr(png_ptr);
    if (mainprog_ptr == NULL) {
        fprintf(stderr, "writepng severe error:  "
                "jmpbuf not recoverable; terminating.\n");
        fflush(stderr);
        exit(99);
    }

    longjmp(mainprog_ptr->jmpbuf, 1);
}
```

Because we have to use a libpng function, however trivial, to retrieve our pointer, there is an extra block of code in our version that makes sure the pointer is not NULL. If it is, we are completely stuck, and our only real option is to exit. But assuming the pointer seems valid (it may have been overwritten with an invalid but non-NULL address, in which case we're going to "exit" whether we want to or not), we use our saved `jmp_buf` and longjump back to the part of our application that most recently invoked `setjmp()`. The key difference from using libpng's error handler is simply the location of the `longjmp()` call. Here we call both `setjmp()` and `longjmp()` within the same application—indeed, from within the same source file. They are therefore guaranteed to have consistent notions of how a `jmp_buf` is defined, so we have eliminated one more potential source of very-difficult-to-debug crashes.

---

* Ford's Model T was also renowned for its wide range of color options.

batch processing. Thus I chose to override libpng's default compression setting (zlib level 6—see Chapter 9, *Compression and Filtering*) with the slower "maximum" setting (zlib level 9):

```
png_set_compression_level(png_ptr, Z_BEST_COMPRESSION);
```

Note that a good PNG-writing program should let the user decide whether and how to override the default settings; options for very fast saves and/or for maximal compression might be reasonable, in addition to the default. In fact, pnmtopng provides options to do just that.

The next step is to convert our notion of the image type into something libpng will understand. In this case, because we support only three basic image types— grayscale, RGB, or RGBA—we have a one-to-one correspondence between input and output types, so setting the PNG color type is easy. For more general programs, libpng provides several PNG_COLOR_MASK_* macros that can be combined to get the color type, with the exception that PNG_COLOR_MASK_PALETTE and PNG_COLOR_MASK_ALPHA are incompatible. We also set the appropriate PNG interlace type if the user so requested:

```
int color_type, interlace_type;

if (mainprog_ptr->pnmtype == 5)
    color_type = PNG_COLOR_TYPE_GRAY;
else if (mainprog_ptr->pnmtype == 6)
    color_type = PNG_COLOR_TYPE_RGB;
else if (mainprog_ptr->pnmtype == 8)
    color_type = PNG_COLOR_TYPE_RGB_ALPHA;
else {
    png_destroy_write_struct(&png_ptr, &info_ptr);
    return 11;
}

interlace_type = mainprog_ptr->interlaced? PNG_INTERLACE_ADAM7 :
                                           PNG_INTERLACE_NONE;
```

At this point, we can set the basic image parameters. We have the option of using several functions, each of which sets a single parameter, but there is really no point in doing so. Instead we set all of them with a single call to png_set_IHDR():

```
png_set_IHDR(png_ptr, info_ptr, mainprog_ptr->width,
    mainprog_ptr->height, mainprog_ptr->sample_depth,
    color_type, interlace_type,
    PNG_COMPRESSION_TYPE_DEFAULT, PNG_FILTER_TYPE_DEFAULT);
```

If we supported palette-based images, this is the point at which we would define the palette for libpng, via the png_set_PLTE() and possibly png_set_tRNS() functions. We can also set any optional parameters the user specified, starting with the gamma value, background color, and image modification time. In the case of

Tweaking Compression

Closely related to compression is filtering, one area in which it is almost always better to leave the decision up to libpng. Repeated tests have shown that filtering is almost never useful on palette-based images, but on everything else it is quite beneficial. Though libpng allows one to restrict its filter selection, this is rarely a good idea; dynamic filtering works best when the encoder can choose from the five defined filter types. But for programmers who want to play with the alternatives, here's an example:

```
/*
    >>> this is pseudo-code
    if (palette image, i.e., don't want filtering) {
        png_set_filter(png_ptr, PNG_FILTER_TYPE_BASE,
            PNG_FILTER_NONE);
        png_set_compression_strategy(png_ptr, Z_DEFAULT_STRATEGY);
    } else {
        >>> leave default filter selection alone
        png_set_compression_strategy(png_ptr, Z_FILTERED);
    }
*/
```

The calls to **png_set_compression_strategy()** actually alter zlib's behavior to work better with the filtered output. Other zlib parameters can also be tweaked, at least in theory; these include the sliding window size, memory level, and compression method. For the last, only method 8 is currently defined, but zlib 2.0 is likely to introduce at least one or two new methods when it is eventually released. Of course, unless and until the PNG specification is revised accordingly, no new compression method can be used within a PNG file without invalidating it.

The window size is the only thing a normal PNG encoder should consider changing, and then only when the total size of the image data, plus one extra byte per row for the row filters, amounts to 16 kilobytes or less. In such a case, the encoder can use a smaller power-of-two window size without affecting compression, which allows decoders to reduce their memory usage. The following fragment shows how to modify these zlib parameters; the values shown are the defaults used by libpng (consult the libpng documentation, specifically "Configuring zlib" and "Controlling row filtering"):

```
/*
    >>> second arg is power of two; 8 through 15 (256-32768) valid
    png_set_compression_window_bits(png_ptr, 15);
    png_set_compression_mem_level(png_ptr, 8);
    png_set_compression_method(png_ptr, 8);
*/
```

the background color, we know that **have_bg** will be true only if the image has
an alpha channel; in this program, that necessarily implies that it's an RGBA
image, not grayscale with alpha or palette-based with transparency. Thus we only
fill in the red, green, and blue elements of the **png_color_16** struct:

```
if (mainprog_ptr->gamma > 0.0)
    png_set_gAMA(png_ptr, info_ptr, mainprog_ptr->gamma);

if (mainprog_ptr->have_bg) {
    png_color_16  background;

    background.red = mainprog_ptr->bg_red;
    background.green = mainprog_ptr->bg_green;
    background.blue = mainprog_ptr->bg_blue;
    png_set_bKGD(png_ptr, info_ptr, &background);
}

if (mainprog_ptr->have_time) {
    png_time  modtime;

    png_convert_from_time_t(&modtime, mainprog_ptr->modtime);
    png_set_tIME(png_ptr, info_ptr, &modtime);
}
```

It is also worth noting that libpng copies most of the data it needs into its own
structs, so we can get away with using temporary variables like **background** and
modtime without worrying about their values being corrupted before libpng is
ready to write them to the file. The only exceptions are things involving pointers,
in which case libpng copies the pointer itself but not the buffer to which it points.
In fact, libpng's text-handling code is an excellent example of that:

```
if (mainprog_ptr->have_text) {
    png_text  text[6];
    int  num_text = 0;

    if (mainprog_ptr->have_text & TEXT_TITLE) {
        text[num_text].compression = PNG_TEXT_COMPRESSION_NONE;
        text[num_text].key = "Title";
        text[num_text].text = mainprog_ptr->title;
        ++num_text;
    }
    if (mainprog_ptr->have_text & TEXT_AUTHOR) {
        text[num_text].compression = PNG_TEXT_COMPRESSION_NONE;
        text[num_text].key = "Author";
        text[num_text].text = mainprog_ptr->author;
        ++num_text;
    }
    if (mainprog_ptr->have_text & TEXT_DESC) {
        text[num_text].compression = PNG_TEXT_COMPRESSION_NONE;
        text[num_text].key = "Description";
        text[num_text].text = mainprog_ptr->desc;
        ++num_text;
```

```
    }
    if (mainprog_ptr->have_text & TEXT_COPY) {
        text[num_text].compression = PNG_TEXT_COMPRESSION_NONE;
        text[num_text].key = "Copyright";
        text[num_text].text = mainprog_ptr->copyright;
        ++num_text;
    }
    if (mainprog_ptr->have_text & TEXT_EMAIL) {
        text[num_text].compression = PNG_TEXT_COMPRESSION_NONE;
        text[num_text].key = "E-mail";
        text[num_text].text = mainprog_ptr->email;
        ++num_text;
    }
    if (mainprog_ptr->have_text & TEXT_URL) {
        text[num_text].compression = PNG_TEXT_COMPRESSION_NONE;
        text[num_text].key = "URL";
        text[num_text].text = mainprog_ptr->url;
        ++num_text;
    }
    png_set_text(png_ptr, info_ptr, text, num_text);
}
```

Here I have declared a temporary array of six **png_text** structs, each of which consists of four elements: **compression**, **key**, **text**, and **text_length**. The first of these simply indicates whether the text chunk is to be compressed (zTXt) or not (tEXt). **key** and **text** are pointers to NULL-terminated strings containing the keyword and actual text, respectively. These pointers are what libpng copies, but the text buffers to which they point must remain valid until either **png_write_info()** or **png_write_end()** is called—we'll return to that point in a moment. The final member of the struct, **text_length**, is used internally by libpng; we need not set it ourselves, since libpng will do so regardless.

Anywhere from one to six of the structs is filled in, depending on whether the main program set the appropriate bit for each of the six supported keywords. Then **png_set_text()** is called, which triggers libpng to allocate its own text structs and copy our struct data into them. Alternatively, we could have used a single **png_text** struct, repeatedly filling it in and calling **png_set_text()** for each keyword; libpng merely chains the copied text structs together, so the net result would have been the same.

The setting of the text chunks is our last piece of non-pixel-related PNG information, so our next step is to write all chunks up to the first IDAT:

```
    png_write_info(png_ptr, info_ptr);
```

Doing this flushes any time or text chunks to the output file, and the corresponding data in the PNG structs is marked so that it is not written to the file again later. I mentioned earlier that text buffers must remain valid until either **png_write_info()** or **png_write_end()** is called, which implies that either

Text Buffers, PNG Structs, and Core Dumps

The issue of libpng's allocation of its own text buffers is worth a closer look, because it indirectly led to a subtle but fatal bug in a popular PNG viewer. The program in question was John Bradley's XV, an elegant and powerful image viewer/converter for the X Window System. Version 3.10a, released late in 1994 and still the most recent release as of this writing, had no native PNG support. But because it was available in source-code form, it was one of the first applications to support the reading and writing of PNGs, thanks to a patch created by Alexander Lehmann in June 1995 and later modified by Andreas Dilger and the author of this book.

This patch was originally written to work with libpng 0.71 and zlib 0.93, beta versions so old they were arguably alpha-level software. At the time, major functionality was still being added to libpng, and the so-called modern "convenience functions" for modifying libpng parameters did not exist. As a result, the patch was designed to access the two PNG structs directly, and later updates to the patch did not completely eliminate this behavior. In particular, all versions of the patch through 1.2d, released in June 1996, allocated their own text structs and plugged them directly into one of the main PNG structs for libpng's use.

Now fast-forward to January 1998, when the final libpng betas were being released. By this time, libpng provided functions not only to allocate and destroy the PNG structs, but also to read from them and write to them. In particular, `png_set_text()` already existed in its present form; i.e., it allocated its own text structs and copied the user-supplied data into them. But one of the changes in libpng 0.97 involved plugging some small memory leaks by freeing these libpng-allocated text structs as part of `png_destroy_write_struct()`. Unfortunately, libpng had no way to track whether it had actually allocated the structs in the first place, and ... well, one can see where this is going. First libpng freed the text structs, then the XV patch—which had allocated them—did so again. Boom: segmentation fault, core dump, an incomplete PNG file, and no more XV.

The moral of this little story is simple: 1995-era programs had no choice but to access libpng structs directly, because that was how libpng was originally written. But modern programs should never do so, not only because of this particular problem, but also for the several other reasons detailed in the previous two chapters. Let's say it again: *Accessing libpng structures directly is just plain evil. Don't do it!*

Ye have been warned.

one can be used to write text chunks to the PNG file. This is indeed the case. Had we wished to put all of our text chunks (or the time chunk) at the *end* of the PNG file, we would have called `png_write_info()` first, followed by one or both of `png_set_tIME()` and `png_set_text()`.

In the case of the latter function,* we could do both—that is, call it with one or more text structs before calling `png_write_info()` and then call it again with one or more new text structs (perhaps a lengthy legal disclaimer to be stored in a zTXt chunk) afterward. Any calls to `png_set_text()` occurring before `png_write_info()` will be written to the PNG file before the IDATs; any calls to it after `png_write_info()` but before `png_write_end()` will be written to the PNG file after the IDATs. And any `png_set_text()` or `png_set_tIME()` calls after `png_write_end()` will be ignored.

Having completed our pre-IDAT housekeeping, we can now turn to our image-data transformations. But unlike our PNG-reading demos, most programs that write PNGs will not require many transformations. In fact, we only call one, and technically there's no point even in that:

```
png_set_packing(png_ptr);
```

This function packs low-bit-depth pixels into bytes. There are no low-bit-depth RGB and RGBA images; only grayscale and palette images support bit depths of 1, 2, or 4. But our main program neither counts colors to see whether a palette-based representation would be possible, nor checks for valid low-bit-depth grayscale values, and it always sets `sample_depth` to 8, so there is currently no possibility of libpng actually being able to pack any pixels. However, pnmtopng does both, and perhaps a subsequent revision of *wpng* will, too.

The only remaining thing for our initialization function to do is to save copies of the two PNG-struct pointers for passing to libpng functions later:

```
mainprog_ptr->png_ptr = png_ptr;
mainprog_ptr->info_ptr = info_ptr;

return 0;
```

Once again, we could have used global variables instead, but this program is intended to demonstrate how a multithreaded PNG encoder might be written.

---

* Recall from Chapter 11, *PNG Options and Extensions*, that only one tIME chunk is allowed.

Interlaced PNG: writepng_encode_image()

Back in the main program, the first thing we do after returning is to free the text buffer, since all of its data has already been written to the PNG file. Then we calculate the number of bytes per row of image data; since we accept only three basic file types, there are only three possibilities for this: either one, three, or four times the image width.

What happens next depends on whether the user requested that the PNG image be interlaced. If so, there's really no good way to read and write the image progressively, so we simply allocate a buffer large enough for the whole thing and read it in. We also allocate and initialize a **row_pointers** array, where each element points at the beginning of a row of pixels, and then call **writepng_encode_image()**:

```
int writepng_encode_image(mainprog_info *mainprog_ptr)
{
    png_structp png_ptr = (png_structp)mainprog_ptr->png_ptr;
    png_infop info_ptr = (png_infop)mainprog_ptr->info_ptr;

    if (setjmp(mainprog_ptr->jmpbuf)) {
        png_destroy_write_struct(&png_ptr, &info_ptr);
        mainprog_ptr->png_ptr = NULL;
        mainprog_ptr->info_ptr = NULL;
        return 2;
    }

    png_write_image(png_ptr, mainprog_ptr->row_pointers);

    png_write_end(png_ptr, NULL);

    return 0;
}
```

One can see that the actual process of writing the image data is quite simple. We first restore our two struct pointers; we could simply use them as is, but that would require some ugly typecasts. Next we set up the usual PNG error-handling code, followed by the call that really matters: **png_write_image()**. This function writes all of the pixel data to the file, reading from the **row_pointers** array we just set up in the main program. Once that is complete, there is nothing left to do but to write out the end of the PNG file with **png_write_end()**. As discussed earlier, this will write any new text or time chunks, but not ones that have already been written; in our case, that means it does nothing but write the final IEND chunk. The second parameter to **png_write_end()** is ordinarily **info_ptr**, but since we have no extra chunks to write, passing a NULL value is a tiny optimization.

Noninterlaced PNG: writepng_encode_row()

If the user did *not* request interlacing, we can read and write the image progressively, allowing very large images to be converted to PNG without incurring a huge memory overhead. In this case, we forego the **row_pointers** array and simply allocate **image_data** large enough to hold one row. Then we start looping over all of the rows in the image (i.e., **height** rows), reading the pixel data into our buffer and passing it to **writepng_encode_row()**:

```
int writepng_encode_row(mainprog_info *mainprog_ptr)
{
    png_structp png_ptr = (png_structp)mainprog_ptr->png_ptr;
    png_infop info_ptr = (png_infop)mainprog_ptr->info_ptr;

    if (setjmp(mainprog_ptr->jmpbuf)) {
        png_destroy_write_struct(&png_ptr, &info_ptr);
        mainprog_ptr->png_ptr = NULL;
        mainprog_ptr->info_ptr = NULL;
        return 2;
    }

    png_write_row(png_ptr, mainprog_ptr->image_data);

    return 0;
}
```

Astute readers will perceive that this function is almost identical to the previous one for interlaced images; the differences are the lack of a **png_write_end()** call (for obvious reasons) and the call to **png_write_row()** instead of **png_write_image()**. **image_data** now acts as our single row pointer.

Once the loop over rows completes, we call one last function to close out the PNG file:

```
int writepng_encode_finish(mainprog_info *mainprog_ptr)
{
    png_structp png_ptr = (png_structp)mainprog_ptr->png_ptr;
    png_infop info_ptr = (png_infop)mainprog_ptr->info_ptr;

    if (setjmp(mainprog_ptr->jmpbuf)) {
        png_destroy_write_struct(&png_ptr, &info_ptr);
        mainprog_ptr->png_ptr = NULL;
        mainprog_ptr->info_ptr = NULL;
        return 2;
    }
```

```
    png_write_end(png_ptr, NULL);

    return 0;
}
```

Again, the function is exactly like what we've seen before except that it calls `png_write_end()`. Alternatively, it could have been combined with `writepng_encode_row()` had we included in our `mainprog_info` struct a flag indicating whether the given row was the last one in the image.

writepng_cleanup()

The last tasks for the main program are to clean up the PNG-specific allocations and the main-program-specific ones, which is accomplished via the `writepng_cleanup()` and `wpng_cleanup()` functions. The former is very similar to the analogous routine in Chapter 14, except that this one calls `png_destroy_write_struct()`, which has only two arguments:

```
    void writepng_cleanup(mainprog_info *mainprog_ptr)
    {
        png_structp png_ptr = (png_structp)mainprog_ptr->png_ptr;
        png_infop info_ptr = (png_infop)mainprog_ptr->info_ptr;

        if (png_ptr && info_ptr)
            png_destroy_write_struct(&png_ptr, &info_ptr);
    }
```

`wpng_cleanup()` closes both input and output files and frees the `image_data` and `row_pointers` arrays, assuming they were allocated. Since both cleanup functions are also called as a result of various error conditions, they check for valid pointers before freeing anything and set NULL pointers for anything they do free.

Getting the Source Code

All of the source files for the *wpng* demo program (*wpng.c, writepng.c, writepng.h,* and makefiles) are available on the Web, under a BSD-like Open Source license. The files will be available for download from the following URL for the foreseeable future:

> *http://www.cdrom.com/pub/png/pngbook.html*

Bug fixes, new features and ports, and other contributions may be integrated into the code, time permitting.

16

Other Libraries and Concluding Remarks

As I mentioned at the beginning of Chapter 13, *Reading PNG Images*, libpng is not the only option for adding PNG support to an application. There are numerous other possibilities, particularly for the Windows platforms; a number of these use libpng themselves.

Cross-Platform Libraries

In the next two sections, I list roughly two dozen PNG-supporting libraries and toolkits, with particular emphasis on those with the greatest cross-platform support or support for some of the less common platforms. For an up-to-date list of PNG toolkits and related code, please check the Toolkits web page and the Source Code and Libraries page at the PNG home site:

> *http://www.cdrom.com/pub/png/pngaptk.html*
> *http://www.cdrom.com/pub/png/pngcode.html*

Note that I have not personally tested any of the libraries or toolkits listed here.

ImageMagick

John Cristy's ImageMagick is a C library that provides a uniform interface to a few dozen image formats. It not only includes a standard C API but also has Perl and Python interfaces. It also provides several powerful utilities, including an X-based viewer called *display*, for which it is probably better known. ImageMagick is freely available in source and binary formats for Unix, VMS, Macintosh, and 32-bit Windows platforms, albeit without the *display* and *animate* tools on the Mac. (An X server is required for those two programs on the other platforms.) It uses libpng and zlib for PNG support and may be modified and distributed freely as long as its copyright is acknowledged.

http://www.wizards.dupont.com/cristy/ImageMagick.html

Image Library

Colosseum Builders' Image Library is a C++ library that supports reading and writing PNGs, JPEGs, and several other image formats. The distribution includes demo apps for encoding, decoding, and viewing images, the accompanying documentation indicates that the library is an alpha release. Also, much of the code is described at length in *The Programmer's Guide to Compressed Image Files*, by John Miano, Image Library's principal author. Borland C++ Builder and Microsoft Visual C++ are explicitly mentioned on the web page, which also claims that the library is written in standard C++, implying that it should work with most compilers. Full source code is freely available, including an independent implementation of the deflate and inflate algorithms, i.e., the core routines of zlib. Image Library may be used without fee in software that is likewise free and distributed with source; otherwise, licensing fees apply. The latest release as of this writing was on July 22, 1998; this version incorrectly rejects PNG images with a zlib window size other than 32 KB.

http://www.colosseumbuilders.com/sourcecode.htm

PaintLib

Ulrich von Zadow's PaintLib is a C++ class library for decoding and manipulating several image formats, including PNG; version 2.0 adds an ActiveX control to the Win32 port. Like several of the available imaging toolkits, PaintLib actually uses libpng and zlib for its PNG support and provides a higher-level, unified interface to its supported formats. Source code is available, and it compiles under at least DOS, Unix, and both 16-bit and 32-bit Windows. The library may be freely used and distributed as long as its use is acknowledged.

http://user.cs.tu-berlin.de/~uzadow/paintlib/

QHTM

QHTM is a 32-bit Windows control from Russell Freeman and Gipsysoft that lies somewhere between an image toolkit and an HTML browser. Specifically, it provides a programming interface that allows one to add HTML support, including PNG images, to an application. (PNG is actually supported via code from PaintLib.) QHTM 1.0 does not yet handle transparency, but support for that is planned. Like PaintLib, QHTM may be freely used and distributed as long as its use is acknowledged.

http://www.gipsysoft.com/qhtm/features.html

ImageVision Library

SGI's ImageVision Library is "a toolkit for creating, processing and displaying images on all Silicon Graphics workstations," to quote from the web page. It actually does not read or write image files itself; all file I/O is handled by SGI's Image Format Library, which is also available for 32-bit Windows (Microsoft Visual C++ 5.0 only). According to the Irix 6.5 documentation, IFL is still based on libpng 0.88 and zlib 1.0, but the Windows version may be more up-to-date. Irix users compiling applications for use with current versions of libpng and zlib should take care that they don't accidentally load the older IFL code.

> *http://www.sgi.com/Technology/ImageVision/*

Imlib

Imlib is another high-level, multiformat image library, currently under development by Red Hat Advanced Development (RHAD) Labs. Though developed under and mainly supported for Linux, it is written as portable Unix/X code, and source code is available for compiling on other platforms. Imlib supports programs based on both plain Xlib and on the GIMP Toolkit (GTK+). Unlike the X frontends for the demo programs presented in Chapters 13 and 14, Imlib has the great advantage of supporting most X displays, including monochrome, pseudocolor (all bit depths from 2 through 8), static color, and truecolor. On the other hand, it treats all images as 24-bit RGB, optionally with a single color marked as transparent. As of this writing, the current release is version 1.9.4, which includes a placeholder pointer for future 8-bit alpha-channel support but no indication of what level of support may eventually show up. The authors indicated in early March 1999 that alpha support was a low priority.

> *http://www.labs.redhat.com/imlib/*

QuickTime

Apple's QuickTime is a high-level, multiformat image (and multimedia) library for Mac OS System 7.0 and later and for 32-bit Windows. Version 3.0, which natively supports reading PNG images, is included as a standard part of Mac OS 8.5, making Mac OS the first operating system for which PNG support is built in.* PNG is also supported unofficially in QuickTime 2.5 via a read-only PNG importer written by Sam Bushell. A future QuickTime release is expected to support writing PNG images.

> *http://www.apple.com/quicktime/*

---

* A developer's release of Apple's next-generation Rhapsody OS also had PNG support, but it has not yet been released as a shipping product.

ImageGear

Accusoft's ImageGear is a commercial imaging library that supports several dozen formats, including PNG. It is available for Unix, OS/2, Macintosh, 16-bit and 32-bit Windows (including a Visual Basic interface), and Java (both as Java classes and as Beans). The web page strongly implies that full alpha transparency is supported, too.

http://www.accusoft.com/Digital_Imaging/ImageGear/IG98_Fr.htm

Java Advanced Imaging API

In November 1998 Sun's Javasoft subsidiary finally added native PNG support to Java. As of the beta release in April 1999, the Java Advanced Imaging API included both read and write support for PNG. The Advanced Imaging API requires the Java 2 SDK (formerly known as JDK 1.2) or later and will presumably be available under the same terms as Java itself.

http://www.javasoft.com/products/java-media/jai/
http://www.javasoft.com/products/java-media/jai/forDevelopers/jai-apidocs/
http://www.javasoft.com/products/java-media/jai/forDevelopers/jai-guide/

Sixlegs PNG

Six-Legged Software's Java package reads and displays PNG images as a Java ImageProducer. It supports full alpha transparency, gamma correction, progressive display, and conversion to grayscale, plus quite a few ancillary chunk types. Write support is expected in a separate, yet-to-be-released package. The current read-only release, as of early April 1999, is version 1.0a and requires JDK 1.1 or later (for zlib). Chris Nokleberg released version 1.0a under the GNU LGPL—formerly the Library General Public License, recently renamed the Lesser General Public License since it allows linking to proprietary code. Full source code is included.

http://www.sixlegs.com/png/

Java Image Content Handlers

The Java Image Content Handlers were originally developed by Justin Couch for his employer, ADI Limited, but the code was subsequently released as free software and is now distributed by Justin's own company, The Virtual Light Company. Several other image formats are supported in addition to PNG, including JPEG, TIFF, NetPBM, BMP, TGA, and GIF. The current release, version 0.9.1, is read-only, but write support is coming. The handlers are written for Java 2 (JDK 1.2) but will work with JDK 1.1 with only minor changes. Full source code is included; as with Sixlegs PNG, the license is the GNU LGPL.

http://www.vlc.com.au/imageloader/

Java PNG

VisualTek's Java PNG library is, as the name suggests, a library for use in Java programs with support for reading and writing PNG images. Its license is somewhat less than clear, however; the web page claims it is distributed under the GNU General Public License, but no source code is available, and another web page refers to a 30-day evaluation period. Apparently it may be freely used in GPL'd programs but must be licensed commercially in other programs.

http://www.visualtek.com/PNG/

JIMI

Activated Intelligence's image toolkit supports a number of image formats, either "natively" or via Java's ImageProducer/ImageConsumer model, with both read and write support for PNG. The web site claims it is quite fast and can handle extremely large images (100 MB or more), subject only to available disk space. The package, currently version 2.0, is commercial, but the Standard edition is royalty-free; i.e., it requires no payment beyond the initial purchase.

http://www.activated.com/products/jimi/jimi.html

Java Vector Graphics (JVG)

Faidon Oy-Ab's Java Vector Graphics package supports reading and writing PNG images, as well as a few other formats. The current release, version 1.0, is shareware, but the older 1.0 beta 1 (with read-only PNG support) is free. A company representative promised in November 1998 that at least the PNG portion of JVG 1.0 "will be freeware soon," mainly due to the fact that Sun is including PNG support in the Java Advanced Imaging API.

http://web.avo.fr/faidon/JVG.htm

Pnglets

Pnglets was a late addition; created by Roger E. Critchlow, Jr., and first released in April 1999, it is written entirely in JavaScript and is capable of creating palette-based PNG images on the fly. Thus it can be included on web pages, allowing the client browser (rather than the web server) to render PNG bitmaps dynamically. The author considered the initial release to be "pre-alpha," but it already appeared to be relatively feature-complete; the main problems noted on the web page included a JavaScript incompatibility with Microsoft's Internet Explorer and the lack of PNG transparency support in current releases of Netscape Navigator. Pnglets is available under the GNU General Public License (GPL), which is more restrictive than the GNU LGPL. The initial version did not appear to include any special wording about how the license might affect user-written JavaScript embedded in a web page that uses

Pnglets, but that will probably be clarified in a subsequent release. (The Pnglets code itself lives in a separate file, *Pnglet.js*, and is "linked in" via the HTML SCRIPT tag.)

> *http://www.elf.org/pnglets/*

Img

Jan Nijtmans's Img is a free image-processing extension to the Tcl/Tk scripting language; it uses libpng and zlib for its PNG support. It works with Tcl 7.5 and Tk 4.1 and later versions* on both Unix/X and 32-bit Windows platforms. Both reading and writing are supported in versions 1.1.4 and 1.2b2, but a patch to Tk is required in order to write PNG images with an alpha channel. Version 1.2 is expected to be released just after the Tcl/Tk 8.1 release, currently scheduled for early May, 1999. Unfortunately, Scriptics was unwilling to incorporate Jan's Tk patch into the official 8.1 release (Tk 8.1 is thread-safe, but the patch is not), so manual patching will remain necessary for some time to come in order to write alpha PNGs.

> *http://home.wxs.nl/~nijtmans/img.html*

Python Imaging Library

As its name suggests, Fredrik Lundh's Python Imaging Library (PIL) provides support for multiple image formats under the Python interpreted programming language on Unix or 32-bit Windows platforms. It can also support Tcl/Tk via the Tkinter package. Though currently still at a suspiciously low beta version (0.3b2), PIL supports both reading and writing PNG images, apparently including alpha channels and some 16-bit-per-sample images (possibly grayscale only). It also includes some support for MNG streams, though this has not been not updated since roughly draft 33. PIL may be freely used and distributed as long as such use is acknowledged.

> *http://www.python.org/sigs/image-sig/Imaging.html*

PNGHandler

Simon Clarke's PNGHandler provides read/write PNG support to the BeOS Translation Kit. It is freely available for both PowerPC and Intel platforms, and it requires BeOS version R3 or later. PNGHandler can read all PNG bit depths with the possible exception of 16-bit-per-sample images (e.g., 48-bit RGB), and it appears to have full alpha support. For writing, it supports only depths of 8, 24, and 32 bits. It appeared that PNGHandler may have been renamed to PNGTranslator as of version 1.20, but version 1.21 is once again called

---

* As of version 8.0, Tcl and Tk share the same version number.

PNGHandler. Nevertheless, if the following link should break, check the PNG home site's Toolkits page, given at the beginning of this section, for updates.

http://www.be.com/beware/Datatypes/PNGHandler.html

SuperView Library

Andreas Kleinert's SuperView Library, part of his SViewII image application, provides read and write support for numerous image formats on the Amiga, in addition to a host of image-manipulation functions. It is not clear from the documentation whether it supports any of the more advanced PNG features such as gamma correction or even transparency. SViewII and the SuperView Library are shareware.

http://home.t-online.de/home/Andreas_Kleinert/sview.htm

Windows-Specific Libraries

ImageLib

Version 4.0, Skyline Tools. This is a 32-bit Windows DLL with Delphi support; version 2.5 also supported 16-bit Windows. It claims "support for most PNG formats" and "image conversion," which implies that it has read/write support for PNGs.

http://www.imagelib.com/

ImageMan ActiveX Suite and *ImageMan DLL Suite*

Version 6.02, Data Techniques. These are suites of ActiveX controls, Visual Basic controls, and DLLs for image manipulation and conversion. They support both 16- and 32-bit Windows and include read/write support for PNGs.

http://www.data-tech.com/imocx/imageman_activex_suite.htm
http://www.data-tech.com/imageman_dll_suite.htm

ImgDLL

Version 4.3, Smaller Animals Software. This is a 32-bit Windows DLL with read/write support for PNGs; it claims to support alpha transparency and gamma correction as well. It can be used with Visual C++, Visual Basic, and so on.

http://www.smalleranimals.com/imgdll.htm

LEADTOOLS

LEAD Technologies. This is a suite of toolkits with image support, including partial read/write support for PNGs. According to the features page, 2-bit PNG images and images with 16 bits per sample are not supported for either reading or writing, and interlacing and alpha transparency are supported only for reading. LEADTOOLS once supported the DOS and OS/2 platforms in addition to 16- and 32-bit Windows, but now only Windows appears to be supported.

>   *http://www.leadtools.com/products.htm*

PiXCL Tools

Version 4.22, VYSOR Integration. This is an "interpreted image-processing and graphics language toolkit" for creating multimedia presentations, demos, and imaging applications, especially for satellite data. It is available for 32-bit Windows, and it includes both standalone tools and a DLL for user programs.

>   *http://www.vysor.com/p40tools.htm*

PixelGraphicLibrary

Version 1.0 beta 5, Peter Beyersdorf. This is an image-manipulation library for either Delphi 2 or 3 under 32-bit Windows, with read/write support for PNGs. It includes a simple demo viewer.

>   *http://www.beyersdorf.com/pgraphe.html*

TwistedPixel

Bananas Software. This is an ActiveX control (OCX) for 32-bit Windows. It includes read/write support for PNGs and a number of other image formats, and it can be used with Visual C++, Visual Basic, Delphi, in web browsers, and so on.

>   *http://home.earthlink.net/~bananasoft/twisted.htm*

Victor Image Processing Library

Version 5.0, Catenary Systems. This is a DLL for 16-bit and 32-bit Windows; it includes read/write support for PNGs and a number of other image formats, though PNG is only supported in the 16-bit Windows version with a separate add-on (freely downloadable). Apparently, only the 32-bit Windows version is still under active development—the last Windows 3.x release was version 4.25. There is also a version 3.7 for DOS, but it has no PNG support, and the PNG add-on does not apply to it.

>   *http://www.catenary.com/victor/*
>   *http://www.catenary.com/victor/download/vicpng.html*

Concluding Remarks

The Portable Network Graphics format represents one more step in the evolution of portable, robust image formats. With good, ubiquitous support just around the corner in web browsers, and with support in image viewing and editing applications not only common but actually expected by customers, PNG's future is bright.

Of course, in the four years since PNG was created, I've learned a few lessons about what works and what doesn't. In the spirit of various publications' "post-game analyses" or "postmortems," here is a quick look at some of the things I did right and some I did wrong, in no particular order.

Alpha transparency

Content developers are justifiably excited about the possibility of using variable transparency, including real anti-aliasing. The fact that PNG can do 8-bit (or smaller) RGBA-palettes is currently underappreciated and decidedly under-implemented, but it will come to be seen as one of PNG's greatest strengths in the next year or two.

Gamma and color correction

Despite rather spotty support in applications to date, gamma and color correction are features designers have been begging for, though not always by name. They will eventually come to be expected, but support in more browsers and image editors (*correct* support!) is necessary before users will begin to notice the difference. And while operating-system support for gamma and color correction isn't absolutely necessary, having it—as in recent releases of Unix/X and Mac OS and rumored future versions of Windows—makes the lives of application developers much easier.

Animation

The lack of a PNG-related animation format early on, and the subsequent delay in finishing and implementing a viable one, was perhaps PNG's greatest failing—certainly it is one of the most oft-heard criticisms. While there was no way the PNG Development Group could have known about Netscape's GIF-animation surprise late in 1995, in retrospect, it is obvious that the group should have begun development on a PNG-like alternative right away.

Allowing the early MPNG project to be swayed too far in the direction of a heavyweight multimedia format was also a mistake; the best course would have been to come up with something just a little better than animated GIF, with the option of extending it later to become more in line with today's MNG. A "thin" PNG animation spec, similar to the capability provided today by ImageMagick, could have been implemented easily by mid-1996 or even the end of 1995. (Starting small and working up is always easier!) Fortunately, recent drafts of the MNG specification have added the concept of "simplicity profiles," so developers finally have the option of supporting a subset of the full PNG/MNG animation spec in a well-defined manner. Versions since 0.93 have actually extracted low complexity and very low complexity subsets into separate documents—MNG-LC and MNG-VLC, respectively—so "starting small and working up" is now not only possible but also actively encouraged.

Open Source–style development

It is difficult to zero in on one feature that counts as PNG's greatest success, but arguably the open, Internet-based development process was (and is) it. Even four years later, creating a robust, portable, extensible, well-specified image format from scratch in *two months* is nothing short of amazing.* The continued infusion of new blood and new ideas has been invaluable. New code is good, too.

Free reference code

When trying to promote the acceptance of a new format in existing applications, nothing succeeds so well as doing some of the developers' work! The availability of free and robust reference libraries (libpng and zlib), with minimal restrictions on reuse and redistribution, was clearly vital to PNG's success.

Decoupled compression engine

Separating the file format, as symbolized by libpng, from the compression engine, symbolized by zlib probably made the format more palatable to programmers. If, for some reason, one were averse to using both libraries (perhaps due to code size), one could choose to implement only the PNG half—which is not nearly so intimidating as rewriting both the PNG library and the deflate algorithm. The fact that zlib's core compression code was already a trusted and familiar component of gzip and the Info-ZIP tools may have helped, too.

Slow browser support

The failure to get good PNG support into the Big Two browsers even four years after PNG's release—and the lack of any support for two-and-a-half years—must count as a strike against the PNG Group, even if it's still not apparent what could have been done differently. At the time, Netscape and Microsoft were in the midst of the so-called Browser War, and one more image format, even one that boasted alpha and gamma support, just wasn't flashy enough to show up on their proverbial radar screens. Personal contacts might have helped, but both companies were large enough that finding the right contact was close to impossible.

Nevertheless, that's (mostly) water under the bridge. As I noted way back in Chapter 1, *An Introduction to PNG*, the 4.0 releases of both browsers have supported PNG files natively since late 1997, and the 5.0 releases are expected

---

* Or perhaps we are just now learning what university professors and Linux enthusiasts have always known: graduate-student-powered development is the way to go. Certainly the author of this book didn't get a whole lot done during the first two months of 1995, when PNG was being designed. (Actually, only about a quarter of the most active members of the PNG Development Group were students at the time, but the remainder achieved honorary grad-studenthood.)

to fully support both alpha transparency and gamma correction. Once that happens, web designers can be expected to begin using (and demanding!) PNGs with alpha and gamma support on web pages within a year or so.

Standardization

Pushing PNG as a standard (Recommendation) of the World Wide Web Consortium was probably key to getting PNG support into the Big Two by the end of 1997. And PNG's inclusion in the VRML97 ISO specification led to its status today as an ISO standards-track format, which is likely both to help speed its acceptance in areas outside the Web (such as medical imaging, perhaps) and to ensure its longevity as a common and useful image format.

Specification

As most implementors know, there are specifications, and then there are *specifications*. PNG's spec has been praised by a number of third parties as being one of the cleanest, most thorough, and least ambiguous image specifications ever written. Partly, this was due to the work of some very good editors, but it owes a lot to the Open Source process, too (the "many eyeballs" effect).

Extensibility

PNG's well-defined method for adding new features in a backward-compatible manner has already proven itself many times over. The addition of the iTXt chunk early in 1999 is the latest example; even 1995-era viewers can still display a PNG image with such a chunk in it. Of course, such a powerful tool cuts both ways, as became apparent when some users mistakenly tried to use PNG images containing Fireworks's huge editing extensions on web pages.

Internal consistency checks

The presence of cyclic redundancy check (CRC) values in every chunk is a positive thing and helps PNG's robustness, but one of the original aims—the ability to verify from a command-line prompt that a PNG image was downloaded properly—turned out not to be particularly useful. The advent of high-speed modems, ubiquitous Internet connections, and, above all, web browsers with smart downloading capabilities, all served to make the command-line feature obsolete before it was ever really put in place. The pngcheck utility discussed in Chapter 5, *Applications: Image Converters*, was originally written for this purpose, but has since evolved into more of a PNG conformance tester.

Overall, PNG has done quite well. Yes, there were a few missed turns, a few mistakes, and somewhat slower acceptance than many of us had hoped. But as Tom Lane has repeatedly reminded us, JPEG didn't catch on any faster, and even GIF took quite a while outside of CompuServe. The fact that PNG is currently one of only three accepted image formats on the Web is quite an achievement. May its next four years be equally exciting!

> *Sun sets over GIF.*
> *With PNG on the horizon,*
> *Web is dark no more.*

—Michael N. Randers-Pehrson

References

In this section we list some of the books, web pages, and other references relevant to each chapter.

Chapter 1

Portable Network Graphics (PNG) home site
> Roelofs, Greg, *http://www.cdrom.com/pub/png/*. This site includes the PNG specification (all versions), the PNG extensions document, sample images, historical information, an extensive list of known PNG-supporting applications, programming information (including a link to the demonstration source code presented in Part III), and even a VRML97 test world.

"Not Just Decoration: Quality Graphics for the Web"
> Lilley, Chris, *http://www.w3.org/Conferences/WWW4/Papers/53/gq-boston.html*. In particular, see the sections on "Anti-aliasing and Transparency" (*http://www.w3.org/Conferences/WWW4/Papers/53/gq-trans.html*), "Gamma Correction" (*http://www.w3.org/Conferences/WWW4/Papers/53/gq-gamma.html*), "Colour Display" (*http://www.w3.org/Conferences/WWW4/Papers/53/gq-gamut.html*).

"PNG and Gamma"
> Lilley, Chris, *http://www.w3.org/Graphics/PNG/platform.html*.

"PNG and Chromaticity"
> Lilley, Chris, *http://www.w3.org/Graphics/PNG/platform2.html*.

"PNG and Color Management"
> Lilley, Chris, *http://www.w3.org/Graphics/PNG/platform3.html*.

International Color Consortium home page
> *http://www.color.org/*. The ICC is responsible for the standard "device profile"

format that allows one to describe the characteristics of display devices very precisely.

sRGB web site
> Hewlett-Packard Company, *http://www.sRGB.com/*.

IEC Technical Committee 100 home page
> International Electrotechnical Commission, *http://www.iec.ch/tc100/*. This is the committee overseeing the standardization of sRGB.

"JPEG—What's New"
> Elysium, Ltd., *http://www.jpeg.org/public/jpegnew.htm*. This site contains news and information about JPEG-LS, among other things.

HP Labs LOCO-I/JPEG-LS home page
> Hewlett-Packard Company, *http://www.hpl.hp.com/loco/*.

"Waterloo BragZone"
> Kominek, John, *http://links.uwaterloo.ca/bragzone.base.html*.

BitJazz home page
> *http://www.bitjazz.com/*.

16million.png
> *http://www.cdrom.com/pub/png/img_png/16million.png*. This is the 113 KB lossless image containing all 16.8 million possible colors in the 24-bit RGB spectrum.

"Win98 Explorer buffer-size bug"
> *http://www.macromedia.com/support/fireworks/ts/documents/ie_bug.htm*.
> When Windows 98's Explorer is set to **View → as Web Page**, it will crash when certain PNG images with large chunk sizes are clicked on, apparently due to a 4 KB buffer limitation in Explorer. This problem first showed up with the intermediate PNG files produced by Fireworks 1.0.

Chapter 2

"Unable to View .png Images with Internet Explorer 4.0"
> Microsoft Corp., *http://support.microsoft.com/support/kb/articles/q174/9/46.asp*. This is the Knowledge Base article that reports that IE 4.0 cannot be used to view standalone PNG images (that is, when a PNG file is double-clicked in Explorer), despite being able to view PNG images on web pages.

"Zeus Server—Webmaster guide: MIME types"
> Zeus Technology, *http://www.zeus.co.uk/products/zeus1/docs/guide/features/mimetypes.html*.

"Apache Content Negotiation"
Apache Group, *http://www.apache.org/docs/mod/mod_negotiation.html*.

"Content Negotiation Explained"
Apache Week, issue 25, July 26, 1996, *http://www.apacheweek.com/features/negotiation*.

Chapter 7

"The GIF Controversy: A Software Developer's Perspective"
Battilana, Michael C., *http://www.cloanto.com/users/mcb/19950127giflzw.html*.

Thomas Boutell's home page
Boutell, Thomas, *http://www.boutell.com/boutell/*.

"MNG-supporting Applications"
Roelofs, Greg, *http://www.cdrom.com/pub/mng/mngapps.html*.

The Data Compression Book, Second Edition
Nelson, Mark, and Jean-loup Gailly, M&T Books, New York, 1996.

"PNG Graphics Specification as Basis for GIF24"
CompuServe, Feb. 14, 1995, *http://www.w3.org/Graphics/PNG/CS-950214.html*.

"Paleo PNGs"
Randers-Pehrson, Glenn, *http://www.rpi.edu/~randeg/paleo_pngs.html*.

"Jonathan Swift–Gulliver's Travels–Dictionary–B"
Jaffe, Lee, *http://www.jaffebros.com/lee/gulliver/dict/b.html#bigend*. The source of "big-endian" and "little-endian" computer jargon explained.

VRML97, ISO/IEC 14772-1:1997; Conformance and minimum support requirements
http://www.vrml.org/Specifications/VRML97/part1/conformance.html.

RFC 2083: "PNG (Portable Network Graphics) Specification, Version 1.0"
Boutell, Thomas, et al., *ftp://ftp.isi.edu/in-notes/rfc2083.txt*.

PNG (Portable Network Graphics) Specification, Version 1.0
Boutell, Thomas, et al., *http://www.w3.org/TR/png.html*. This is the "W3C Recommendation *01-October-1996*."

PNG (Portable Network Graphics) Specification, Version 1.1
Randers-Pehrson, Glenn, et al., *http://www.cdrom.com/pub/png/spec/*. This link will always be updated to point at the latest version of the PNG specification. See also *http://www.cdrom.com/pub/png/pngdocs.html* for pointers to other versions and formats for the specification (plain text, PostScript, etc.).

MNG (Multiple-image Network Graphics) Format, Version 0.95
> Randers-Pehrson, Glenn, *http://www.cdrom.com/pub/mng/spec/*. This link will always be updated to point at the latest version of the MNG specification. See also *http://www.cdrom.com/pub/mng/mngdocs.html* for pointers to other formats for the specification (plain text, PostScript, etc.).

Chapter 8

"Colour in Computer Graphics: Student Notes"
> Lilley, C., F. Lin, W. T. Hewitt, and T. L. J. Howard, Manchester Computing Centre and Department of Computer Science, University of Manchester, *http://www.man.ac.uk/MVC/training/gravigs/colour/*. In particular, see Chapters 2 and 3. Follow the freely available link to the student notes and six color-plate links in the "Lecture course" section.

"The JPEG Still Picture Compression Standard"
> Wallace, Gregory K., *ftp://ftp.uu.net/graphics/jpeg/wallace.ps.gz*.

Encyclopedia of Graphics File Formats, Second Edition
> Murray, James D., and William vanRyper, O'Reilly and Associates, 1996.

Chapter 9

"zlib Technical Details"
> Adler, Mark and Jean-loup Gailly, *http://www.cdrom.com/pub/infozip/zlib/zlib_tech.html*.

"Source Code"
> Colosseum Builders, *http://www.colosseumbuilders.com/sourcecode.htm*. This is the location for an independent PNG and zlib implementation in C++, by John Miano.

The Programmer's Guide to Compressed Image Files
> Miano, John, ACM Press/Addison Wesley Longman, 1999.

International Telecommunication Union (ITU) home page, *http://www.itu.int/*.

"JPEG Related Links"
> Elysium, Ltd., *http://www.jpeg.org/public/jpeglinks.htm*. This page contains links to various JPEG and FAQ lists, information about JPEG 2000 and JPEG-LS, software, and so forth.

"JPEG-LS Public Domain Code"
> Signal Processing and Multimedia Group, Department of Electrical and Computer Engineering, University of British Columbia, *http://spmg.ece.ubc.ca/research/jpeg/jpeg_ls/jpegls.html*.

See also the Chapter 1 entries for the HP Labs LOCO-I/JPEG-LS home page and the "Waterloo BragZone."

Chapter 10

"Color Technology"
Poynton, Charles, *http://www.inforamp.net/˜poynton/Poynton-colour.html.*

A Technical Introduction to Digital Video
Poynton, Charles, John Wiley & Sons, 1996, *http://www.inforamp.net/˜poynton/Poynton-T-I-Digital-Video.html.*

"The colour gamut of a sample monitor (an HP A1097C)"
Lilley, Chris, *http://www.w3.org/Conferences/WWW4/Papers/53/hp3.png.* This is the chromaticity diagram used in Figures 10-1 and C-4.

International Commission on Illumination (CIE) home page
http://www.cie.co.at/cie/.

"ICC Profile Specifications"
International Color Consortium, *http://www.color.org/profiles.html.*

"Color-related stuff—icclib"
Gill, Graeme, *http://web.access.net.au/argyll/color.html.* This page provides source code to a library capable of reading, writing, and doing color conversion on ICC profiles.

See also the Chapter 1 entries for additional links on gamma, chromaticity, color management, sRGB and the International Color Consortium home page, and see the Chapter 8 entry for "Colour in Computer Graphics: Student Notes."

Chapter 11

RFC 822: "Standard for the Format of ARPA Internet Text Messages"
Crocker, David H., et al., August 13, 1982, *ftp://ftp.isi.edu/in-notes/rfc822.txt.* This standard, as amended by RFC 1123 below, includes the date format recommended for use in PNG's Creation Time text chunk.

RFC 1123: "Requirements for Internet Hosts — Application and Support"
Braden, R. (editor), October 1989, *ftp://ftp.isi.edu/in-notes/rfc1123.txt.*

"HTTP Specifications and Drafts"
World Wide Web Consortium, *http://www.w3.org/Protocols/Specs.html.* These standards define the official URL format recommended for use in PNG's unofficial URL text chunk.

RFC 1766: "Tags for the Identification of Languages"
Alvestrand, Harald, March 1995, *ftp://ftp.isi.edu/in-notes/rfc1766.txt.*

Assigned Language Tags
Internet Assigned Numbers Authority, *ftp://ftp.isi.edu/in-notes/iana/assignments/languages/.* This ftp directory contains all of the RFC 1766-format language tags registered to date (not counting those that were implicitly registered by RFC 1766 itself). See the file *tags* for a brief summary.

RFC 2279: "UTF-8, a Transformation Format of ISO 10646"
Yergeau, François, January 1998, *ftp://ftp.isi.edu/in-notes/rfc2279.txt.*

Unicode Consortium home page
http://www.unicode.org/.

The Unicode Standard, Version 2.0
Unicode Consortium, Addison Wesley, 1996, *http://www.unicode.org/unicode/uni2book/u2.html.*

"Introduction to Widescreen: Aspect Ratios"
Killian, E., *http://www.clapro.com/widescreen/aspect/aspect.html.*

"Graphics Interchange Format(sm), Version 89a"
CompuServe, 1990, *http://www.wotsit.org/wgraphic/gif89a.zip.*

Chapter 12

Multiple-image Network Graphics (MNG) home site
Roelofs, Greg, *http://www.cdrom.com/pub/mng/.* This site includes pointers to the full MNG draft specification, a list of all known MNG-supporting applications, and related information and images. Glenn Randers-Pehrson is a major contributor of material.

libjpeg
Independent JPEG Group, *ftp://ftp.uu.net/graphics/jpeg/.* Source code for the current libjpeg release as of this writing, version 6b, is in the archive *jpegsrc.v6b.tar.gz.* The directory also contains plain text and PostScript versions of the JFIF 1.02 specification.

Independent JPEG Group home page
http://www.ijg.org/.

See also the Chapter 7 entry for the MNG (Multiple-image Network Graphics) Format, Version 0.95.

Chapter 13

"PNG Source Code and Libraries"

> Roelofs, Greg, *http://www.cdrom.com/pub/png/pngcode.html*. This is the (relatively) official home page for *libpng* and many of the free PNG-conversion utilities.

zlib home site

> Roelofs, Greg, *http://www.cdrom.com/pub/infozip/zlib/*. This is the official home for *zlib*, maintained on behalf of Jean-loup Gailly and Mark Adler. Please contact them for anything except broken links.

"A Standard Default Color Space for the Internet—sRGB, Version 1.10"

> Stokes, Michael, Matthew Anderson, Srinivasan Chandrasekar, and Ricardo Motta, November 1996, *http://www.w3.org/Graphics/Color/sRGB* .

Chapter 15

"NetPBM (PBMPLUS) Toolkit"

> *http://www.arc.umn.edu/GVL/Software/netpbm.html*. There is no official NetPBM home page yet, but the Graphics and Visualization Laboratory's site is a very good substitute.

RFC 1345: "Character Mnemonics and Character Sets"

> Simonsen, Keld, June 1992, *ftp://ftp.isi.edu/in-notes/rfc1345.txt*. This document provides mappings for a large assortment of 1-byte character sets.

Character Maps

> Simonsen, Keld, *ftp://std.dkuug.dk/i18n/charmaps/*. This is a directory of 1-byte character sets and is probably more complete than RFC 1345. The parent directory contains still more information on international character sets.

"Representation of ISO 8859-1 characters with 7-bit ASCII"

> Kuhn, Markus, February 20, 1993, *http://fileserver.hrz.uni-marburg.de/komm/ tin-1.30/html/iso2asc.txt*.

Chapter 16

See also the entry for John Miano's book in the section for Chapter 9.

Glossary

This section defines some of the technical terms and acronyms used throughout the book. More glossary entries may be found in Section 11 of the *PNG Specification, Version 1.1*. Terms in italic are defined in this glossary.

alpha channel

A special *channel* that associates transparency (or opacity) with an image. An image without an alpha channel is considered to be completely opaque; an image with an alpha channel may be opaque in some areas, fully transparent in other areas, and partially transparent in still others. There are two types of alpha, associated and unassociated. Associated (or premultiplied) alpha replaces all of the nonalpha (color or grayscale) information in the image with the values it would have if the image were displayed against a black background; for example, in an *RGB* image with a premultiplied alpha channel, all RGB values in completely transparent regions are replaced by black pixels. This form can be rendered faster (especially against black backgrounds, where the alpha channel can be completely ignored), but it amounts to a lossy transformation of the image data. Unassociated alpha leaves the nonalpha values untouched; this is the kind supported by *PNG*.

ANSI

American National Standards Institute, the U.S. standardization body responsible for such standards as the ANSI C programming language.

anti-aliasing

A procedure for reducing the appearance of jaggedness around high-contrast features such as lines or text in a *raster image*. Anti-aliasing effectively involves reducing the contrast slightly by mixing the two contrasting colors along their boundary. For example, a diagonal black bar on a white background would be rendered with some shades of gray along the edges, according to how the ideal geometric representation of the bar was situated relative to the positions of the *pixels* in the image.

ASCII

American Standard Code for Information Interchange, a 7-bit code (which originally included an 8th bit for parity) that has become the de facto character standard for English text and programming languages. ASCII is also the least common denominator in other character sets, including Latin-1 (*ISO/IEC 8859-1*) and Unicode UTF-8.

aspect ratio

The ratio of a rectangle's width to its height. The aspect ratio of most computer monitors is 4:3, while that of U.S. high-definition television displays is 16:9. Individual *pixels* may also be considered to have an aspect ratio. On a 4:3 monitor that is displaying at the same ratio (for example, 1024 × 768 or 800 × 600), the pixels are square and therefore have a 1:1 aspect ratio. When such a monitor displays at 1280 × 1024, however, its pixels are slightly flattened and have an aspect ratio of 16:15.

big-endian

A data format in which multibyte values are stored with the most significant values lowest in memory. This is the format used on Apple Macintosh computers and most Sun workstations, for example.

Big Two

Informal name for Netscape Navigator and Microsoft Internet Explorer, the two most influential web browsers in the world. Their support (or lack of it) for *PNG* was and is a critical factor in PNG's acceptance as an image format for the Web.

channel

The collection of all information (specifically, *samples*) of a given type in an image. For example, the collection of all red samples defines one type of channel. *RGB* images have red, green, and blue channels.

chromaticity

The color components of an image or a *color space*, not including intensity information. In a *YUV* image, for example, Y is the intensity value; U and V are chromaticity values.

chunk

The fundamental building block of a *PNG* file and the means by which the specification may be extended in a backward- and forward-compatible way.

CIE

Commission Internationale de l'Éclairage, or the International Commission on Illumination, an international standards-making body.

CMYK

Cyan, magenta, yellow, and black (the letter B is reserved for blue), the four pigments most often used in printing. Cyan, magenta, and yellow are the complements of red, green, and blue on the traditional color wheel.

color correction

Adjustment of the color values in an image in order to compensate for variations in the color output of various display devices—for example, between two monitors made by different manufacturers, or between a monitor and a color printer.

color depth

See *pixel depth*.

colormap

Another name for a *palette*; that is, a table of *RGB* color values (usually no more than 256) that is referenced by index in the main part of the image.

color space

A conceptual space in which colors are represented by discrete numerical values, almost always with a basis in the human visual system. *RGB*, YC_bC_r, *YIQ*, *YUV* and *CIE XYZ* are all examples of three-dimensional color spaces; *CMYK* is a four-dimensional example. Physical color, as in sunlight reflecting off leaves, can only be approximated by discrete values;* it is more accurately modeled as a function—specifically, intensity as a function of wavelength.

compression

The act of encoding data into a smaller representation than its original form. See *RLE* for a simple example.

content negotiation

A handshaking procedure carried out between a web server and a web browser in order to determine the best format for a given piece of data. In the context of images, a server might have *PNG, JPEG, GIF,* and *TIFF* versions of the same image; content negotiation between the server and client determines which of the four formats is sent to the browser.

---

* Actually, one could imagine measuring the wavelength of every photon; the sum of all such measurements over a given interval of time (the "exposure") and at a given location on electronic film (a "*pixel*") would be a *humongous* list of discrete values. Within the limits of quantum mechanics (for a given pixel size, the wavelength can only be measured to a certain precision), it would be a completely accurate representation of physical color.

CRC

Cyclic Redundancy Check (or, more rarely, Cyclic Redundancy Code), an efficient means of checking for accidental corruption of data. The most common version, including that used in *PNG*, is 32 bits ("CRC-32"), but 16-bit CRCs were common in older applications.

CRT

Cathode-ray tube, the principal component of traditional monitors and television displays. Often used synonymously with "monitor."

dithering

The process of mixing dots (or *pixels*) of different colors together in the same region in order to give the appearance of other colors; often performed after an image has been *quantized* to a reduced number of colors, in order to spread the errors around more evenly. The procedure tends to reduce the contrast of sharp features and may introduce noticeable patterns in the image (as in the case of an *ordered dither*); it also reduces the compressibility of the image considerably, especially in the case of an *error-diffusion dither*.

error-diffusion dither

A specific *dithering* method in which *quantization* errors are diffused spatially in a quasi-random manner. This tends to be much slower than the usual alternative (an *ordered dither*), but the results generally look much better. The Floyd-Steinberg method is an example of an error-diffusion dither.

FAQ

Frequently Asked Question list (or a single such question), a format for providing commonly requested information in public forums and on the Web. Sometimes also interpreted as "Frequently Answered Questions."

filter

In *PNG*, a method of reversibly transforming the image data so that it will compress better when fed to the main *compression* engine. In the context of operating systems with command-line interfaces, a program that processes and optionally modifies the data within a command pipeline. For example, in the following pipeline, ppmquant acts purely as a filter, modifying the output of tifftopnm and feeding the results to the input of pnmtopng:

```
tifftopnm foo-24.tiff | ppmquant -floyd 256 | pnmtopng > foo-8.png
```

In the context of an *LCD* screen or other light-emitting device, a filter is simply a material that is transparent to some wavelengths of light (say, green) and opaque or nearly opaque to all others.

floating point

The usual means of storing very large or very small numbers, or numbers with a fractional part; when encoded in machine-readable form, the method involves a sign bit (positive or negative), a fractional part (the mantissa), and an exponent (in base 2). Other machine encodings for numbers include integer (the most common), fixed point, and plain text.

fractal

Of or pertaining to an object with fractional dimension and self-similarity at many or all scales; also, the name of such an object. The most famous fractal is the Mandelbrot set, which is basically a two-dimensional blob with a boundary of dimension greater than one but less than two. Around the boundary are tiny, distorted copies of the main blob, and each copy has its own copies nearby; this attribute is called self-similarity, and it is the basis for fractal *compression.*

FTP

File Transfer Protocol, one of the oldest means of transferring files over a network. It has been largely superseded on the Web by *HTTP.*

gamma correction

Adjustment of the intensity values of an image (loosely speaking, a combination of brightness and contrast) in order to compensate for variations in output devices. For example, images displayed on a standard Macintosh must be gamma-corrected to appear the same way they do on a standard PC, and vice versa.

GIF

Graphics Interchange Format, an image format designed by (and a service mark of) CompuServe. The GIF format is technically capable of storing 24-bit images, but only crudely; in practice, it is only an 8-bit, *indexed-color* format.

GIMP

GNU Image Manipulation Program, an open Source image editor similar to Photoshop; originally called the General Image Manipulation Program. In this book we've referred to it as "Gimp" for readability (similar to "Unix"), but it is an acronym.

GNU

GNU's Not Unix, a recursive acronym for the project led by Richard Stallman and the Free Software Foundation to create an entire Unix-like operating system (and associated tools) using only freely available, freely modifiable, and freely redistributable software.

GTK, GTK+

GIMP Toolkit, a graphical toolkit originally designed for the Gimp image editor under Unix and the X Window System. Subsequently split off as a separate, application-independent project, GTK+ is currently being ported to 32-bit Windows, as well. GTK+ is in some ways similar to the Motif toolkit for X (for those who are familiar with that), but unlike Motif, GTK+ is freely available in source-code form and may be integrated, distributed, and modified without license fees or royalties.

HTML

Hypertext Markup Language, the format used for web pages.

HTTP

Hypertext Transfer Protocol, the most common means by which web pages, images and other associated files are transferred between machines. A related but older protocol is *FTP*.

IANA

Internet Assigned Numbers Authority, the official registration authority for such things as Internet media types (e.g., `image/png`).

ICANN

Internet Corporation for Assigned Names and Numbers, the presumed successor to *IANA*.

ICC

International Color Consortium, an industry body whose goal is to promote and standardize cross-platform color management.

IEC

The International Electrotechnical Commission, an international standards-making body. See also *ISO*.

IESG

Internet Engineering Steering Group, the administrative body of the *IETF*. Members of the IESG manage groups of IETF working groups.

IETF

Internet Engineering Task Force, an open development group whose purpose is to evolve and standardize the Internet and its protocols.

indexed color

Another term used to describe palette-based images; synonyms include *color-mapped* and *pseudocolor*.

interlacing

A method of reordering image data so that an approximate version of the whole image may be displayed quickly, and later refined as more of the image data becomes available.

ISO

The International Organization for Standardization, perhaps the best-known international standards-making body. The ISO and *IEC* often collaborate on standards of mutual interest; JTC 1 is one of their Joint Technical Committees.

ITU

International Telecommunication Union, an international standards-making body specializing in telecommunications networks and services.

JFIF

JPEG File Interchange Format, the most common file format for *JPEG* images. (*TIFF* is another file format that can be used to store JPEG images, and *JNG* is a third.) JFIF is not a formal standard; it was designed by a group of companies (though it is most often associated with C-Cube Microsystems, one of whose employees published it) and became a de facto industry standard.

JNG

JPEG Network Graphics, the name of the subset of *MNG* that can be used to store JPEG images with an optional *alpha channel*.

JPEG

Joint Photographic Experts Group, the informal name for the group that defined the image-encoding standard that bears their name. JPEG (the standard, which is also known as *ISO/IEC* 10918-1) is capable of compressing photographic ("continuous-tone") images quite highly with little or no visible degradation of quality—that is, without visible artifacts or loss of detail. JPEG itself is not a file format, however; see *JFIF*, *JNG*, and *SPIFF*.

JPEG-LS

A new standard for *lossless* and near-lossless *compression* of photographic images, also known as *ISO/IEC* 14495-1 and *ITU* Recommendation T.87. See also *LOCO-I*.

LCD

Liquid crystal display, a technology used in most notebook displays and, thanks to its flat geometry and relatively light weight, more and more desktop displays.

little-endian

A data format in which multibyte values are stored with the least significant values lowest in memory. This is the format used on standard Intel (x86-based) PCs and Digital workstations, for example.

LOCO-I

Low-Complexity Lossless *Compression* for Images, an algorithm developed at Hewlett-Packard Laboratories that forms the basis for the *JPEG-LS* standard.

look-ahead buffer

A block of yet-to-be-encoded data that is scanned as part of a "greedy" algorithm, in order to see whether a better choice (*compression*-wise) is just ahead, so to speak.

lossless compression

Any *compression* method that allows for the exact reconstruction of the original data, bit for bit. This is the type of compression used in *PNG* and essentially all compressors of textual data, such as Zip and gzip.

lossy compression

Any *compression* method that allows only an approximate reconstruction of the original data. Common forms of *JPEG* fall into this class.

LUT

Lookup table, a means of storing data that would otherwise require an unreasonable amount of resources. For example, a *palette* is a type of lookup table that allows image data to be encoded indirectly, thereby reducing its overall space requirements. *Gamma correction*, on the other hand, has potentially large computational requirements, since it involves the use of exponential functions. Calculating the exponentials once for every possible *sample* value and storing the results in a lookup table is almost always more efficient than computing an exponential for every sample in the image.

LZ77, LZ78, LZSS, LZW

A class of *lossless compression* algorithms deriving from two seminal papers by Jacob Ziv and Abraham Lempel, first published in 1977 and 1978.

MHEG

Multimedia/Hypermedia Experts Group, the informal name for the group that defined the *HTML*-like standard that also bears their name. MHEG (the standard, which is also known as *ISO/IEC* 13522) may be thought of as a next-generation teletext with graphics, video, and interactive capabilities in addition to text. MHEG-5 is the small-footprint subset that is designed to work well on digital set-top boxes; it has been adopted in parts of Europe and is expected to be used in Asia as well. The United Kingdom's profile for MHEG-5 on digital terrestrial television defines precisely what data formats are allowed within the MHEG-5 framework, and one of the two formats it allows for bitmapped images is *PNG*.

micron

One-millionth of a meter; also known as a micrometer and abbreviated μm.

MNG

Multiple-image Network Graphics, *PNG*'s multi-image extension. MNG can be used for animations, slide shows, collections of image parts (such as *palettes*) or even single images that are generated algorithmically.

Moore's Law

An empirical prediction first made in 1965 by Intel's Gordon Moore, who observed that the capacity of memory chips had increased by a factor of two every 12 months or so. The law was later applied to microprocessors and revised slightly to its current (unofficial) form, which states that computational power increases by a factor of two every 18 months. It is now so well established that it may actually amount to a self-fulfilling prophecy, due to chip-makers' fears that their competitors will maintain such a rate of improvement. So far, it has held for 17 doublings, representing a performance increase of more than five orders of magnitude since 1971. See *http://www.intel.com/intel/ museum/25anniv/hof/moore.htm* for a 1997 graph of the trend and *http://mason.gmu.edu/~rschalle/moorelaw.html* for a nice historical overview.

MSIE

Microsoft Internet Explorer, a web browser.

ordered dither

A specific *dithering* method in which color values are modified in individual blocks of *pixels*, usually of sizes between 4 × 4 and 16 × 16. This method is quite fast but tends to leave the image with a very grainy, patterned appearance; an *error-diffusion dither* will almost always look better.

Paeth predictor

One of the filter types used in *PNG* as a precursor to *compression*; invented by Alan W. Paeth.

palette

A table of *RGB* color values that is referenced by index in the main image data. Since a table of 256 or fewer colors can be referenced by an 8-bit index, a large *palette*-based (or *colormapped*) image can be stored in roughly one-third the space of the corresponding RGB version. For very small images, the overhead of a 768-byte palette may outweigh the savings due to smaller pixels (that is, 8 bits per pixel instead of 24). And images with more than 256 colors either need a larger palette (and therefore larger indices) or must be edited to use 256 or fewer colors in order to be stored in a palette-based format. *PNG* supports palettes of 256 or fewer colors.

phosphor

A chemical compound that emits visible light when struck by energetic electrons, which is the usual arrangement within a cathode-ray tube, or *CRT.* Cathode rays are, in fact, electrons accelerated via high-voltage plates to an energy capable of exciting the three phosphor types at the front of a monitor.

pixel

A single grid point (or "dot") in a *raster image*; composed of one *sample* from each *channel*. Most computer images are composed of pixels.

pixel depth

The total number of bits used to represent a single pixel. In a *truecolor* or grayscale image, with or without an *alpha channel*, the pixel depth is therefore equal to the product of the *sample depth* and the number of *channels*. For example, an *RGBA* image (four channels) with 16 bits per sample would have a pixel depth of 64 bits. In the case of channels with unequal sample depths, simply add the number of bits for each channel; e.g., on a typical PC "high-color" display, the number of bits for red, green, and blue channels is usually five, six, and five bits, respectively, resulting in 16-bit pixels. *PNG* channels in a given image always have equal sample depths.

PNG

Portable Network Graphics, the subject of this book. Version 1.0 of the specification was the first *W3C* Recommendation ("01-October-1996") and Internet *RFC* 2083. Version 1.1 was approved by the *PNG Development Group* in October 1998 and released publicly on December 31, 1998. A subsequent version, differing only in editorial structure, formatting, and the addition of one more recently approved *chunk* (iTXt), is currently under review by Joint Technical Committee 1, Subcommittee 24, of the *ISO/IEC*; it will become version 1.2 of the PNG spec and officially will be known as ISO/IEC 15948 upon approval as an international standard.

PNG Development Group

The Internet-based working group that designed *PNG* in 1995 and continues to discuss and occasionally approve extensions to it, usually in the form of new *chunk* types. Development takes place via two mailing lists, and interested parties may join by following the instructions at *http://www.cdrom.com/ pub/png/pngmisc.html.*

PPP

> Point-to-Point Protocol, a networking protocol commonly used in computers connected to the Internet with modems.

pseudocolor

> Another name for *palette*-based images, also known as *colormapped* or *indexed color*. In contrast, an *RGB* image is known as *truecolor*. (Grayscale images are simply grayscale.)

quantization

> The process of reducing an image with many colors to one with fewer colors, usually in preparation for its conversion to a *palette*-based image. As a result, most parts of the image (that is, most of its *pixels*) are given slightly different colors, which amounts to a certain level of error at each location. Since photographic images usually have extended regions of similar colors that get converted to the same quantized color, a quantized image tends to have a flat or banded (contoured) appearance unless it is also *dithered*.

raster image

> An image composed of a rectangular array of colored or grayscale dots (see also *pixel*). This is the only type of image officially supported by the *PNG* format. Such images have a fixed size (as measured in dots) and can be enlarged or reduced only imperfectly.

ray-tracing

> A computationally intensive method of generating photorealistic images, by tracing virtual rays of light back from the image plane into the scene and calculating their behavior in reverse. Reflection, refraction, and shadows can be modeled quite nicely, although one can use a "radiosity" program for even more realistic images.

RFC

> Request for Comments, the *IETF*'s name for its standards, recommendations, and technical notes. RFCs fall into two categories, Internet Standards and Informational RFCs; the *PNG* 1.0 specification was approved as one of the latter, which are less formal. As with most such bodies, the IETF recognizes other standards organizations such as the *W3C* and *ISO*, and it will refuse to accept a format or protocol for its own standardization process if another standards body has already done so for the same content.

RGB

> The most common *color space* in computing, representing colors as combinations of red, green, and blue values. This model matches the design of color monitors and *LCD* panels, which use red, green, and blue *phosphors* and *filters*, respectively.

RGBA

Red, green, blue, *alpha*. This is the usual format for partially transparent color images.

RLE

Run-length encoding, a very simple *compression* method in which runs of repeated bytes are replaced by (length,value) pairs. For example, the 12-byte sequence 0 0 0 0 0 9 9 9 9 9 9 9 could instead be encoded as the 4-byte sequence 5 0 7 9, which would be interpreted as "five zeros followed by seven nines."

sample

One of the values associated with a single *pixel*, for example, the red value of a given pixel is a sample. *RGB* images have three samples per pixel; *RGBA* images have four; grayscale images have one. In a *palette*-based image, samples are associated with the palette, not the pixels.

sample depth

The number of bits used to store a *sample*. For example, a 24-bit *RGB* image uses 8 bits per sample; a 48-bit RGB image or 16-bit grayscale image uses 16 bits per sample. Thus, the sample depth has to do with the precision of each color value—that is, the extent to which it can differ from its nearest neighbors. In a *palette*-based image, the sample depth refers to the palette entries; it is always 8 bits in *PNG*, even if the *pixel depth* is smaller.

scientific notation

A means of compactly representing very large or very small numbers as the product of a decimal value (between 1 and 10) and a power of 10. For example, there are 86,400 seconds in a day; in scientific notation, that value would be written 8.64×10^4. A much larger example is Avogadro's number (from chemistry), which is approximately 6.02×10^{23}. On the other end of the scale, the mass of an electron is roughly 9.11×10^{-31} kilograms.

sliding window

A central component of the *LZ77* class of *compression* algorithms, in which a window of fixed width is imagined to slide over already-processed data as the current location is advanced. This window indicates the region in which LZ77's relative pointers (or [distance,length] pairs) are valid.

SPIFF

Still Picture Interchange File Format, the successor to *JFIF* and an official standard for *JPEG* image files.

sRGB

Standard *RGB* color space, a means of specifying precisely how any given RGB value should appear on a monitor or printed paper or any other output device. sRGB was promoted by the *ICC* and submitted for standardization by the *IEC*.

suggested quantization

If a *truecolor* image will be viewed on systems capable of displaying only 256 (or fewer) colors, an encoder may take the additional step of finding one or more preferred sets of colors to which the image may be *quantized* most effectively. This avoids the necessity of decoders on such systems having to scan the entire image before displaying anything; with the suggested quantization (or "suggested palette"), they can immediately begin mapping image colors to the reduced set and display the image data without delay.

texture-mapping

In 3D rendering engines where performance is limited by the number of polygons visible in any given scene, texture-mapping is a computationally inexpensive means of applying a pattern to an otherwise basic polygon in order to make it appear more complex and/or realistic. For example, a simple rectangle can be made to look like a brick wall by applying the image of a repeating (tiled) brick pattern to it; such an image is called a texture. Secondary textures, such as light (or shadow) maps and bump maps, can add even more realism, at minimal rendering cost.

TIFF

Tagged Image File Format, a file format designed by Aldus (now Adobe). TIFF supports virtually every image type and *color space* imaginable, with a file structure that is practically arbitrary and half a dozen possible *compression* methods. As such, it is not fully supported by any application in the world, and it has been plagued by incompatibilities over the years. A subset is widely supported by scanner and image-editing software on multiple platforms, however.

transfer function

In general terms, the functional relationship between two quantities, such as an input voltage and an output light intensity, or an input range of digital values and an output range of digital values. This is a useful concept for describing the pipeline an image takes, say, from light entering a camera lens to *RGB* data in computer memory to voltages in a *CRT* to the light emitted from the monitor.

truecolor

Another name for *RGB* images; that is, capable of representing a very large number of colors (usually anything up to 16.8 million, or even more) without resorting to *quantization* and *dithering*.

URL

Uniform Resource Locator, the standard means of specifying networked resources such as web pages. The format typically involves a protocol name (e.g., `http` or `ftp`), an Internet hostname or IP number, an optional port number, and a path specification on the given host; these parts are separated by certain punctuation (colons, forward slashes, etc.).

UTC

Coordinated Universal Time, the standard time reference for Earth and the human race. Knowing the UTC time and one's timezone offset from it, it is possible to calculate the local time—for example, 1:00 PM UTC corresponds to 3:00 AM Pacific Standard Time (on the same day). UTC is almost the same thing as Greenwich Mean Time (GMT), which was originally used as the standard time reference.

VAG

VRML Architecture Group, the body that drove the design and standardization of VRML 2.0 (also known as VRML97).

vector image

An image whose most basic elements consist of lines, arcs, polygons, and so forth. Such an image can be scaled arbitrarily without introducing fuzziness or other artifacts. Many PostScript images fall into this category, though PostScript also supports *raster images*. Windows metafiles and Adobe Type 1 fonts are other examples of vector images.

VRML

Virtual Reality Modeling Language, the current standard for 3D objects and animations on the World Wide Web.

W3C

World Wide Web Consortium, a commercially funded body that standardizes (via Recommendations) protocols and formats for the Web. *PNG* and *HTTP* are examples of such standards.

XYZ

A standard *color space* for more than half a century. Like *RGB*, YC_bC_r and others, XYZ has its basis in the human visual system; unlike most of them, however, it is a device-independent color space and is the preferred intermediary for conversions between other color spaces.

Y10K

The year 10,000, an impending problem for software that stores years as four *ASCII* digits (as in the string `"1963"`).

Y2038

The year 2038, an impending problem for many current Unix systems, which store dates as four-byte, signed integers representing the number of seconds since January 1, 1970. At roughly 3:14 AM *UTC* on January 19, 2038 (which is either January 18 or January 19 elsewhere in the world, depending on one's timezone), such systems will flash back to December 1901. Unix systems that store dates as unsigned four-byte integers are OK until early February, 2106.

Y2K

The year 2000, an impending problem for software that stores years as two *ASCII* digits (as in the string `"63"`). This particular problem has been generating a great deal of excitement (money to be made), fear (problems) and loathing (lawsuits) lately.

YC_bC_r, YIQ, YUV

Three *color spaces* that approximately model how color is interpreted by the human visual system, with an intensity value and two color values. Color *JPEG* images almost always use the YC_bC_r color space instead of *RGB*.

Index

About the Author

Greg Roelofs (*http://pobox.com/~newt*) is a senior researcher at Philips Electronics, specializing in compression, graphics, 3D, and audio software. He helped design the PNG image format, maintains its official web site, and writes free software in his spare time. Greg holds a doctorate in astrophysics from the University of Chicago.

Colophon

Our look is the result of reader comments, our own experimentation, and feedback from distribution channels. Distinctive covers complement our distinctive approach to technical topics, breathing personality and life into potentially dry subjects.

The animal on the cover of *PNG: The Definitive Guide* is a kangaroo rat. There are about 20 species of kangaroo rat (genus *Dipodomys*, family *Heteromyidae*) found in western North America. Some of these species are endangered. These small mammals are equipped with long, narrow feet that enable them to get about with long, strong hops. They can travel as far as two meters per hop. Their tufted tails, which are approximately as long as their bodies, are used as rudders. The forearms of kangaroo rats are so short that they often disappear within their fur. Most kangaroo rats have a color similar to the sand or soil of their environment, with black or white facial markings and two stripes running down the back. Albino kangaroo rats do occasionally appear. Like all of their relatives in the *Heteromyidae* family, kangaroo rats have large, fur-lined pouches in their cheeks into which they stuff food to carry back to their nests. They eat grass, plant greenery, and seeds. It is not uncommon to find evidence of a visit by a kangaroo rat in vegetable gardens. Remarkably, they are able to obtain all the water they need from the food that they eat. Kangaroo rats are able to live their entire lives without ever drinking water.

Kangaroo rats are nocturnal animals. They tend to be antisocial and belligerent. Kangaroo rat fights frequently occur. During these fights they jump in the air and kick at each other with their powerful legs. Kicking, in this case kicking sand, also comes in handy when cornered by enemies such as rattlesnakes or coyotes. While the enemy has sand in its eyes, the kangaroo rat makes his hopping getaway.

Kangaroo rats build their subterranean nests beneath small bushes or trees. They line the nests with leaves or grass, and build in numerous tunnels and escape outlets.

Nancy Kotary was the production editor and copyeditor for *PNG: The Definitive Guide*; Norma Emory was the copyeditor; Madeleine Newell was the proofreader; Nicole Gipson Arigo, Jane Ellin, and Sarah Jane Shangraw provided quality control. The illustrations that appear in this book were produced by Robert Romano and Rhon Porter using Macromedia FreeHand 8 and Adobe Photoshop 5. Seth Maislin wrote the index.

Edie Freedman designed the cover of this book, using a 19th-century engraving from the Dover Pictorial Archive. The cover layout was produced with Quark-XPress 3.32 using the ITC Garamond font. Whenever possible, our books use RepKover™, a durable and flexible lay-flat binding. If the page count exceeds RepKover's limit, perfect binding is used.

The inside layout was designed by Nancy Priest and Alicia Cech and implemented in troff by Lenny Muellner. The text and heading fonts are ITC Garamond Light and Garamond Book. This colophon was written by Clairemarie Fisher O'Leary.

Perl

Perl Resource Kit—UNIX Edition

By Larry Wall, Nate Patwardhan,
Ellen Siever, David Futato &
Brian Jepson
1st Edition November 1997
1812 pages, ISBN 1-56592-370-7

The *Perl Resource Kit—UNIX Edition* gives
you the most comprehensive collection of
Perl documentation and commercially
enhanced software tools available today.
Developed in association with Larry Wall, the creator of Perl,
it's the definitive Perl distribution for webmasters, programmers,
and system administrators.

The *Perl Resource Kit* provides:

- Over 1800 pages of tutorial and in-depth reference
  documentation for Perl utilities and extensions, in 4 volumes.
- A CD-ROM containing the complete Perl distribution,
  plus hundreds of freeware Perl extensions and utilities—
  a complete snapshot of the Comprehensive Perl Archive
  Network (CPAN)—as well as new software written by Larry
  Wall just for the Kit.

Perl Software Tools All on One Convenient CD-ROM

Experienced Perl hackers know when to create their own, and when
they can find what they need on CPAN. Now all the power of CPAN—
and more—is at your fingertips. The *Perl Resource Kit* includes:

- A complete snapshot of CPAN, with an install program for
  Solaris and Linux that ensures that all necessary modules are
  installed together. Also includes an easy-to-use search tool
  and a web-aware interface that allows you to get the latest
  version of each module.
- A new Java/Perl interface that allows programmers to write
  Java classes with Perl implementations. This new tool was
  written specially for the Kit by Larry Wall.

Experience the power of Perl modules in areas such as CGI,
web spidering, database interfaces, managing mail and USENET
news, user interfaces, security, graphics, math and statistics,
and much more.

Programming Perl, 2nd Edition

By Larry Wall, Tom Christiansen &
Randal L. Schwartz
2nd Edition September 1996
670 pages, ISBN 1-56592-149-6

Coauthored by Larry Wall, the creator of
Perl, the second edition of this authoritative
guide contains a full explanation of Perl
version 5.003 features. It covers Perl
language and syntax, functions, library
modules, references, and object-oriented features, and also explores
invocation options, debugging, common mistakes, and much more.

Perl Resource Kit—Win32 Edition

By Dick Hardt, Erik Olson,
David Futato & Brian Jepson
1st Edition August 1998
1,832 pages, Includes 4 books & CD-ROM
ISBN 1-56592-409-6

The *Perl Resource Kit—Win32 Edition* is
an essential tool for Perl programmers who
are expanding their platform expertise to
include Win32 and for Win32 webmasters
and system administrators who have discovered the power and
flexibility of Perl. The Kit contains some of the latest commercial
Win32 Perl software from Dick Hardt's ActiveState company, along
with a collection of hundreds of Perl modules that run on Win32,
and a definitive documentation set from O'Reilly.

Advanced Perl Programming

By Sriram Srinivasan
1st Edition August 1997
434 pages, ISBN 1-56592-220-4

This book covers complex techniques for
managing production-ready Perl programs
and explains methods for manipulating data
and objects that may have looked like magic
before. It gives you necessary background
for dealing with networks, databases, and
GUIs, and includes a discussion of internals to help you program
more efficiently and embed Perl within C or C within Perl.

Web Programming

CGI Programming on the World Wide Web

By Shishir Gundavaram
1st Edition March 1996
450 pages, ISBN 1-56592-168-2

This book offers a comprehensive explanation of CGI and related techniques for people who hold on to the dream of providing their own information servers on the Web. It starts at the beginning, explaining the value of CGI and how it works, then moves swiftly into the subtle details of programming.

Dynamic HTML: The Definitive Reference

By Danny Goodman
1st Edition July 1998
1088 pages, ISBN 1-56592-494-0

Dynamic HTML: The Definitive Reference is an indispensable compendium for Web content developers. It contains complete reference material for all of the HTML tags, CSS style attributes, browser document objects, and JavaScript objects supported by the various standards and the latest versions of Netscape Navigator and Microsoft Internet Explorer.

Frontier: The Definitive Guide

By Matt Neuburg
1st Edition February 1998
618 pages, 1-56592-383-9

This definitive guide is the first book devoted exclusively to teaching and documenting Userland Frontier, a powerful scripting environment for web site management and system level scripting. Packed with examples, advice, tricks, and tips, *Frontier: The Definitive Guide* teaches you Frontier from the ground up. Learn how to automate repetitive processes, control remote computers across a network, beef up your web site by generating hundreds of related web pages automatically, and more. Covers Frontier 4.2.3 for the Macintosh.

JavaScript: The Definitive Guide, 3rd Edition

By David Flanagan & Dan Shafer
3rd Edition June 1998
800 pages, ISBN 1-56592-392-8

This third edition of the definitive reference to JavaScript covers the latest version of the language, JavaScript 1.2, as supported by Netscape Navigator 4.0. JavaScript, which is being standardized under the name ECMAScript, is a scripting language that can be embedded directly in HTML to give web pages programming-language capabilities.

Learning VBScript

By Paul Lomax
1st Edition July 1997
616 pages, includes CD-ROM
ISBN 1-56592-247-6

This definitive guide shows web developers how to take full advantage of client-side scripting with the VBScript language. In addition to basic language features, it covers the Internet Explorer object model and discusses techniques for client-side scripting, like adding ActiveX controls to a web page or validating data before sending to the server. Includes CD-ROM with over 170 code samples.

Web Client Programming with Perl

By Clinton Wong
1st Edition March 1997
228 pages, ISBN 1-56592-214-X

Web Client Programming with Perl shows you how to extend scripting skills to the Web. This book teaches you the basics of how browsers communicate with servers and how to write your own customized web clients to automate common tasks. It is intended for those who are motivated to develop software that offers a more flexible and dynamic response than a standard web browser.

How to stay in touch with O'Reilly

1. Visit Our Award-Winning Web Site

http://www.oreilly.com/

★ "Top 100 Sites on the Web" —*PC Magazine*
★ "Top 5% Web sites" —*Point Communications*
★ "3-Star site" —*The McKinley Group*

Our web site contains a library of comprehensive product information (including book excerpts and tables of contents), downloadable software, background articles, interviews with technology leaders, links to relevant sites, book cover art, and more. File us in your Bookmarks or Hotlist!

2. Join Our Email Mailing Lists

New Product Releases
To receive automatic email with brief descriptions of all new O'Reilly products as they are released, send email to:
listproc@online.oreilly.com
Put the following information in the first line of your message (*not* in the Subject field):
subscribe oreilly-news

O'Reilly Events
If you'd also like us to send information about trade show events, special promotions, and other O'Reilly events, send email to:
listproc@online.oreilly.com
Put the following information in the first line of your message (*not* in the Subject field):
subscribe oreilly-events

3. Get Examples from Our Books via FTP

There are two ways to access an archive of example files from our books:

Regular FTP
- ftp to:
  ftp.oreilly.com
  (login: anonymous
  password: your email address)
- Point your web browser to:
  ftp://ftp.oreilly.com/

FTPMAIL
- Send an email message to:
  ftpmail@online.oreilly.com
  (Write "help" in the message body)

4. Contact Us via Email

order@oreilly.com
To place a book or software order online. Good for North American and international customers.

subscriptions@oreilly.com
To place an order for any of our newsletters or periodicals.

books@oreilly.com
General questions about any of our books.

software@oreilly.com
For general questions and product information about our software. Check out O'Reilly Software Online at **http://software.oreilly.com/** for software and technical support information. Registered O'Reilly software users send your questions to: **website-support@oreilly.com**

cs@oreilly.com
For answers to problems regarding your order or our products.

booktech@oreilly.com
For book content technical questions or corrections.

proposals@oreilly.com
To submit new book or software proposals to our editors and product managers.

international@oreilly.com
For information about our international distributors or translation queries. For a list of our distributors outside of North America check out:
http://www.oreilly.com/www/order/country.html

O'Reilly & Associates, Inc.
101 Morris Street, Sebastopol, CA 95472 USA
TEL   707-829-0515 or 800-998-9938
          (6am to 5pm PST)
FAX   707-829-0104

TO ORDER: **800-998-9938** • **order@oreilly.com** • **http://www.oreilly.com/**
OUR PRODUCTS ARE AVAILABLE AT A BOOKSTORE OR SOFTWARE STORE NEAR YOU.
FOR INFORMATION: **800-998-9938** • **707-829-0515** • **info@oreilly.com**

Titles from O'Reilly

International Distributors

UK, EUROPE, MIDDLE EAST AND AFRICA (EXCEPT FRANCE, GERMANY, AUSTRIA, SWITZERLAND, LUXEMBOURG, LIECHTENSTEIN, AND EASTERN EUROPE)

INQUIRIES
O'Reilly UK Limited
4 Castle Street
Farnham
Surrey, GU9 7HS
United Kingdom
Telephone: 44-1252-711776
Fax: 44-1252-734211
Email: josette@oreilly.com

ORDERS
Wiley Distribution Services Ltd.
1 Oldlands Way
Bognor Regis
West Sussex PO22 9SA
United Kingdom
Telephone: 44-1243-779777
Fax: 44-1243-820250
Email: cs-books@wiley.co.uk

FRANCE

ORDERS
GEODIF
61, Bd Saint-Germain
75240 Paris Cedex 05, France
Tel: 33-1-44-41-46-16 (French books)
Tel: 33-1-44-41-11-87 (English books)
Fax: 33-1-44-41-11-44
Email: distribution@eyrolles.com

INQUIRIES
Éditions O'Reilly
18 rue Séguier
75006 Paris, France
Tel: 33-1-40-51-52-30
Fax: 33-1-40-51-52-31
Email: france@editions-oreilly.fr

GERMANY, SWITZERLAND, AUSTRIA, EASTERN EUROPE, LUXEMBOURG, AND LIECHTENSTEIN

INQUIRIES & ORDERS
O'Reilly Verlag
Balthasarstr. 81
D-50670 Köln
Germany
Telephone: 49-221-973160-91
Fax: 49-221-973160-8
Email: anfragen@oreilly.de (inquiries)
Email: order@oreilly.de (orders)

CANADA (FRENCH LANGUAGE BOOKS)

Les Éditions Flammarion ltée
375, Avenue Laurier Ouest
Montréal (Québec) H2V 2K3
Tel: 00-1-514-277-8807
Fax: 00-1-514-278-2085
Email: info@flammarion.qc.ca

HONG KONG

City Discount Subscription Service, Ltd.
Unit D, 3rd Floor, Yan's Tower
27 Wong Chuk Hang Road
Aberdeen, Hong Kong
Tel: 852-2580-3539
Fax: 852-2580-6463
Email: citydis@ppn.com.hk

KOREA

Hanbit Media, Inc.
Sonyoung Bldg. 202
Yeksam-dong 736-36
Kangnam-ku
Seoul, Korea
Tel: 822-554-9610
Fax: 822-556-0363
Email: hant93@chollian.dacom.co.kr

PHILIPPINES

Mutual Books, Inc.
429-D Shaw Boulevard
Mandaluyong City, Metro
Manila, Philippines
Tel: 632-725-7538
Fax: 632-721-3056
Email: mbikikog@mnl.sequel.net

TAIWAN

O'Reilly Taiwan
No. 3, Lane 131
Hang-Chow South Road
Section 1, Taipei, Taiwan
Tel: 886-2-23968990
Fax: 886-2-23968916
Email: benh@oreilly.com

CHINA

O'Reilly Beijing
Room 2410
160, FuXingMenNeiDaJie
XiCheng District
Beijing, China PR 100031
Tel: 86-10-86631006
Fax: 86-10-86631007
Email: frederic@oreilly.com

INDIA

Computer Bookshop (India) Pvt. Ltd.
190 Dr. D.N. Road, Fort
Bombay 400 001 India
Tel: 91-22-207-0989
Fax: 91-22-262-3551
Email: cbsbom@giasbm01.vsnl.net.in

JAPAN

O'Reilly Japan, Inc.
Kiyoshige Building 2F
12-Bancho, Sanei-cho
Shinjuku-ku
Tokyo 160-0008 Japan
Tel: 81-3-3356-5227
Fax: 81-3-3356-5261
Email: japan@oreilly.com

ALL OTHER ASIAN COUNTRIES

O'Reilly & Associates, Inc.
101 Morris Street
Sebastopol, CA 95472 USA
Tel: 707-829-0515
Fax: 707-829-0104
Email: order@oreilly.com

AUSTRALIA

WoodsLane Pty., Ltd.
7/5 Vuko Place
Warriewood NSW 2102
Australia
Tel: 61-2-9970-5111
Fax: 61-2-9970-5002
Email: info@woodslane.com.au

NEW ZEALAND

Woodslane New Zealand, Ltd.
21 Cooks Street (P.O. Box 575)
Waganui, New Zealand
Tel: 64-6-347-6543
Fax: 64-6-345-4840
Email: info@woodslane.com.au

LATIN AMERICA

McGraw-Hill Interamericana
Editores, S.A. de C.V.
Cedro No. 512
Col. Atlampa
06450, Mexico, D.F.
Tel: 52-5-547-6777
Fax: 52-5-547-3336
Email: mcgraw-hill@infosel.net.mx

O'REILLY®

O'REILLY™

O'Reilly & Associates, Inc.
101 Morris Street
Sebastopol, CA 95472-9902
1-800-998-9938

Visit us online at:
**http://www.ora.com/
orders@ora.com**

O'REILLY WOULD LIKE TO HEAR FROM YOU

Which book did this card come from?

_____

Where did you buy this book?
- ❏ Bookstore
- ❏ Direct from O'Reilly
- ❏ Bundled with hardware/software
- ❏ Other _____

- ❏ Computer Store
- ❏ Class/seminar

What operating system do you use?
- ❏ UNIX
- ❏ Windows NT
- ❏ Other _____

- ❏ Macintosh
- ❏ PC(Windows/DOS)

What is your job description?
- ❏ System Administrator
- ❏ Network Administrator
- ❏ Web Developer
- ❏ Other _____

- ❏ Programmer
- ❏ Educator/Teacher

❏ Please send me O'Reilly's catalog, containing
a complete listing of O'Reilly books and
software.

Name _____ Company/Organization _____

Address _____

City _____ State _____ Zip/Postal Code _____ Country _____

Telephone _____ Internet or other email address (specify network)

Nineteenth century wood engraving
of a bear from the O'Reilly &
Associates Nutshell Handbook®
Using & Managing UUCP.

BUSINESS REPLY MAIL
FIRST CLASS MAIL   PERMIT NO. 80   SEBASTOPOL, CA

Postage will be paid by addressee

O'Reilly & Associates, Inc.
101 Morris Street
Sebastopol, CA 95472-9902

‖‖‖‖‖‖‖‖‖‖‖‖‖‖‖‖‖‖‖‖‖‖‖‖‖‖